D1236388

Yale Western Americana Series, 32

Mario T. García

Desert Immigrants

The Mexicans of El Paso, 1880–1920

New Haven and London   Yale University Press

All photographs are courtesy of the
El Paso Public Library, Aultman Collection.

Designed by James J. Johnson
and set in IBM Press Roman type.
Printed in the United States of America by
Halliday Lithograph, West Hanover, Mass.

Library of Congress Cataloging in Publication Data

García, Mario T.
  Desert immigrants.

  (Yale Western Americana series ; 32)
  Bibliography: p.
  Includes index.
  1. Mexican Americans—Texas—El Paso—History.
2. El Paso, Tex.—Ethnic relations. 3. El Paso,
Tex.—History. I. Title. II. Series.
F394.E4G36   976.4′96   80-36862
ISBN 0-300-02520-3 (cloth)
      0-300-02883-0 (paper)

10 9 8 7 6 5 4 3 2

To Nama and Tanaca
To Mama and Pop

Contents

Tables

Acknowledgments

Numerous persons and institutions must be thanked for contributing to this study. First and foremost, I am deeply indebted to Ramón Eduardo Ruiz, who believed years ago that I could become a historian. This study would not have been possible without him. Others who offered sound advice in the early stages were Michael Parrish and Harry Scheiber. Carlos Blanco and my other *compañeros* at the Third College at the University of California, San Diego, helped form my social conscience, which aided in conceiving this study. For help in the final revising period I am thankful to Professor Ruiz and my colleague at the University of California, Santa Barbara, Alexander B. Callow, Jr. In addition, Albert Camarillo, Carl Harris, Elliot Brownlee, Mary Brownlee, Ileana Rodríguez, Richard García, and Francisco Lomelí have in various ways assisted me in the organization and preparation of parts of this study.

Institutions that provided financial support and facilities for the development of this study are the Ford Foundation through its Graduate Fellowship Program for Mexican Americans; the National Chicano Council on Higher Education for a postdoctoral grant in 1978; the University of California, Santa Barbara, for Faculty Research Grants including a Regents' Fellowship in 1976, and for released time from teaching in order to complete this study; the National Endowment for the Humanities for a Summer Research Grant during 1976; and the Rockefeller Foundation, the Andrew W. Mellon Foundation, and the NEH (Grant no. FC 26278-76-1030) for their financial assistance during my tenure at the Center for Advanced Study in the Behavioral Sciences in Stanford, California, where the final draft was completed. Of course I must give my thanks to the center and its director, Gardner Lindzey, for providing a most helpful and stimulating environment during 1978-79.

In particular, I appreciate Barbara Witt's meticulous typing at the center.

In addition, research institutions that must be mentioned for their assistance include the Chicano Studies Library, University of California, Berkeley; the Southwestern Collection, El Paso Public Library; the University of Texas at El Paso Archives; Professor Oscar J. Martínez and his staff at the Institute of Oral History at the University of Texas at El Paso; Marvin Shady at the El Paso Central Labor Council, who gave me access to his collection of the *Labor Advocate*, El Paso's labor newspaper; the El Paso Public School System for allowing me to examine early school board records; the Bancroft Library at the University of California, Berkeley; the Federal Records Center in East Point, Georgia; the National Archives in Washington, D.C.; the Secretaría de Relaciones Exteriores in Mexico City; and the AFL–CIO Library in Washington, D.C.

Finally, for their support, encouragement, and love I would like to give special thanks to my family and, of course, to Ellen.

Desert Immigrants

Map 1. United States–Mexico Border Region. Adapted from Nestor Valencia, "Twentieth Century Urbanization in Latin America and a Case Study of Ciudad Juarez" (M.A. thesis, University of Texas at El Paso, 1969, in UTEP Archives, no. 518), p. 29.

1

Introduction

Although many Americans are only now becoming aware of the
Mexican presence in the United States due to the current controversy over undocumented immigrant workers, Mexicans are no
strangers to American history. They have lived and worked in the
Southwest and California, ironically, far longer than Anglo-Americans who captured this previously Mexican territory during the
Mexican War (1846–48). Those Mexicans who remained north of
the new border following the conflict not only lost their family
and communal lands but became subject to racial and political discrimination as well as cultural erosion. Their eventual second-class
status set the pattern for the later treatment of Mexican immigrants.
Hence, the nineteenth-century experience is fundamental to understanding race relations in these regions. The early Spanish-speaking
settlements, nonetheless, represented only the beginning of the
Mexican saga within the United States. Of far greater importance
has been the immigrant story commencing in the late nineteenth
century, which is inextricably linked with the growth of American
industrial capitalism.

The rise of the American industrial state during the post-Civil
War period set the stage for the arrival of thousands of Mexicans in
the United States. As a result, Mexican immigration can be seen
as one chapter in that momentous migration of foreign-born peoples
to this country during the late nineteenth and early twentieth centuries. Immigration from the neighboring republic was part of a larger
historical process: the acquisition of new sources of labor by Yankee captains of industry. Yet while immigration was directly tied to
industrialization, it had regional characteristics. In the industrialized
East and Midwest, for example, immigration gave rise to an industrial working class. Regions such as the South, Southwest, and West,

1

on the other hand, remained less developed and supplied agricultural products and industrial metals—economic activities necessitating a different form of labor supply. In this regional division of labor the Southwest became integrated into the American industrial system by the turn of the century. Limited in industrial production, the Southwest was in special need of unskilled railroad hands, farmworkers, mine and smelter laborers, and a variety of other forms of menial labor. Lacking a local labor market and finding it difficult to recruit European and Asian immigrants owing to geographic distance and racial prejudices, entrepreneurs soon discovered a profitable and acceptable labor supply south of the border. Together, industrialization, regional economic specialization, and Mexican immigrant labor launched an economic boom in the Southwest and in the process created new and enlarged Mexican communities within the United States. Mexican immigration, as such, is rooted in late nineteenth-century American economic developments associated with the growth and expansion of American capitalism. It is this interrelationship between American capital and Mexican immigration that constitutes the larger framework for this study.

Since the late nineteenth century Mexican immigrants, unlike their European and Asian counterparts who crossed vast oceans, have traversed an expansive desert frontier to reach the United States. Rather than steamships it was the iron horse that provided the transport for their arduous journey. The new arrivals were the forebears of today's Mexican Americans and Chicanos.* This is the story of those early desert immigrants who settled in El Paso, the most important American city along the United States–Mexican border. El Paso symbolized to Mexicans what New York had represented to European immigrants: the opening to what they believed would be a better life. Besides being the largest port of entry, this border site between 1880 and 1920, the years of its greatest economic growth, supplied jobs for large numbers of unemployed Mexican workers as it surged from an obscure desert town to an "instant city." As El

---

*In this study the term *Mexican* refers to all persons of Mexican descent but in particular immigrants from Mexico. The term *Mexican American* refers to Mexicans born in the United States. The term *Spanish surnamed* refers to all persons of Mexican descent. Finally, *American* or *Anglo* refers to all non-Mexicans, especially white citizens of the United States.

Paso and the Southwest contributed to the new industrial state, Mexican immigrants augmented its swelling multiracial working class.

Mexican immigration to the United States, however, must be seen in the light of El Paso's and the Southwest's economic infrastructure. Owing to its geographic and border location, El Paso became not only the main arrival terminal for Mexican immigrants but a significant railroad, smelting, ranching, and commercial center with both national and international importance in that it linked the southwestern region with the rest of the United States as well as with Mexico. The penetration of the railroads into the border desert area in the early 1880s made this possible, and thousands of enterprising Americans and Mexicans flocked to El Paso in search of better lives. Second in importance only to the railroads, the El Paso Smelter best exemplified the city's economic boom. El Paso's railroad connections and proximity to Mexican and southwestern mines made it a perfect site to receive ores from surrounding fields. By World War I the smelter employed as many as 3,000 workers, mostly Mexicans, and made El Paso a major smelting center. Trade with Mexico represented a third leading enterprise. With the Mexican Central Railroad opening Mexico's interior to El Paso's trade, by 1910 the border city became the focal point for increased international commerce. El Paso also became a major cattletown as both southwestern and Mexican ranchers used it as their main shipping point. These four economic sectors in turn stimulated various additional local enterprises such as the wholesale and retail trade, manufacturing, tourism, and construction. In less than half a century El Paso had become, according to its boosters, the Queen City of the Southwest.

Yet the southwestern boom would not have been possible without the availability of cheap Mexican labor. Mexicans migrated to the United States because of the possibilities of jobs but also as the result of dislocation in their own country. Forced off their individual and communal lands by dictator Porfirio Díaz's shortsighted policies aimed at benefiting national as well as foreign investors in agriculture, thousands of poor Mexicans first migrated to the northern Mexican states such as Chihuahua, Sonora, and Coahuila, where employment could be found with the railroads, mines, and ranches. However, owing to the 1906 recession in Mexico plus the ravaging effects of the Mexican Revolution of 1910, many Mexicans, jobless and homeless, crossed the border into the American Southwest, in many cases enticed by labor-scarce Yankee enterprises. Lax American immigration policies and practices, moreover, including a special exemption for some Mexicans from the Immigration Act of 1917, further encouraged this movement of both immigrants and political refugees. Between 1880 and the beginning of the Great Depression almost 1 million Mexicans entered the United States, thousands first arriving in El Paso. Here venturesome and unscrupulous labor contractors, both American and Mexican, greedily pounced on the newcomers and contracted them for work throughout the Southwest as well as in other parts of the country. El Paso, as a regional marketplace of cheap labor, became unmatched along the U.S.–Mexican border.

Besides supplying Mexican immigrant workers to other areas, El Paso profitably employed great numbers of them in local industries. The economy of the city in fact became dependent on the Mexican *obreros*—the workers. Mexicans could be found in every major economic activity: transportation, smelting, manufacturing, the retail trade, construction, and a variety of services. In addition to men, some Mexican women found employment outside the home and formed a significant addition to El Paso's working class. Limited in the types of jobs available to them, Mexican women monopolized domestic work and laundering. Still others found work in the city's early garment factories and as clerks in both American- and Mexican-owned stores. Yet not all Mexicans in El Paso were wageworkers. To service the growing Mexican population an active business sector sprang up. Segregated in the *barrios* (Mexican neighborhoods) and restricted in capital because of the meager earnings of the Mexican workers, *comerciantes* (merchants) owned and operated a variety of small businesses such as grocery stores, restaurants, tailor shops, barbershops, and community newspapers. These small businessmen, along with a lesser number of professionals, formed a lower middle class and exercised political and cultural leadership within El Paso's Mexican community. As workers and as businessmen, Mexicans, both men and women, contributed to El Paso's economic growth. Moreover, success in finding jobs made it easier for Mexicans to adapt to life north of the border. Conditions were hard but at least most had work whereas almost none had existed in Mexico.

Once across the border, however, Mexicans were occupationally restricted by the economic character of the Southwest and by the historic discrimination against Mexicans in the region. The booming southwestern economy, largely extractive and agricultural, provided immigrants with mainly menial work. Needing only a minimum of skilled personnel, the railroads, mines, smelters, and farms expanded and prospered because of their use of unskilled Mexicans. In El Paso the relationship between the economy and the condition of Mexican immigrants is visible. Based on the region's underdevelopment limiting job advancements for workers, a class society functioned with distinct racial divisions. Mexicans were primarily blue-collar workers whereas Americans were mostly white-collar employees, businessmen, managers, and professionals. Such a system produced profits and privileges for the city's employers while restricting wages for all workers—both Mexicans and Americans—although nonetheless dividing them along racial lines. The small and weak local American Federation of Labor, for example, consistently fought against the employment of alien labor in El Paso and directed its animosity and frustration more at Mexican workers than at American bosses. This interaction among class, race, and labor in El Paso involved occupational distribution, wage standards, and the relationship of organized labor to the Mexican working class.

Education might have helped to close the economic gap between Mexicans and Americans but so-called Mexican schools in the barrios only contributed to the disparity. The El Paso public school system from the very start followed a policy of segregating Mexican children. School administrators argued that until Mexicans learned an adequate amount of English, they would have to remain in their own schools, which provided classes solely through the early grades. However, most who did learn English failed to enter integrated classes after the sixth grade because they had to seek work by then to augment the family income. Consequently, school officials believed that the Mexican schools should direct their attention to manual and domestic education that would help the students to find jobs. Carpentry, sewing, laundering, and domestic science become regular parts of a Mexican student's training in comparison to the better-rounded curriculum offered in American neighborhood schools. Besides manual training the schools stressed the need to instruct

Mexicans in the ideals and ethics of American society. "Americanization" would make for a more loyal and disciplined future work force and citizenry. Patriotism, ethics, cleanliness, and English were the foundations for the socialization fostered in the Mexican schools. What little schooling the Mexicans did acquire, moreover, took place in highly congested buildings in the southside Mexican districts. Aoy School, for instance, represented not only the largest school in El Paso but the largest for Spanish-speaking students in the United States. Essential as manual workers, Mexicans in El Paso received the type of education that would best serve the labor requirements of local industries and businesses.

Mexicans in El Paso likewise lived apart from Americans. Although obviously many preferred to live in familiar cultural surroundings, occupational and wage discrimination along with racial prejudice kept them segregated in the Mexican slums. Chihuahuita, the central barrio in the southern half of the city, was the principal and initial settlement for Mexican immigrants. It further served as a labor pool where nearby railroads, construction firms, downtown retail stores, laundries, and other employers, even American housewives, found needed workers. Mexicans lived in overcrowded homes with little or no sanitation, high infant mortality rates, many cases of tuberculosis and other diseases, and the highest rate of crime in the city. Still, Mexicans successfully adjusted due to their prior experiences with poverty and to their adamant belief that El Paso represented only a temporary stay until they could return to Mexico with enough savings to start a better life. Such adjustment, however, left them vulnerable to exploitation. By 1920 the Mexican neighborhoods had expanded but were still "south of the tracks," along the border, and separate from the better-off American northside districts. Although some local reformers worked to improve living conditions among the Mexicans, they failed to promote the removal of the Mexicans' de facto segregated living conditions and they did not focus on a major cause of such problems: the persistence of Mexicans as a cheap labor force. Hence, the continued reliance by El Paso and the Southwest on cheap labor from Mexico assured the survival of Chihuahuita and the other congested barrios of the city.

No less than the employers, politicians came to value the concentration of Mexicans in El Paso. Astute politicians, especially in the

stalwart Democratic machine—the Ring—recognized that control of
the Mexican vote would ensure political dominance. Through the
use of Mexican American politicos, patronage, and by literally buying the Mexican vote, the Ring monopolized the Mexican electorate
and remained in office. For example, the Second Ward, encom-
passing most of Chihuahuita, not only contained the city's largest
number of voters but regularly provided Ring candidates with substantial margins over their opponents. Although a key to the Ring's
success, Mexican-American politicians were no mere lackeys of the
machine. Instead, with their ability to deliver the Mexican vote they
helped organize a Mexican-American pressure group within the Ring
that assisted in obtaining jobs as well as ethnic protection. Ironically, most Mexicans had little interest in American politics. Living
close to their homeland and hoping to eventually return, they saw
no reason to give up their Mexican citizenship and to actively participate in local politics other than by accepting much needed money
for their votes. For the majority of Mexicans one's country still
meant Mexico, not the United States.

Conscious of themselves as Mexicans, immigrants in El Paso became even more aware of their country and of their loyalties to it
with the impact of the Mexican Revolution of 1910. In fact all of El
Paso became involved in the revolution when the El Paso–Ciudad
Juárez area proved to be perhaps the most strategic site for all revolutionary actions. El Paso was a logical haven for political exiles. They
could receive support from the large local Mexican community and
owing to the city's border location could easily purchase arms
from American suppliers and transport them across the boundary.
The revolution also affected Mexican–Anglo relations as racial
tensions soared along the border, especially during the American occupation of Veracruz in 1914 and Pancho Villa's raid on Columbus,
New Mexico, in 1916. Despite the hazards, many Mexicans concerned themselves with events in *la patria* and in their own small
ways aided the different revolutionary juntas that operated out of
El Paso. The Mexican Revolution revealed El Paso's unavoidable
ties with Mexico and the nationalist consciousness of the Mexican immigrant.

Culturally, Mexicans remained distant from the American population due to residential segregation and cultural discrimination.

Mexicans also successfully retained many native traditions and values because of their proximity to the border. Such cultural retention aided in their adjustment to immigrant life. Immigrants found within the family, the church, mutual societies, and other social institutions transferred from Mexico a familiar and secure cultural environment. Yet among El Paso's large Mexican population contrasts in life-styles existed as more acculturated Mexican Americans, educated and sophisticated Mexican political refugees, and the mass of poor Mexican immigrants comprised diverse cultural enclaves although linked by common traditions. Together, Mexicans of different backgrounds enriched the cultural life of El Paso. At the same time, they were not immune to certain Americanizing influences, especially because their children attended American schools. Cultural continuity and cultural change characterized the Mexican community and produced a distinct Mexican border culture.

One hundred years after the commencement of large-scale Mexican immigration to the United States, most Mexicans still suffer economic, political, and social disparities in contrast to Americans in El Paso and throughout the Southwest despite some advances. Continued immigration from Mexico together with racial and cultural discrimination helps account for this inequity along with the persistence of a southwestern economy characterized by a slower pace of industrialization using labor-intensive conditions and cheap labor from both sides of the border. Class, racial, and cultural divisions are rooted in the particular economic development of El Paso and the surrounding country. The Mexican experience, however, is not unique although this study concentrates on El Paso and its Mexican population. Mexicans share a common historical legacy, notwithstanding racial and cultural differences, with other Americans of immigrant backgrounds, especially those who entered the United States during the same critical period of the late nineteenth and early twentieth centuries. Early Mexican immigrants were part of a larger historical experience resulting from the growth of American industrial capitalism and its need for new sources of cheap and manageable labor. Not marginal to the history of the United States, despite long neglect by American historians, Mexican immigrants and their offspring have been major contributors to this country's past and present.

2

Out of the Desert

The immigration of Mexican workers to the United States and the
formation of Mexican settlements (barrios) in cities such as El
Paso coincided with rapid economic growth in the Southwest during
the late nineteenth and early twentieth centuries. Specializing in
mining, ranching, and agriculture, the Southwest experienced an economic boom. Yet, due to its dominant extractive character, the
economy remained less developed than other industrializing sections
of the United States. Some manufacturing took place, but the railroads transported most of the area's raw materials to be processed in
the East and Midwest. Into this setting Mexicans entered and filled
a basic labor need: unskilled manual workers. In the Mexican, southwestern employers found a cheap, manageable, and extensive source
of labor. Mexicans migrated to the border by the thousands and
accepted jobs in mines, smelters, farms, and cities. Once employed,
however, most Mexicans stayed as unskilled workers owing to the region's simple labor requirements as well as racial and cultural discrimination. As a result the economy of the Southwest formed the
foundation for the particular experiences of Mexican immigrants.

The southwestern boom, of course, did not occur in a vacuum.
Instead it followed national as well as worldwide economic trends,
especially the growth of post-Civil War industrial capitalism in
the United States. American industrialization had preceded the War
between the States, but the Union victory secured its predominance.
Between 1865 and the turn of the century the United States, like
Western Europe, underwent tremendous growth in industrial production. New factories turned out iron, steel, electricity, chemicals,
foodstuffs, textiles, and sundry other industrial and consumer items.
Besides employing armies of workers, capitalists installed new
and improved manufacturing techniques, such as Frederick Taylor's

9

assembly-line methods. Late-nineteenth-century American industrialization flourished due to abundant natural resources, a large supply of cheap labor, especially from Europe, the availability of investment capital from earlier mercantile enterprises (augmented by
European capital), a favorable political climate, and a growing
industrial culture, characterized as "Yankee ingenuity." Of these factors the discovery of additional industrial raw materials assumed
greater importance as production thrived. To locate and transport
such freight, entrepreneurs expanded and modernized the nation's
railroad and transportation system, which assisted in the exploitation
of virgin areas. Consequently, industrialization fostered a pattern of
regional economic specialization. While most factories remained
in the Northeast and parts of the Midwest, the South and West served
them with agricultural and mining resources. The South grew cotton,
tobacco, and rice; the Midwest and Pacific Coast supplied grains;
the Great Plains raised cattle; the Lake Superior region mined iron
and copper; and the Pacific Northwest shipped lumber. In addition
the South and West had other natural materials desired by "captains of industry." Too profitable as exporters of such resources, the
South and West built few industries. The West's total annual value
of manufacturing by 1914 amounted to only $80 million, less than 5
percent of the national total. Manufacturing in these two regions
involved either the processing of raw materials or small-scale production for local markets. Southern and western manufacturers found
themselves restricted due to several conditions: sparse populations
with limited markets; strong competition from eastern manufacturers;
scarce eastern and foreign capital, which preferred mining and
agricultural investments; and discriminatory transportation costs.[1]
Integrated by the railroads into a national industrial economy, the
South and West developed primarily as producers of raw materials.

In the historical context of industrial capitalism's need for
new domestic as well as foreign supplies of raw materials, the Southwest along with northern Mexico received attention for their valuable resources. The investment of outside capital and technology
sponsored a regional economy but one inextricably linked with
eastern industries.[2] The border city of El Paso reflected these regional, national, and international developments that supported a
southwestern economy based on mining, ranching, commerce,

agriculture, tourism, and transportation. From a small village in 1880 El Paso blossomed into a desert metropolis of almost 100,000 forty years later. One scholar, in his study of San Francisco and Denver, terms such rapid urbanization the "instant city."[3] The economic growth of El Paso and the old Mexican Cession, in turn, affected their political, cultural, and racial character as Americans as well as Mexican immigrants flocked to the border looking for a better life.

In its economic transition El Paso made use of its traditional geographic and economic resources. Appropriately named, El Paso served as a natural passageway for the Spaniards as they explored the mountains that separate the immense Chihuahua Desert from the Rio Grande Valley of Upper New Mexico. The Mission of Our Lady of Guadalupe founded by the conquistadores in 1659 along the banks of the Rio Grande together with the settlement of Paso del Norte served as a rest and supply center on the tortuous route between Santa Fe and Ciudad Chihuahua throughout the Spanish (1659–1821) and Mexican periods (1821–46).[4] Among the first Americans to visit Paso del Norte was the explorer Zebulon Pike. Captured by Spanish officials in New Mexico in 1807, Pike, on his way to a Chihuahua prison, observed the trade between New Mexico and Chihuahua through Paso del Norte. He later reported that each year New Mexico sent about 30,000 sheep to Chihuahua plus tobacco, dressed deer, skins, fur, salt, and wrought copper vessels of superior quality. In return, Paso del Norte received dry goods, arms, iron, steel, ammunition, and European liquors. Pike also recorded that New Mexico obtained gold, silver, and cheese from Sinaloa. Expanded commerce saw additional American visitors in Paso del Norte after the Santa Fe trade between Missouri and New Mexico opened in the 1820s. From Santa Fe, American merchants took their wares to Ciudad Chihuahua by way of Paso del Norte. New Mexico *hacendados*, moreover, continued to drive their sheep and cattle to Chihuahua. Between 1839 and 1850 about 200,000 head of sheep crossed the Rio Grande at Paso del Norte.[5]

The economic and strategic importance of the Old Chihuahua Trail resulted in its capture by United States forces during the Mexican War. As part of this operation American troops under the command of Colonel Alexander Doniphan occupied Paso del Norte in December 1846. During their stay the Yankees enjoyed the fine wine and fruits grown in the surrounding valley. John T. Hughes, a member of the Doniphan expedition, reported to the secretary of war on the Mexican settlement's agricultural potential. Hughes noted that about 8,000 Mexicans lived in the town and grew pears, peaches, apples, figs, and grapes from which they made some of the finest wine he had ever tasted. Hughes believed that if "energetic" Americans farmed the valley it would yield ten times the fruit and wine the Mexicans produced. To encourage settlers Hughes suggested a turnpike, railroad, or other forms of communication between Paso del Norte and the populated sections of the United States.[6]

Despite Hughes's enthusiasm, agriculture played a minimal role after El Paso, as the American side of the Rio Grande was called, became the westernmost part of Texas. Instead its geographic location kept it as a transportation and supply site. In 1850 the Butterworth Mail Company established a route between San Antonio and El Paso, and eight years later the Overland Stage Company operated a line through El Paso that connected St. Louis to San Francisco.[7] Other stage firms also found it convenient to have El Paso on their runs and by the end of the Civil War this former Mexican settlement had direct stage connections with Santa Fe, San Antonio, and Chihuahua. An early American in El Paso, W. W. Mills, later reflected on the importance of these stage routes. "These mail coaches," he wrote,

> were the forerunners of the "Limited Express" and the Pullman sleeper of the present day; and the rough, brave men who drove and managed them and protected the stations, fighting Indians the while, were the pioneers, the Daniel Boones . . . of this frontier! They opened the way for the Southern Pacific, the Mexican Central, the "Sunset" and the Santa Fe.[8]

However, this transportation network did not lead to a heavy migration of Americans to the border. Indeed, El Paso was not really a *pueblo* or town in any strict sense during the post-Mexican War period. Most Mexicans, for example, continued to live on the left bank of the Rio Grande in Paso del Norte rather than on the American side. Those who remained in El Paso were few, scattered, and worked as farmers and farmworkers. Mills estimated in the late 1850s that the population of El Paso was 300 and consisted mostly of Mexicans. The small number of Americans tended to be either merchants with stores on both sides of the border or operators of gambling halls. Both catered to Mexicans as well as to Americans on their way to the California goldfields. For the most part, Americans fostered good relations with the Mexicans as a way of enlarging their trade. In addition many Americans had Mexican wives or mistresses. Hence, the postwar period came to be characterized by small numbers of Mexicans and Americans coexisting peacefully in an adobe hamlet. No set pattern of racial or labor exploitation appears to have existed because outside the retail trade and saloons Mexicans and Americans had no direct economic connections. The only major ethnic tension occurred in 1877 as a result of El Paso's "Salt War" (see chap. 8), which involved Mexicans from the lower valley towns of Ysleta and San Elizario rather than from El Paso. By 1880 the El Paso census recorded a population of only 736, mainly Mexicans, with a few American merchants.[9] Nevertheless, El Paso's stage ties and border location gave it commercial importance. After the War Department built posts in West Texas and New Mexico, El Paso became a military supply center. Cattle ranchers, from both sides of the border, furnished the American military and used El Paso as a market. Moreover, its proximity to Paso del Norte (later renamed Ciudad Juárez in 1888) across the border further strengthened El Paso's role as a cattletown.[10]

Yet, investments in southern Arizona copper provided a greater impetus to the early growth of El Paso during the Gilded Age. Acquired in the Gadsden Purchase of 1853, this portion of Arizona possessed some of the richest copper ores in North America. "That sixty mile drop in the [boundary] line," one historian wrote in 1924, "gave the United States the control of the richest copper deposits in the world and made El Paso what it is today." The discovery of copper and other metals in Arizona, as well as Sonora, Chihuahua, and New Mexico, enhanced El Paso's position as a commercial center. The mining boom, in turn, raised the demand for cattle and extended rangelands in West Texas, New Mexico, and

Chihuahua. El Paso's new prosperity was soon mirrored in the border town's numerous gambling halls, theaters, and saloons. It has been estimated that in 1882 there existed a barroom for every 200 persons in El Paso.[11]

While mining stimulated El Paso's economy, the extension of railroads into the Southwest and northern Mexico connecting their mineral deposits with American industries proved to be the principal catalyst in the region's boom. "If a town were to realize its dream of greatness," a railroad historian observes of the Southwest, "it was not only necessary to get a railroad, but to be the first to obtain one."[12] Due to its geographic and border location and previous history as an avenue of trade, four American railroads began to build toward El Paso in 1878: the Atcheson, Topeka, and Santa Fe; the Southern Pacific; the Texas and Pacific; and the Galveston, Harrisburg and San Antonio (G.H. & S.A.).[13] Banker C. R. Morehead understood what the railroads would mean for this desert town. "Plenty of room here for a big city," Morehead wrote in his diary in 1881, "which it will be in time after the railroads come. It is the natural pass from East to West, North to South, and it may become a mining center."[14] The Southern Pacific had the honor of entering El Paso first, on May 19, 1881, followed by the Santa Fe on June 11, 1881. Jay Gould's Texas and Pacific completed its line from Texarkana to El Paso six months later and the Galveston, Harrisburg and San Antonio arrived from Houston on January 12, 1883. In addition, the Mexican Central from Mexico City, which would transport thousands of Mexican immigrants, finished its route to the border in March 1884. The *Lone Star*, one of El Paso's first newspapers, noted that the Mexican Central connected El Paso with the "Paris of America" and it encouraged the town's businessmen to increase their trade with Mexico's interior.[15] The completion of this railroad network complemented the town's previous importance as a trade and supply settlement and yet represented a new economic era for El Paso with national and international implications.

With the railroads came American merchants, miners, businessmen, lawyers, and gamblers. Railroad officials encouraged this migration by publicizing the region's economic potential. Consequently, El Paso was transformed from a "sleepy Spanish-American

village" to a "brawling, lawless border town of ten thousand."[16] In a
study of early Jewish merchants in the area, one scholar observes
that the basic motivation that brought Americans to the area consisted of the "old hunger for El Dorado."[17] One early historian,
likewise, believed that Yankee enterprising spirit differentiated the
new American residents from the older Mexican inhabitants. "If
we are right in our surmise," he wrote, "El Paso got the railroads
with their shops and their payrolls because the Americans in the
town went after the business, while the Mexicans . . . sat around following the shade from one side of the house to the other."[18] Although such a racial view is questionable, the railroads did initiate a
period of prosperity making the *El Paso Daily Times* boast in 1901:
"What Horace Greely intended to say was 'Go to El Paso, young man,
and grow up with the city.'"[19]

El Paso's railroads made the border city and its surrounding
countryside into a regional satellite. Exporting raw materials, El Paso
became closely tied to eastern capitalists who provided capital,
markets, technology, skilled labor, and manufactured products. Yet
railroads also made the city into a regional metropolis dominating
its own economic satellites, such as the mining and ranching sectors
of West Texas, southern New Mexico, eastern and southern Arizona, and parts of northern Mexico, particularly Chihuahua. As a
regional metropolis, El Paso performed a middleman function between the resources of its hinterland and the flourishing industries
of the nation.[20] One historian of western "instant cities" notes
that they represented "integral parts of the widespread society that
they served and, consequently, provided a focus for many aspects
of life: seat of authority, center of culture, place of refuge, hub of
transportation, communication, mobility, and industry."[21] El
Paso's regional, national, and international dimensions involved four
of the border city's major economic activities: railroad transportation, mining, trade with Mexico, and ranching.
    With the railroads El Paso emerged by World War I as a major
southwestern city. The coming of the iron horse allowed El Paso to
tap its broad hinterland. Although the railroad brought modernized transportation, it did not represent a total break with the past.
The railroads were built on the Spanish and Mexican trails that

crisscrossed the Southwest and made El Paso a commercial stop on the Old Spanish Trail. Nevertheless, the railroads symbolized the new American era, modernizing the economy and changing the town into a railroad, mining, ranching, and labor center. The *Times*, noting this transformation, observed in 1902 that El Paso's commercial ascendancy could be credited both to its location and to the railroads. From the four major railroads that entered El Paso, the city's transportation network increased to eight American and Mexican lines by 1920.[22] Railroads brought to El Paso and the Southwest what one scholar calls a "more coherent functional region."[23] In this integrated economy Mexico was considered of major significance. A Santa Fe line official predicted in 1878 that the construction of a railroad along the United States–Mexican border would create "another Texas from the territory of old Mexico."[24] Although political annexation did not occur, W. H. Plant, the president and general manager of the Plant Railroad and Steamship System, expressed the commercial interest of all railroad men in Mexico by 1900. He stressed that business between the United States and Mexico had substantially increased and that the railroads wanted part of it. El Paso had a major stake in this trade, Plant concluded, since in order for railroads to penetrate Mexico, they needed to enter through the border city. Four years later an agent of the Development Company of America submitted a report on Chihuahua emphasizing that despite a general ignorance in the United States about Mexico, the neighboring republic offered outstanding advantages for investments and industries due to its varied resources, mild climate, productive soil, and immense territory. Mexico lacked only railroads to reduce transportation costs. Moreover, Americans could easily invest in Mexico because of its geographical proximity: "almost a part of the United States—and one of which a few energetic foreigners are just beginning to take advantage."[25]

Besides the Mexican trade the railroads opened other southwestern areas to El Paso's commerce. The *Modern Traveler*, a railway journal in Chicago, described El Paso's position as the central focus of a vast underdeveloped region containing bountiful natural wealth and the distributing point for the cattle and mining industries. The *Traveler* believed that few cities had a more favorable commercial location than El Paso. "Four gigantic railroads from four major cities," the journal graphically portrayed El Paso's rail connections, "at four points of the compass enter the city of El Paso like the four spokes of a great wheel converging to the hub."[26]

The railroads likewise became major employers of labor in El Paso. The *Times* reported in 1902 that railroads in the city paid out each month nearly $200,000, most of which remained in the El Paso economy. The Southern Pacific that year, for example, employed 500 men and had a monthly payroll of $10,000. The Texas and Pacific had 200 men in El Paso and paid out $14,000 every month. The Mexican Central employed 150 men and had a payroll of $6,000 a month. Finally, the Sierra Madre line had 110 employees and a payroll of $9,000. By 1914 the assessed valuation of the railroads in El Paso reached $3,683,480. In El Paso railroads also hired thousands of Mexican immigrants to work in construction and maintenance crews throughout the Southwest.[27]

Next to the railroads, mining best exemplified the economic boom. With the employment of large numbers of Mexican immigrant workers, Arizona, for example, increased its copper production from 23,274,965 pounds in 1883 to 719,035,514 pounds in 1917 and by World War I led all states in the extraction of this valuable industrial metal. In demand as a conductor of electricity, especially for the expanding telephone, telegraph, and cable systems, copper represented the "queen" of southwestern metals. Eastern corporations, such as Phelps-Dodge, reaped profits from investments in copper extraction, particularly in Arizona. With mines and smelters at Bisbee, Morenci, Douglas, and Nacozari in Sonora, Phelps-Dodge's copper output rose from approximately 14 million pounds in 1890 to 186 million pounds in 1918. Besides copper, deposits of gold, silver, coal, lead, and zinc were also mined in Arizona, New Mexico, and northern Mexico.[28] The *Mexican Mining Journal,* an American publication in Mexico City, acknowledged in 1907 that Mexico ranked as the largest producer of silver, second to the United States in copper production, fourth in lead, and fifth in gold. Investor Robert F. Ames of Chicago, interviewed by the *Times* in 1902, admitted that mining expansion in the Southwest had attracted eastern capital to this remote section of the country. A few years earlier, he pointed out, much capital had been invested in northwestern mining fields, but this had changed with recent dis-

coveries in the Southwest and northern Mexico. Twelve years later
Charles M. Pepper, the special correspondent of the *Washington
Star,* wrote from Torreón that Americans represented the "mainstay"
in Mexican mines. "It is in the mining localities," Pepper informed
his readers, "that the American characteristics come out most strongly. No mining proposition has been too difficult or too risky for some
American group of capitalists to take hold of it."[29]

In El Paso the ore discoveries made the city a mining center. The
Times had predicted in 1892 that mines would contribute the most
to El Paso's prosperity. The wealth of the Rocky Mountains and the
Sierra Madre, the paper postulated, would arrive in El Paso and
construct not only another Denver but the "proudest" international
city in the world. Yet the same newspaper understood that mining
prosperity depended on national developments. In 1900 the newspaper correctly observed that federal support for the extraction
industry had been partly responsible for El Paso's growth. "Brass is
the backbone of the administration," the *Times* reported, "and
the price of copper has certainly helped this district."[30]

El Paso supplied machinery and goods for the mines. "The city
is full of mining men," the *Times* proclaimed in 1900. "Look out
for big deals." Miners purchased various products shipped from the
East to El Paso that helped the city's retail business. Boots, shoes,
clothing, flour, grains, groceries, pianos, automobiles, and other lux-
uries were bought by miners and mining companies on trips to the
border city. Mining supply companies also established headquarters
there. In 1900 the International Machinery Company of El Paso
reported doing a large business in mining machinery throughout Mexico as well as New Mexico and Arizona. Besides these firms many
mining enterprises opened offices in El Paso to facilitate their supply
operations. The *International Industrial Record* in 1901 listed
several mining companies in the city. These included the Pass City
Copper Company, assessed at $100,000 and with mines in Chi-
huahua, and La Fortuna Mine and Milling Company, worth $199,950
and with mines in Sonora.[31]

The impact of mining on El Paso was not restricted to commerce.
With the aid of Mexican workers the city became a major smelting
location. Its railroad connections and proximity to Mexican mines
made El Paso a perfect site to receive ores from the surrounding

fields. In 1883 the *Lone Star* observed that it would not benefit El
Paso to receive vast quantities of ore, especially after the Mexican
Central's completion, if they could not be smelted locally. "We only
lack a man or a body of men with sufficient capital," the *Times*
emphasized in its sponsorship of a smelter, "to make these natural
advantages properly available." Smelter entrepreneurs agreed.
"There is no reason why any camp in New Mexico and Arizona
should send its ores to Colorado," one smelter official in El Paso
stated. "El Paso is the legitimate market of the mining districts
east of Los Angeles and south of Santa Fe and north of Parral, Mexico."[32] The El Paso Smelter, one of the town's largest industries,
began operations in 1887 approximately 2½ miles northwest of El
Paso and was the property of an outside interest: the Kansas City
Consolidated Smelting and Refining Company of Argentine, Kansas.
Incorporated at $3 million, the smelter hired a work force of 250
with skilled workers from other parts of the country and common
laborers from Mexico. The principal source of ore consisted of
lead–silver primarily from Mexico and its most unique feature was a
100-foot wooden chimney. "Because of El Paso's location at the
crossroads (where American ore moved east and Mexican ore north),"
a historian of the Mexican mining industry concludes, "and the
prevalence of cheap labor, which offset fuel and transportation costs,
the financial success of the plant was assured."[33]

In 1899 the El Paso Smelter expanded and joined the mining
empire of the American Smelting and Refining Company (ASARCO).
This giant corporation had been organized to own and manage
properties of seventeen companies and one partnership and controlled
sixteen smelting plants, eighteen refineries, and numerous western
and Mexican mines. Despite these extensive holdings ASARCO did
not possess a smelting monopoly in the West due to the presence
of the Guggenheim family, whose interests included smelters and
mines in the West and Mexico. While ASARCO announced in 1899 a
profit of $3½ million, the Guggenheims had gained as much but
with fewer holdings. ASARCO, however, had debts of $7 million. In-
tense competition plus ASARCO's financial problems led to a mer-
ger of both corporations in 1901.[34] As part of this new smelting and
mining monopoly, the El Paso Smelter bought all classes of gold,
silver, lead, and copper ores. With reconstructed plant facilities by

1902, moreover, it employed 900 workers with a yearly payroll of half a million dollars and a production capacity double the old plant. One year later the chamber of commerce noted a greater growth and announced that the smelter ranked among the largest in the world as it employed 1,500 men and had a payroll of $60,000 a month. In addition it paid shippers of metals $800,000 to $1 million per month. One mine alone sent to the smelter in a year $1 million worth of ore. Receiving ores from New Mexico, Arizona, West Texas, Chihuahua, Sinaloa, Durango, Coahuila, and Lower California, the smelter contributed a million dollars each month to the city's economy.[35]

Unfortunately the financial panic of 1907 slowed the smelter's operations as lead and silver prices plummeted. Additional problems arose when the Mexican Revolution of 1910 cut off ore supplies from Mexico, leading to an increase of lead shipments from Colorado, Arizona, and New Mexico to offset the loss. The prolonged revolution in Mexico forced the smelter to concentrate more on copper smelting since it could easily acquire this metal from its open-pit Santa Rita Mines in New Mexico. By 1913 the lead capacity of the smelter was down to 1,000 tons per day while that of copper was 15,000 tons per day. The need for lead and copper during World War I helped to compensate further for the decline it sustained because of the Mexican Revolution. To meet the heavy war demand, the smelter employed a work force of between 1,300 and 3,000 with a payroll of $75,000 a month.[36] Not only did the smelter serve as El Paso's largest employer, especially of Mexican immigrant workers, but it tied the city's economy even closer to regional and national markets.

"As is Gibralter [*sic*] to the Mediterranean in naval operations," the *Lone Star* proclaimed in 1881, "so is El Paso to the trade and commerce of the United States with Mexico." The newspaper believed that the border town's geographic location plus its railroad system would make it a major trade center. Mexico's importance to El Paso's economy was revealed when trade increased between the southern republic and the United States. American exports to Mexico rose dramatically from $4,012,827 in 1850 to $61,029,681 in 1910, while Mexican imports grew at an even greater rate. From $575,200 in 1850, imports from Mexico swelled to $105,357,236 in 1910. As a result Mexico showed a favorable trade balance on the eve of the

1910 revolution, and despite decreased commerce during the civil
war a substantial trade pattern had already been established. On
the border El Paso became a principal port of trade between the
United States and Mexico. The business sector of El Paso recognized
the city's dependency on this international activity. As the *El Paso
Herald* put it in 1916: "El Paso is a city and will continue only
as a city because she is an international point—cut out the boundary
line and everything that has made her a city goes with the wiping
out of the boundary line." Besides its role as an import–export hub,
El Paso served as a distribution and marketplace for American investments in Mexico.[37] These early transactions involved railroads,
mines, ranches, and commercial farming as well as smaller investments in a variety of other enterprises. United States capital represented 38 percent of all foreign investments in Mexico by 1911, a far
larger share than any other country's, and was concentrated in railroad construction and the extractive industry. With the exception of
the Federal District, the northern Mexican states of Chihuahua, Coahuila, Nuevo León, and Sonora received the largest share of American capital. In its international edition of 1903 the *Times* bluntly
emphasized El Paso's interests in these investments:

> Mexico, the land of romance, of sunshine, of the Aztecs, the
> Moquis, the Yaquis, the home of the adobe, the serape, the re-
> boso; the nativity of the chile, the enchilada and the frijole [*sic*] ;
> Mexico, the El Dorado of Cortez, of Alvarado, of Acquila; the
> land of gold and silver and copper; is before us for study, for
> inspiration, for reflection and, perhaps, more than anything else
> for profit.[38]

A good indication of El Paso's role in international trade can be
seen in customs figures for both El Paso and Juárez. In 1893 the port
of El Paso had the largest receipts, $740,047.23, of any port in
Texas, followed by Galveston, $131,062.52, Brownsville, $129,062.52,
and Corpus Christi, $13,830.95. Within a decade El Paso had be-
come the ninth largest port of entry in the United States and the *Times*
predicted that in another ten years El Paso would rival Baltimore
and Boston. This commercial traffic also made Juárez the principal
Mexican port along the border. To justify a salary increase plus

an additional clerk, United States Consul J. Harvey Brigham informed Washington in 1886 that the Mexican town already represented a "first class consulate." Brigham noted that during the previous year exports to the United States passing through Juárez amounted to over $7 million and exceeded those of Honolulu and Hong Kong.[39] By 1910 despite a substantial decline due to a faltering Mexican economy, the result of the 1907 recession, El Paso's imports still reached over $2½ million and its exports over $5½ million. Although the revolution in Mexico temporarily halted trade, it recovered by 1917 and reached its prerevolutionary level.[40]

These customs figures indicate the growth in trade as well as the level of economic development in both countries. Although it underwent economic growth under dictator Porfirio Díaz (1876–1910), Mexico remained an underdeveloped nation. Consequently, most of her imports through El Paso consisted of manufactured products, especially for the railroads, mines, and haciendas of the north. In 1900, for example, $1,265,090 worth of machinery and machine parts entered Mexico at El Paso. On the other hand Mexico exported to the United States raw materials such as ores, cattle, hides, cotton, and coffee. The United States consul in Juárez observed in 1890 that total exports of precious metals from Mexico the previous year had amounted to almost $18 million and more than two-thirds of it had passed through his port.[41] While commerce exposed Mexico's lack of industrialization, it also showed increased American attention to Mexico's natural resources as a basis of trade and investment. "By 1911 Mexico," according to one historian, "was truly an economic satellite of the United States."[42] For El Paso this international dimension meant that its economy depended not only on national conditions but on international ones also. The *Mexican Mining Journal* emphasized the internationalization of American investment capital when it declared in 1911:

> There is an increasing tendency of American capital to seek investment in foreign countries and particularly in the Spanish-American countries of Mexico and Central America which are its nearest neighbors and the natural field for the investment of American capital. Up until recent years the development of the western part of the United States offered a more attractive

field for the investor than could be found in a foreign country, but this day is passing. The gradual taking up of the vacant lands of the West is one of the principal causes that have rendered the West a less attractive field for investment than heretofore. American capital must seek foreign investment just as the American manufacturer must seek a foreign market for his products and the countries of Spanish-America with their wealth of underdeveloped natural resources is the natural field for the investor and the market for the manufacturer.[43]

As with railroads, mining, and trade with Mexico, the livestock industry helped incorporate El Paso into a regional and national economy. The city's location and its railroads made it a shipping point for cattlemen in West Texas, New Mexico, and northern Mexico, where large rangelands existed. The *Lone Star* commented in 1885 that in a nine-month period more than 60,000 head of cattle, horses, and sheep had been transported through El Paso. Of the surrounding region Chihuahua supplied the largest number of cattle to El Paso. "The demand for Mexican cattle," reported the United States consul in 1898 from Juárez, "has almost exhausted the supply." Two years later the value of imported cattle and other live animals was $419,720, which next to ores represented El Paso's chief imports. "Almost all the land in northern Chihuahua that is available," stated an American consular official, "is used for ranching purposes."[44] Into the new century, moreover, shipments of cattle from Chihuahua remained heavy. In 1909 the value of exported cattle from Juárez to El Paso reached $1,160,312. This represented, according to the El Paso Chamber of Commerce, 76 percent of the entire cattle imports of the United States. One year later 174,530 head of cattle valued at $2,460,681 entered through El Paso, and the chamber of commerce proudly announced that this was the largest shipment in El Paso's history and more than 80 percent of total cattle importations into the country. The Mexican Revolution considerably reduced the supply of Chihuahua livestock, and cattle imports dropped to 81,068 in 1919. An increase in cattle raising in West Texas and New Mexico, however, compensated for the decline and over $14 million worth of cattle passed through the border city in 1917.[45] The growth of the livestock industry also led to the construction of small packing houses. National organizations such as Swift, Armour, and Morris along with other firms built facilities in El Paso to take advantage of nearby cattle ranges, as well as the availability of cheap labor.[46]

Not a traditional cattletown because of its other sources of income, El Paso nevertheless became closely tied to the livestock industry of the Southwest and northern Mexico. The 1920 city directory observed that ranching would continue to affect El Paso more than any other southwestern city. Despite the border city's prominence as a mining and trade center the directory concluded that El Paso "owes much of her wealth to the cattle industry, many of El Paso's wealthiest citizens having made their fortunes on the range; and she is grateful."[47]

As a result of these regional, national, and international connections, El Paso's internal economic institutions substantially grew between 1880 and 1920. However, such growth still reflected limited industrial development based on the extraction and processing of raw materials as well as the city's reliance on eastern investments and markets. Seven areas exemplify this condition: wholesale and retail trade, manufacturing, tourism, business and home construction, banking, agriculture, and population growth.

Railroads stimulated El Paso's wholesale trade. The *Lone Star* correctly observed in 1881 that with the completion of the Mexican Central, El Paso merchants would profit from the Mexican trade. To take advantage of this opportunity, the paper stressed that El Paso needed large wholesale houses stocking cotton and woolen goods, hats, boots, shoes, agricultural and mining machinery, furniture, liquors, "and, in short, everything that the United States has for sale to Mexico." By 1910 wholesale interests held investments of over $13 million consisting of 75 wholesale houses with 200 traveling salesmen. Despite some losses during the Mexican Revolution the wholesale business in 1916 was worth $50 million and the chamber of commerce believed that more prosperity was around the corner once the conflict in Mexico subsided. The chamber emphasized that Mexico would need millions of dollars worth of goods and that because of its location El Paso "should handle the lion's share of this great business."[48] By 1918 wholesale houses employed more

than 400 salesmen, who covered an immense trade territory extending
300 miles east and north, 600 miles west and northwest, and as
far south as Durango. Two years later, however, total wholesale investments had dropped due to the general post-World War I recession
and the conclusion of the Mexican Revolution, which ended large
sales of arms and supplies across the border. Still El Paso remained
in 1920 the major wholesale center in the Southwest and the total
volume of business done that year included: dry goods, $4 million;
groceries, $7 million; drugs, $400,000; jewelry, $100,000; boots and
shoes, $500,000; hardware, $6 million; and toys, $200,000.[49]

Mexico's establishment in 1885 of a duty-free zone in Ciudad
Juárez had initially hurt El Paso retailers, but its removal in 1905 due
to pressure from American merchants, Mexican merchants in the
interior, and general economic recession inaugurated a boom period
for El Paso stores.[50] The retail business grew as a variety of stores
serviced both El Paso residents and shoppers from the Southwest and
Mexico. "El Paso is quite a shopping point," observed one shopper
from New Mexico. "The town is full of Southern New Mexico's
ladies today on shopping tours. I am a great believer in the patronage
of home merchants and of fostering every kind of home [market], but
it must be conceded [that] El Paso's merchants carry a line of goods
superior to anything found this side of Albuquerque."[51] The *Times*
observed that El Pasoans no longer had to order goods from St. Louis
or Chicago because local stores now carried complete stocks. In
1910 when retail sales reached $2 million, the El Paso Retail Mer-
chants League commended merchants for their enterprise in acquiring
new business. This reflected what the league called "the El Paso
Spirit."[52]

Although wholesalers and retailers enjoyed prosperity, El Paso
desired to provide more than services. The *Lone Star* in 1881 concluded that El Paso should not remain what the newspaper termed an
"accidental city." "Instead of simply *attracting* capital," it emphasized, "we must be prepared to *create* it; otherwise we shall be
consumers only and soon exhaust what little advantages nature has
vouchsafed us without any effort on our part." Twelve years later
the *Times* commented that the city, besides being a railroad center,
needed to build factories. Non-El Pasoans concurred with this
opinion. William H. Thompson, the president of the St. Louis Bank

of Commerce, told the *Times* in a 1900 interview that because El Paso already supplied a large territory, it could become an important manufacturing site, especially since it faced no competition from other southwestern towns. Thompson believed that in two or three years the railroads would promote manufacturing in El Paso as a way of multiplying the wholesale market. "It will amaze you," he predicted, "the number of large and small industries that will spring up here as soon as the railroads conclude they can help themselves by helping your city."[53]

To encourage manufacturing, the chamber of commerce at the turn of the century negotiated with eastern industries about locating in El Paso. The chamber insisted that industries related to mining, besides smelting, could profit in the city. It pointed out that $5½ million worth of mining machinery had passed through El Paso in 1899 on its way to Mexico and that no reason existed why the city could not manufacture such machinery. As a result of the chamber's efforts, by 1910 El Paso acquired three foundries that produced mining and smelting equipment. The *Times* joined the chamber's efforts to industrialize El Paso but emphasized that the city required small industries as well as large ones. According to the paper, big industries could not produce for the entire needs of the population. Diversified industries, the border newspaper stressed, would help make El Paso self-sufficient and employ more men with larger payrolls. To reach such a goal, the chamber of commerce in 1909 began a "smokestack campaign" to attract industry. Praising the attempt, the *Times* pointed out that whatever type of manufacturing could be secured, El Paso offered excellent transport facilities for markets in the United States, Mexico, and the Orient. "They will each bring business, capital, population to the City," it stated, "offer employment for labor and be a factor in the creation of Greater El Paso."[54]

One year later the chamber of commerce announced that in five years more than $5 million had been invested in El Paso manufacturing. Among the plants built were the Southwestern Portland Cement Company costing over $1 million and producing more than 500,000 barrels of cement per year. Other industries included cigar manufacturing, turning out more than 4 million cigars each year from imported Mexican tobacco that El Pasoans believed to be

superior to Cuban cigars. Some of the city's residents also raised
a $50,000 bonus in 1911 to construct the Pearson Box Factory, which
employed a number of workers.[55] In 1920 the municipal directory
listed 286 manufacturing plants including the smelter and railroad
facilities with 5,000 workers—10,000 in good times—and with a
total value of $17 million.[56] Although impressive, El Paso's manu-
facturing industries did not replace transportation, smelting, and
commerce as the keystones of the border city's economy. Moreover,
these small-scale industries were the direct result of the regional
boom in transportation, mining, and ranching and hence prospered
only because of the need for southwestern raw materials. Too,
El Paso's manufacturing plants possessed a limited regional market
and did little to provide greater job mobility since they employed
either only small numbers of skilled workers or, by contrast, mostly
unskilled labor.

Tourism represented an additional border enterprise. The railroads made this possible and El Paso built substantial facilities for
visitors such as hotels and restaurants. In 1881 the *Lone Star* advocated the construction of a $50,000 hotel to house the many vis-
itors the railroads would bring. It warned that unless El Paso took
immediate steps to improve hotel accommodations, the town would
face serious problems. To induce tourists and conventions, El Paso
promoted its sunny and dry desert climate with warm tempera-
tures throughout most of the year. "The altitude of El Paso is 3700
to 3900 feet," a chamber of commerce advertisement read. "Because of this medium altitude there is less tendency to sleeplessness,
hemorrhages, headaches, and heart emotions that are so prone to
develop in extreme altitudes." The *Times* noted in 1891 that El Paso
had already become a popular winter resort and that hundreds of
eastern health seekers would arrive during the coming cold season.
This migration of health seekers represented, according to one historian, an important factor in nineteenth-century population movements. "A pragmatic, century-long search for a health-restoring and
disease-free area led inevitably," he points out, "to the early discovery and subsequent development of what many pioneers referred
to as nature's sanatorium, the elevated, moistureless, sun-drenched
plains and mountains health frontiers in the lower Southwest."
One visitor to El Paso believed, however, that local residents did not

realize that their city could become one of the world's great health resorts. Stressing health as a source of income, he urged construction of parks and sanitary facilities.[57] El Pasoans and eastern capitalists agreed and helped build hotels to house health seekers as well as tourists. The *Times* announced in 1900 that St. Louis and Chicago entrepreneurs had agreed to finance new hotels in the city. It further noticed that during winter months an average of 700 visitors arrived each day and that they paid for the best hotels available. Still, southwestern cities such as El Paso, San Antonio, Tucson, and Phoenix became favorite rest centers with only a minimum of publicity and few health facilities. Besides health seekers and tourists, many travelers and businessmen also stopped in El Paso on their way in and out of Mexico. In addition, shoppers from Mexico, West Texas, New Mexico, and Arizona visited every day. Because of the flow of people the number of hotels increased from 11 in 1889 to 29 in 1920.[58]

Along with the climate, El Paso used its Mexican connection to entice tourists. It advertised that they could easily cross the border at El Paso and visit Ciudad Juárez and other locations in northern Mexico. Here they would find a new cultural experience. An 1890 travel description emphasized that strangers had to make a trip to Juárez. Everything in the old Mexican town would be of great attraction, including the houses, streets, the old church, and the system of irrigation. "The habits, customs, and life of this primitive people are undescribable as a whole," this review stated, "but very interesting."[59] A later chamber of commerce article entitled "El Otro Lado" (The Other Side) assured potential tourists that Ciudad Juárez was "typically Mexican":

To the visitor who approaches the Mexican border for the first time "the other side" is the chief point of attraction. Ciudad Juárez lies just across the river from El Paso, and is reached by a ten-minute drive or electric car ride. Juárez, with its 8,000 people, is typically Mexican. The old church—centuries old, one of the oldest on the continent—with its massive adobe walls; the amphitheater for bull-fighting, the plaza, the streets, the business houses and dwellings, the curio shops, the vehicles from the surrounding country, the personal appearance, dress and customs of the people are all full of novelty and interest to the

American visitor. Our Mexican neighbors are accustomed to
being made the target of curious American eyes. The Mexican
is nothing if not courteous, and the humblest peon will meet
and converse with you with a degree of manly dignity and
courtesy that commands not merely respect but admiration.[60]

As a tourist attraction Ciudad Juárez also benefited certain American businessmen. Owing to the closing of El Paso's red-light district
and gambling houses by 1910, many American operators shifted
their trade across the border and helped initiate Juárez's dependency
on tourism from El Paso and the United States. "The town's well
being," one border historian writes, "rested upon the uncertain in-
flow of American visitors." Aware of Juárez's, as well as other
Mexican border towns', uneven economic development in comparison to El Paso, the *Revista Internacional* of Juárez observed in 1917:

> Our towns live in poverty, being wholly tributary to our
> neighbors. We have no industry, no agriculture, and lack a means
> of support. Other than what the local braceros [commuters] earn,
> in addition to the bull fights, the cock fights, the lotteries,
> liquor and curio shops which delight the tourists who visit us.[61]

Besides commerce, manufacturing, and tourism El Paso's physical
expansion represented the most visible sign of economic growth. An
important employer of unskilled Mexican workers, the construction
industry built many businesses, schools, churches, and homes. As an
example of this building boom the number of contractors and
builders increased from 11 in 1889 to 101 in 1919. The *Times* revealed in 1903 that large eastern syndicates had so much confidence
in the city's stability and future greatness that they wanted to invest in real estate that they considered a "gilt edge security."[62] Observing that construction in that year had reached a new high, the
Times believed that the building industry exemplified El Paso's
transition from a frontier town of adobe homes, dance halls, and
gambling houses to a desert metropolis. From $369,884 in 1898 the
total value of building permits jumped to $4 million in 1916. The
sharpest rise occurred during the Mexican Revolution and indicates
that the civil disruption across the border did not irreparably harm the

city's economy. El Paso moved from being fifth in building permits issued by Texas cities in 1913 to first place two years later, ahead of Houston, Dallas, Fort Worth, and San Antonio.[63]

In addition to eastern capital the banks of El Paso helped finance internal growth. From the establishment of the State National Bank in 1881, El Paso's banks expanded to eight in 1919 with resources of over $39 million. The most significant deposits occurred between 1910 and 1920 and can be attributed to both industry and trade as well as the movement of Mexican money to El Paso because of the revolution. For example, in 1911 the Mexico Northwestern Railway Company of New York advised its El Paso general manager to transfer its Chihuahua account to an American bank in the border city. This amounted to about $100,000 in gold deposited in the State National Bank. The availability of local capital allowed businesses to borrow easily for construction and expansion. Hence, accelerated financial activity increased bank clearings from $32,610,396 in 1907 to $308,861,839 in 1919. "El Paso has the most substantial and liberal banking houses to be found in the west," proclaimed an El Paso storeowner in 1901, "and our merchants— well, they all have a nice balance on the credit side of their bank accounts, and are fixed to do business on a cash basis."[64]

In contrast to other economic activities El Paso agriculture proved a disappointment. Situated in one of the most arid regions of the United States, El Paso did not receive enough rainfall to support agriculture. Moreover, the federal government did not complete construction of the Elephant Butte Dam in southern New Mexico until 1917; in later years the dam provided irrigation for agricultural production. In anticipation of this vital irrigation system the chamber of commerce had pointed out in 1910 that the Rio Grande Valley of El Paso possessed one of the most remarkable valleys on the American continent. Walled in by mountain ranges on both sides of the border, the valley, according to the chamber, was absolutely perfect from a farmer's point of view. With their natural fertilizers the waters of the Rio Grande enriched the soil and made the valley equal if not superior to the Nile's. The chamber concluded that a variety of grasses, vegetables, and fruits could easily be cultivated on the area's 200,000 acres. Consequently, despite limited irrigation El Paso's agricultural production grew, although it

remained a small enterprise. The total value of farm property in El
Paso County increased from $2,848,859 in 1900 to $8,726,633
in 1920. Hay and forage were the most cultivated crops; their production rose from a value of $309,530 in 1910 to $1,037,502
ten years later.[65] Some farmers also cultivated fruit. "There were
extensive pear orchards between El Paso and Ysleta [down river],"
a local resident, who arrived in 1917, remembers.[66] The 1920 census
listed 542 farmers in the county and only $569,056 as farm expen-
ditures for labor. As a result El Paso remained dependent on other
areas for most of its agricultural needs.[67]

Finally, as El Paso's economy grew, the city underwent a vast
shift in population. Businessmen, lawyers, railroadmen, miners,
merchants, craftsmen, and teachers as well as thousands of Mexican
laborers migrated to the Gateway City seeking profits and a higher
standard of living. Hence, the population of El Paso soared from 736
in 1880 to 77,560 in 1920 and probably closer to 100,000 because
the census failed to count many Mexicans. The border city became
the fifth largest urban center in Texas and the most populated in
West Texas, New Mexico, and Arizona. El Paso, moreover, believed
that its population expansion was proof of its ascendancy over
potential competitors. "Anybody not an idiot," the *Times* emphasized as early as 1891, "knows that El Paso is destined to be the
great city of the southwest; and when Albuquerque has more population than now, including 50,000,000 mosquitoes, El Paso will be a
city of 15,000 people."[68]

As the population increase indicated, the economic growth of El
Paso and the Southwest constituted a remarkable accomplishment.
From a sparsely inhabited area, El Paso became a large urban oasis in
40 years. Besides responding to the impact of the railroads, mining,
ranching, and trade with Mexico, El Paso also operated as an important commercial, banking, and tourist center. In the process El
Paso and its surrounding economic region became integral parts of
American industrial capitalism. By World War I the Southwest
functioned as a leading supplier of industrial metals, agricultural
products, and livestock and in turn consumed eastern manufactured products. Still, although the Southwest and El Paso prospered
in this relationship, the extractive and agricultural nature ot the
region's economy retarded industrial development. Although this

economic pattern has changed considerably since World War II due to accelerated industrialization, many southwestern areas retain earlier economic characteristics. One critic, for example, noted in the late 1940s that El Paso represented a "semi-amateur metropolis. . . . Except by strictly local standards," he observed, "it has no big business really its own. As metropolis it is chiefly a convenient operational stage through which bigger interests back East, or whatever they are, function regionally."[69] It is this economic infrastructure, historically characterized by extractive-related industries with low-skilled labor-intensive conditions, that has in turn shaped the politics and culture of a distinct region and has influenced racial patterns, for perhaps El Paso's most significant role lay in its service as a market for unskilled Mexican labor. Thousands of Mexicans crossed the border and not only swelled the city's population but also provided a large and cheap labor supply. Hence, an additional but little known aspect of American immigrant history began.

3

Desert Immigrants

While El Paso reflected the economic development of the Southwest in transportation, mining, ranching, and commerce, it also mirrored the great need for cheap labor by southwestern industries.
Employers met much of their labor requirements, as in the East and
Midwest, through immigration. Initially employing a varied assort-
ment of European, Asian, and Mexican workers, by the turn of the
century southwestern enterprises relied almost exclusively on neighboring Mexico for their supplies of hired hands.[1] Between 1880
and 1920 large numbers of Mexicans entered southwestern labor
markets. Because of its location as the termination point of the Mexican Central, El Paso played a key role in the process and represented
the foremost labor supply center in the region. In El Paso the railroads and other industries contracted thousands of newly arrived
Mexican immigrants and transferred them throughout the Southwest as well as other sections of the country. At the same time, economic changes in Mexico along with the disruption of the Mexican
Revolution (1910–17) forced Mexicans to travel north in search of
jobs. The Mexicans' need for work complemented the desire by
southwestern enterprises for a large supply of cheap, unskilled, and
manageable workers.

Mexico's limited economic development became the major internal cause for the emigration of Mexicans between 1876 and 1910.
During the presidencies of Porfirio Díaz significant advances took
place in railroad construction, mining, the commercialization of agriculture, oil production, and the establishment of industries, textiles
in particular. In this transformation foreign investments were an indispensable source of capital and technology. The *El Paso Times* reported on the eve of Díaz's downfall in 1910 that the total amount

33

of capital invested in Mexico between 1886 and 1906 had been more than 2 billion pesos; foreign capital represented almost 70 percent of it. Americans invested in railroads, mines, ranches, farms, and other concerns prior to 1910. These investments, along with European ones, helped to stimulate sustained economic growth in Mexico under Díaz, whose open invitation to foreign capital made Mexico, according to a contemporary slogan, "the mother of foreigners and the stepmother of Mexicans."[2] Mexico's economic growth led many observers to see a new era of order and progress for it as a result of Díaz's leadership. "Our sister republic of Mexico stands upon the threshold of the dawning century," the *Houston Post* commented in 1900, "with wonderful social, political, and industrial development to its credit." The *Post* believed that the railroads, modern business methods, expanded industries, and modernization of the legal and educational system constituted the foundation for Mexico's economic take-off.[3]

Yet, Mexican policy, which in theory worshipped industrial gods, in practice left the ageless hacienda in control of the countryside. Its tentacles, nearly everywhere in rural Mexico until 1910, displaced the rural population due to changes in land tenure. Before Díaz, the communal villages had characterized the densely populated central regions; however, between 1876 and 1910 Díaz and his henchmen in office sanctioned the theft of village lands by wealthy hacendados. Meant to encourage foreign investment in order to stimulate exports in such items as cotton, coffee, and henequen, Díaz's land policy proved disastrous to dirt farmers as hacendados and at times foreigners acquired "public lands," previously communal properties (*ejidos*) owned by *campesinos.* One estimate places the number of dirt farmers who lost communal lands at 5 million. Moreover, a growing population, the result of improved health measures, served to exacerbate land shortages and rural poverty. Between 1875 and 1910 Mexico's total population multiplied by more than 50 percent. Díaz's short-sighted policy and the population explosion left a large class of landless rural laborers eager to move north to find jobs in industry, agriculture, and mines in the lightly populated provinces of northern Mexico.[4]

Mobility characterized this new worker. He not only could find employment on the cotton or cattle haciendas, but when he needed to he could work in railroad construction and maintenance or in the mines as a manual laborer. Clearly, the jobless went in search of work and better wages.[5] Chihuahua and Sonora, for example, paid among the highest wages in Mexico. By 1900 a common laborer earned about 88 cents (U.S.) in Ciudad Juárez compared to 23 cents (U.S.) in Mexico's interior. But, nevertheless, across the border similar work in Texas paid $1 a day.[6] Eventually, owing to the 1907 recession in Mexico and the Mexican Revolution of 1910, when much unemployment occurred, many workers crossed the border into the United States. A sample of World War I draft registration cards for El Paso reveals that the majority (72%) of Mexican immigrants were born in the northern Mexican states, especially Chihuahua.[7] The governor of Arizona, commenting on increased Mexican immigration to his state in 1907, observed that high wages in the mines, smelters, railroads, and ranches tempted Mexicans to leave their homeland.[8] The opportunities for jobs that had produced the migration of landless workers to Mexico's northern borderlands motivated the first great wave of Mexican immigrants to the United States.

It is difficult to determine the exact number of Mexicans entering the United States between 1880 and 1920 because immigration officials did not keep adequate records for every Mexican who crossed the border. Moreover, it appears that many Mexicans crossed and recrossed the frontier several times due to seasonal employment in the United States. In a 1912 article Samuel Bryan, writing for the *Survey*, noted that until 1908 immigration figures on Mexicans "are so obviously incomplete as to be of little value." Many also crossed illegally at various points along the lengthy and unguarded desert boundary. Table 3.1 lists official immigration figures from 1894 to 1920. Although showing increased immigration, the data represent smaller figures than those published by El Paso newspapers. Furthermore, Mexican immigration records reveal a much higher volume of migration, in some cases more than double the American numbers for a given year. The 1930 census, the first to record a category for Mexicans, estimated that the Mexican population of the United States grew from 367,510 in 1910 to 700,541 in 1920, although these figures did not include "illegals" or those counted as "whites." Between the turn of the century and the start

Table 3.1.   Mexicans Admitted to the United States, 1894–1920

1894	109	1908	6,067
1895	116	1909	16,251
1896	150	1910	18,691
1897	91	1911	19,889
1898	107	1912	23,238
1899	161	1913	11,926
1900	237	1914	14,614
1901	347	1915	12,340
1902	709	1916	18,425
1903	528	1917	17,869
1904	1,009	1918	18,524
1905	3,637	1919	29,818
1906	1,997	1920	52,361
1907	1,406		

Source: U.S. Immigration reports as quoted in Charles H. Hufford, *The Social and Economic Effects of the Mexican Migration into Texas*, p. 33. For Mexican immigration figures see Ricardo Romo, "Mexican Workers in the City: Los Angeles, 1915–1930," p. 65.

of the Great Depression, more than 1 million Mexicans arrived. Owing to its proximity to the border and its economic boom, Texas received more than half the Mexican immigrants.[9]

Many of them entered the United States through El Paso via the Mexican Central Railroad. "Probably more Mexican laborers enter the United States through El Paso," an American government official reported in 1908, "than cross the border either east or west of that city." Charles Armijo, who arrived in El Paso with his family in 1910, remembers that a fare on the Mexican Central did not cost much. Available information, however, indicates that railroad passage to the border from central Mexico was between 10 and 15 American dollars, undoubtedly causing some hardship on immigrants from the interior. Large numbers found jobs in El Paso and added to the border city's population growth. By 1920 El Paso had the second largest (next to San Antonio) Mexican population of any American city and was the only major southwestern metropolis with more Mexicans than Americans.[10]

Mexicans emigrated to the United States in two definable periods between 1880 and the conclusion of World War I. The first included unrestricted movement across the border up to 1917; the second involved immigration limited for work in specific industries as a result of the Immigration Act of 1917. Until that year the only Mexicans who could not enter the country were the physically and mentally handicapped, paupers, beggars, all persons not capable of earning a living, convicted criminals, polygamists, anarchists, and prostitutes. Since 1885 immigration officials also had prohibited contract labor. Even under the 1907 Immigration Act immigrants from Mexico did not have to pay a head tax or any other entrance fee, causing a *Times* reporter to remark that "Mexicans can come in easier than any other class of immigrants." Armijo recalls that immigrants could enter and leave without passports and whenever they pleased. According to El Paso historian Cleofas Calleros, who arrived with his family at the turn of the century, "All you had to do coming from Mexico, if you were a Mexican citizen, was to report at the immigration office on the American side . . . give your name, the place of your birth, and where you were going to."[11]

During the 1890s Mexicans, entering in smaller numbers, did not cause any considerable notice or alarm. In 1894 a Mexican newspaper in El Paso, *El Defensor*, commented that the availability of work had promoted the immigration of Mexicans. Railroads—or the *traques* as the Mexicans called them—operating along the border between the Gulf of Mexico and the Pacific Ocean contracted almost all their manual laborers in El Paso. The *Arizona Silver Belt* editorialized in 1898 that railroad construction crews in Arizona consisted mainly of Mexicans and Indians. "It is difficult to get white men to work," the editor wrote, "the wages being only $1.50 a day, and board $5 per week with some minor charges, which reduce a man's net earnings." The employment of Mexican railroad workers in the border city increased the prosperity of local merchants since most of the workers' families lived in El Paso and, in turn, economic expansion reinforced the city's attraction for new immigrants. *El Defensor* also observed that some of the immigrants entered the United States illegally by walking across the often dry Rio Grande at El Paso.[12]

According to one early immigrant, the railroads did not allow Mexican employees to take their families with them on the job.

However, after a laborer had worked at least six months, the railroads provided free transportation for his family to the job location. Those who left families in El Paso or Mexico received three-week passes to visit their wives and children every six months. The Dillingham Commission, established by the United States Senate to investigate immigrant conditions throughout the country, calculated from data acquired from nine Western railroads between 1907 and 1909 that 58.2 percent of the wives of Mexican railroad laborers lived in the United States. No other immigrant railroad workers in the West, such as southern Europeans and Asians, could match this figure and the commission suggested, although without evidence, that "the conditions under which section hands live are less uninviting to the Mexican women than to the women of any other race." By 1910 one railroad line, the Santa Fe, encouraged the migration of Mexican families in order to stabilize the line's work force. As one Santa Fe engineer put it, hiring married men produced a "better trained and steadier class of laborers."[13]

As more immigrants with their families arrived during the first decade of the new century, concern began over the flow of Mexicans into El Paso. The chief of the Bureau of Immigration in El Paso, General Malloy, told the *Times* in 1902 that for several months "hordes of Mexicans of every age have been pouring over the border, seeking the benefits of United States citizenship." According to Malloy, during the month of May an unusually large number of Mexicans entered. In one week between 400 and 500 Mexicans had been admitted and an average of 250 per day had made applications for admission. Malloy noted that even boys and old men and women could be found among the immigrants and that labor contractors herded the Mexicans and transported them to be used as cheap labor in railroad grading camps. The Mexican consulate confirmed Malloy's statements and its secretary commented that immigration had occurred because of a drought in Mexico, forcing many farmers and campesinos to leave Mexico and enter the United States in search of work.[14]

One year later the El Paso Medical Association complained that unrestricted immigration of Mexican "peons" had caused a potential health problem for El Paso as well as the whole country. It recommended rigid enforcement of federal immigration laws for a period of twelve months in order to protect the United States against the bubonic plague striking Mexico. "We understand well enough," a spokesman for the association stated, ". . . that half a dozen government inspectors cannot prevent poor Mexicans from crowding into the country." The association believed that the "most objectionable class" of Mexicans did not cross over the international bridges but illegally waded across the Rio Grande. To prevent the illegal entrance of paupers and the diseased, it called upon state, territorial, and city officers to serve as immigration inspectors. "The sheriffs, deputy sheriffs, constables and policemen," the association's representative stressed, "would detect the stranger and they could be escorted back to the Mexican side of the line." The association further urged a one-year ban on Mexican "peon" immigration.[15]

No such restriction was placed and four years later the *Times* reported that in the 1906 fiscal year 32,465 immigrants had arrived in El Paso, a gain of 7,575 over fiscal 1905. Of those admitted, 31,358 were Mexicans. Twenty Mexicans came to the United States for every American who went to Mexico. A Mexican newspaper in El Paso pointed out one year later that 22,000 Mexican men between the ages of 19 and 45 had crossed into El Paso during 1906. They came because of oppression at the hands of hacendados and *caciques* (political bosses), who forced them to work for almost nothing. "It is only natural," the Mexican newspaper *El Paso del Norte* emphasized, "that the 'Supreme Law of Necessity' obliges all these people to emigrate to a foreign land in search of higher wages and better treatment." El Paso newspapers printed various other accounts of Mexican immigration to El Paso prior to the Mexican Revolution. In September 1907, for example, the *Times* reported that 400 Mexican laborers had been admitted by local immigration officials. These workers had arrived in Ciudad Juárez on two Mexican Central trains on a Friday and by the next day had crossed into El Paso. "These immigrants appear at the border in sombrero, sarape, and sandals," observed one federal official, "which, before crossing the river, they usually exchange for a suit of 'American' clothing, shoes, and a less conspicuous hat."[16]

The Dillingham Commission noted the increased migration and employment of Mexican labor in the Southwest. The Senate investigating body estimated that Mexicans represented 17.1 percent of all common laborers employed in the maintenance of way departments of nine western and southwestern railroads. Most of the Mexicans worked close to the border. Of the railroads examined, the Santa Fe and the Southern Pacific hired the majority of Mexicans. Out of its 2,672 common laborers, the Santa Fe engaged 2,599 Mexicans. One historian has suggested that many Mexicans chose to work for the Santa Fe because of the religious symbolism the railroad's name conveyed.[17] The Southern Pacific employed 2,714 Mexicans in a work force of 12,592 laborers; however, the bulk of the Mexicans toiled in the railroad's Southwest division. "The number of Mexican section hands employed in the Western States," the commission emphasized, "has more than doubled since 1900 in spite of the fact that roads, e.g., the Rock Island operating in other States, have begun to employ them and are paying higher wages." According to the Senate report, although Mexicans had displaced other groups of cheap labor, such as the Chinese and the Japanese, the new immigrant workers formed an additional source of low paid labor. From its data the commission revealed that the railroads paid Mexican workers only $1 a day, except for a short period before 1907, when they received $1.25 per day. Senator Dillingham's commission concluded that railroads like the Santa Fe and Southern Pacific preferred Mexicans because they possessed more physical strength than the Japanese yet were known for their tractability and "passive obedience." In addition, Mexicans "are easily satisfied, and there is no fear of concerted action by them."[18]

During the Mexican Revolution, political as well as economic immigrants came to El Paso. Hundreds of political refugees, both rich and poor, fled Mexico to escape persecution by the different warring factions. Prior to Francisco Madero's capture of Ciudad Juárez in May 1911, for example, large numbers of Mexicans from the strategic border town and surrounding region fled to safety in El Paso, including many young men escaping impressment into Díaz's army. "The hotels and rooming houses of the city are filled with the families of Juárez's most exclusive social circles," one observer reported. Two years later as civil war erupted once again after Madero's assassination, more political refugees found a haven in the border city. A *Times* correspondent, witnessing the entrance of 500 refugees, remarked that most were women and children from the wealthiest families in Chihuahua.[19] Arriving at the age of nine with his parents and three brothers and sisters, Jesús Moreno later remembered that "there were a lot of people coming to that city (El Paso) because of the Revolution. . . . We came to the United States to wait out the conclusion of the Revolution. We thought it would be over in a few months."[20]

The largest and most controversial influx of political refugees occurred in January 1914 following the defeat of Mexican federal troops at Ojinaga on the Texas–Coahuila border southeast of El Paso. Thousands of *federales* and their camp followers fled to Presidio, Texas, to escape capture at the hands of Francisco "Pancho" Villa. Once the fugitives were in American territory, United States military forces captured them under an 1899 international convention governing belligerent troops crossing into a neutral country. Unable to provide adequately for their care in Presidio, however, officials transferred the refugee army, totaling more than 5,000, to Fort Bliss on the outskirts of El Paso. General Hugh L. Scott, the commander of the base, attempting to calm fears that the detainment of such large numbers would cause disease or social disorders, assured the city council that the Mexicans had been vaccinated and would be closely guarded in a tent camp surrounded by wire fences and electric lights. To assuage local discontent, the general further pointed out that over $1,000 a day in provisions would have to be purchased from El Paso merchants to maintain the camp.[21]

Unconvinced by Scott, Americans expressed alarm and anger at having to host the Mexican refugees. One El Paso physician in a letter to the *Times* warned against the dangers to public health and morals from what he considered the unsanitary and immoral nature of the female camp followers. "They are aliens, civilians, indigent, unhygienic and liable to become public charges," he emphasized, "in fact are obnoxious to every law governing the admission of aliens into the United States." Another El Pasoan complained that Mexicans, whether refugees or not, did not appreciate American charity and generosity; consequently, the United States had no obligation to take care of those fleeing from their own civil war. "I cannot understand what the United States is coming to," J. C. Jarvis wrote, "when it allows a foreign disturbing element to come to this country and break all the laws and go unpunished, as they do in El Paso." Furthermore, one American failed to comprehend why the United States allowed refugees into the country when so many Mexicans already had glutted the local labor market, causing unemployment among Americans. Finally, one letter writer to the *Times*, signing himself as "O," declared that the refugees endangered El Paso's peace. Because most of them supported Madero's assassin, General Victoriano Huerta, "O" argued that antifederal forces led by Villa would undoubtedly retaliate against El Paso if the refugees posed a threat. The refugees, he concluded, were a menace. Reinforcing such fears, the American consul in Ciudad Juárez suspected imprisoned Mexican officers of directing revolutionary plots along the border and suggested to the State Department that 200 or 300 of them be removed from El Paso. However, the *Times* urged patience and good will. In an editorial entitled "Refugees Welcome," the border publication reminded El Pasoans that in earlier, more peaceful days Mexicans arriving to patronize city stores had been a welcome sight and comprised a significant group of consumers. Refugees, the paper contended, continued to be important shoppers as well as law-abiding residents. Astutely recognizing the economic value of the Mexican population to El Paso's fortunes, the *Times* concluded by calling for racial harmony: "The *Times* is glad to have this opportunity to voice as it feels it does voice, the practically unanimous judgment of the intelligent and hospitable people of El Paso, that the presence of this large number of the citizens of Mexico is not a menace, but a source of prosperity and happiness to the people of this city."[22]

The *Times* attempted to alleviate further tensions by publishing accounts indicating that sanitary and peaceful conditions existed in the refugee camp at Fort Bliss. Reporter Julia A. Sharp wrote one piece suggesting that Americans should be neither concerned nor sentimental about the refugees including the women and children; not only were they used to harsh conditions, but they had a number of conveniences. Sharp informed her readers that army officials provided the Mexicans with sufficient food, clothing, medical care, and shelter. She indicated that some children had no clothes but that this caused no problem because the majority of children in Mexico, ages two to five, were accustomed to having no clothes. Hence,

El Pasoans need not worry about them. The fact that these children possessed no clothes during cold desert days in January did not appear to bother reporter Sharp either. She also expressed an opinion on the hardiness of the female camp followers. "What would be death to an American woman," Sharp subjectively stated, "is an appetizer to the class of Mexican women found at Fort Bliss and while our sympathies go out to the mother weeping over the death of her little one or to the wife sorrowing for a husband lost in battle, we must take into consideration that it is their own fight and not ours; that we did not send women trailing over the desert wastes, and last and not least that we could not prevent them going even if they were offered good homes." Whether concerned or not, El Pasoans were relieved of the refugees in April, when officials transported them to Fort Wingate in southern New Mexico. A few months later the American government released the noncommissioned officers, privates, and camp followers, who returned to Mexico. During the brief existence of the Fort Bliss refugee camp 5,296 Mexicans had been detained including 1,237 women and 532 children.[23]

Despite the political character of many immigrants, between 1910 and 1920 most Mexicans arrived seeking jobs not political sanctuary, although the civil war at times made it difficult to leave the country. The *Times* observed in 1911 that for two months there had been a decrease in the number of Mexican immigrants through El Paso. F. W. Berkshire, the Chief of Immigration Inspectors in the city, stated that for the previous three or four years there had been an average of 2,000 Mexican immigrants per month in El Paso from February to May. They came to work on the railroads of the Southwest, but not one Mexican had entered since January due to the breakdown of train communication between El Paso and the Mexican interior caused by the revolution. Yet by late spring the Mexican Central resumed operations and more than 1,000 Mexican laborers arrived during the first days of June. Once the Mexicans were admitted, contractors immediately sent them to work in Arizona and California railroad camps. The *Times* further noted that every train that arrived in Juárez during June brought about 300 men to work on railroad section gangs in the Southwest.[24]

In 1914 the *Times* reported that a "horde of strange Mexicans" had been discovered wandering through south El Paso, bordering the river. Policemen found about 300 Mexicans camped in an alley who stated they were farmers from the vicinity of Mexico City and that they had left their homes because of the revolution. They informed the *Times* that another 700 *compañeros* remained in Juárez but would cross the border in the next few days. Most of the men said they had left their families in Mexico while they came to the United States looking for jobs. After only one day in El Paso the majority of these immigrants had been shipped out by employment offices to work on New Mexico railroads. Years later a St. Louis labor contractor observed that Mexicans in the United States often received news of jobs through several channels: in restaurants; barbershops; poolhalls; hotels; labor offices; from merchants; correspondence from other Mexicans in railroad camps; from Mexican newspapers in the United States; and in some cases one Mexican would leave a railroad camp to bring other workers back with him.[25]

As increased fighting broke out in the north-central parts of Mexico between 1914 and 1916, thousands of Mexicans entered El Paso. In one June week in 1916 immigration officials admitted 4,850 Mexicans into the city. American miners forced to leave Torreón reported that officers of General Venustiano Carranza's army granted free transportation to El Paso to families along the route of the Mexican Central. Torreón and other towns of the area had become short of food and little or no work could be found. Félix Urdiales, who lived in Juárez at the time, recalled that farm production had ceased in northern Mexico, resulting in widespread hunger. The *El Paso Herald* received reports in August of people dying of hunger in Zacatecas and Torreón, and the Reverend José Márquez, who directed charity activities in Juárez, stated that 200 destitute men, women, and children arrived in the Mexican border city every week from the interior.[26] Observing that many Mexican immigrants remained in El Paso "to glut the labor markets and keep down wages," the *Survey* also commented on their depressed condition:

Refugees before one band of marauders after another, homeless, poverty stricken, chronically hungry, alien in speech, manners, habits and ideas, they have proved a heavy burden for so young a community as El Paso to carry. For El Paso, 'Gateway to Mex-

ico,' has found its wickets opening in since Díaz fell. And El
Paso, like New York, gets more than its share of the weak among
incoming aliens.[27]

The large movement of Mexicans into El Paso caused officials to
fear a major epidemic. To prevent it, all Mexicans who crossed the
border, whether immigrants or residents of Juárez who worked in El
Paso, had to receive vaccinations against typhus. In order not to
offend the Juárez commuters, the *Herald* pointed out that they did
not represent the source of the health hazard. The problem, according
to the paper, did not consist of the productive and sober men and
women who worked in El Paso and lived in Juárez but in the migrants
from Mexico's interior who arrived in poverty and poor health.[28]

In addition to vaccinations the city health department inspected
all areas of Chihuahuita, the largest Mexican district in El Paso
and adjacent to the border, for any contagious diseases. A room-to-
room search uncovered no such problems, but the inspectors
burned all rags and bedding infested with lice. Immigration officials
also increased their surveillance of illegal entrants and captured
large numbers of Mexicans who smuggled themselves across the river.
Captain L. L. Hall of the El Paso Police Department emphasized
the problem at a Rotary Club luncheon in March and warned that
the city faced a severe crisis because 2,000 Mexican immigrants desired to enter El Paso, but the city, customs, and immigration
officials could not cope with these numbers. Many had already crossed
illegally downriver from Washington Park in the city's eastern section and upriver from the cement plant in the western part of El Paso.
Hall announced that assistance had been requested of General John
Pershing's troops then stationed in the city but that Pershing, lacking
instructions from Washington, refused. By June 1916 the problem
became worse and U.S. immigration officers at the Santa Fe bridge
connecting El Paso with Ciudad Juárez began turning back hundreds
of Mexicans. The immigrants had to pass rigorous physical examinations, which many failed. Despite these rejections Mayor Tom Lea
of El Paso cautioned that unless these strict entrance requirements
continued, he would be forced to declare a quarantine against Mexican immigration. The danger of the spread of typhus had become
too great to take chances, the mayor stated, hence the hundreds of

Mexicans seeking entry to El Paso had to be considered a health menace and kept out.[29]

A quarantine did not have to be enforced and immigration authorities reported that not one case of typhus or any other dangerous disease had been found among 2,000 immigrants who entered El Paso in three days. They observed that no more than 1,500 who remained in Ciudad Juárez desired to enter the country. "The large numbers of Mexicans that are asking for admission to the United States are apparently healthy, in good physical condition and some are not wholly destitute," said the supervising inspector at the international bridge. "Some say they have not had anything to eat for several days."[30] Nevertheless, continued reports of typhus and smallpox in Zacatecas and Aguascalientes made El Paso officials consider a quarantine until the danger abated by year's end. By then the special El Paso population census taken in 1916 reported that out of a total population of 51,898, Mexicans represented 52 percent, or 32, 724 people. In addition, 7,051 refugees—almost all Mexicans—resided in the city.[31]

The Immigration Act of 1917 temporarily reduced the movement of Mexicans into the United States. Although its literacy test and $8 head tax had been intended to restrict Europeans, it also affected Mexican immigration. The number of Mexicans who entered in 1917 dropped to 25,000, nearly half the figure for the previous year. Moreover, although as aliens they could not be subjected to American conscription laws, many Mexicans returned to their homeland during World War I for fear of being drafted.[32] This decline in addition to war manpower shortages led employers in El Paso and the Southwest to complain of a lack of labor. The *Herald* reported a dearth of Mexican workers at a time when the region badly needed railroad, farm, and factory laborers. Instead, Mexicans had started to return to Mexico at the rate of 100 a day out of fear and ignorance of the new immigration law, and the *Los Angeles Times* warned of a serious exodus with particular dire consequences for agricultural and ranching interests along the Texas border. Even El Paso housewives felt the effect of the restrictions because the law barred Mexican servants who could neither read nor write from employment, forcing many housewives to do their own work.[33]

Opposed to these regulations, the executive committee of the
Arizona Council of Defense requested its state representatives in
Congress to seek a suspension of the literacy test and head tax
provisions in order to facilitate immigration from Mexico. The council claimed that the railroads of southern Arizona needed 5,000
laborers and that the shortage could total 16,500 within a year. It
believed that the maintenance of the railroads should be considered a military priority and entitled to Mexican workers. Besides
the railroads, other Arizona industries insisted that they needed
Mexican unskilled labor, especially the farmers of the Salt River Valley, who desired hands for their harvest of grain, alfalfa, cotton,
and other crops. The mines also reported a shortage of labor. "Mexico is therefore the country to which Arizona must look for unskilled
labor," asserted the *Herald* in an editorial supporting the Arizona
council. The El Paso paper affirmed the council's contention that
both the literacy test and the head tax represented an effective barrier
against men desiring jobs in the United States. California farm grow-
ers concurred, and according to a member of the California Fruit Grow-
ers' Exchange the 1917 restrictions threatened to create a workers
shortage for the Southern California harvest.[34] The demand by southwestern economic interests for liberal immigration laws constituted a
traditional request by American industries, especially in "good times."

The efforts of the Arizona council succeeded as well as those of
agricultural interest groups throughout the Southwest. The Department of Labor announced in June 1917 that the immigration law
would be suspended in part to allow Mexican laborers to enter for
agricultural work. According to the decree, the secretary of labor
waived the literacy test, the $8 head tax, and the 1885 prohibition of
contract labor. The *Herald* praised this decision but noted a serious
flaw in the suspension. "This leaves the railroads out in the cold," the
paper stated, "and they are most in need of men." It observed that
one line alone estimated an immediate need for 5,000 laborers. Other
southwestern employers also reported a desire for Mexicans. The
Herald believed that it might not be too late for the secretary of
labor to modify his position to include more industries employing
Mexican workers, and that perhaps they could be shifted from one
area to another—wherever the demand became greatest. "For instance," it pointed out,

at one time it might be desireable [*sic*] to have a large number of Mexicans available for the cotton picking. At another time they might not be needed on the farm but would be in demand in the section gangs on the railroads. At still another, the mines and smelters might be in need of ordinary labor and secure some hundreds or even thousands of men from the railroads and farms.[35]

Although the Department of Labor did not immediately extend the suspension, in August the *Herald* reported that the first positive results of the waiver could be seen in the movement of trainloads of Mexicans to sugar beet factories in California and cotton fields in Arizona. It further believed that the suspension had already proved to be a blessing both for American farmers and for the Mexicans, many of whom had lost their jobs due to the shutdown of copper mines and smelters in Sonora. The *Herald* emphasized that the waiver had helped alleviate the region's labor shortages.[36]

Despite the entrance of agricultural workers, total immigration from Mexico declined during 1917 because of the immigration law. J. B. Gwin, the Secretary of the Associated Charities of El Paso, observed some results of the new restrictions. Mexicans who applied at an employment agency now had to present an immigration card to show they had been legally admitted. Yet the enforcement of the law led to an increase in illegal crossings, especially below Ysleta (a few miles down the river from El Paso), where some persons hauled Mexicans in boats to the American side, charging 50 cents per person. Gwin believed that the decline in immigration had made Chihuahuita a healthier place to live since the law kept "the worst class of Mexicans out," although he observed that the application of the literacy test had been made as lenient as possible. All applicants for admission at the El Paso port of entry had to read twenty lines in the Bible in some language. On the other hand, immigration officials strictly enforced the head tax provision. Finally, those admitted had to be bathed and their clothes and baggage sterilized by immigration authorities. A reporter noted that inspectors used gas to disinfect baggage since normal steam cleaning would ruin their contents. According to Félix Urdiales, who obtained a passport to enter the United States at the time, border officials, including a contingent of Texas Rangers stationed at El Paso, also required Mexican

commuter workers from Ciudad Juárez to be bathed every eight
days. In exchange for a bath, commuters received a receipt certifying
they had been cleaned that day.[37]

Persistent demands by the railroads and mines for Mexican labor
resulted in an 1918 amendment to the immigration law of the previous year. The amendment extended the waiver to Mexicans entering
to work in railroad maintenance and coal mining. These aliens could
remain in the United States no longer than the duration of the war
and had to secure employment before crossing. In addition, employers had to file job applications with immigration authorities at the
port of entry. Laborers admitted under the amendment received iden-
tification cards and labor contractors employing them had to be
responsible for their transportation to the place of work. George J.
Howe, chief inspector at the port of El Paso, predicted that the
new modifications would bring immediate relief from labor shortages
in the Southwest. However, the *Herald* reported a week later that
no dramatic increase in Mexican immigration had occurred. It believed
that many laborers in Mexico desired to work in the United States
but that ignorance of the new waiver held many back. Apparently
some Mexicans did not hesitate, for Tom Bell, the deputy commissioner of the Texas Labor Department, commented that the
efforts of his office and other agencies to recruit Mexicans to pick
the cotton crop had met with success. According to Bell, the Mexican workers arrived in El Paso at the rate of 90 per day and were
shipped out as fast as possible to the interior of the state. Some of
them went to Colorado and California to work in the sugar beet
industry, where Bell asserted they had been assured of good wages
and wholesome food.[38]

By July 1918 the number of Mexican immigrants entering El
Paso had definitely increased, although demand still exceeded the
supply. W. H. Robb, the senior examiner of the United States
Employment Service, on a visit to El Paso observed that 500 laborers
had arrived in Juárez but had to wait while American officials took
their photographs and filled out forms before the Mexicans could
cross the border. These procedures took too much time, the *Times*
complained, at a moment when employers immediately needed
workers. To compound matters, other areas of the country expressed
an interest in the Mexicans. Representatives of the Pennsylvania

Railroad, for example, arrived in El Paso and reported that they could use several thousand laborers.[39]

The desire for Mexican workers seemed inexhaustible. During 1918 Texas farm groups maintained that the suspension of the 1917 law did not provide sufficient laborers and requested that all restrictions on Mexican immigration be dropped. In San Antonio a July conference of Texas officials and agricultural interests petitioned Secretary of Labor William B. Wilson to lift for 90 days the immigration law for Mexican labor. The conference reported that South Texas farmers required 40,000 Mexicans. The *Herald* supported the San Antonio meeting and stressed the acute labor shortages in Texas and the Southwest due to the war effort. Because of its seasonal nature, agriculture felt this shortage more than other enterprises and the *Herald* pointed out that in some southwestern areas women had to work in the fields "helping with slender muscles but stout hearts to do the work for which there is an insufficiency of men." It emphasized the lack of laborers for mines, factories, and offices in the region and that even these concerns had to employ boys and elderly men. A great service could be rendered, the *Herald* concluded, if Washington would waive all restrictions against Mexican labor with the exception of health and wartime measures.[40]

The request did not meet the approval of federal officials, although they did extend the waiver to include Mexicans working in any type of mining or as common laborers in federal construction projects. Affecting only immigration district no. 23, covering Texas, New Mexico, Arizona, and California, this latest order from the Department of Labor, the *Herald* noted, would relieve labor shortages to some extent. The paper claimed that military aviation fields and army camps in Texas had been in urgent need of manual workers. The Arizona copper mines suffered from a lack of Mexicans, and the railroads found it difficult to maintain an adequate work force for the section gangs "whose groups of houses dot the desert from here to Los Angeles."[41]

The end of the war terminated the special exemptions of the 1917 immigration law. Yet southwestern industries still insisted that they would be seriously hurt if the waiver did not continue. Sympathetic to their interests, the Labor Department ruled that employers who had contracts for Mexican laborers prior to December

15, 1918, could import them until January 15, 1919. The regulation permitted Mexican laborers in agriculture, on the railroads, in government construction work, and in the mines to remain in the United States until they were no longer needed or their contracts expired. Moreover, persistent pressure by these industries kept these exemptions in force until 1921. The survival of the suspensions after the war meant that the economy of the Southwest continued to be supplied with cheap Mexican labor despite earlier declarations that the waiver had been only a wartime necessity. The Immigration Bureau announced that twice as many Mexicans entered the United States during fiscal 1919 than in any previous year since 1900. In view of the increase, some immigration officers expressed doubts about the Southwest's lack of unskilled labor. Indeed, the 1920s would witness an even larger immigration and importation of Mexicans until the 1929 depression put a stop to it.[42]

In 1912 a *Times* editorial asserted that southwestern industries had found it difficult to obtain the labor they needed and that "the cry of the hour is continually for more dependable labor." Unable to acquire American workers—or so they claimed—these industries turned to El Paso as their supply center for cheap and manageable Mexican labor. "Of the border cities," observed a federal labor inspector, "El Paso is the only one that is a real labor depot."[43] A significant example of El Paso's role in meeting the labor demands of the Southwest can be seen in the activities of the city's labor contractors, the *renganchistas* as the Mexicans called them. Four types of contractors could be found in El Paso: individual contractors; El Paso-owned employment agencies; representatives of southwestern and national corporations; and government-operated employment offices.

Individual contractors played a prominent role during the early, unregulated period of Mexican immigration. Although it is difficult to determine how many operated in El Paso, a number of them were Mexicans, who may have been American citizens. As early as 1891 the Mexican newspaper *El Latino-Americano* noticed that an El Paso labor contractor, Aurelio Pérez, desired to employ Mexican servants and laborers. Disregarding the prohibition of contract labor, individual contractors like Pérez as well as employment agencies and corporations disobeyed immigration law in hiring Mexican workers. Soon after the completion of the El Paso Smelter in 1887, for example, a federal court found smelter vice-president Robert S. Towne guilty of violating the 1885 contract labor law. According to testimony, Towne and a smelter agent had visited Santa Rosalía, Chihuahua, where they hired 40 Mexicans at a peso (50 cents) a day for three months at the El Paso Smelter. Towne admitted contracting the Mexican workers but claimed he was unaware of the new contract labor law at the time. When informed, he dismissed the Mexicans before they crossed the border. Some of the Mexicans testified that their contracts had been terminated at Paso del Norte but that Towne had told them they could still secure work at the smelter and even provided free transportation from the border to the large plant. G. W. Dickey, a smelter foreman, informed the court that the 40 Mexicans had been hired at the smelter. Dickey further stated that Towne had given instructions to keep the new workers separate from other Mexican laborers, who received higher wages, "so that they could not compare notes as to wages." In addition Towne had insisted that the recruits not be dismissed until they had paid off their fares from Santa Rosalía. Despite Towne's claim of innocence the jury agreed with the district attorney that the smelter executive had adopted a subterfuge to avoid the law and hence declared Towne guilty and fined him $1,000. The *Times* observed that the court had pending six similar cases.[44]

Twelve years later county officials jailed Paromino Contrara on a charge of importing contract labor into the United States. Contrara admitted to securing Mexican laborers for railroad work but denied he got them in Ciudad Juárez. According to Contrara he recruited among the Mexicans who hung around El Paso's plaza. He acknowledged being hired by the Southern Pacific as well as other lines to obtain Mexicans for grading, track, and section work. With no proof against him the court acquitted Contrara. Three years later officials arrested another contractor, Ricardo Velásquez, on a similar charge. In his arraignment U.S. officers claimed that Velásquez had entered Juárez and "lured" several Mexicans for work on railroads running out of El Paso. Velásquez maintained, however, that a section foreman had instructed him to do so and that he had been ignorant of any unlawful conduct. American consular authorities also observed

numerous violations of the contract labor law by the turn of the
century. United States consul T. T. Edwards, for example, informed
the State Department in 1905 that he had reason to believe that
Mexicans, contracted for work in the United States, had been crossing
the border in large numbers at El Paso.[45]

Perhaps the best known contractor in El Paso was R. G. González, who ran an office in the Mexican barrio. As a Mexican,
González had an advantage over his American competitors since he
could more easily convince Mexican immigrants to sign with him.
This made González a valuable contractor, especially for the railroads,
his biggest customers. In 1905 the *Times* reported that González
had shipped 75 Mexicans to Douglas and Bisbee to work on the
Southwestern Railroad in southern Arizona. Three years later he received a telegram requesting 1,000 Mexican laborers immediately
for work in the construction of the Galveston, Harrisburg and San
Antonio Railroad. Although most of his business came from southwestern lines, González also had contacts in other areas. He informed
a reporter in 1907 that he had just completed a contract with a midwestern line to supply 2,500 Mexican section hands for summer
work.[46]

Although González and other Mexican labor contractors provided
jobs to immigrants in search of work, they sometimes came in for
criticism. *El Clarín del Norte* of El Paso in an article entitled "Los
Enganchadores" (The Contractors) attacked the labor contractors
for their maltreatment and abuse of *los pobres surumatos* (the poor,
uncultured Mexicans) and warned that it would notify the police
of these practices. Either the police paid no attention to *El Clarín*
or the newspaper failed to follow through on its threat, for González and the other contractors continued in business. Longtime El
Paso resident José Cruz Burciaga recalls that by 1920 contractors
sent out every day numerous *enganches* (gangs of contract labor) of
between 50 and 100 men. Although it is not known if Mexican
workers had to pay El Paso labor contractors, Jesús Garza, who arrived in San Antonio in the early 1920s, remembered paying $1 to a
renganchista for railroad work.[47]

Besides individual contractors, various employment agencies took
advantage of the desire for Mexican labor throughout the Southwest
and in other sections of the country. The *Survey's* Samuel Bryan

reported in 1912 that El Paso's employment agencies "are well organized and supply a large number of immigrants to the various railroad companies operating in the Southwest, and to employers in other industries." Most agencies operated as close as possible to the border to contract the Mexicans as they entered El Paso. Murray and Reedy, for example, had their office at 916 South El Paso and advertised in 1906 for 1,000 men to work in new railroad construction. It needed laborers, drillers, tunnel men, rockmen, hammermen, trackmen, teamsters, and section hands and offered $2 a day plus free transportation. Murray and Reedy placed men with mining companies in the region although railroads hired most of "their" Mexicans. In 1910 the *Times* disclosed that several hundred Mexicans had been sent daily to various parts of the country by employment firms and that some went as far as Illinois and Nebraska. All railroads into El Paso had placed large orders with the contractors. One agency provided nearly 1,500 Mexicans in a few days and had requests for an additional 5,000. El Paso historian Calleros remembered that such agencies as the Zárate and Avina, the Hanlin Supply Company, and the Holmes Supply Company contracted laborers for the Santa Fe and Southern Pacific railroads. "Now those laborers," according to Calleros, "were hired for $1 a day." One correspondent further noted that employment agencies made much of their profits by charging board on the trip from the border to the immigrant's work destination. In addition, agencies held food and supply concessions at company stores. To pay for such provisions, employers deducted money from workers' first wages.[48]

The demand for Mexican laborers became so great that the agencies' biggest problem was insufficient numbers to fill their orders. This condition worsened after the financial panic of 1907. During the depression, railroads repatriated large numbers of Mexicans for lack of work; consequently, when good times returned, labor demands exceeded the supply. Nevertheless, the Dillingham Commission revealed that between July 1908 and February 1909, five labor agencies in El Paso transported 16,471 Mexicans to several railroads. P. W. Geary announced during the summer of 1910 that he had an order for 1,000 men for railroad work in central Texas and southern Oklahoma but could not secure enough Mexicans to fill it. The revolution in Mexico also hurt the contractors, and one agent

reported in 1911 that his firm had been unable to answer a demand
for 4,000 railroad laborers in Arizona, New Mexico, and California.
Another stated that he had an appeal for 500 workers in New Mexico
but could send only 50 men. That year a *Times* survey of all the
labor agencies in El Paso revealed that they had on hand requests for
a total of 9,000 railroad workers. If these could not be filled by
Mexicans, the contractors stated that they and the railroads would
have to search elsewhere for their labor needs.[49] Fortunately for
them, this became unnecessary because the disruption of Mexican immigration proved to be only temporary.

Because of larger orders, employment offices engaged in intense
competition along the border. To defeat their opponents some of
them dispatched Mexican agents to neighboring Chihuahua, where
they promised laborers from $1.25 to $2.00 per day for railroad
work if they migrated to El Paso and signed with their agency. If
successful, those agents received from 50 cents and up for every man
they secured. The agencies claimed that such tactics did not violate
the contract labor law. In their zeal to hire Mexican workers, Arizona
agencies even encouraged Mexicans to cross illegally rather than go
to a port of entry. An El Paso agent believed that the situation in
Arizona resulted from the lack of immigration stations along the border. However, this was not necessary in El Paso, where adequate
immigration facilities existed. There agents denied infringements of
the contract labor law but admitted employing Mexicans in Ciudad
Juárez, where immigrants agreed to sign with particular firms on
their arrival in El Paso.[50]

The competition became so aggressive that the agencies stationed Mexican employees at the Santa Fe Bridge, where they literally pounced on the immigrants as they crossed the border. "Come,
I'll get you a job," El Paso resident Mauricio Cordero remembers
the labor agent's appeal to incoming Mexicans. "Come, come, I'll
hire you."[51] The *Times* reported that strong and healthy young
Mexicans did not need much money to enter the United States since
as soon as they stepped foot on American soil, labor contractors
hired them. This led the newspaper to give the immigrants the title
of "King Peon":

In fact the despised and lowly peon becomes something of

an autocrat as soon as he crosses the line. His wants are provided for and a close watch kept upon him to see that he does not get lost. When ready for shipment, each is provided with a number and they are herded down to the Union Station not unlike cattle. It is needless to say that Pullman cars are not provided for their transportation.[52]

The scene at the bridge became almost ludicrous at times. In September 1907 the police arrested eleven Mexican agents at the Santa Fe crossing on charges of "pushing their business too zealously, for blocking the streets and for disturbing the peace." While most of them pleaded not guilty,

> officer Rubio testified that there had been but 10 or 12 Mexican laborers, surrounded by at least 14 "pullers in" of as many employment agencies and that each agency had seized on his victim. One tried to pull his laborers one way and another another. One had a laborer by the coat, another by his sleeve, and another by his hair, each voicing in loud tones, with a "noise like a rough house," the advantages of his particular agency. In a compact mass the group swayed back and forth, completely blocking the sidewalk on South El Paso Street as well as attracting quite a crowd.[53]

According to the police report, additional agents from the Holmes Supply Agency arrived and secured all the laborers for their office. After the court inquired about the condition of the Mexican immigrants, it fined each agent $1. The police, however, could also be of assistance to labor contractors. Although no similar information exists for El Paso, one San Antonio recruiter years later admitted he had contracted Mexicans jailed in Fort Worth for having no jobs. "If I get you out, will you work?" the contractor asked the Mexicans. "They said yes, and I have taken them out and put them to work."[54]

Between 1927 and 1930, when economist Paul S. Taylor compiled data for his seminal studies on Mexican labor in the United States, several El Paso labor contractors talked to him about their early activities. R. P. Zárate of the Zárate–Avina Labor Agency recalled that his company started providing Mexican labor in 1902

to railroads between El Paso and Chicago. Another agent at the
Zárate–Avina office also remembered that whereas in 1904 the agency
had transported from El Paso about 700 Mexicans, one year later
it sent out 1,300 and the numbers continued to multiply. W. H.
Talbot of the L. H. Manning Company with offices in El Paso, Tucson, and Los Angeles informed Taylor that the decade 1910 to 1920
represented a "fill-up period" when Mexicans replaced other na-
tionalities as the Southwest's major labor source. According to Talbot,
the Southern Pacific employed Mexicans from El Paso to San Jose
and Stockton. B. J. Kerley of the Hanlin Supply Company, which began contracting Mexican labor in 1912, stated that his firm preferred
Mexicans because "you can fire one or two without losing your
whole gang." C. R. Howard of the Holmes Supply Company further
stressed the attraction of Mexican labor to southwestern employers.
"Mexicans are not subject to agitators," Howard commented. "They're
not organized. They're peaceable . . . and will work on the desert
or anywhere the Santa Fe wants to put them." Finally, an agent of
the Holmes Company summarized the value of Mexican immigrant
workers, especially to El Paso contractors:

> El Paso is a primary labor market. L. A. is secondary. Mex-
> ican labor is good. It is the best common labor in California.
> It isn't rapid, either mentally or physically, but it is steady. The
> Mexicans will take a vacation from their work every once in a
> while. The Mexican father says, 'My son will take care of me
> (in my old age).' The Mexicans are peculiarly adapted to agricul-
> ture. They are good miners and the best track labor available.[55]

In addition to individual contractors and employment offices,
the railroads and other industries of the Southwest had their own labor agents in El Paso. The Southern Pacific opened an office in 1894
and its agents, crossing the border, encouraged Mexicans to enter
the United States, where they could find employment. Once in El
Paso the agency contracted them and promised the immigrants $1.25
per day as well as free passage back to the border. The Southern
Pacific also had offices in Tucson, Los Angeles, and Wilcox, Arizona,
that supplied the railroad line from Bakersfield to El Paso with Mexican laborers. In return the railroad paid each agency $1 per head.

At times railroad representatives also utilized the Help Wanted columns of the newspaper to advertise for workers. One such ad in 1901 read: "Wanted—one hundred men on railroad work." A year later four different railroads had agents in El Paso during one week looking for "able-bodied" men for work in California, Colorado, Oklahoma, and East Texas. The Santa Fe man reported in 1908 that he needed 200 men for track work in Kansas, Colorado, and California. The Southern Pacific and the Rock Island representatives stated they could use about 500 more men. "The roads as a rule work Mexican laborers," the *Times* commented, "and there seems to be a scarcity of that kind of labor at present."[56]

One such period occurred during Francisco Madero's siege of Ciudad Juárez in the spring of 1911, when the number of Mexican immigrants to El Paso declined. As a result, one railroad agent considered a more drastic measure to obtain workers. L. H. Manning of Tucson, a representative of the Southern Pacific as well as other lines in Arizona, New Mexico, and California, arrived in April searching for 2,000 laborers. When told that Madero might disband his army in a few days after he captured Juárez, Manning stated that he would be prepared to "take the whole of Madero's army and 'stake' the men to picks and shovels if they were ready to get on the job." Apparently, some of Madero's men accepted Manning's offer—or at least more Mexicans arrived in El Paso—for two days later 150 Mexicans left El Paso on a Southern Pacific train for work in Arizona.[57]

During World War I railroads outside the Southwest also had their men in El Paso. The agent of the Pennsylvania Railroad, for example, announced in 1916 that he sought 200 Mexicans for "a labor experiment." Moreover, owing to the 1917 immigration restrictions the demand for Mexican labor heightened. One agent believed that Mexican labor had become scarce and yet the railroads could use between 5,000 to 10,000 Mexicans. After the Department of Labor ruled that Mexicans could enter the United States for railroad work, the Baltimore and Ohio along with other eastern lines quickly dispatched agents to the border. Besides being used as manual laborers, Mexicans were employed as strikebreakers by some of the railroads, such as the Chicago and Alton Railroad, which imported Mexicans to break a strike in 1918 only to have the Mexicans refuse to work after they learned of the dispute.[58]

Agricultural interests took advantage of the 1917 and 1918 waivers and contracted workers in El Paso. The Continental Sugar Company of Toledo, Ohio, sent C. G. Pinto to the border to secure 1,000 Mexican laborers, although a reported embargo on labor from Mexico by the government of General Venustiano Carranza prevented him from doing so immediately. Pinto stressed that "the labor problem is a serious one . . . and getting hands for as large a concern as ours is a big job." According to the labor agent his company required 5,000 laborers to work 25,000 acres of sugar beets in Ohio and Michigan. Previously labor had been plentiful in the East and Midwest, but since the war the company had turned to Mexico "and now apparently that is cut off." A few days after Pinto's arrival, other sugar beet representatives came to El Paso. The *Herald* reported that hundreds of Mexican agricultural laborers had been admitted for the sugar beet fields of Idaho, Colorado, and Utah and that a group of them had left El Paso for southern Utah accompanied by agents of the Utah-Idaho Sugar Company. These contractors had been in session for several days with immigration officials arranging the recruitment of workers; their negotiations completed, the sugar men left. In 1919 the *Times* observed that 150 Mexicans from Ciudad Juárez with their families, furniture, and pets had been hired by a Colorado sugar beet company for work in beet fields and sugar refineries. However, one agent of the sugar beet industry did not have as much success. Mexican authorities arrested him for soliciting Mexicans at the international bridge. Carranza officials claimed that Antonio Salas had illegally contracted the Mexicans on the Juárez side of the border, although witnesses told a *Herald* reporter that the recruiter had remained at least 10 feet from the boundary line. The Mexicans finally released Salas along with another agent, who had been arrested on the same charge a few days before. By 1919 various sugar beet interests operated labor agencies in El Paso including the Great Western Sugar Company, Holly Sugar Company, Belmond Isle Company, Utah-Idaho Company, Amalgamated Sugar Company, and Dominion Sugar Company of Ontario, Canada.[59]

The last and least important type of labor contractors consisted of government-operated labor agencies that were organized out of the loud clamor for Mexican labor during the war years. The Texas

Bureau of Labor Statistics, for example, employed labor commissioners to assist Texas industries, especially agriculture, to secure
Mexican workers. In June 1918 Tom Bell and M. A. Domínguez,
deputies of the bureau, appeared in El Paso to arrange with Mexican
officials in Ciudad Juárez for a supply of 3,000 workers from Chihuahua for the fields of north and central Texas. That same year an
office of the United States Employment Bureau of the Department of
Labor in cooperation with El Paso officials opened in the basement
of the city hall. It proposed to supply the labor needs of El Paso
and vicinity although it also delivered workers to railroads such as
the Santa Fe. The bureau placed Mexicans—as well as some Americans—as farm laborers, carpenters, manual laborers, stenographers,
and clerical assistants. Yet its major service was the employment
of Mexican domestics in El Paso homes. Figures released by the bureau in November 1919 indicate that Mexican women accounted
for most of its applicants. During the first 19 work days of that
month, the bureau interviewed 14 American women and directed 6
of them to work. On the other hand, it interviewed 1,740 Mexican
women during the same time and dispatched 1,326 of them to work.
The bureau had 647 American male applicants but found jobs for
only 69. Of 869 Mexican men it sent 176 to jobs. Besides the El Paso
office, the Department of Labor operated 23 similar ones in Texas
and New Mexico: 18 in Texas and 5 in New Mexico. "The people of
El Paso and vicinity," stated Henry W. Walker of the local agency,
"are just beginning to appreciate the scope of the work undertaken
by the Department of Labor in opening free employment offices
throughout the country."[60] Besides the bureau, a special El Paso office of the Department of Labor opened in September 1918. The
department considered this post essential in order to assist Mexican
laborers as they entered the United States and to provide for their
welfare after they had gone to work.[61]

Despite the Department of Labor's concern, Mexican immigrants
as well as Mexican consular officials in the United States at times
complained of deceptions and mistreatment of workers by border
inspectors and labor contractors. Upon crossing in 1910, several
Mexicans informed the Mexican consul in El Paso of an immigration
official's attack on a fellow worker. The Mexicans protested that
every day immigration officers at the Santa Fe Bridge crossing

committed abuses against Mexicans desiring to enter the United States for work. According to the workers the officer in this particular case detained a "poor Mexican worker" and demanded the surrender of a bottle he possessed. The bottle contained nothing, the immigrants told the consul, but when their friend refused to give it up the officer escorted him into the inspection station. "In a little while," explained the Mexicans, "we heard blows and to our surprise we witnessed the officer striking our countryman with a thick stick and stating he was going to deliver him to the authorities who would imprison him for five years." The immigrants appealed to the consul to intervene in behalf of their arrested compañero and, believing that similar attacks would continue, requested that their complaint be sent to the Mexican government. Five years later, moreover, the Mexican consul at El Paso wrote the secretary of foreign relations in Mexico City that quite often there had come to his attention cases of fraudulent offers involving Mexican immigrants. In one instance a railroad agent had offered a large number of Mexican laborers six months' work in Philadelphia at $1.80 a day including free round-trip transportation from the border. The consul had learned, however, that the railroad had repudiated the agreement and refused free transportation back to the border. "This is not the first case of this kind," emphasized the consul, "and I therefore wish to urge Mexicans to investigate the facts before contracting." The consul further suggested that his warning be published in Mexico City newspapers so that potential immigrants would not be "deceived by flattering offers and leave our country."[62]

To protect against the nonfulfillment of labor agreements between immigrants and labor contractors, consul Soriano Bravo advised in 1917 that workers obtain written contracts. Although the consul believed that Mexican immigration should be limited due to increased population pressures on Mexican border cities, Soriano Bravo hoped that those who crossed the frontier would be aware of their rights. In a memo addressed to "The Mexican Workers" the consul stressed that every immigrant insist on a written agreement stipulating the duration of the contract, the wages to be paid, and free transportation back to El Paso. Soriano Bravo offered to counsel immigrants about contracts. In addition the Mexican diplomat wrote to all El Paso labor contractors about the necessity of a written contract and enclosed an English translation of a sample contract. "I would suggest," he told the contractors, "that you put into use this form and furnish every Mexican laborer that you engage with one of them." Besides specifying the work period, wages, and transportation, the sample contract provided that in case of a job-related injury, the employer would transfer the worker to an "adequate hospital." Unfortunately, the efforts of Soriano Bravo, as well as other Mexican consuls along the border, appear to have had little impact and few—if any—labor contractors gave written contracts to Mexican workers.[63]

However, economic instability in Mexico and the Mexicans' need for jobs overcame the hardships associated with emigration to the United States. With such a readily available army of labor, the different types of contractors transferred to work thousands of Mexicans throughout the Southwest as well as other sections of the country. The Dillingham Commission, in its investigation of specific western industries, reported that in 1910 foreign-born Mexicans represented 7.1 percent of all workers in metalliferous mining, including 26.4 percent in Arizona; and in western smelting and refining, foreign-born Mexicans were 12.8 percent of the total with 60.5 percent in Arizona. By 1917 Mexican miners in the Grand Canyon State numbered 16,000.[64] As early as 1904, moreover, a Mexican newspaper in the city, *El Paso del Norte,* had noted that various Mexican families had left the city to work on Mississippi plantations, and in 1911 a news dispatch from New Orleans stated that an increase in Mexican laborers had occurred in Louisiana and other southern states. According to the report, Mexicans had been found—along with Italians—to be best adapted to the hot Louisiana climate and their work had been more than satisfactory. They labored in cane fields, sugar refineries, lumber and turpentine camps, and as manual workers. Furthermore, "Spanish is heard almost as frequently as English on the docks where Mexican and Central American laborers principally are employed." A valuable asset of the Mexicans, the dispatch concluded, was their ability to get along with black workers. "Despite the fact that the Mexican is displacing the Negro in many occupations," the dispatch reported, there seems to be no resentment on the part of the black race. One of the reasons for the esteem in which Mexican laborers are held is due to the fact that they are not divided into factions among themselves as are the Italians, and still can labor side by side with negroes without friction, a condition impossible between the American laborers and the colored races.[65]

Mexicans could also be found in midwestern meat packing houses and related industries. In one plant in Nebraska City the Mexicans had displaced so many American workers that a campaign to get rid of the Mexican began. Warnings posted on building walls read: If You Are a Mexican, Leave the City by Sunday Night. This wide geographic mobility of the Mexicans reflected to a large degree their employment by the railroads, which distributed them throughout various sections of the country. By 1912 Mexicans were the main source of labor for the railroads west and south of Kansas City and could be found in large numbers in Missouri, Iowa, and Illinois. An immigration officer in Houston recalled in the late 1920s that by 1915 "south and west of St. Louis practically all the [railroad] laborers were Mexicans but not much north except on the Burlington and Rock Island." From railroad construction and maintenance the Mexicans often shifted to other jobs in agriculture or industry. Having entered as an economic migrant, the Mexican remained one in the United States.[66]

Although Mexican immigrant workers adjusted to harsh working and living conditions and became indispensable to the economic development of the Southwest and, in particular, El Paso, they nevertheless felt the burden of their toil. Reflecting their relationships with labor contractors as well as their labor on the railroads, some composed songs conveying their worst feelings about work north of the border. One such song a Mexican immigrant worker entitled "Los Enganchados" (The Hooked Ones): [translated]

On the 28th day of February
That important day
When we left El Paso,
They took us out as contract labor.

When we left El Paso
At two in the morning,
I asked the boss contractor
If we were going to Louisiana.

We arrived at Laguna
Without any hope
I asked the boss
If we were going to Oklahoma.
        .   .   .

We arrived on the first day
And on the second began to work.
With our picks in our hands
We set out tramping.

Some unloaded rails
And others unloaded ties,
And others of my companions
Threw out thousands of curses.

Those who knew the work
Went repairing the jack
With sledge hammers and shovels,
Throwing earth up the track.

Eight crowbars lined up,
We followed disgusted;
To shouts and signs
We remained indifferent.
        .   .   .

Said Jesús, "El Coyote,"
As if he wanted to weep,
'It would be better to be in Juárez
Even if we were without work.'

These verses were composed
By a poor Mexican
To spread the word about
The American system.[67]

4

Obreros y Comerciantes

The commercial, semi-industrial character of El Paso's economy largely determined the types of jobs Mexicans obtained. Requiring large numbers of manual workers, employers hired Mexicans. Between 1880 and 1920 the economy became dependent on the Mexican *obreros*—the workers. Their significant numbers alone formed the labor base upon which the city's development rested. As one scholar likewise notes of southern black migration into Chicago during the early twentieth century, immigration produced a Mexican proletariat in El Paso.[1] Mexicans, in both unskilled and some skilled jobs, could be found in every major economic activity: transportation, smelting, industry, the retail trade, construction, and a variety of services. "Some have said that half of the population of El Paso is Mexican," wrote an American" and if that is not quite true it is because the rest cannot possibly edge in." According to the writer, El Paso's greatest asset lay in its Mexican population, which could be used to develop numerous industries. "And with such a mass of good, faithful and speedily efficient labor at your door and within your border," this astute observer concluded, "it is a sad neglect of a golden opportunity not to hasten to provide the employment that will make of that labor ample consumers of home products."[2]

El Paso enterprises recognized the economic benefits to be derived from the city's pool of Mexican labor. The El Paso Smelter, for example, employed more Mexicans than any other firm. City directory listings show that between 1900 and 1910 the number of Spanish-surnamed smelter workers went from 811 (84% of the total) to 1,017 (90% of the total). Ten years later the 1920 directory recorded a slight decrease in Spanish-surnamed workers at the

65

smelter, although they still formed a substantial majority. Of 917 employees, 768 (or 87%) had Spanish surnames. Although the city directories did not include every worker, the decrease may have resulted from lower production after World War I. Besides their large numbers it appears that the smelter employed the Mexicans chiefly as manual laborers. Most Mexican smelter employees listed in El Paso World War I draft records worked as laborers. In contrast, Americans monopolized the limited skilled occupations in this labor-intensive industry. The smelter paid the Mexicans a wage that ranged from $1.00 a day in 1902 to $1.50 a day in 1914. The average salary for American workers cannot be determined, but wages for skilled workers in El Paso in 1911 ranged from $3.50 to $6.00 a day. For their pay the Mexicans worked twelve-hour days until 1914, when the company began three eight-hour shifts. Since El Paso's "blue laws" did not affect the smelter because of its location just outside the city limits, many of the Mexican workers also labored on Sundays.[3]

In El Paso the railroads hired not only thousands of Mexicans for work throughout the Southwest but also many for their shops in the border city. While the 1900 city directory had listed only 29 Spanish-surnamed employees of the railroads out of 834, twenty years later it had counted 1,010 Spanish surnames, or 37 percent of 2,753 railroad workers. Many of these remained in El Paso and worked in the shops. Although the largest number of Mexicans were manual laborers, the railroads utilized some in numerous other capacities, as table 4.1 shows. The railroad's need for skilled and semiskilled workers plus the large number of Mexicans allowed a minority to be trained as machinists, machinist's helpers, boltmakers, car repairmen, and truckers. A small number held clerical and foreman positions, presumably over other Mexicans.[4] Charles Armijo, who arrived in 1910 at the age of 30, found employment as a Pullman conductor due to his higher level of education than most other immigrants. "I ran between here (El Paso) and Los Angeles, between here and Albuquerque, and several places," he recalled. "They used to switch me around." Cleofas Calleros, who began work for the Santa Fe line in 1912 as a messenger boy, advanced to a chief line clerk fourteen years later. Calleros remembered, however, that Mexicans rarely could be found in the offices.[5] Almost no Mexi-

Table 4.1 Occupations of Spanish-Surnamed Railroad Workers in El Paso as Listed by the 1920 City Directory

Occupation	Persons with Spanish Surname	Occupation	Persons with Spanish Surname
Laborer	188	Truckman helper	3
Machinist helper	97	Mechanic	3
Boltmaker helper	60	Tank helper	3
Machinist	56	Engineer watchman	2
Car repairman	55	Fire helper	2
Car repairman helper	49	Stevedore	2
Coach cleaner	48	Porter	2
Truckman	37	Oil man	2
Blacksmith helper	36	Engineer	2
Wiper	28	Engineer inspector	2
Stripper foreman	27	Timekeeper	2
Handyman	26	Special agent	2
Boltmaker	21	Wheel pressman	2
Clerk	20	Airman helper	2
Printer's helper	16	Ash pitman	2
Fireman	13	Craneman	1
Gateman	12	Toolman	1
Car carpenter	11	Car repairman helper	1
Machinist apprentice	11	Hammer boy	1
Car repairman apprentice	9	Assistant manager	1
Hostler helper	8	Switchman	1
Helper	8	Labor foreman	1
Coppersmith helper	8	Track repairman	1
Painter	7	Engineer equipper	1
Hostler	7	Wiper foreman	1
Blacksmith	5	General cashier	1
Trackman	5	Towerman	1
Pipeman helper	5	Machinist inspector	1
Stripper	4	Hammer operator	1
Tinner	4	Brakeman	1
Supplyman	4	Drill pressman	1
Sweeper	4	Carpenter helper	1
Coppersmith	4	Pipeman	1
Apprentice	4	Mill helper	1
Tankman	4	Wheel press helper	1
Messenger, telegraph dept.	3	Airman	1
Subforeman	3	Air brake repairman	1
Painter apprentice	3	Coppersmith helper	1

Source: El Paso City Directory, 1920. Other persons with Spanish surnames were listed as working for a railroad, but no occupations were recorded.

cans, moreover, held the few engineering or managerial jobs because these occupations remained in American hands.

In a report for the Department of Labor in 1908, one federal official outlined what he believed were characteristics making the Mexican attractive to railroads. "As a laborer the Mexican immigrant is said to be unambitious, physically not strong, and somewhat indillent [sic] and irregular," he wrote, "but against this is put the fact that he is docile, patient, orderly in camp, fairly intelligent under competent supervision, obedient, and cheap. His strongest point with the employers is his willingness to work for a low wage."[6] That same year the *Times* pointed out that owing to the national downturn in the economy, the El Paso and Southwestern Railroad had reduced the pay of their laborers in El Paso to 10 cents an hour. "Many of the men employed," the paper observed, "who for the most part are Mexicans, are greatly dissatisfied, and there was considerable talk of their quitting. None of them, however, quit Saturday night, and it is thought that, in view of the scarcity of work, that few, if any, will leave."[7] The cheapness of Mexican workers and their ability to be used in unskilled, semiskilled, and even skilled occupations made them attractive employees for the railroad shops. Lines such as the Southwestern and the G.H. & S.A., for example, hired large percentages of Mexican workers in both their machine shops and roundhouses. One old-time resident, who worked as a downtown store clerk, remembers seeing many Mexican employees of the Southern Pacific and other railroads going to lunch with their greasy overalls and caps.[8]

Because of the building boom in El Paso, construction companies depended heavily on Mexican workers, especially for common labor. The *Lone Star* reported in 1885 that the boom had provided jobs for large numbers of laborers. In addition to business and home construction, Mexicans worked as laborers for the building of the streetcar system and for such firms as the Asphaltite and Bituluthic companies, which paved many of the city's streets.[9] One federal official remarked that Los Angeles and San Antonio contractors also employed Mexicans for street grading. In 1908 San Antonio Mexican street workers received wages of $1.25 and $1.50 a day. Some of El Paso's builders utilized the services of labor contractor R. G. González, who advertised in 1912 that he could promptly supply the construction firms with laborers. Moreover, construction accidents reported in the newspapers often involved Mexicans such as one in 1904 on Overland Street that injured several Mexican workers.[10] Other industries employing Mexicans included the El Paso Milling Company with 90 Spanish-surnamed employees in a work force of 119 in 1917. The Darbyshire Harvie Iron and Machine Company listed 113 Spanish surnames out of 129 workers that same year. Finally, in 1917 the El Paso Brass Foundry had 28 employees, 18 with Spanish surnames.[11]

While most of these firms hired Mexicans as manual laborers, some taught a minority particular skills or hired Mexican craftsmen who had migrated to the border. This became necessary not only because Mexicans worked for lower wages but also because it was difficult to recruit American skilled workers to El Paso and the rest of the Southwest. In 1905 the *Times* noted that a lack of plasterers, brick masons, and carpenters had delayed construction of the Union Station for the railroads. According to the paper the unavailability of craftsmen had become a problem throughout the city. In order to alleviate this condition, employers began using Mexicans in these positions. Still other concerns hired Mexicans who had specific skills such as boilermakers and pressmen. One sample of occupational distribution in El Paso by surname reveals that Mexicans employed as skilled workers in 1920 represented 10.5 percent of Mexican workers.[12]

The Kohlberg Cigar Factory, producer of La Internacional cigars, hired a large percentage of skilled Mexican workers. Founded in 1886 by a German Jewish immigrant, the plant from its start employed Mexican and some Cuban cigarmakers. Originally located on El Paso Street, it moved to a new building at Santa Fe and Second streets in 1911 that the *Times* called "one of the best equipped and most modern cigar factories in the southwest." On the second floor of the factory, workers rolled the cigars, turning out an average of 15,000 per day. One of the features of such activity involved an old cigarmakers' custom. While the men worked, one read aloud newspapers and books as a form of education and entertainment for the workers. Several other cigar factories also operated in El Paso for short periods but the Kohlberg firm remained the largest and best known. In 1917 it had 113 employees, 110 with Spanish surnames.

One Mexican, whose father came to El Paso in 1910, recalled that his father had worked for La Internacional after having been a cigar worker in Puebla, Veracruz, Havana, and Tampa.[13]

Besides being employed in industries, many Mexicans were hired by El Paso merchants. The need for Spanish-speaking clerks arose because of the significant numbers of Mexican consumers from both sides of the border who patronized the local stores. Consequently, the sign Se Habla Español (We Speak Spanish) became a common sight throughout the downtown shopping district. Want ads in the newspapers often appeared reading:

Help wanted—
Four neat Spanish salesmen that can deliver the goods; no others need apply. Ask for Mr. Pat Ochoa, room 5, Stevens Bldg.[14]

In 1916, one of the largest dry goods stores, the Popular, employed nearly 100 Mexicans, half its employees. The founder of the Popular, Adolph Schwartz, early had recognized that if he wanted to prosper in El Paso he had to learn Spanish. Many of the Popular's more important customers included numerous Mexicans, presumably wealthy ones from Chihuahua, who often stopped to chat with Schwartz in his office. "His knowledge of Spanish," one study notes of Schwartz, "had helped him to attract and maintain this clientele." Furthermore, his use of Mexican clerks helped in sales to the Mexican shoppers. A 1920 Popular ad in the Spanish language *La Patria* emphasized that all store departments had Spanish-speaking personnel. "We have twenty-six years experience," the ad boasted, "of good treatment of Mexican customers." Besides prominent stores such as the Popular, Mexican clerks worked in a variety of smaller ones owned by both American (mostly Jewish) and Mexican merchants. One former clerk recalls that he first worked in a store on South El Paso Street called La Buena Suerte (The Good Luck). As a salesman he received $6 a week, a wage comparable to that of a laborer.[15] In a few cases some Mexicans, such as Francisco G. Maese, who sold sewing machines for the Singer Company, worked as salesmen for national firms. "For two generations he [Maese] was a familiar sight on El Paso streets," wrote Calleros, longtime resident and historian. "His buggy with a sewing machine strapped to

the back was everywhere."[16] The extent of the Mexican clerical
force can be seen in one study which calculates that the percentage
of Spanish surnames in low white-collar occupations rose from
12.0 percent in 1910 to 19.8 percent ten years later. As an indication
of this growth, 75 Mexican clerks in 1913 organized the International Clerk's Protective Association with 191 Mexican members.[17]

Mexicans also worked in additional business establishments as
teamsters, waiters, cooks, dishwashers, and janitors. The Mills Building
in downtown El Paso, for example, employed a Mexican as an extra
elevator operator for 20 cents an hour. Others found jobs as janitors
with the city public schools. Some Mexicans, such as Juan Baca, became self-employed. He owned a carriage and transferred goods
between Ciudad Juárez and El Paso for $3 to $5 a day. Chris P. Fox,
longtime El Paso resident, remembered that some Mexicans operated express wagons called *expresitos*, hauling furniture and other
items for different stores. According to Fox, the Mexicans "could
load more furniture on one of those little old wagons that you can in
a van today." In the early 1880s the *Lone Star* noted El Paso's dependence on Mexican fruit and vegetable "hucksters" who regularly
crossed the border to sell their produce. The paper further observed
that "Mexican ice cream vendors are numerous." The *Times* reported
in 1913 that a group of Mexicans worked as individual garbage men
hauling trash on their wagons from the American northside to their
homes in Chihuahuita, where city sanitation wagons picked up the
load.[18] Moreover, by 1915 a few Mexicans made a living as jitney
drivers, although this involved them in a controversy with the El Paso
Electric Railway Company, facing competition from the jitneys. In
a patriotic letter "To Our Fellow El Pasoans," the streetcar company
attacked the Mexicans. It appealed to antialien sentiments by emphasizing that Mexican refugees owned many of the jitneys. Consequently, the streetcar officials argued that the Mexicans represented transients who would take their money with them when they
left. The streetcar company pointed out that the jitneys charged
10 cents, double a streetcar ride, and that while American operators
were clean and courteous, the Mexicans were not. "Take many
of the 'jitne' drivers," the company charged, "and you will see them
collarless, shirt-sleeved, their clothing greasy from the oil of their

machines, a cigaret between their lips, the smoke blown into the faces of passengers. Is this courtesy?" A supporter of the streetcars in a letter to the *Herald* asked: "Who are the jitne drivers? Can they read and speak English? If a sign ahead should read, 'Stop; Real Danger Ahead' can the jitne driver read it quickly?"[19]

In addition to private employers, public agencies employed Mexicans. In 1886 the city council paid $3 to certain Mexicans for cutting brush on the sewer system survey line. Three years later the council minutes recorded a total payment of $12 to ten Mexican laborers for street maintenance. The city further employed Mexicans at $1 a day for park work. Besides using Mexicans for common labor, officials hired them for cooking in the pesthouse and city jail. In their wagons Mexicans often hauled patients to the pesthouse or hospital.[20] Furthermore, the city's major "scavenger job"—head of the sanitation department—was a Mexican patronage position that the Democratic Ring bestowed on a loyal Mexican American politician who helped deliver the Mexican vote. Frank Alderete, who with his brother, Ike, headed the Ring's Mexican faction, held the job for part of the period and employed Mexicans for the city. In a letter to the city council in 1908, Mayor Joseph Sweeney praised Alderete's ability. "I think," Sweeney wrote, "that the Sanitary Commissioner, Mr. Alderete, is entitled to your thanks and that of every citizen in El Paso, for the efficient and capable Department he has established."[21] In 1912 more than a hundred Mexican employees of the city (many apparently American citizens) organized a political club called the Círculo de Amigos and struck a bargain with the city not to hire any laborers except club members.[22] Public utility companies such as the El Paso Water Company also employed Mexican common laborers. Although the Mexicans worked long and hard hours, one utility official believed they sought any excuse not to work. "When a Mexican laborer wants to take a day off," claimed superintendent W. H. Watts of the water company,

> he can be relied on to dig up a saint or some kind of anniversary to celebrate. On St. John's day all my Juans are out celebrating, and the Josés, Pedros, et al, get out of their work on St. James' and St. Peters' days. But a new anniversary was rung in on me this morning. One of my men was missing and I asked Louis Behr

[*sic?*] what saint's day he was celebrating. Louis said the man
was not celebrating any saint today, but was celebrating the
anniversary of the burning of his house; that he was remaining
home today to prevent fire from repeating the performance.
Next they will be celebrating the anniversary of the death of
some pet dog or burro.[23]

Not all Mexicans found public employment jobs as laborers. Some
(often for political favors) acquired positions on the police force.
The 1890 payroll of city employees included Santiago Alvarado, who
received $60 a month as the sole Mexican police officer in a 12-man
department. Earlier that year lawyer O. A. Larrazolo had presented
the city council a petition on behalf of Alvarado and another Mexican
policeman. It noted that both men received smaller wages compared
to American officers of similar rank. For their services the Mexicans requested a wage of $75 per month. Although the council appar-
ently did not approve the salary increase, its minutes reveal that
another Mexican policeman received $75 a month in 1894. Two years
later 5 Mexican officers worked on a 16-man police force. These
Mexican policemen served as street patrolmen, mounted policemen,
and special officers. During the next several years the city hired
additional Mexican policemen, but surprisingly by 1918 only 3 were
listed out of 90 men in the police department. The decline may have
resulted from increased racial tensions and heightened prejudice in
the city due to the Mexican Revolution and the fear of war with
Mexico. Besides being a minority on the police force, Mexican officers received beats in Chihuahuita but rarely in the American sections of the city. A policeman from 1901 to 1905, Ramón González
years later recalled that his own beat included the corner of Utah
Street (now Mesa Avenue) and Third Street on the southside, from
where he could keep an eye on the red-light district, officially
sanctioned by the city.[24]

Besides the police force Mexicans received other types of public
appointments. Mexicans in El Paso represented a major political
asset to the Democratic Ring, which controlled the city and county
governments throughout most of the period. Although most Mexicans did not possess American citizenship, the ring literally "voted"
their Mexicans, ensuring itself of victory over reform Democrats and

a weak Republican party. As part of the process the ring rewarded
Mexican American politicos such as Ike Alderete, who served as
district clerk until he fell into political disfavor with the Ring. The
record for political longevity, however, went to Crispiano Aranda,
better known as Cris Aranda, who was deputy county clerk for
42 years. When Aranda died in 1930, an El Paso newspaper eulogized that his death ended one of the most remarkable public careers
in the county's history. Next to him, J. A. Escajeda stood as the
staunchest Mexican American supporter of the Ring. He held a
variety of offices including district clerk from 1887 to 1931. The
ring also appointed or elected Mexican Americans as county commissioners, justices of the peace, and constables.[25] Despite this
patronage the Ring never supported any Mexican American for a
major political position such as mayor or county judge, and Mexican
Americans did not play a significant role in the decision-making
procedures of the Democratic party.

While the city and county governments provided most public
employment for Mexicans, some managed to receive federal appointments as well. Pedro Candelaria, for example, held a job as distributing clerk in 1896 at the El Paso Post Office and according
to historian Calleros, "Pete was a faithful servant in the community."
Pilar A. Maese entered the postal service in the 1880s and became
an assistant postmaster. In 1901 the *Times* noted that J. M. García
worked as a U.S. customs inspector and a year later the paper
reported that Antonio Sierra had been named official interpreter
at the El Paso Bureau of Immigration. The *Times* also carried a
story in 1904 about one of the first Mexicans to hold a federal job.
"Cristóbal Beserra, 102 years old," the paper stated, "and who
came to El Paso sixty years ago, wants a pension. He worked for
the government many years ago and is now too old to earn a living."[26]

In addition to men, some Mexican women found employment
and became a significant portion of the Mexican working class of
El Paso. Because entire families as well as single men had arrived
from Mexico, many females, especially daughters or other young
female relatives, had to find work to augment the earnings of the
men. Moreover, some women had lost their husbands and consequently had become the main source of income for their children.

A sample of 393 El Paso households from the 1900 manuscript
census reveals that almost one-fifth (17.11%) of Mexican households
contained a working woman. American women also had to enter
the labor force and the census sample recorded 11.21 percent of
American households with a female worker. Mexican women
who worked, according to the census sample, were unmarried daughters, wives with no husbands, or single women. Married Mexican
women, on the other hand, both foreign and native born, within a
nuclear or an extended family, did not work outside the home. In
no case in the sample did a woman with an employed husband have a
job.[27] Because both the census and city directories failed to count
many Mexicans it may well be that a larger percentage of Mexican
women, including married ones, worked, especially at part-time
labor and laundry or sewing. In any event, fewer married women
appear to have had jobs than unmarried ones. Age and fertility
help explain this condition. In the 1900 sample, more than three-
fourths of married Mexican immigrant women were between fifteen
and forty years of age, a period when women generally gave birth
and had children at home. Indeed, more than three-fourths of all
married Mexican immigrant women in El Paso, based on the sample,
had children twelve years of age or under or children listed as attending school; of these, more than one-third had children five years of
age and under.[28] If having children kept married women in the home,
so too, apparently, did the attitude of many Mexican men, who resented women, especially wives, working or wanting to work. Most
males believed that their work was a man's duty but that women's
consisted of raising children and keeping house.[29] As one working-
class newspaper in Mexico during the age of Porfirio Díaz emphasized: "To be a wife is to be a woman preferably selected amongst
many other women, for her honesty, for her religiousness, for her
amiability, . . . for her industriousness [and] for her docility."[30]

Nevertheless, despite such attitudes the Mexican family in the
United States did not remain static. Over the years more Mexican
women, especially daughters, became wageworkers to augment
the family income. Also, as the economy expanded, El Paso and
southwestern industries and services began to recruit more Mexican
women workers. The increase in Mexican female wageworkers in El
Paso by 1920 can be seen in census figures for that year. The census

reported that 3,474 foreign-born females, almost all Mexicans, ten years of age and older were engaged in a gainful occupation. Foreign-born female wageworkers represented half of all females ten years and over who held jobs in El Paso. Most female workers in El Paso (3,112 females, or 45% of all employed women) did "women's work." The two largest occupations, familiar to women in Mexico, were servant (1,718) and laundress (710), where the majority of Mexican working women could be found.[31] Owing to deficiencies in skills and schooling, as well as to prejudice against them, few Mexican women, unlike their American counterparts, were in such skilled professional occupations as teaching, nursing, or office work.[32] Table 4.2 shows the number and percentage of Spanish-surnamed women listed as domestics and laundresses in the city directories of 1889, 1910, and 1920.

Victor S. Clark, a Bureau of Labor inspector, noted in 1908 that Mexican "immigrant women have so little conception of domestic arrangements in the United States that the task of training them would be too heavy for American housewives."[33] Yet domestic work proved to be the most readily available source of jobs for Mexican women. Still, Clark correctly recognized that women from preindustrial cultures might have difficulty adjusting to the new electrical devices of middle-class American homes, although he failed to understand that the employment of Mexican maids saved southwestern housewives from having to buy the new appliances. Mexican domestics did their work by hand. Elizabeth Rae Tyson, who grew up in El Paso, remembered the extent of Mexican maids used by American families. "Owing to the large Mexican majority," she recalled,

> almost every Anglo-American family had at least one, sometimes two or three servants: a maid and laundress, and perhaps a nurse-maid or yardman. The maid came in after breakfast and cleaned up the breakfast dishes, and very likely last night's supper dishes as well; did the routine cleaning, washing and ironing, and after the family dinner in the middle of the day, washed dishes again, and then went home to perform similar service in her own home.[34]

An examination of the city directories, listing both home and work

Table 4.2   Number and Percentage of Spanish-Surnamed Domestics and Laundresses, 1889, 1910, 1920

	Number	Percentage of total workers (Mexican and American)
Domestics		
1889	61	49.73
1910	447	65.37
1920	1,528	76.18
Laundresses		
1889	40	34.90
1910	220	64.48
1920	516	92.17

Source: El Paso City Directories, 1889, 1910, 1920. The 1890 city directory was not used, because no copies for that year could be found. The discrepancy between the 1920 census figures and those of the city directory is probably the result of a more limited survey by the city directory.

addresses, indicates that the Mexican maids left their homes in the barrios in the morning to work in American neighborhoods during the day and then returned in the afternoon or evening to the Mexican districts. In some cases Mexican domestics had living quarters with their employers. One newspaper account reported that the hours of "house girls" went from seven in the morning to five in the afternoon, and in 1907 they received from $3 to $6 per week for this. Most, apparently, were hired by American middle-class families.[35]

Mexican women, besides working as servants, found other employment opportunities. Many worked as washerwomen, either in American homes or in their own as well as in the various laundries of El Paso. In laundries they learned such other skills as the use of sewing machines and received from $4 to $6 a week. In 1917 the largest in the city, the El Paso Laundry, employed 134 Spanish-surnamed workers out of a total of 166, and Mexican women, mostly doing collar and flatwork, comprised what appears to have been more than half the Mexican employees. That same year the Elite Laundry had 76 Spanish-surnamed female workers out of a total of 128. Another of the larger laundries, the Acme, employed 75 Spanish-surnamed females out of 121 employees in 1917. The same pattern prevailed in the smaller laundries. For example, the Post Laundry had 33 Spanish-surnamed women in their work force of 49. While many of these laundresses lived in El Paso, some came from Ciudad Juárez. The daughter-in-law of Frank Fletcher, who owned the Acme Laundry, remembers that when she arrived in 1926, a laundry truck picked up the Mexican women at the border, took them to work, and returned them in the evening to the international bridge. The use of nonresident Mexican women limited already low wages.[36]

In addition to service jobs some Mexican women labored as production workers, especially in El Paso's early garment factories. In 1902 Bergman's factory, which turned out shirts and overalls, reported that it had 3 American women and a large number of Mexican females. Yet, according to a newspaper account, Bergman concluded that he could get more and better work out of his Americans and consequently paid them $10 to $14 a week while the Mexicans received no more than $9 a week. Several years later, in 1919, the El Paso Overall Company advertised in a Spanish-language newspaper that it needed Mexican women for sewing and for general work. Mexican women likewise worked in the Kohlberg Cigar Factory. Mostly boxing cigars, 22 Mexican women out of 113 employees labored in the plant in 1917. Some women also found jobs as clerks and sales personnel in the downtown stores. A *Times* ad in 1905 read: "Wanted—5 experienced American and Spanish salesladies." The Mexican newspaper, *El Día*, in 1919 praised Panchita Salas for her "work and charm" at the El Globo Department Store run by the Schwartz family. That same year the White House Department Store, one of El Paso's largest, publicized in *La Patria* that it needed young women clerks in all its departments. Still other Mexicans worked as cooks or dishwashers in restaurants. In more unfortunate cases Mexican women sold food on the streets of Chihuahuita.[37]

Finally, as in other societies, some women inhabited the saloons and gambling halls of the red-light district. The *Lone Star* in 1885 expressed shock over a twelve-year old Mexican girl's activities. "It is rumored," the newspaper sermonized, "that she is a prostitute and most any hour of the day she can be seen in the streets with different men." When the city government enforced an ordinance in 1903 to move the district farther from the center of El Paso, the *Times* reported that many of the prostitutes "proposed to go across the river, among the number being Mexicans, which include the dance hall girls." Two years later, when Lou Vidal attempted to open his dance hall, police raided and arrested his employees, which included dance hall girls María González, Josefa González, Lola Beltrán, and Senida García.[38]

While men and women formed the bulk of the Mexican workers in El Paso, many children between 10 and 15 had to find jobs to help their families, although it is difficult to calculate their exact numbers. Guillermo Balderas, whose family arrived after 1910, recalls that most Mexican boys worked after completion of the sixth grade. Some, such as Augustine Romero, labored in the railroad yards. He had a job as an oil boy at the G.H. & S.A. roundhouse when accused in 1908 of assault against the son of a railroad laborer. Others sold newspapers, shined shoes on El Paso streets, or delivered packages for merchants. Some worked as water boys at the El Paso Smelter. In 1914 George Harper, the city sanitary commissioner, noted that some Americans paid Mexican boys 25 cents to cart off garbage from their backyards. Mexican girls also worked, and included among the large number of servants could be found girls in their early teens.[39]

Although most Mexicans in El Paso were workers, there did develop an active business sector (comerciantes) servicing the Mexican population. It appears that among the immigrants as well as among Mexican Americans some had sufficient capital to operate small-scale enterprises. Moreover, wealthier political refugees invested in El Paso businesses after 1910. The majority of these establishments, however, tended to be small, service oriented, and located in the Mexican barrio of Chihuahuita. Consequently, Mexican businessmen functioned separately from the general business community. Between 1900 and 1920 only a handful of Spanish surnames appeared on the membership rolls of the chamber of commerce. The Retail Merchants League organized in 1910 contained no Mexican members and the Retail Grocers Association had only one Mexican participant.[40]

Advertisements in the Spanish-language newspapers of El Paso called attention to the variety of Mexican businesses in the city. These included restaurants, general stores, tailors, photographers, bakeries, labor contractors, laundries, clothing stores, bookstores, meat markets, interpreters and translators, real estate salesmen, watchmakers,

furniture stores, drugstores, saloons, and moneylenders. The Calderón Brothers' ad in *La Patria* in 1919 showed the Mexicans'
new material tastes in that they sold phonographs and records including "the most popular tunes for dancing." One of the
largest Mexican stores, the Calderón Brothers incorporated for
$50,000 in 1916 and sold stock at $10 a share.[41] Finally, ads
appeared for Mexican silent movie houses on South El Paso Street,
such as the Teatro Alcázar, the Teatro Iris, and the Teatro Hidalgo.
These theaters belonged to the International Pictures Company
headed by J. de la C. Alarcón of El Paso. "People laughed at me and
said my ideas were crazy when I entered the moving pictures field
here six years ago," Alarcón stated in an interview, "but I succeeded,
and I am far more certain of success in my new and bigger undertaking." Alarcón had been a printer and newspaperman in Ciudad
Juárez with little money when he crossed the border in 1913 and
entered the theater business. In a short time he had prospered and in
1919 operated six theaters in El Paso, two in Juárez, and four in
Chihuahua besides offices in New York and Mexico City distributing
American films throughout Mexico.[42]

An appealing characteristic of these Mexican establishments was
their use of colorful store names. They symbolized not only cultural
traditions but also a nationalistic and ethnic consciousness among
Mexicans in El Paso. Besides those already mentioned, Mexican stores
had such names as: Cantina El Palacio, La Puerta del Sol, La Estrella,
Cantina El Toro, Las Tres Piedras, La Perla, La Azteca, Agencia
Hispano-Americana, Gran Fotografía Mexicana, and Carnicería Mexicana.[43] At times, these titles expressed more than just a cultural
and nationalist sentiment. "The magnificent success obtained by my
newspaper La Patria," boasted editor Silvestre Terrazas before the
Ad Club of El Paso in 1920, "is largely due to its name, its motto and
the engraving you see in these cards, with national colors; my traveling agents, specially in New Mexico and Arizona, tell me that cards
like these, with the picture of Father Hidalgo, advertising *La Patria*
(The Fatherland), are being displayed in nearly every home."[44]

Besides aiding business sales, newspaper advertising led to an
important Spanish-language press in El Paso. Between 1890 and 1920
more than 20 Mexican daily and weekly newspapers appeared in the
border city. Some, like *Sancho Panza* published in 1891, had only

a brief tenure, while others, such as *La Patria*, operated for several years. Although each newspaper possessed a particular ideological perspective, many represented commercial enterprises rather than political organizations. In addition to local, national, and international news along with literary sections, the Spanish-language press carried numerous advertisements by both Mexican and American merchants. Publishers stressed that businesses would increase their sales and profits if they advertised in the Mexican press. *El Hispano-Americano* in 1893 pointed out that the "intelligent and enlightened Spanish reading public" of the Southwest read El Paso's "cheapest and only Spanish daily on both frontiers." Consequently, it informed American manufacturers that the Mexican population constituted a large consuming market. To assist American merchants, *El Hispano-Americano* translated all advertisements free of charge. "Here is a new field for the manufacturer and businessmen to increase business and profits," the Mexican paper concluded. Impressed by these arguments, a number of corporations bought space in Mexican newspapers in El Paso and throughout the Southwest. That these firms had found a new consumer in the Mexicans can be seen in an ad by the Sears, Roebuck and Company published in *El Correo del Bravo* in 1913. "Atención: Mexicanos," the notice appealed to Mexican customers. "With the objective of making it more convenient for our Mexican friends in the United States to buy our merchandise," Sears announced, "we have just established a Special Department to attend all requests made in the Spanish language."[45]

The ability of Silvestre Terrazas, who had arrived as a political refugee, and other Mexican publishers to acquire extensive advertising made El Paso's Mexican press among the most widely circulated Spanish-language newspapers in the Southwest and northern Mexico. For example, in addition to agents north of the border, Terrazas employed a Chihuahua advertising manager for *La Patria's* international editions, which, according to Terrazas, furthered commercial relations between the United States and Mexico.[46] The Mexican press of El Paso through its national and local advertisements influenced Mexican buying habits and mediated the immigrants' acceptance of American business and consumer values.

As a further indication of the growth of Mexican businesses, the city directory of 1900 had listed only 3 Spanish-surnamed

barbers, yet twenty years later El Paso had 57 barbershops run by
Mexicans. A similar increase involved the Spanish-surnamed boot-
and shoemakers, whose shops grew from 8 in 1900 to 56 in 1920.
Moreover, the number of Spanish-surnamed retail grocers listed
by the directory rose from 19 in 1900 to 446 in 1920. One year
earlier the *Times* reported that El Paso's Mexican grocers had organized a Spanish Speaking Retail Grocers Association with 129 members. Although the spread of grocery stores was significant, most
remained small and operated out of the Mexicans' homes. Some grocers also had to work as laborers to make a living.[47]

Despite the number of barrio stores, few Mexicans could be
found in more lucrative and established business occupations. The
city directory of 1920 listed no Mexican advertising agencies, no
Mexican auto dealers, no Mexican gas stations, 5 Mexican contractors
out of a total of 101, and only 7 Spanish-surnamed real estate and
land agents out of 92.[48] In addition the retail apparel and dry goods
stores owned by Mexicans could not compare to large department
stores such as The Popular and The White House. Limited in capital
and located only in the Mexican districts, Mexican businesses remained dependent on the small wages and basic needs of immigrants.

One major exception was Félix Martínez, the most prominent
Mexican in El Paso. Unlike most Mexicans, however, Martínez had
been born and educated in New Mexico. At Las Vegas he had published a Democratic newspaper, *La Voz del Pueblo*, besides owning
considerable property. According to one account, Martínez had
lost most of his money in politics by the time he moved to El Paso
in 1897. Yet he must have retained some funds, for on his arrival
El Monitor noted that Martínez had acquired a real estate office, a
notary public service, a hotel, and various other properties. Impressed, *El Monitor* believed that the Mexican community of El
Paso would gain from the presence of such a distinguished man as
Martínez: "a gentleman of honor, fame, and of charitable feelings."
From his arrival to his death in 1916 at the age of 58, Martínez
accumulated what appears to have been a significant amount of
wealth. He owned or had interests in the Martínez Publishing Company, the El Paso–Juárez Railway Company, the International
Real Estate Office and General Brokerage firm, the Southwestern
Portland Cement Company, the Central Building and Improvement

Company, the East El Paso Town Company, and the International
Water Company. Martínez also held substantial property investments throughout the city. When a reporter inquired of one of
Martínez's daughters in 1963 if she knew the entire business activities
of her father, she replied: "It's hard to say. They were extensive and
he was in many business ventures with his friends. I really don't
know what his dealings were."[49]

Not restricting himself to business, Martínez served on the board
of directors of the chamber of commerce and as president of the
El Paso Fair Association, promoting the city. The chamber also
appointed "Don Félix" to its Committee on Lands and Irrigation,
which assisted in the construction of Elephant Butte Dam in southern
New Mexico. Because he was involved in Democratic politics, many
regarded him as a major political figure in El Paso. His political
as well as economic and civic influence led to his selection by President Woodrow Wilson in 1915 as chairman of the United States
Commission to South America and to the Panama Pacific International Exposition held that year in San Francisco. Prior to this
appointment, Wilson had named Martínez a director of the Federal
Reserve Bank for the bank's Eleventh District, covering Texas.
At his death, mourners included important El Paso as well as Chihuahua officials who in their top silk hats and fine suits paid final
respects as the body lay in state in the chamber of commerce for two
days under police guard.[50]

Unlike businessmen who played a significant role because they
catered to the essential needs of the Mexican population, few professionals were found in the barrios due to the poverty of the people
and the lack of educational opportunities. In 1900 the city directory
listed 50 dentists and physicians; only 1 had a Spanish surname.
Twenty years later, out of 182 dentists and physicians 11 had Spanish surnames. Some Mexican physicians practiced in El Paso only
because they had fled as political refugees from the Mexican Revolution. Dr. M. N. Samaniego, for example, not only represented
the small number of Mexican professionals but was one of the first
dentists in the city with his office on El Paso Street in 1895. Dr. Juan
C. Rechy, however, was the most highly respected Mexican physician during the early years and specialized in *enfermedades del
pulmon*—pulmonary diseases. Rechy held a variety of medical

positions in Mexico before he came to El Paso and had traveled in both the United States and Europe. From his office in Chihuahuita, Rechy treated numerous Mexican patients from El Paso and Chihuahua and twice a week administered vaccine shots to children, charging 50 cents for each child but at no cost to the poor. Mexicans also utilized the services of Dr. Antonio de la Campa, who had an office near Chihuahuita in 1897. That same year *El Clarín del Norte* carried a notice for Dr. Santiago González, specializing in heart and blood diseases. Ten years later Professor S. A. Arrieta advertised his practice in the *Herald*. Arrieta emphasized that he had been trained by European specialists, had 16 years experience in Mexico City hospitals, and excelled in Swedish, German, English, and French massages.[51]

Lawyers and other professionals were as scarce as physicians among Mexicans in El Paso. Of 39 attorneys in the 1900 city directory, no Spanish surname appeared and in the 1920 directory only 9 Spanish-surnamed lawyers were listed out of 165. Reginaldo Valenzuela, one of the few Mexican attorneys, advertised in 1897 that he practiced law in both Texas and New Mexico. "I speak perfect English," he informed Mexican readers of *El Monitor*. Other professionals who placed ads in the newspapers included Genaro Ramonet, offering his services as a mining engineer; T. C. Valenzuela, teaching English and Spanish in his school located in the Central Hotel; and José de la Luz Venzor, giving music lessons in the violin and mandolin in his home.[52]

Whether as workers, merchants, or professionals, Mexican immigrants were occupationally and economically restricted by the meager resources of their community and, more importantly, by El Paso's economy, which stressed labor-intensive enterprises requiring mostly cheap manual labor. Still, Mexican workers, male and female, proved essential to the city's economic growth. Mexican labor changed the face of El Paso. Easy accessibility to jobs, moreover, aided the immigrants' own economic and cultural adjustment. Mexicans, although exploited in their work, tolerated hard working and living conditions because at least they had jobs, whereas few existed south of the border. Nevertheless, the relationship between obreros and employers formed a class structure that maintained the material advantages and social privileges that American bosses derived from a large pool of cheap Mexican labor.

5

Class, Race, and Labor

Although Mexicans and Americans, as we will see, adjusted to each
other in El Paso, unequal occupational divisions existed between
both groups. Based on the region's underdeveloped economy, which
limited job advancements for workers, a class society functioned
with distinct racial stratifications: Mexicans primarily as blue-collar
workers along with a minority of American craftsmen and Americans
mostly as white-collar employees, businessmen, managers, and
professionals. Yet even within the city's working class, composed
of both Mexicans and Americans, distinctions are obvious. Clearly,
the need by southwestern enterprises for cheap unskilled labor
coincided with the availability of Mexican immigrants to produce
a class system tainted with racial prejudice. Such a system, moreover,
produced profits and privileges for the region's employers and their
managers, while limiting wages for all workers and, unfortunately,
dividing them along racial lines. Economically the subcategorization
of Mexican workers involved occupational distribution, wage standards, and their relationship to organized labor.[1]

Occupational divisions between Mexicans and Americans can be
observed in table 5.1 covering the period 1900 to 1940.* Almost
three-fourths of the Mexicans in 1900 worked either as laborers, service workers, or operatives. Fewer than one-quarter, however, of
the non-Spanish-surnamed workers—almost all whites since few blacks
lived in El Paso—could be found in these jobs. The 1900 sample reveals that a little more than 20 percent of the Mexicans worked
as craftsmen/foremen and clerical workers. On the other hand, more
than half the non-Spanish-surnamed workers were in these two

Spanish surnamed is used to designate both foreign-born Mexicans and Mexicans born
in the United States. Most Spanish-surnamed adults during this period were foreign born.

Table 5.1   Occupational Composition of El Paso, Texas, by Ethnicity, 1900, 1920, 1940 (Percent)

Occupational group	1900 SS	1900 NSS	1920 SS	1920 NSS	1940 SS	1940 NSS
Professionals	3.03	12.59	3.31	13.82	2.42	18.50
Managers	3.64	13.20	2.00	15.79	2.42	14.45
Clerical	10.91	26.90	14.57	38.82	18.55	24.28
Craftsmen/ foremen	10.91	25.38	12.58	10.53	11.29	9.25
Operatives	9.70	8.12	9.93	5.92	10.48	13.29
Service workers	16.36	10.66	39.07	11.48	36.29	18.50
Laborers	45.45	3.05	18.54	3.29	18.55	1.73
Total	100	100	100	100	100	100
	N= 165	N = 197	N = 151	N = 152	N = 124	N = 173

Source: El Paso City Directories, 1900, 1920, 1940: Taken from unpublished paper by Alma María García, "The Occupational Distribution of El Paso by Ethnicity, 1900–1940," p. 10. García's methodology involves the following description: "A random sample was obtained using the city directories for the years 1900, 1920, and 1940. This was done in the following manner. Fifty numbers were selected from a table of random numbers. By knowing the total number of pages in each directory the table was used according to the amount and range of digits. An estimation was then made of the number of names per page and using the table of random numbers approximately six names were drawn from each of the fifty pages. The desired sample size for each year was 300. This process was repeated for the 1920 and 1940 volumes of the city directory of El Paso. Ethnicity was operationalized in this study according to the following criterion: Spanish surnamed or non-Spanish surnamed. Occupation was coded using the 1960 census of Population Alphabetical Index of Occupations and Industries (revised edition)."

Note: SS, Spanish surnamed; NSS, non-Spanish surnamed.

areas. Moreover, only 6.67 percent of the Mexicans in 1900 held professional or managerial positions as opposed to 25.89 percent of the non-Spanish-surnamed persons.[2]

Yet between 1900 and 1920 Mexicans appear to have enjoyed some mobility within El Paso's economic structure. Although the majority continued as manual workers, there seemed to be a shift from laborers to service workers. More Mexicans also gained in craftsmen/ foremen and clerical occupations.[3] "It is not necessary," editorialized the *Herald* in 1917 on the economic potential of the Mexican population, "to spend too much time training for stores and offices and professions; far more important is it that we build up here a great reservoir of trained labor."[4] El Paso's economic growth not only created considerable employment for Mexicans as unskilled laborers but allowed some to acquire skills. The Dillingham Commission in its 1909 study of immigrant labor in western railroad shops noted that a larger percentage of Mexicans than Japanese became skilled workers. "But this fact is not due to any superiority of the Mexicans," the commission emphasized, "so much as to the fact that he is employed where white men are difficult to obtain on account of social and climatic conditions."[5] Above the level of skilled labor, however, the exclusion of Mexicans is evident. This can be seen in professional and managerial occupations, where a decrease among Mexicans took place in 1920: only 5.31 percent of the Spanish surnamed held such jobs in comparison to 29.61 percent of the non-Spanish surnamed.[6] "There were no Mexican men or women, boys or girls, working in the banks," Cleofas Calleros recalled of pre-Depression El Paso. "None in the electric company, the gas company, the water company. American offices, like insurance offices . . . they never hired Mexicans."[7]

The rural and small town background of many Mexican immigrants played a part in the occupational division between Mexicans and Americans. The persistence of these differences through 1940 and beyond, however, raises doubts about their nature and cause. In his study of Boston, Stephen Thernstrom discovered a similar job dichotomy between blacks and whites. He concluded that although the black culture may have influenced such a distinction, the more important factor seemed to be what he refers to as active and structural discrimination. "In virtually every area of the economy," Thernstrom writes, "it appears that the main barriers to black achievement have been not internal but external, the result not of peculiarities in black culture but of peculiarities in white culture."[8] In El Paso these "peculiarities" involved not only racism toward Mexicans but also a limited economy based on the extractive industry, transportation, and commerce that created few skilled jobs. The most basic labor need in El Paso and throughout the Southwest was for unskilled manual workers. As a result, occupational advancement for Mexicans was confined and restricted to working-class positions. On the other hand, Americans dominated the better paying but scarce skilled and clerical jobs as well as the managerial and professional ones.

A second measure of occupational division appears in table 5.2 taken from one scholar's study of urbanization and social change in the Ciudad Juárez–El Paso area revealing a substantial difference between Mexicans and Americans over a much longer period of time (1910–70). According to this sample, Mexicans experienced some mobility between 1910 and 1920 in semiskilled, service, and low white-collar jobs but declined in skilled blue-collar ones. Moreover, the majority of Mexicans continued after 1920 to be heavily employed in unskilled, semiskilled, and service work, whereas fewer than one-fourth of Americans held such jobs. The percentage of Mexicans in white-collar jobs has risen over the years, yet that of non-Spanish-surnamed persons has also grown, especially in high white-collar occupations, which remain practically closed to Mexicans.[9] The persistence of these differences between Mexicans and Americans over three-quarters of a century provides evidence for both the existence of active and structural racial discrimination in the El Paso labor market and the lack of adequate economic development, necessitating a more trained labor force to close the occupational gap.

Occupational distinctions between Mexicans and Americans can further be seen in wage differentials that increased profits for El Paso industries and restricted the mobility of Mexicans. In a 1911 wage scale printed by the chamber of commerce (see table 5.3) designed to attract industry, the chamber pointed out the abundance of Mexican common labor in El Paso at low wages of $1.25 to $1.50 a day. Moreover, complaints from organized labor suggest that Mexican skilled labor worked for wages lower than those paid Americans. Wage figures for Mexican craftsmen could not be found, but the 1900 census and World War I draft records reveal that almost all Mexicans listed in a craft occupation continued living in poor sections of the city such as Chihuahuita. One economist in the late 1920s discovered that in the El Paso area Mexican carpenters received $3.50 or $4.50 a day compared to American carpenters, who obtained $8 a day.[10] While racial and cultural prejudice supported residential restriction, occupational and wage discrimination did also.

Table 5.2 Occupational Distribution of the El Paso Labor Force by Surname, 1910–70
(Percent)

	1910		1920		1930		1940		1950		1960		1970	
	SS	NSS	SS	NSS	SS	NSS	SS	NSS	SS	NSS	SS	NSS	SS	NSS
High white collar	1.6	17.0	3.8	21.6	1.8	25.9	1.8	18.4	1.8	17.8	3.4	21.7	6.3	27.4
Low white collar	11.2	47.2	18.5	45.9	17.6	44.9	18.4	47.2	26.4	49.4	28.6	50.4	29.2	50.6
Skilled blue collar	12.8	15.6	10.5	12.5	13.1	11.2	12.6	9.6	11.2	12.4	12.2	8.1	7.4	3.6
Semiskilled and service workers	17.0	16.0	21.0	16.9	19.7	16.3	25.8	22.0	33.2	15.6	27.6	13.2	33.7	17.3
Unskilled laborers and menial service workers	57.4	4.2	46.2	3.1	47.9	1.8	41.4	2.8	27.4	4.8	28.2	6.5	23.5	1.2

Source: Random samples of 500 Spanish-surnamed and 500 non-Spanish-surnamed persons for each year covered, taken from the El Paso *City Directories,* 1910–70. Occupational categories are patterned after Stephen Thernstrom, *The Other Bostonians,* appendix B, pp. 290–92. Cited in Oscar J. Martínez, *Border Boom Town: Ciudad Juárez Since 1848,* appendix table 6, pp. 164–65.

Note: SS, Spanish surnamed; NSS, non-Spanish surnamed.

Table 5.3   Daily Wages Paid for Skilled and Unskilled Labor in El
Paso, 1911

Plumber	$6.00
Steam fitter	$6.00
Machinist	$4.00
Carpenter	$3.50–4.00
Mason	$5.00–6.00
Bricklayer	$5.00–6.00
Blacksmith	$3.00–5.00
Painter	$3.00–5.00
Electrician	$3.50–4.00
Teamster	$2.00–2.50
Farmhand, with board	$1.00–1.25
Common labor	$1.25–1.50

Source: El Paso Chamber of Commerce, *Prosperity and Opportunities in El Paso and El Paso's Territory for the Investor–Manufacturer–Jobber–Miner–Farmer–Home Seeker,* p. 19.

Although it did not specify the El Paso labor market, the Dillingham Commission observed wage discrepancies along racial lines in various western industries. Table 5.4 illustrates that in its survey of western railroads, the commission detected that 86.1 percent of Mexican employees earned less than $1.25 per day in 1909. No other nationality rivaled the Mexicans in low earnings. While only 5.3 percent of the Mexicans received $1.50 or above, 84 percent of native-born Americans obtained such wages. In addition a substantial percentage of other foreign-born groups received $1.50 and over. The commission in its examination of the Clifton and Douglas smelters in Arizona also found significant wage differences between Mexican and non-Mexican employees. While most Mexican smelter workers were paid between $2 and $2.50 per day, the majority of both native-born and other foreign-born workers earned over $2.50 a day. "The differences in the wages paid Mexicans and the native-born and north Europeans employed as general laborers," the Senate investigators explained, "are partly due to differences in the places held by individuals of these races as general laborers, but they are largely accounted for by discrimination against the Mexicans in the payment of wages."[11] One study of Mexican labor in Arizona reports that as early as the turn of the century a two-scale wage system between Mexicans and Americans had become

Table 5.4   Percentage of Male Employees 18 Years of Age and
Older Earning Each Specified Rate per Day in Western Railroads,
by General Nativity and Race, 1909

	<$1.25	$1.25–1.49	$1.50+
Native born	10.3	5.7	84.0
Foreign born			
English	0	5.4	94.6
German	0	85.5	14.5
Greek	0	8.2	91.8
Irish	0	2.5	97.5
Italian, north	0.7	56.7	42.6
Italian, south	0.7	56.0	43.3
Japanese	19.0	80.5	0.5
Korean	0.0	100.0	0.0
Mexican	86.1	8.6	5.3
Norwegian	0	2.5	97.5
Asiatic	0	43.7	56.3

Source: Dillingham Commission, pt. 25, vol. III, pt. I, p. 19. The commission noted that
the 10.3% of the native born who earned less than $1.25 included a number of Mexican
Americans.

"traditional." During World War I, moreover, Phelps-Dodge in its
Bisbee mines paid Mexican laborers $2 a day and American laborers,
miners, timbermen, and mechanics $2.50 to $6 a day.[12]

More attention to wage differences between Mexican and
American workers occurred as the result of hearings held in El Paso
in November 1919 by the Texas Industrial Welfare Commission.
Although the hearings did not investigate the wages of Mexican
males, they did focus on Mexican women. During three days of
testimony by female employees as well as employers, the commission discovered that Mexican women in the laundries and factories of the city received less pay than American women in other
Texas industries. The Mexicans also obtained less than the salaries
of laundry and factory workers in other Texas cities performing
similar work but not facing Mexican competition. According to the
commission these differences made it more difficult to set a general
minimum wage throughout the state. The problem, the commission believed, was in the Mexicans' lower standard of living, a
condition deemed beyond remedy.[13] Members of the commission
concluded, although without evidence, that "the Mexican workers

find it possible to 'live comfortably' on a wage that American workers would regard as 'starvation wages.'"[14] The commission suggested
that the only possible solution would be to establish different wage
zones in Texas, taking into consideration these different living standards.[15]

El Paso employers testifying before the commission supported
lower wages for Mexican female workers. F. B. Fletcher, the general
manager of the Acme Laundry, presented a statement prepared by
the owners of the Acme, El Paso, Troy, and Elite laundries covering
their wage policies. Fletcher pointed out that due to its location on
the border El Paso acquired large numbers of unskilled Mexican workers who performed almost all the unskilled labor in the laundries. On
the other hand, skilled positions such as markers, sorters, checkers,
supervisors, and office assistants went to "English speaking women of
American birth." The laundries paid Mexicans an average of $6 a
week, while Americans received $16.55 a week. "This difference in-
dicates," Fletcher states, "that in this industry the minimum wage
can only be fairly fixed for Mexican female help and for the American entirely different and distinct." Fletcher admitted, however,
that in certain cases Mexicans were used as skilled workers although
apparently still at lower wages. He emphasized that efforts had
been made by the laundries to secure more American workers but
that they had not succeeded and consequently "trouble is found
in filling even the best positions and so the Mexican help has to be
used, with its unquestionable limitations."[16]

Although the laundries probably profited from their use of
cheaper Mexican workers, Fletcher defended lower wages for them
on the basis that their racial and cultural disadvantages did not
allow them to produce as much as the Americans. "We are confront-
ed with the deep seated differences in temperament existing between
the Anglo-Saxon and mixed Latin races," the laundry official told
the commissioners, "the differences between the progressiveness, ini-
tiativeness and energy of the former and the backwardness of the
Mexican." He believed that the Mexican women possessed no "material desire" to learn and progress and he informed the commission
that in one plant the Mexicans refused to use the bathroom because
they feared other workers would use the time to steal their lunches,
shoes, or clothes. The Mexican females, according to Fletcher, did not

represent reliable workers and hence did not advance to responsible positions. "These remarks do not constitute an indictment against Mexican female workers," the general manager insisted, "but a plain statement of facts." Fletcher concluded that American workers in other cities were more efficient than Mexicans. He alleged that the rate of finished shirts turned out by American women averaged 45 per hour for 3 operators while the Mexicans averaged 25 shirts per hour with 4 operators, "or about six shirts per hour per operator as against 15 for American help." Fletcher contended that in collar work it took at least double the number of Mexican operators, and that for flatwork most American laundries averaged 40,000 pieces a week for a crew of 6 women; yet in El Paso it took 20 Mexican women to produce the same amount of work per week.[17]

In addition to the laundries, the department stores of the city defended lower wages for Mexican women. Adolph Schwartz, owner of the Popular Dry Goods, testified that he paid his saleswomen an average of $19.63 a week. This, however, involved two types of workers. Those women, apparently Americans, working on the main floor received more pay than those in the basement departments, who, according to Schwartz, "are mostly Mexicans." The basement employees received from $10 a week minimum to $20 a week. On the other hand Schwartz pointed out that the highest paid saleswomen received salaries of $37.50 to $40 a week. He justified lower wages for Mexican women by their lower standard of living. Admitting that Mexican females constituted 20 percent of the Popular's employees, Schwartz emphasized that those Mexicans who spoke English received better jobs, apparently as clerks. The others worked in the alteration department.[18]

Other employers testifying included the owners of garment factories. B. H. Hollander of the El Paso Manufacturing Company claimed that his firm paid union scales for piecework, which meant $18 to $20 a week. However, Hollander contradicted himself when he said that he had 22 Mexican females on piecework averaging $9.50 a week. Like the other "bosses," Hollander defended these wages because of the claimed unproductiveness of the Mexicans: "American girls will beat the best of them [the Mexicans] about 50 percent, but we cannot get the Americans of experience here. Our machines are electrically driven, capable of making 2200 stitches per minute and efficient and steady help can do more than [it] is now doing." B. N. Haywood of the El Paso Overall Company supported Hollander and argued against a minimum wage. Haywood alleged that he paid his Mexican female employees union wages but only if they worked adequately. Moreover, Haywood stated that his "turnover" ran about 200 percent.[19]

However, Mexican women who appeared before the commission refuted the charges that owing to a lower standard of living they did not need higher wages. One group of laundry workers, striking for higher wages, testified that the laundries had paid them from $4 to $5 a week. When asked what they would consider a reasonable wage, the women had different answers but their estimates ranged from $8 to $15 a week.[20] Manuela Hernández, who had worked several years at the Acme Laundry, told the commission in Spanish that she received $11 a week as a worker. While her wages were the highest paid Mexican women in the plant, American women averaged $4 to $6 more than Mexican workers although she did not specify if the Americans did similar work. "I find it difficult to live on my wages," Manuela commented, "which I turn in to the family budget." She concluded that it would take $16 a week for her family to live comfortably." María Valles testified that she worked at the Elite Laundry and received $4.50 a week. She lived with her family and supported a nine-year-old girl. "I have to support her and myself," she stated, "but I have to make great sacrifices, some days going without food, for lack of means." For her wages Valles told the commission she worked at times ten or twelve hours, six days a week. She believed she could live comfortably on $15 a week. An employee of the American Laundry, Guadalupe Espejo, expressed the problem of low wages and high prices for the Mexicans:

> I am getting $7 a week at the American Laundry in a collar machine. I have one dependent. My room rent is $5 a month; groceries cost $5.50 a week and I cannot buy a coat a year or one in two years. My clothing costs $10 to $12 a year and two pairs of shoes a year cost $4.50 a pair. The coat I have on I bought 10 years ago on the installment plan. I think $15 a week would be needed to live on comfortably.[21]

At $28 a month and with expenses that totaled $27 a month not including clothes and other items, Guadalupe Espejo barely received a subsistence wage.

Mexican women employed in the El Paso Overall Company also made statements urging higher wages. The *Herald* described one of these workers, Daniela Morena, as a "woman along in years" who testified that she made $7 to $8 a week and supported her mother and two children. She believed that she required at least $15 a week, "but if alone might get along with $8 or $9 a week, as she 'dressed very humbly.'" Eloise Alcalá, who had worked for almost a month at the El Paso Manufacturing Company, explained that she received $8 a week. She felt that she could not adequately care for herself and her children on this wage and would need at least $25 a week. When one of the commissioners inquired what she would do with the additional money, Alcalá replied, "I think I would spend it all for groceries." Another woman at the same plant, Josefa Gandara, commented that she folded clothing at $6 a week and turned her money over to the family budget. She thought she could not live alone on this salary but would require no less than $18 or $19 a week, "although she said she knew nothing about it except the difficulty of meeting the family expense."[22]

In support of the Mexican women, representatives of some civic and labor organizations argued that the wages paid these workers should be raised. Henry Walker of the employment bureau told the commission that his office supplied many Mexican servants at wages from $4.70 to as high as $8 but that most turned down the lower wages claiming they could not live on them. Employers would reap the rewards of more efficient workers, Walker advised, if they paid higher wages. Increased salaries would also elevate the Mexican women's standard of living. As for the belief that Mexican women felt satisfied with their economic conditions, Julia S. Roldán, a Mexican YMCA teacher, rebutted such a contention. Mexican girls are just as anxious to live comfortably as American girls," Mrs. Roldán informed the commission. She insisted, moreover, that although Mexican women did not complain they had many dissatisfactions with their living conditions. "Give the Mexican girl the same chance," the YMCA teacher concluded, "and she will show equal efficiency with the American girl." W. J. Moran of the *Labor*

Advocate, the official newspaper of the Central Labor Union, also endorsed a raise for the Mexicans because it would help "Americanize" them. "I believe," he told the commission, "that if the Mexican girl had proper food and living her mind would get to functioning as does that of her Anglo-Saxon sister." Moran suspected, however, that due to long years of suppression it might take the Mexicans "more than a generation for their minds to get to functioning like the Anglo-Saxon." The labor leader concluded that it would be to the advantage of employers to support a minimum wage because it would force exploiters of cheap labor to do likewise.[23] Yet, since almost all El Paso employers exploited cheap labor, Moran's arguments as well as those of the Mexican women and their supporters fell on deaf ears. Persistent low wages for all Mexicans, men and women, whether for economic or racial reasons, continued to characterize El Paso's economy.

Low wages for Mexicans, especially immigrants, plus their employment at times as skilled workers also hurt organized labor, as represented by the American Federation of Labor. "Mexican wages" lowered wages for all workers, including Americans. Besides taking jobs from Americans in some cases skilled Mexican workers were used by employers to intimidate labor unions and break strikes. However, rather than uniting with Mexicans to uplift conditions for all workers, organized labor in El Paso pursued a policy of separation. Two basic factors encouraged this development: the historic tradition of the AFL emphasizing skilled craft unions to the exclusion of unskilled workers and, secondly, the particular threat of unorganized Mexican workers to the AFL in El Paso. These conditions provoked intense antagonism toward Mexican immigrants by the AFL but, ironically, weakened organized labor as well.

The major goal of the AFL since its organization in 1886 had always been to establish unity among skilled workers. This the AFL attempted to do in El Paso when it established the Central Labor Union (CLU) in 1909 with 27 unions covering more than a thousand workers.[24] These unions included the carpenters, printers, musicians, machinists, plumbers, sheet metal workers, electrical workers, and railway clerks.[25] In racial terms the membership of the AFL in El Paso consisted primarily of Americans because most Mexicans

were unskilled. The expressed principle, however, of the CLU was
not racial exclusion. Although in 1902 and 1910 southwestern delegates to AFL national conventions had expressed concern over the
presence of "pauper labor" from Mexico, the *Labor Advocate*
stated in 1910: "This newspaper stands for the improved conditions
of all workers without regard to nationality. We all have to work,
and since we work together, we should unite, Mexican and American, for our mutual benefit."[26]

Indeed, a minority of Mexican Americans did belong to the craft
unions. Unlike Mexican immigrants, whom it excluded, the El Paso
AFL made efforts to organize Mexicans who were American citizens and skilled workers. Although they constituted only a small percentage of the city's Mexican population, some Mexican Americans
had learned skills as a result of El Paso's economic growth and employers' willingness to tap their large Mexican work force for both
untrained and trained labor. The AFL's acceptance of Mexican
American skilled workers led to both segregated as well as integrated
unions. In an occupation, for example, including a significant percentage of Mexican Americans as well as American employees, the
AFL endorsed segregated locals. The best example involved the
retail clerks. Seventy-five Mexican American clerks employed in retail stores with a large Mexican clientele organized in 1913 the
International Clerk's Protective Association with 191 members. The
union hoped to gain an early closing hour. With the assistance of
the CLU and some sympathetic civic associations, the movement succeeded and most of the stores signed agreements to close at 6 P.M.
during the week and 9:30 P.M. on Saturday. These included some of
the more prominent department stores, such as the Popular and the
White House. After their victory and acceptance into the CLU,
the Mexican American clerks stayed in their own local, the Retail
Clerks' Union No. 1372, while American clerks organized a separate local, No. 1339.[27]

A second type of Mexican American participation in the AFL involved those occupations dominated by them. One of these, the
Unión de Tabaqueros, affiliated with the Cigar Workers Union, the
Mexican cigar workers organized in 1901. The Hod Carriers Union
formed another predominately Mexican American union.[28] Perhaps the best example, however, of the AFL's attempt to organize

a "Mexican occupation" involved the laundry workers. In October 1919 some of the Mexican women together with state and local AFL organizers established the Laundry Worker's Union, a federal union of unskilled workers affiliated with the AFL. They organized workers —almost all Mexican women—in the Acme Laundry of El Paso. When this plant refused to accept the union and fired two of the women organizers, the rest of the almost 200 workers went on strike until employers rehired their co-workers. When three other laundries attempted to do the work of the Acme Laundry, Mexican women at these plants joined the strike. Owners of more laundries at first agreed to recognize the union but then changed their minds. The women at these places also struck. In a few days between 300 and 575 workers, including some men, had gone on strike against all El Paso's laundries. At a meeting of the CLU the Mexican women unanimously agreed to stand by their union. "Truly this was a sight that would do the heart of any one good to see these girls and women," the *Labor Advocate* reported, "some of them hardly in their teens and some of them bent with age, standing up and solemnly promising that no matter what may come or what may happen, they would stand together for the mutual good of their fellow worker."[29]

In its organizational effort the AFL emphatically pointed out that this movement did not involve alien workers, for most of the women held American citizenship. In an editorial the *Advocate* asserted, "The strike of the Laundry Workers in our area is somewhat unique, for too often we have taken it for granted that these workers were practically all Mexicans, hence we gave but little concern, but this is not the case. True it is, that they are nearly all of Mexican origin but they are by no means all of Mexican citizenship. The large majority are residents of El Paso and citizens of the nation, but nevertheless, let us look at the facts that are fundamentally the cause of this strike." Besides the nonrecognition of the union by the laundries and the dismissal of the women organizers, the strike occurred over the low wages paid the workers, which ranged from $4 to $6 a week. In comparison, laundry workers in Fort Worth, Dallas, Galveston, Houston, and San Antonio averaged $14 a week. "There is no question," the *Advocate* stated, "but that the treatment of the laundry workers of El Paso has been disgraceful and disgrace rests upon the laundry owners."[30]

During the strike the AFL supported the laundry workers with money collected from members of the CLU. The fund was further augmented by contributions from several Mexican social organizations who saw the strike as a means of self-protection for their fellow *Raza*. The CLU also brought in a special AFL organizer, C. N. Idar of San Antonio, to work with the women. "Mr. Idar," the *Advocate* pointed out, "is himself a Mexican and understands the language and customs of the Mexican and will be able to help them in a great way." In addition the laundry union purchased the American Laundry and began to operate it under union conditions. The *Advocate* believed that such a move would be more beneficial than to spend union funds in strike benefits and "idleness."[31]

Unfortunately for organized labor, and the laundry workers, the distinction that the AFL made between Mexican American workers and alien Mexican workers hastened the strike's defeat. The laundries simply hired other Mexicans, apparently recent immigrants as well as commuters from Ciudad Juárez, to replace the strikers. The labor newspaper noted that even though 486 workers, mostly women, had gone on strike hundreds of additional Mexicans had asked for jobs in the laundries.[32] How many of these were citizens and how many were not is impossible to determine. Nevertheless, as long as the AFL maintained its separation from the larger and more important immigrant working class, the weaker organized labor's position became. As the laundry strike clearly revealed, Mexican immigrants could be used not only as cheap labor but as strikebreakers as well.

Besides participation in de facto segregated locals, a minority of Mexican Americans was integrated into some predominantly American unions. Those with Mexican American members included the El Paso Typographical Union, the Painter's Union, the Carpenter's Union, the Musician's Union, the Brewery Workers, the Pressman's Union, the Sheet Metal Workers, and the Freight Handlers. Although it is difficult to know how many Mexican Americans belonged to these unions, a few acted as union officials or as delegates to the CLU; no Mexican American, however, was elected to a major office in the CLU. For example, in 1914 the Brewery Workers selected Fred Téllez as vice-president, Rosa Meléndez as recording secretary, and Frank Fuentes as doorkeeper. P. A. Carvajal of the

Bartenders International Alliance was a charter member of his local and served as its president and as delegate to the CLU. In 1916
the union selected Carvajal to be a member of its delegation to
the State Federation of Labor Convention in Houston. "In his
union," the *Advocate* said of the Mexican American bartender, "he
has been a building force, always a diligent worker, pleasant and
agreeable, but tenacious for the right. 'Tony,' as he is familiarly
called by most everyone in El Paso, has ever been a popular fellow,
which accounts for his being an enthusiastic member of the El Paso
Eagles and other fraternal orders."[33]

Although some Mexican American craftsmen were organized
by the AFL they represented only a small portion of El Paso's
work force. The AFL itself covered only a minority of the working
class. In 1910, for example, the Brewery Workers had only 30
members; the Bricklayers, 40; the Sheet Metal Workers, 25; the
Carpenters, 45; the Typographical Union, 35; and the Painters, 45.
The El Paso Smelter, on the other hand, alone employed more
than 1,000 unskilled and unorganized Mexicans, mostly immigrants.
Consequently, the AFL's selective organizing policy left the great
majority of Mexicans out of unions. Such disregard, however, ran
counter to the expressed sentiment of President Samuel Gompers and
the national body, which stressed in 1916 that unorganized Mexican nationals in the Southwest should be organized by AFL locals.
"Internationalization of capital," Gompers correctly emphasized,
"has made necessary the internationalization of the labor movement."[34] At its thirty-sixth annual convention in Baltimore, the AFL
adopted a resolution calling attention to the fact that employers
used Mexican workers not only as strikebreakers but as low wage laborers, retarding the progess of organized labor in the Southwest.
"This problem must be met," the Baltimore resolution stated, "by
the development of the organized labor movement in Mexico and
by the organization of the Mexicans within our country." One year
later, as a response to the labor shortage of World War I and to
Gompers's attempt to secure the support of labor in Mexico for a
Pan American Federation of Labor, the AFL reiterated its support
of extending membership to Mexican immigrant workers.[35] Yet,
despite the national organization's resolutions, the AFL in El Paso

stubbornly refused to organize Mexican immigrants, holding them responsible for the city's low wages, even among union members, and considering them organized labor's biggest obstacle to a viable movement. Unfortunately, while the AFL's analysis of border labor conditions was largely correct, its policy of excluding immigrants instead of organizing them served only to promote anti-union conditions and to undermine the effectiveness of union building in El Paso.

Besides the use of Mexican immigrants as strikebreakers, the major complaint of organized labor against them was their effect on wage scales. Unions in Arizona, for example, warned that increased Mexican immigration threatened the two-wage system between American and Mexican workers.[36] In El Paso, union wages were much lower than in southwestern cities that did not face the competition of cheap Mexican labor. According to the *Advocate*, laborers in the border city received 10 to 20 percent less pay than their counterparts in other cities of similar size. Moreover, the cost of living in El Paso ranged from 10 to 20 percent higher. The El Paso Electric Railway Company, using Mexicans for construction and maintenance, paid its American employees wages 10 to 25 percent lower than other cities. "The streetcar men," the *Advocate* exaggerated, "in exactly the same capacities as the engineer and conductor on a limited passenger train, do not get as much in wages as do the Mexican track greasers." The newspaper also observed in 1916 that the cost of living in El Paso during the previous six months had jumped 30 to 80 percent, but only three craft unions had received wage increases of from 9 to 18 percent. The *Advocate* pointed out four years later that in any city within 600 miles of El Paso unskilled labor received from $3.50 to $5.00 per day. In El Paso, employers paid unskilled workers from $1.25 to $2.00 owing to the proximity of the border "and our local Mexican population." Obviously, the newspaper stated, a fallacy existed that business in El Paso could not pay higher wages because other southwestern cities did. Moreover, criticizing a *Times* editorial calling for the unemployed to be put to work on Rio Grande Valley farms, the *Advocate* correctly explained that the city's labor problem was not a scarcity of workers but the fact that employers did not pay a living wage. "The editor of this paper," the *Advocate* emphasized, "could supply all the laborers wanted in 48 hours notice, right here in El Paso; and who are citizens of El Paso county, many taxpayers and having families to support—if living wages were paid."[37]

Because a direct link existed between low wages and Mexican immigration, the AFL aimed much of its wrath at the Immigration Bureau. At the thirteenth convention of the Texas State Federation of Labor held in Galveston in 1910, the El Paso delegation supported a resolution accusing the Immigration Bureau of showing no concern over the admission of Mexican laborers who competed with organized labor in the Southwest. More than 1,000 Mexican aliens, the resolution stated, entered the United States every month. They included not only common laborers but musicians, carpenters, painters, tinners, and other skilled workers. The resolution condemned labor contractors and employers who used Mexican agents to recruit laborers from across the border and denounced the Immigration Bureau for permitting the practice. In addition the El Paso AFL heavily criticized the railroads for violating the contract labor law. "One of the subterfuges resorted to by the railroads to pull wool over the eyes of the Immigration authorities at the border," the *Advocate* informed its readers, "and make it appear that these vast hordes of peons come here on their own notion looking for work, is to employ shipping agents on this side of the river, in the guise of 'employment agent' to meet at the immigration station each consignment sent up to them by the real and original employer, the secret agent in Mexico." These "employment agents," the newspaper angrily declared, met the "peons" at the international crossing, gathered them up and shipped them to their job locations. In turn the agents received a deduction from the Mexican's wages.[38]

Such real threats to the position of organized labor in El Paso, perpetuated by employers, led to a heated but unsuccessful campaign against both the employment of Mexican nationals and the immigrants themselves. The *Advocate* attacked the Mexicans for being parasites, paupers, "criminals of the most dangerous types," bearers of diseases, immoral, and sexually irresponsible. In a letter to the *Advocate*, F. M. Barker, a traveling salesman, expressed sentiments toward Mexican immigrants apparently shared by many union men. "There is a general complaint all over the Southwest," Barker wrote,

about the reckless way this class of people are being scoured and
all the worthless and criminal class were being brought here and
shipped out on different roads, where the people claim that they
finally settle down in the towns and refuse to work at any price,
but live off of the money their women can make, where the men
practice polygamy, adultery, and every other class of crime
against morality. I heard one man was shipped out of El Paso
three times, and every time he brought out a different woman as
his wife.[39]

Not only did the AFL attack the moral character of the Mexicans, it
also used racial and chauvinistic "standards" in its attempt to convince employers not to hire them. "Cheap labor," the *Advocate* indig-
nantly exclaimed,

yes, at the sacrifice of manhood of homes and all that go to
build up and sustain a community.

Cheap labor—at the cost of every ideal cherished in the heart
of every member of the white race, utterly destroyed and buried
beneath the greedy ambitions of a few grasping money gluttons,
who would not hesitate to sink the balance of society to the
lowest levels of animalism, if by so doing they can increase their
own bank account.

True Americans do not want or advocate the importation of
any people who cannot be absorbed into full citizenship, who
cannot eventually be raised to our highest social standard, but
help to raise that standard to even higher planes; where the
avariciously inclined will be relegated to the nether darkness
from which they drew their blackened souls.[40]

The *Advocate* urged El Paso businesses and industries to employ
only American citizens and not Mexican nationals who came to work
for short periods of time and then returned to Mexico, or those
living across the river in Ciudad Juárez and commuting to work in El
Paso each day. "Go down to the bridge any morning and see the
horde of pauper labor from four to six hundred," the *Advocate*

pointed out, "that daily cross over on this side and work, and take our American dollars and go back on the other side at night and spend them over there. Thus throwing out home labor and lessening the business of the El Paso merchant."[41]

During a 1914 strike of American streetcar conductors, the *Advocate* claimed that although the conductors possessed great responsibilities for the lives of their passengers, they received salaries similar to Mexican aliens in other jobs. "Take a look at him up there in the front of the car," the paper emphasized,

> with the responsibility of your life and the lives of many others in his care. Then turn around in your seat or across the aisle and take a look at some ugly visaged, peon Mexican laborer from the smelter or the cement plant. Compare the two. There is the American motorman or conductor, true Americans, yet paid a slave's wage. Those Mexicans who can neither read, write the English language and can hardly think, are paid as much as are these men upon whom the company places a burden of responsibility greater than their wages.[42]

Although the AFL correctly criticized employers as well as city and county governments for their anti-union practices, their most venemous charges were directed at Mexican nationals and by implication all Mexicans. "Is it a pretty sight to see men," the *Advocate* told the contractors of El Paso, "brawny American men with callouses on their hands and empty stomachs—sitting idly on benches in the plaza, while slim-legged peons with tortillas in their stomachs, work in the tall building across the way? Do you prefer the name Fernández, alien, to the name James, citizen, on your payroll?"[43] In 1919 William T. Griffith of the CLU notified the AFL national convention meeting in Atlantic City of the "alien threat" to organized labor along the border. Griffith informed his fellow delegates that the U.S. Army at nearby Fort Bliss had hired Mexican commuter workers from Juárez for carpentry and other forms of skilled labor at wages below the scales set by the War Labor Board. These men, Griffith stressed, were un-American, nonunion, owed their allegiance to another country, and "have as a class on numerous occasions proven themselves unfriendly to the United States." To correct this condition the El Paso unionist urged the hiring of "red-blooded American citizens" at Fort Bliss.[44]

In addition to its nativistic campaign the AFL used other methods to end the employment of Mexican aliens. The federation argued that it hurt business to pay low wages to Mexicans who spent most of their money in Mexico and not in El Paso. This proved to be a weak charge, however, since only part of the income of merchants' sales came from local consumption. Of greater importance were the surrounding railroad, mining, ranching, and agricultural interests, many of which purchased their supplies in El Paso. Moreover, despite the AFL charge it appears that most Mexican commuters patronized El Paso stores. Finally, the AFL attempted to pressure the political establishment by threatening to use the labor vote against politicians who supported the employment of Mexican nationals. Yet this tactic also failed because the same bankers, contractors, merchants, and other employers who profited from the availability of cheap Mexican labor to southwestern enterprises also controlled the city and county governments through the Democratic Ring's manipulation of the Mexican vote. Clearly, Mexican votes were more valuable to political bosses, both Democratic and Republican, than those of organized labor. Not only was the AFL in El Paso economically weak but it had little political leverage.[45]

The AFL in El Paso exemplified organized labor's traditional weak and vulnerable condition along the U.S.–Mexican border. Unlike employers, unions profited little, if any, from the exploitation of cheap Mexican labor. Although unions protected certain skilled jobs for their members it seems that organized labor in El Paso received lower wages than did craftsmen in other regions. Small in numbers due to the border economy's limited industrial growth, the AFL was surrounded by vast numbers of unskilled, and even skilled, Mexican immigrant workers. While its best policy to uplift labor conditions may have been to help organize all workers, Americans and Mexicans, citizens and noncitizens, skilled and unskilled, the AFL regrettably succumbed both to economic self-interests and to a racist ideology that, ironically, aided only employers and kept the working class divided. Although it may have been difficult to organize immigrant workers, given their limited interest in American society, still class unity rather than class separation, an unsuccessful tactic, might have proved more fruitful. Calling for the establishment of all-Mexican AFL locals in the Southwest, Mexican labor organizer Antonio I. Villarreal in 1918 expressed the belief that Mexican workers in the United States would not shun unionization if they could retain their Mexican citizenship.[46] However, the exploitative labor conditions of El Paso and the Southwest, instead of acting as a catalyst for the AFL to organize in a progressive fashion, only strengthened its traditional conservatism.

Although exploited by employers, the Mexicans' response to their conditions must be seen in light of their motives for having left Mexico. Mexicans had come to El Paso and the United States in search of jobs and with the hope of a quick return as soon as they had accumulated sufficient savings. Of course, the proximity of Mexico fostered this attitude. Unlike overseas immigrants, Mexicans could easily return to their homeland when economic and political conditions improved or visit relatives and friends. Although no records exist to document this migration, it nevertheless appears that such traffic occurred. At most, the possibilities for a return were less a matter of dreams and more a question of practicality. Hence, few Mexicans sought citizenship in the United States. Out of a total number of foreign born in El Paso in 1920 some 30,073, or 90 percent, remained aliens.[47] "I have always had and now have my home in El Paso," one immigrant commented in the 1920s, "but I shall never change my [Mexican] citizenship in spite of the fact that there [El Paso] I have greater opportunities and protection."[48] Consequently, Mexicans tolerated their economic subordination in El Paso because they had only a limited interest in American society: to get a job, make money, and return to Mexico. Moreover, because so many found employment, they saw their jobs as a significant improvement over their previous lower paying or unemployed positions in Mexico. Years later when asked why his family never returned to Mexico even though they had intended to, Charles Armijo replied: "Because we liked it here. We made a better living here."[49] As one scholar correctly observes about immigrant workers to the United States, they compared themselves not with American workers but with those left behind. In the United States they had jobs.[50] Grateful, Mexicans, like other newcomers, endured both long hours of hard work and squalid living conditions.

This does not mean, however, that Mexicans were incapable of struggling against exploitative conditions. Although fear of being fired and deported restrained most from engaging in open protests, some occasionally did resort to strikes when threatened with loss of jobs, when they believed employers cheated them out of better wages, and when labor organizers assisted them in their grievances. Besides the laundry strike of 1919 other work stoppages involving Mexicans took place. In 1901, for example, almost 200 Mexican construction workers employed by the El Paso Electric Street Car Company struck for a pay increase from $1.00 to $1.50 per day for ten hours' work. The workers claimed that they all lived in El Paso and that Mexicans from Ciudad Juárez had been hired by the streetcar line to replace them. The company agreed to employ only residents but refused the wage increase. Although not all construction workers accepted the offer, they had little choice after the company used El Paso policemen to protect their strikebreakers and to arrest some of the strikers. A similar walkout by streetcar workers occurred again four years later with almost identical results. The Mexican smelter workers also struck for better wages. In 1907 almost 150 left their jobs and requested a raise from $1.20 to $1.50 per day. After they replaced some of the strikers with additional Mexicans, smelter officials conceded a 20 cent increase, but about half the smelter workers refused the agreement and left for other work in Colorado.[51]

In addition, Mexican smelter workers participated in 1913 in one of the largest strikes in El Paso's early history. The Mexicans asked for a wage increase of 35 cents, giving them $1.75 per day. Furthermore, some of the workers desired a reduction of hours from twelve to eight. When the company refused, about 100 Mexicans went on strike. The following day an additional 300 Mexicans joined them and by the third day 650 Mexicans had left their jobs along with 5 carpenters, the only Americans in the strikers' ranks. During the strike, the Mexicans displayed good organization, which prevented attempts by smelter officials to divide them and hire replacements. To maintain unity the strike leaders held mass meetings to keep the men informed of negotiations with the company. The presence of Industrial Workers of the World organizers (apparently Mexicans) may have been an additional and important factor in the strike, although the exact role of the "Wobblies" cannot be determined. Their appearance, however, prompted the Central Labor Union to support the

strike and attempt to convince the Mexicans to join the more conservative Western Federation of Miners. CLU officials, moreover,
refuted a claim by one El Paso newspaper that the strike had been
initiated by the IWW. "The statement made in today's *Herald*,"
responded W. G. Griffin of the CLU, "that union labor men of El
Paso blame the IWW for the strike at the smelter is untrue." According to Griffin, the IWW had nothing to do with the strike. Rather,
the Mexican workers themselves had launched it. Yet upon closer
questioning, the CLU spokesman admitted that IWW organizers had
arrived in the city and had unsuccessfully attempted to recruit the
Mexicans. Consequently, CLU agents had likewise gone to a smelter
meeting to urge the strikers to unite with the Western Federation
of Miners.[52]

Although the striking smelter workers did not join either labor
organization, they did attempt to continue resistance until the smelter
met their demands. Unfortunately their efforts were unsuccessful
because the company used a variety of tactics to destroy the strike.
To protect their strikebreakers the company brought in the Texas
Rangers. In one particular incident a ranger shot a striker in the
leg after Mexicans began to pelt the rangers with stones because they
had allowed strikebreakers to enter the smelter. Company managers
also put additional pressure on the Mexicans through a court order
evicting them from their homes, which they rented from the smelter.
Finally, the company's ability to import a sufficient number of
scabs broke the strike. Besides more Mexicans, the smelter brought in
temporary black workers from Louisiana and East Texas. "They have
been coming in on practically every train from East Texas," the *Times*
noted, "and it is now reported that at least 350 negroes are employed at the smelter." Faced with defeat, some of the Mexican
strikers returned to their jobs, but the smelter refused to rehire
many of the others.[53]

Other Mexicans who went on strike included the employees of
the city water department in 1911, the Mexican retail clerks in 1914,
and the Mexican garbage collectors and park employees in 1919.[54]
In all these strikes Mexicans attempted to improve their economic
conditions. Although these actions did not involve a class consciousness, they did involve an ethnic one. Mexican immigrants did not
see themselves as members of a proletariat class but as Mexicans tem-

porarily in a foreign land; hence, they organized and protected themselves along ethnic lines. Furthermore, the issues in these strikes
concerned disputes over wages and did not include a class ideology
such as that articulated by the IWW. According to one scholar, immigrant workers in the United States engaged in labor conflicts but
only over narrow wage terms and not in "broader areas involving
general changes in the institutions governing the allocation of scarce
rewards."[55] Strikes among immigrant workers could be consistent
with the limited interests they had in American life: jobs and savings.
Nevertheless, most Mexicans in El Paso and throughout the Southwest avoided labor agitation. They, as well as other immigrants to the
United States, had not come for such purposes. "The real cause [for
migration]," one immigrant historian rightly observes of Slavic immigrants in Pennsylvania, "was probably the hope of acquiring income
to reestablish the peasant in his old position in the village. He intended his migration to be temporary, just long enough to win
American money to restore his status as a self-sufficient old-country
landowner."[56] The same could be said of many Mexican immigrants. Adjustment not resistance characterized their stay in the
United States.

6

The Mexican Schools

Important mainly as an unskilled labor force, Mexicans in El Paso
and throughout the Southwest received only a minimal education
through Mexican schools located in the barrios. Education along the
border, as elsewhere, serviced the specific economic and intellectual
needs of the larger community. In El Paso the type of training provided Mexicans by racially segregated public schools complemented
the labor requirements of industries and businesses for manual
workers from the Mexican population. The schools also functioned
as a means of social control through their attempts to Americanize the Mexicans in order to make them loyal and disciplined
future employees. Limited in schooling, Mexican immigrants and their
children did not have access to educational opportunities that would
permit them to close the economic gap between themselves and most
Americans.

From their inception El Paso public schools segregated most
Mexican children. When the first schools opened in 1883 it appears
that only a few Spanish-speaking children attended, despite a school
census reporting 116 Mexicans of school age. While poverty and migratory habits adversely affected their enrollment, Mexicans also
faced a language barrier. The school board refused to teach any child
who did not know English; consequently, only a small number of
Mexicans studied in the early schools.[1] To alleviate this condition,
some concerned parents supported the efforts of Olivas V. Aoy,
an elderly Spaniard, who in 1887 began teaching English to Mexican children in order to prepare them for entrance into the public schools. Commencing with 29 pupils, Aoy could barely meet his
expenses with the small tuition he charged. As a result the school
board one year later voted to incorporate Aoy's school into the public

system but on a segregated basis. Faced with a growing Mexican school-age population, with future economic and social consequences for El Paso, the school board believed that Aoy (whose school became known as the Mexican Preparatory School) could provide a useful service. The school board, unwilling and unprepared to teach English to Mexican children in the regular schools, hired Aoy to perform that function. Mexican students would first learn English under Aoy and when adequately prepared could transfer to another school.[2] By the early 1890s Aoy with two Mexican assistants was instructing almost 100 students in the first and second grades. Unfortunately, and to the sorrow of many Mexican parents and children, Aoy died in 1895. The superintendent of the public schools, however, pledged that the Mexican school would continue and urged every child who had attended Aoy's school to contribute flowers to the Spaniard's grave in honor of "the teacher who has labored so earnestly for the Mexican children of this city."[3]

Following Aoy's death, the school board appointed W. H. T. López principal of the Mexican Preparatory School, whose enrollment continued to soar as more immigrants arrived in El Paso. In 1897 the southside school had 200 pupils but only 3 teachers. To relieve overcrowded conditions the school board authorized construction of a new six-room building, named after Aoy, that would accommodate 300 students. Yet in its decision the board stressed that its policy remained to segregate Mexicans at least through the fourth grade before transferring them to American schools. At the same time, the board emphasized that due to the cost of maintaining the Mexican school it could provide Aoy only with the first four grades. The new school, regrettably, quickly became congested. At the turn of the century 500 Mexicans studied in double sessions at Aoy, which had the highest enrollment of any El Paso school.[4] Ironically, it graduated few Mexicans to other public schools with higher grades since, despite a new knowledge of English, most Mexican children had to seek work after the early grades to augment the family income. Hence, a distinct pattern of school segregation and educational underdevelopment for Mexicans became accepted in El Paso's school system on the eve of the great period of immigration from south of the border. During the next 30 years more Mexicans would attend schools but still apart from American children and in overcrowded and inferior facilities.

Although most Mexican students after 1900 left school between the fourth and sixth grades to find work to augment the family income, school officials argued that because of the need for Mexican children to work at an early age the Mexican schools should direct their attention to manual and domestic education that would best assist the students to find jobs. On the other hand the schools in American neighborhoods presented a better-rounded curriculum with both practical and academic training. In his report to the school board in 1908 school superintendent F. M. Martin stressed the difference between Mexican and American schools. The problem of the Mexican children, Martin stated, had to be considered separate from that of American children. He believed that the best manual training should be introduced to American elementary students including cardboard construction, clay modeling, sand table work, weaving, and other activities emphasizing individual initiative as well as laying the foundation for advanced academic work. However, according to Martin even this type of nonacademic training would not be possible for Mexican students. The superintendent admitted that such a curriculum might be taught in the Mexican schools if the students completed the grammar grades; yet, almost all the Mexicans left school by the sixth grade. Martin concluded that the most that could be expected of the average Mexican child, whose parents could not afford more than four years of education, would be for the child to become fairly proficient in English and to be able to solve simple arithmetical problems, such as those he would face in everyday life. Consequently, Martin advised that teachers in the Mexican schools concentrate on the "practical side of education" and that "the supervisor of manual training be instructed to devise proper means by which to direct the activities and latent energies of the Mexican children into channels which will lead them in after life to be more useful, and incidentally to become happier in the exercise of these God given faculties." To the superintendent, sewing represented one activity that he believed "worth while" for Mexican children.[5]

Martin's assessment of the Mexican child's educational potential became the accepted belief of many other Americans in El Paso. The *Times* in 1909, for example, stated that the large Mexican population posed a "peculiar problem" for the city's schools. This consisted of the fact that the public schools taught 1,800 Mexicans, most of whom knew little English and who remained in school for no more than four years before they had to leave and find work. "The great question," stressed the *Times*, "is how to accomplish the greatest good for these children in the short time that they remain in school." The solution, it believed, involved the school board's curriculum for the Mexican schools, which covered elementary manual training; habits of truthfulness and honesty; reading, writing, and speaking English; and some arithmetic. Such a course of study, the *Times* reasoned, would meet the particular needs and capacities of the Mexican students, "and it is the purpose of our system to lift up these children to higher ideals and to better living, to the end that they may be happy themselves, and more useful to the city in which they live." The Women's Civic Improvement League expressed not only the view of the limited mental capacities of the Mexicans but also of the benefits for some Americans to be derived from manual training in the Mexican schools. The league noted that in the public schools 2,000 Mexican children learned English and other practical skills such as reading and writing. In addition it observed that the schools instructed them in morals, cleanliness, and truthfulness. The league believed, however, that more advanced instruction could be provided for older Mexican students. A well-equipped manual training school for these pupils, it suggested, would benefit the entire community. According to the league the "house-girls" for the entire city came from the Mexican settlement and if they could be taught housekeeping, cooking, and sewing, every American family would benefit. The Mexican girls would likewise profit since their services would improve and hence be in greater demand. "These children are particularly apt in whatever they can do with their hands," the league emphasized, "they write well and draw well, and naturally take to finger work, sewing, weaving, etc." The league proposed that if a significant number of Mexicans could be taught English, domestic science, and manual training, El Paso would solve a major economic problem by adding to the productivity of its Mexican population.[6]

Commissioned by the school board to survey the city schools,

Paul W. Horn, the superintendent of American schools in Mexico City, further recommended in 1922 vocationally oriented education for El Paso's Mexican children. Horn believed that besides English the Mexican child should receive instruction in those activities in which he or she was especially gifted. These included music and handiwork. Horn also advocated for the Mexican "training of an industrial nature especially suited to his needs and capacities." As an example the American educator stressed that special provisions could be made to teach cooking and sewing in the first three grades of the Mexican schools since, unlike in American districts, Mexican girls of thirteen and fourteen could be found in these grades. Horn believed that such vocational subjects would meet the most important curriculum needs of the Mexican schools. "After these subjects are taught," his report concluded, "it will not make so much difference if less emphasis is placed upon the other subjects of the conventional elementary school curriculum."[7]

As a result of such views, the Mexican schools pursued a curriculum emphasizing the need to train Mexicans in simple skills and to socialize them to American norms and values. Woodshops, sewing rooms, laundry rooms, and domestic science rooms became regular settings for a Mexican student's training. Despite the stress on manual training, however, the southside schools did not receive as much financial support for this aspect of their curriculum as did the American schools. Aoy, for example, received only $125.50 a month in 1910 for manual training expenses compared to Lamar in the American northside, which obtained $340.90. Clearly, although manual training played a major role in the Mexican schools, it was intended to teach only limited skills for children who would fill jobs as laborers, servants, and laundresses.[8]

The Mexicans' educational experience in El Paso was not, of course, unique. Similar stress on vocational education existed in other southwestern areas, as it did indeed throughout the United States, especially in urban areas with high concentrations of industrial workers, both native born and foreign born. In 1911 J. C. Ross, writing in the *New Mexico Journal of Education*, recommended industrial education for the Spanish-speaking population of New Mexico. Not only would this form of education provide Mexicans with a trade but also, according to Ross, would teach the "intrinsic value" of all work. Pearl I. Ellis in her *Americanization Through Homemaking* emphasized in the 1920s that Americanization programs among the Mexicans, besides raising their standard of living and their morals, would teach skills that would indirectly serve certain industries. Because Mexican girls, Ellis alleged, possessed a fondness for sewing and because few of them entered high school, she concluded that their ability as seamstresses had to be developed in the elementary schools. Kimball Young's *Mental Differences in Certain Immigrant Groups* pointed out that due to the assumed inability of the Mexican child to compete intellectually with the American, the curriculum of the Mexican schools had to accommodate the type of work available when these children entered the job market. Young proposed changes that would provide Mexicans with "training for occupational efficiency; habits and attitudes as make for social cooperation," and finally "training for appreciation of the arts and sciences for satisfaction and happiness."[9]

The importance of industrial education for Mexican children throughout the Southwest was also justified by "intelligence tests" developed by scholars, who argued that certain races were inherently more intelligent than others. In 1915, for example, Lewis Terman at Stanford University observed that his tests showed that a low level of intelligence "is very, very common among Spanish, Indian and Mexican families of the Southwest, and also among negroes. This dullness seems to be racial, or at least inherent in the family stocks from which they come." A few years later another scholar writing in the *Journal of Educational Psychology* stated that in his opinion Mexicans were mentally inferior to Anglo-Saxons and that the factors contributing to their retardation included irregular school attendance, the transient character of the Mexican family, and the "native capacity, or intelligence of the Mexican people." Still others proposed that the Mexicans' problem in learning English indicated an inferior mental capacity. Indeed, B. F. Haught in a 1931 article in the *Journal of Applied Psychology* concluded that the command of English was the supreme indicator of intelligence. Teachers of Mexican children likewise alleged inferiority on the part of Mexicans. In 1929 a California teacher stated that "Mexican children are usually of inferior intelligence in comparison with

American children." According to him, Mexicans did not possess the intelligence to go beyond the third grade. Very few of these reports, however, mentioned language or poverty as a factor in the low scores achieved by Spanish-speaking children in tests as well as in their poor performance in school. Nevertheless, by 1920 school boards and administrators used such measures to place Mexicans in slow-learning classes and in vocational educational centers that produced manual laborers for employers.[10]

In his study of Mexican schools in the Los Angeles area Gilbert González notes that by the early 1930s vocational training had become the core curriculum of these institutions. In El Monte the district school superintendent not only segregated Mexican children until their thirteenth birthday but offered them special course offerings including woodwork, domestic science, and other subjects that would help them take their place in society. The San Bernardino School District dealt with its "Mexican problem" by establishing a segregated barrio school emphasizing vocational education. "It was thought," González writes, "that this type of education would lead to habits of thrift and industry, and to ability to make necessary contacts with the industrial world." Besides concentrating vocational education in eastside Mexican schools, Los Angeles schools closely cooperated with local industries in developing an efficient vocational program for Mexicans as well as other working-class children. Businessmen expressed a natural interest in Los Angeles schools, stressed the manager of the Industrial Department of the Chamber of Commerce in 1922, not only because they helped pay the bills but also because their workers came from the public schools and hence their efficiency depended on the schools' training methods.[11]

As a result of efforts by Los Angeles garment manufacturers, the chamber of commerce, and the public schools, a cooperative trade school opened in the early 1920s that businessmen and educators hoped would meet the city's need for semiskilled workers. The establishment of this trade school made it possible to train future workers, a task the factories found to be "impossible."[12] In addition to providing skills, the Mexican schools hoped to instill an acceptance of industry's hierarchical order. As one Los Angeles teacher put it:

Before sending boys and girls out to accept positions they
must be taught that, technically expert though they may be, they
must ever keep in mind that their employers carry the responsibility of the business and outline the work, and that the employees must be pliant, obedient, courteous, and willing to help
the enterprise.[13]

"Their practice," González writes of Southern California school districts, "placed Mexican pupils 'into a course of study suited to their
needs which, of course, meant a non-academic curriculum emphasizing manual training. For these children, their education was pro-
grammed to control their experiences rather than to enlarge their
opportunity to change them." This form of education, devised by
progressive educators, also affected other racial and cultural minor-
ities in the United States by reinforcing class divisions in an industrial
society.[14]

Besides the view that both southwestern employers and the Mexican children could best be served by manual training, the schools
stressed the need to instruct Mexicans in the ideals and ethics of
American society. Complementing the progress of the Mexican schools
in the county, the school superintendent of El Paso in 1913 stated
that the first thing Mexican children needed to learn was patriotism.[15] El Paso schools claimed, however, that the Mexican family
and culture hindered their attempt at socialization. For example,
principal Katherine Gorbutt of Aoy believed that the Mexicans' lack
of a sense of time increased school absenteeism. "In years past," she
recalled, "there was the problem of getting children to school on
time. Few homes had clocks and the excuse for lateness on a cloudy
day would be, 'No hay sol, y el sol es mi reloj,' [There is no sun today and the sun is my clock] so one can imagine how many would
be tardy during dark mornings." As future urban wageworkers,
Mexican children needed to learn punctuality because time would
indeed mean money. Yet Gorbutt did not consider the innate
or cultural characteristics of the Mexicans to be all bad. "There
are many things in which a Mexican excels," she stated, "in his

painstaking capacity for little things, in his ability to make the best of a bad bargain, and in his philosophy that is 'why worry about what cannot be helped.' The Mexicans are particularly gifted in art work and music. They make good athletes because they like to play. Aoy school has won many trophies in sports."[16]

Most American teachers shared Gorbutt's racial stereotypes and blamed the Mexican family for the perpetuation of ignorance and immorality. Mrs. F. W. Egan, a visiting teacher in El Paso in 1916, told the school board that an order which had closed the saloons and gambling halls in Ciudad Juárez had reduced, in her opinion, the number of Mexican truants from the schools. Before the saloons and gambling places had closed, said Mrs. Egan, many Mexican children from El Paso could be found on the other side under the influence of liquor. She also alleged frequently finding the children's mothers in the same establishments.[17] In addition to drunkenness, some southwestern teachers believed that Mexican children found it more difficult to repress sexual urges than did Americans. "Authorities on the Mexican mind agree" one Los Angeles school supervisor wrote in the 1920s, "that often the age of 12–14 causes educational and other higher ambition to turn to inclinations of sex impulse."[18]

Because the schools judged Mexicans to be "culturally disadvantaged," officials developed great pride in their ability to Americanize them. "It is impossible to estimate the general good that this school is doing and has done among these benighted Mexican people," the school report for 1903–04 emphasized,

> Yearly there are over six hundred children who attend regularly this school. They come from the humblest homes, where in years past, a knowledge of English and habits of cleanliness and refinement were unknown. . . . Among the first lessons instilled into these children when they enter the school room is cleanliness. It is not an uncommon sight here to see a kind hearted school marm standing in the lavatory room by one of these home neglected urchins, and supervising the process of bringing about conditions of personal cleanliness as he applys [sic] with vigor to rusty hand, dirty ears and neck, unkempt face and head the two powerful agencies of American civilization, soap and water.[19]

In addition to cleanliness and ethics, the schools considered the teaching of English to Mexican children a vital ingredient in the Americanization process. One school board member in 1903 praised American teachers at Aoy for having accomplished wonders in teaching English to Mexican children and pointed out that because of this success, the language was increasingly spoken in many Mexican families. As such, Mexican children acted as socializing agents within their families. To learn English, Mexican children had to remain segregated in the Mexican schools until they had been assimilated into public school work. Whereas almost all the Mexican students knew no English when they entered school, they encountered instruction in English from the very start. Moreover, only a handful of Mexican teachers taught in the Mexican schools and it does not appear that the Americans knew much Spanish.[20] Yet, even if they did, the schools did not encourage the use of Spanish in the classroom. What effect the cultural shock had on the Mexican children cannot be determined, but it may account for the lack of educational mobility among them. In a report on the public schools of El Paso in 1906 the superintendent of the state department of education supported the practice of hiring only teachers in the Mexican schools who did not know Spanish. According to the superintendent, many Mexicans who had learned English in the El Paso public schools had gone on to important positions in El Paso stores. Moreover, whenever the teachers did not know the pupils' language, the children had been forced to learn English. "Teachers who teach children of foreign parentage should not convey instructions in any other than the English language," the superintendent concluded, "this is law and logic."[21] Calling for special English instruction for the Mexican child, Horn in his 1922 survey noted that the Mexican's most essential need consisted of learning English, as well as Anglo-Saxon ideals and standards of living.[22]

Not only in El Paso but throughout the Southwest, schools used English as a key socializing agent. In numerous articles on education and the Mexican population, scholars and teachers expressed much concern over language. Besides advocating English as fundamental to the learning process, they believed that if Spanish was retained over English, Mexican children would pose a future threat to the social order. The director of elementary education in San

Antonio, for example, wrote in 1929 that "the first step in making a unified nation is to teach English to the non-English speaking portion of the population." English, in addition to its ideological value, would also serve a practical economic function. It would make Mexicans better workers as the economy expanded, requiring a more trained and socialized labor force. According to one El Paso teacher, English was not too important for unskilled jobs, but it was for "better positions." Both ideologically and economically the teaching of English proved essential in fulfilling the goals of mass education. English was the common denominator between Mexican children and American teachers.[23]

At the same time, however, schools emphasized Spanish as a practical language for American students to learn owing to El Paso's border location. As early as 1882 the *Lone Star* advocated a "Spanish school" in El Paso that would help Americans prepare for business careers in a bilingual community. For those Americans interested in becoming clerks, the newspaper believed, a good knowledge of Spanish was equal to good letters of recommendation in towns like El Paso, where so much commerce involved Mexicans. Americans, in addition, needed to know Spanish in order to improve business opportunities in Mexico. "It is as little as the state school system should do for the youth of Texas," editorialized the *Times* in 1899, "to fit them to a large extent for such work by instructing them in Spanish." By 1913 the school board authorized the teaching of Spanish but only in predominantly American schools and beginning in the sixth grade. The most pressing curricular need, the superintendent of schools stressed, was for Spanish instruction. "Spanish, for commercial reason if no other," he told the school board, "should be taught in the grammar grades." Emphasizing that the acquisition of a language was more easily accomplished during childhood, the head of the school system concluded that pure Castilian was not necessary; the language of the "better classes" of Mexicans would suffice.[24]

The need to use Spanish as a means to penetrate Mexican markets as well as its significance to El Paso merchants meant that the schools could not totally indict what they believed to be the "unprogressiveness" of Mexican culture. Moreover, the economic and political importance of the local Mexican population deterred such an attempt. Nevertheless, the schools left little doubt that the partial education of the Mexicans served a twofold purpose. It not only helped to meet El Paso's major labor needs, but through the Americanization process it functioned as a form of social control over Mexican aliens, especially children, and helped direct their loyalties to the United States and to American principles. "Boys and girls who then were half dressed, half fed waifs," the school report of 1903–04 concluded, "now speak English, hold positions as clerks in stores, bookkeepers, teachers, interpreters, do all kinds of work where intelligent labor is required, dressmaking, laundrying, cooking, housekeeping, blacksmithing, work in foundries, railroad shops, carpenter shops, factories, etc., and have become so Americanized that the influence they exert for good upon this city in point of sanitation and morals can scarcely be estimated."[25]

Almost 20 years later Horn in his survey likewise praised the work of the Mexican schools. Besides complimenting their work in manual training, the American educator pointed out that in such subjects as spelling and arithmetic the children of the Mexican schools compared favorably with the Americans. In Horn's opinion El Paso had no choice but to continually stress the education and Americanization of its Mexican population. "The future of the city of El Paso," he informed the school board, "depends upon the prosperity and enlightenment of both its native born citizens and its citizens of foreign birth." To underscore what success had already been accomplished in the acculturation of the Mexican child, Horn terminated his report by quoting a letter he received in 1921 from Fidel Barron, a fifth grader at Aoy. "I am very happy because you visited Aoy School," young Fidel wrote,

and also other schools of El Paso.

I am going to tell you the things that I like about the United States.

The first thing that I am obliged for is education that the United States gives me. I like its libraries, the parks, and especially the swimming pools where in the summer one has a very happy time. Also I like the scenery, the climate, the people and the government.

I hope you will come and visit our school again.[26]

Indeed, American teachers in the Mexican schools took great pride in their work among the Mexicans. One principal even compared her faculty to missionaries. "I consider the establishment of the schools for the Mexican children of El Paso my greatest achievement," stated former superintendent G. P. Putman in 1936. According to Putman, prior to his tenure as head of the El Paso schools nothing had been done for the Mexicans, who were growing up illiterate. Principal Gorbutt of Aoy at her retirement in 1941 concluded that seeing Mexican children grow up to be patriotic Americans had been one of her major accomplishments.[27] Yet, what socializing success the Mexican schools gained over the years would also bring forth a key contradiction imbedded in the school system. Intended to turn out hard-working and disciplined blue-collar workers, the Mexican schools at the same time instilled egalitarian ideals and a success ethic, the "American dream." Having accepted these principles, Mexicans, as they grew to maturity, began to demand their rightful place in American society and greater opportunities for economic and social mobility. Unlike their immigrant parents, a Mexican American generation by the 1930s saw themselves increasingly as Americans, not Mexicans, and questioned obstacles to full assimilation. Consequently, the Mexican schools, as the institutions that came to be most directly associated with the lack of economic opportunities, would in later years become one of the major battlegrounds in the Mexican Americans' quest for equality.

Although Americanization programs to a large extent succeeded, the schools in the Mexican district from the very beginning faced many problems, particularly overcrowded conditions due to the large number of Mexicans who attended the early grades. "The greatest congestion," school superintendent N. R. Crozier told the school board in 1912, "exists in the Mexican schools."[28] Horn also observed in his study that while all El Paso's schools faced problems due to the city's rapidly expanding economy and population, the Mexican

schools remained in worse shape. At Aoy, for example, Horn discovered that no playground existed. In addition the southside
schools had double the number of part-time classes that the American ones had; as a result, larger numbers of Mexican children could
attend school only part of the day. While throughout much of the
period Mexicans represented more than half the total school enrollment, they also studied at fewer schools than the American
children. The school census of 1908 reported that of 6,529 pupils
in the El Paso public schools, 3,675 were Mexicans. In 1914 the
number of Mexican students had doubled to 7,545 out of a total
public school population of 11,863. Two years later the special
1916 census for El Paso revealed that of school-age children between
7 and 16, Mexicans constituted 63.1 percent. Mexicans attended
as regularly as Americans, which only added to their overcrowded
classrooms. Attendance at Aoy, for example, in 1913 stood at 97
percent while the average for all the schools came to 95.5 percent.[29]

One contributing factor to this heavy enrollment in the southside schools seems to have been the attitude of Mexican parents.
Although they themselves arrived with little or no education, many
parents eventually supported schools as a way of helping their children acquire jobs in the United States or in Mexico, if the family
ever returned. Some parents, for example, wanted their daughters
to learn enough English so they could get jobs as domestics in
American neighborhoods. If Mexican parents had concerns over
the effects of Americanization on native culture, they seem to have
repressed them in the hope of material gains for their children.
Furthermore Mexican newspapers in El Paso published notices
alerting their readers to the opening dates of public schools and urging parents to enroll their children. Likewise, Mexican social organizations joined in this encouragement. In a letter to the school
board in 1919 a group of Mexican clubs pledged their support to
"any effort to advance the cause of public education in the city."
Some Mexicans also advocated night schools for adults where certain skills as well as English could be learned. Grateful for the education the Beall School provided Mexican children, one refugee
wrote to the *Herald* in 1917: "The progress that the children make,
the good discipline enforced, and the splendid professional spirit
of the teachers appears doubly commendable on account of the fact

that nearly all the children are Mexican children, and many of them refugees from Mexico."[30]

With such support, Mexican attendance became concentrated largely in the racially segregated schools "south of the tracks." The earliest school in the area, Aoy at Seventh and Kansas, was the largest school in the city as well as the largest one for Spanish-speaking students in the United States. It multiplied from 200 pupils in 1897 to 1,364 in 1919. Other schools heavily attended by Mexicans included the Alamo School at Hills and Fourth and the Franklin School at the corner of West Overland and Leon. Faced with growing Mexican enrollment in these two schools as the barrio expanded, American parents petitioned the school board in 1910 for permission to send their children to the predominantly white San Jacinto School. The board approved the recommendation but rescinded it a few days later after Mexican parents protested what they believed to be a discriminatory act.[31] As the Mexican settlement spread, however, American families moved to better neighborhoods in other sections of the city and left these schools to the Mexicans. "It may be observed in passing," Horn pointed out in 1922, "that while these races are not segregated by any order of the school board they tend largely to segregate themselves on account of the districts in which the children reside."[32] The public school at the smelter also contained mostly Mexicans as did the Beall School in East El Paso due to its location near the railroad yards at Piedras and Rivera.[33] "At the Bell [Beall] school there wasn't a single American nor black," ex-alumni Guillermo Balderas recalls. "Everyone, 100% at the Bell [Beall] school was Mexican."[34] Including the smelter school these five Mexican schools in the El Paso district contained almost half the total school enrollment in 16 public schools during the 1919–20 academic year.[35]

Besides overcrowding, the Mexican schools possessed only the early grades up to the sixth with the exception of the Beall School, which had eight. The American neighborhoods, on the other hand, by 1920 contained six schools with eight grades. Although a larger number of Mexican students could be found in the seventh and eighth grades by 1922, Horn observed that whereas in the first grade the children of the Mexican schools outnumbered those in the American ones by almost three to one, the exact reverse held true for the seventh graders. With few students able or encouraged to go beyond the fifth or sixth grade, educational mobility for the Mexicans was quite limited. High school figures show that between 1898 and 1920 only 22 Spanish-surnamed students graduated from the El Paso High School compared to 812 Americans.[36] And not until 1927 was a Mexican high school, Bowie, available in the barrios. "What was the use of a Mexican going to high school," Calleros remembered of those years, "when he couldn't get a decent job?" Balderas recalls that upon finishing the sixth grade in 1922 one of his teachers told the class they should not plan on going to high school because Mexicans worked only as laborers. "Your people are here to dig ditches," the longtime El Paso resident remembers the teacher's words, "to do pick and shovel work. . . . I don't think any of you should plan to go to high school."[37]

The educational programs of the Catholic Church did not substantially improve the economic opportunities of most Mexicans, and the role of the Church will be examined more thoroughly in a later chapter. The complete records of the early parochial schools in the southside no longer exist, but what remains reveals that the schools were limited in enrollments throughout the period in comparison to the public schools. Moreover, it appears that parochial school students came from slightly better off Mexican families, many of them political refugees, who could afford the tuition charged by the schools, which in the case of Sacred Heart amounted to 50 cents a month per child. In 1907 Sacred Heart on South Oregon Street had 300 Mexicans, but by 1920 this had declined to a little over 200. St. Ignatius on Park Street contained 650 Mexican students in 1917 and represented the largest parochial school in El Paso. A third school, Guardian Angel, opened by 1920 to service the Mexicans in East El Paso. A few Mexicans also attended the predominately American St. Mary's school in the central part of the city. Of the Mexican parochial schools, Sacred Heart and St. Ignatius had the full eight grades.[38] Although these efforts by the Church meant that an additional number of Mexicans could attend schools, they did not alter in general the educational discrimination and racial segregation that was aimed at Mexican children in El Paso and that reinforced a lower rate of economic advancement for the Mexican working class. Clearly, Mexicans have not had a history of educational neglect but a history of limited schooling, which has, in turn, supported the desire of southwestern employers for menial, cheap, and manageable labor.

El Paso, 1883.

Santa Fe Bridge, looking south connecting Ciudad Juárez and El Paso, 1911, patrolled by U.S. troops because of Mexican Revolution.

Mexican refugees entering El Paso, 1914.

Mexican refugees at Fort Bliss Camp, 1914.

Mexican laborers at Southwest Portland Cement Company, early 1910s.

Mexican construction workers in El Paso, between 1900 and 1910.

Mexican boys working at the El Paso Smelter, early 1910s.

Mexican cigar makers at the Kohlberg Cigar Factory, 1915.

Mexican women boxing cigars at the Kohlberg Cigar Factory, 1915.

Mexican *comerciante* in El Paso, around 1910.

Mexican store in El Paso, early 1910s.

Aoy School, first Mexican school in El Paso, 1910s.

Beall School, one of several Mexican schools in El Paso, 1910s.

View of downtown El Paso, background, and Chihuahuita, foreground, 1912.

Mexican children in Chihuahuita, early 1910s.

View of the El Paso Smelter with shacks of workers in foreground, early 1910s.

Mexican settlement at the El Paso Smelter, early 1910s.

Mexican worker and his family at the smelter settlement, early 1910s.

Mexican homes in Stormsville, early 1910s.

Chopin Hall and the paying off of Mexican voters, early 1910s.

Félix Martínez,
prominent El Paso businessman and
political figure, early 1910s.

Mexican revolutionaries in Ciudad Juárez, across from the El Paso Smelter, 1911.

Troops of Pancho Villa entering Ciudad Juárez, 1911.

7

The Barrios

Unlike job relationships where some contact between Mexicans and Americans occurred, living arrangements were characterized by an almost total racial separation. While no legal restrictions prohibited Mexicans from living in the better homes found in American neighborhoods (although most Mexicans preferred to live among one another because of racial and cultural affinity), occupational and wage discrimination, in addition to racial and cultural prejudice, kept them tied to the Mexican slums where the worst housing existed. Mexicans lived in overcrowded homes with little or no sanitation, high infant mortality rates, many cases of tuberculosis and other diseases, and the highest crime rate in the city. These conditions posed many problems, but Mexicans adjusted because they knew poverty and because they hoped they would reside only temporarily in El Paso. Unfortunately, their adjustment left them vulnerable to exploitation not only in housing but in other activities as well.

The large-scale employment of Mexicans as unskilled labor plus intensive Mexican immigration determined the location of the barrios in El Paso. The proximity of the city, for example, to the United States–Mexican border made Chihuahuita—as the Mexicans called the central barrio—in the southern half of the city the principal and initial settlement for immigrants.[1] Moreover, the location of industries and businesses that found it profitable to hire Mexican labor also influenced where Mexicans lived. Chihuahuita represented a labor pool where the nearby railroads, construction firms, downtown retail and wholesale stores, laundries, and other employers, as well as American housewives, found needed workers.[2] Outside Chihuahuita, Mexicans resided in two other major areas. The smelter community of the American Smelting and Refining

127

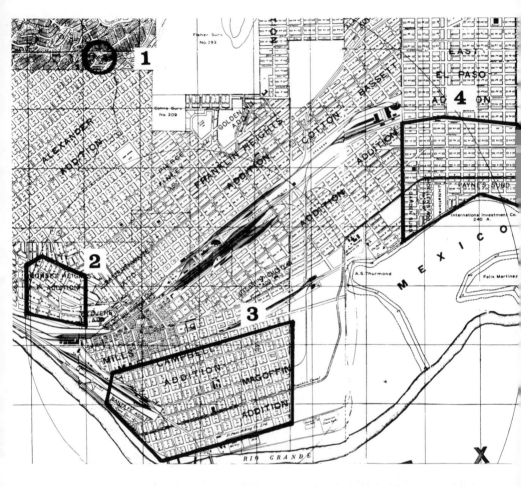

Map 2. Mexican Barrios in El Paso, 1914. *1*, Stormsville; *2*, Sunset Heights; *3*, South El Paso (Chihuahuita); *4*, East El Paso. Adapted from the Chandler Map of El Paso, Texas, copyright 1914 by Fred J. Feldman, El Paso, Texas.

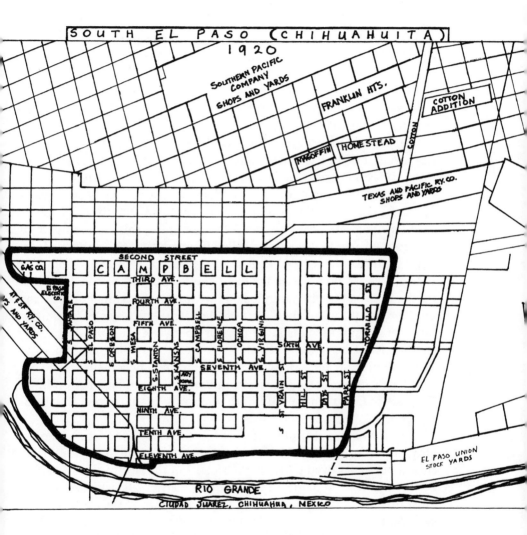

Map 3. South El Paso (Chihuahuita) 1920. Map illustration by Victoria Hogan,
Chicano Studies, University of California, Santa Barbara.

Company was one such settlement outside the western limits of El Paso and along the Rio Grande River. In the southeastern part of the city, East El Paso, Mexicans found work in the adjacent yards of such railroads as the El Paso and Southwestern and the Galveston, Houston and San Antonio line. In addition the El Paso Foundry in the area hired a number of Mexicans. These three locations "south of the tracks" and along the river border became the most densely populated sections of the city between 1880 and 1920, and beyond, and the centers of Mexican daily life.[3]

Besides the valley agricultural communities of Ysleta and San Elizario east of El Paso, Mexicans in the city had traditionally resided along the Rio Grande. No pueblo, however, had ever existed in this area because the main Mexican settlement had always been in Paso del Norte (Ciudad Juárez) on the Mexican side of the river. By the 1890s as more Mexicans migrated to the border, this section north of the frontier, which came to be called Chihuahuita, also expanded. In 1900 Chihuahuita covered almost all the Second Ward (El Segundo Barrio), whose boundaries included the land south of the Texas and Pacific Railroad tracks, bounded on the west by the Santa Fe yards and on the east by the riverbed. Part of the barrio known as El Chamizal, however, represented disputed territory between the United States and Mexico. Due to a sudden change in the Rio Grande channel in 1852, about 600 acres of Mexican property had become located north of the new channel. Nevertheless, El Paso exercised jurisdiction in this part of Chihuahuita until both countries finally settled the issue in 1963.[4]

The 1900 manuscript census reveals the early concentration of Mexicans in south El Paso. The great majority of Mexican workers and small merchants lived either in district 19 in the southwestern half of the city by the Santa Fe yards or in district 20, which covered most of Chihuahuita, the Second Ward, and part of the central city. As a result the southern extensions of such streets as South El Paso, South Oregon, and South Stanton in addition to the cross streets from Second to Tenth contained predominantly Spanish surnames. The rest of the census districts possessed few Mexicans. District 21, for example, which included streets in central and east El Paso such as San Antonio, Olive, and Magoffin, had 266 families, of which only 39 gave Spanish surnames. Some of them lived as

servants in American homes. While most Americans in this district
were professionals or craftsmen, the Mexicans worked as manual
laborers or domestics. In district 22, which covered the north-central
and northeastern portions of the city (with such streets as San
Antonio, San Francisco, and Mesa), the census numbered 391 families, 49 of which had Spanish surnames and lived mainly at the city
limits near the G.H. & S.A. tracks. While the Mexicans in this area
were laborers, the Americans held professional or craft occupations.
District 23 included the northside of El Paso and streets such as
Mesa, California, and Franklin and counted 419 families, but only 11
with Spanish surnames, who lived on either Main or Franklin street.
The Mexican male heads of households apparently worked as railroad
laborers. On the other hand, most Americans listed had jobs as skilled
railroad employees. Finally, district 24 included the northwestern
section of the city. Four hundred thirteen families lived there, of
which 176 had Spanish surnames. Yet of this number, 167 had homes
in the so-called Mexican settlement on San Francisco Street. While
American skilled workers, merchants, and professionals resided in the
area, the Mexicans worked as laborers. Of 219 occupations listed for
the Spanish-surnamed males over 18 on San Francisco street, 166 were
laborers. Revealing the relationship between Mexican residential patterns and immigration, most Mexicans listed in the 1900 census had
recently arrived in the United States. Approximately 86 percent of the
Spanish-surnamed household units in the 1900 sample were foreign born.[5]

Two years after the completion of the 1900 census, the city
directory reported that 60 percent of the Mexican population lived
south of Overland Street, which together with San Antonio and
Second streets plus the railroad tracks formed the northern barriers
between *gringo* El Paso and Chihuahuita. During the next 20 years
the rigidity of this boundary forced the Mexican district to grow in
an eastward direction but still south of the tracks and along the
border. Evidence of this expansion can be seen in the location of the
Catholic churches and public schools, which served the Mexican
population. Dedicated on June 9, 1893, Sacred Heart Church on
South Oregon between Fourth and Fifth streets administered to the
center of Chihuahuita. Major floods in the area four years later and
new immigration led to an easterly movement of Mexicans to the area
of Second and Park streets, where by 1904 St. Ignatius Church

assisted close to 150 Mexican families as the parish extended from Second Street to the river. By 1908 the flow of Mexicans had continued to the east and reached the suburbs of the Cotton, Bassett, and East El Paso additions, where the El Paso Diocese established Guardian Angel Church for the Mexicans of this district. Within the borders of these three parishes lived the largest number of Mexicans in El Paso.[6]

The development of de facto segregated public schools for the Mexicans also reflected an easterly movement. Built in 1899 at Seventh and Kansas, Aoy School in the center of Chihuahuita was the first Mexican school. Seven years later Attorney Adolph Huffman, who completed a school census of the city, reported to the school board that south El Paso had been almost totally filled with Mexicans and that not more than 20 American families remained south of Third Street. Consequently, the Alamo School at Hill and Fourth in the eastern section of Chihuahuita had become a Mexican school. Moreover, Huffman pointed out that many Mexican families had settled in the neighborhood of the Franklin School on West Overland in the southwestern extremities of the city. The school superintendent in 1908 further noted the rapid growth of the Mexican population. At the Aoy School 837 Mexicans constituted the entire school population. The Franklin School contained 100 Mexicans out of a total enrollment of 163 students. Of 517 pupils the Alamo School listed 500 Mexicans. The superintendent likewise observed that the Beall School in East El Paso taught 300 Mexicans in a total enrollment of 324. Although the American families in these neighborhoods protested at times to the school board about Mexican encroachment, most Anglos by 1910 had left these districts and moved to the north and northeastern areas of El Paso.[7]

In addition to Chihuahuita and the southeastern suburbs, which contained the majority of the Mexican population, other smaller Mexican settlements developed in El Paso. For example, beginning in the 1890s many smelter workers rented houses near the smelter. In 1897 the Spanish-language newspaper *El Monitor* observed that *Towne*—as the smelter settlement was called—had grown rapidly and that the Mexican *colonia* had about 2,000 inhabitants. Two years later St. Rosalie's Catholic Church (later renamed San José Del Rio) opened for the Mexican workers and their families at the smelter.

Although the construction of a smelter line by the streetcar company in 1902 made it possible for some workers to live in Chihuahuita and commute to the smelter, many Mexicans chose to remain in Towne. It has been estimated that in 1923 about 5,000 Mexicans and a few Americans resided in the settlement.[8]

Two other pockets of Mexicans could be found in El Paso during this time. Owing to severe flooding of the Rio Grande River in 1897 some Mexicans left Chihuahuita and squatted on Kern's Place in the sparsely populated northern foothills of the city. Here they paid squatter's rent to D. Storms, the owner of the property, which consequently was called Stormsville.[9] Besides their homes the Mexicans erected a chapel: Nuestra Señora de la Luz. Charles Armijo, who arrived in El Paso from Chihuahua in 1910, recalls that about 500 Mexicans lived in Stormsville. "Some worked for the city, garbage company," Armijo noted, "wherever they could find work."[10] The Mexicans remained in the area until 1928, when the city condemned their homes for sanitary reasons and relocated them in the southside. At their departure Stormsville consisted of five blocks of houses with 75 families and almost 400 persons.[11] One historian has written that the Mexicans had built their homes of adobe except for the church and that the settlement contained no sewers and only four toilets. After their removel a newly organized Rim Road Company purchased the land and the "purchase marked the beginning of what came to be the residential showplace of El Paso. It has been said, and correctly so, that no plot of ground in the Southwest has known such extremes—in people, culture, worldly goods, architecture, etc., as has Rim Road, El Paso."[12]

The last Mexican settlement took place in Sunset Heights in the northwest section of El Paso, one of the older and more elegant neighborhoods. With enough money to purchase or rent homes, several wealthy Mexican families who had fled the Mexican Revolution settled in the area after 1910. "They bought property in Sunset Heights," remembers old-time resident Enrique L. Acevedo, "and many rich people, some millionaires from Torreón, Guadalajara, and Chihuahua came to live in the area for many years, although many returned." Mario Acevedo, who arrived in El Paso in 1916, recalls that prominent Mexican physicians such as Domitilo Argüelles, Domitilo Rodarte, Don Edmundo Argüelles, and Andres Villarreal settled in Sunset Heights. Some of their descendants continue to live in the area around Porfirio Díaz Park on Upson and Mundy streets. To care for the spiritual needs of these political refugees, Holy Family Church on West Missouri opened in 1914. The Americans of Sunset Heights apparently tolerated their new Mexican neighbors because of their small numbers and because they were a more "cultured" group than the working-class Mexicans of the southside. Nevertheless, as more Mexicans moved into the district after 1920, many Americans left.[13]

Although Mexicans spread to the southwest of Chihuahuita, but more importantly to the southeast, evidence of individual geographic mobility could not be obtained. A sample of Spanish surnames from the 1900, 1909, and 1915 city directories proved inconclusive due to the inability to trace most individuals. While the lack of information may reflect flaws in the directories, it could also indicate frequent changes of address by the Mexicans or their short stay in El Paso. However, a sample of Spanish-surnamed males from the two El Paso draft boards during World War I reveals that most Mexicans continued to live in the area of Chihuahuita and the southeastern suburbs. Out of a total sample of 274 Spanish-surnamed persons, 66 percent resided in south El Paso, while 25 percent lived primarily in the southeastern suburbs of the Cotton, Bassett, and East El Paso additions, although a few did list homes in the northern half of the city. In addition the draft cards did not contain addresses for 8 percent of the sample. The residential division between Mexicans and Americans can also be seen from a draft board sample of 304 persons with non-Spanish surnames. Only 33 had homes in south El Paso, of which 17 were blacks. The rest with non-Spanish surnames resided in the central district, Sunset Heights, the northern parts of the Cotton and Bassett additions, or in the new northeastern suburbs of Franklin Heights, Golden Hill Addition, Alexander Addition, and Highland Park. Moreover, by 1920 Anglo families had spread farther north and east to include still other suburbs such as Manhattan Heights, Altura Park Addition, and Government Hill Addition. Although Mexicans worked in many of these new neighborhoods as laborers for the construction firms, they could not afford to live there. In some cases, real estate companies refused to rent to those few Mexicans who appeared to have the money for one of the new apartments built after 1910 in the American sections. One advertisement in the *Herald* in 1916 read: "Three room modern Apt. Americans only."[14]

Despite the growth of the Mexican settlement by 1920, geographic mobility resulted only in the enlargement and perpetuation of the barrios. Furthermore, Chihuahuita continued to serve as the major settlement for recent immigrants and consequently contained the largest number of Mexicans. Some of the older residents of the area apparently moved to the eastern sections of the Second Ward or to the southeastern suburbs; however, newly arrived immigrants quickly replaced them. In addition the suburbs and the smelter settlement had both old and new immigrants attracted by the availability of jobs in these locations. The combination of large-scale Mexican immigration and economic underdevelopment effectively segregated Mexicans and produced one of the worst housing, health, and crime conditions in the city.[15]

In 1900 Lewis Gilbert of Missouri on a visit to El Paso described to the *Vicksburg Dispatch* one of the first sights a stranger saw in the border city:

> As he glides into the city over the Texas Pacific railway in its free palatial reclining chairs, his vision encounters numerous huts built of adobe, a species of mud made into slabs of about 12 X 8 inches and from two to three in thickness, laid on in rows with mortar used as a cement and built to a height of about twelve feet—in some instances much lower.

Gilbert reported that these huts contained from one to three rooms and were the homes of Mexicans "who to remain and work in the United States must reside within its borders hence the great Mexican and Indian population of El Paso." In sharp contrast to the dirthouse, the Missourian noted the better homes and businesses of Americans. These included numerous public and office buildings, apartment houses, schools, churches, and banks. Despite "horrible sidewalks," Gilbert observed that Americans build their houses of bricks, unlike the "dobe" homes of the Mexicans.[16]

Few sanitation facilities existed in Chihuahuita and the other

barrios where the *jacales* (as the Mexican adobe homes were called)
were built of mud with dirt floors. Mexicans used the Rio Grande
River for bathing as well as recreation. Although for many this
marked no departure from previous practices, many Americans expressed distaste for the "immorality" of the Mexicans. The *Times*
observed in 1892 that several Mexican boys had been arrested for
nude bathing in the Rio Grande and "indecently exposing themselves." Yet without sufficient water pumps in Chihuahuita, these
early Mexican families had little choice but to use the river. At times,
this led to tragedy. In 1903 twenty-two-year-old Gilberto Terrazas
drowned in the river, and according to the *Times* he was one of many
who had died while bathing or swimming. Terrazas had been a hard-
working young man, the paper eulogized, and had been employed by
some of the local contractors. To prevent other such accidents, the
chief of police in the summer of 1905 prohibited swimming, bathing,
or washing in the river between sunrise and sunset, "and also in-
decent exposure of person." Those violating this order would be subject to a fine not to exceed $100, which Chief F. J. Hall hoped
would reduce the number of drownings from 37 in 1903 and 17 in
1904. Yet three days later the *Times* reported that apparently the
Mexicans had not understood the prohibition as large numbers continued to use the river. Hearing of the violations, police officials
dispatched an officer to the southern portion of the city with orders
to arrest any bathers. "When the officer arrived at the river," the
reporter noted, "he found a great crowd of men, women, and children disporting themselves in the water in various stages of undress,
and ranging from a Mother Hubbard, in the case of women and a
pair of trousers in the case of men, to absolute nudity." Three wom-
en and three small boys were arrested and escorted to the city
jail.[17]

Unable to prevent Mexicans from using the river and faced with
major health problems that might affect American neighborhoods,
the city council one week later discussed the construction of sewer
connections in Chihuahuita. One obstacle to this plan, however, was
who would be taxed for the improvement. The city physician reported that although some progress had been made in sanitary conditions by installation of water connections, the majority of Mexicans
did not have the money to pay for additional sanitation. Mayor

Charles Davis agreed and stated that the property owners (mostly Americans) who rented to the Mexicans should be forced to pay. The mayor further urged that the matter be settled as quickly as possible, for both the health of the city and that of southside residents depended on it.[18]

Yet real estate dealer H. R. Wood argued that landowners in Chihuahuita could not contribute to these facilities. Wood claimed that the 50 cent per month rent paid by Mexicans for the use of the land on which they constructed their jacales did not produce any profit. Consequently, Wood believed that the Mexican owners of the houses, not the property owners, should be made to pay. One alderman disagreed and emphasized that land in Chihuahuita did bring a profit. He pointed out that in many cases six or more houses could be found on a single lot, which greatly increased rent revenues. Property in the area was a good investment, the alderman remarked, and paid 18 percent. Despite the disclosure, the city council compromised and ordered the health department to install as many water connections as possible on each lot and both owners and tenants to pay for the work.[19]

Besides the lack of an adequate water system residents of south El Paso had no heating facilities during cold weather; instead, they gathered firewood from the timber that flowed down the Rio Grande. As in the case of bathing and sanitation the Mexicans' adaptability sprang from their rural and small-town background and from the force of circumstances beyond their control. Nevertheless, some of the more educated Mexican American leaders appeared before the city council in 1910 to protest the unsanitary nature of the Chihuahuita neighborhood. "These people may be poor," Dr. J. A. Samaniego appealed to the council, "but they are human beings, entitled to humane treatment; and you gentlemen will agree with me that it is not right that the alleys around their homes should be made a dumping ground for the trash and filth gathered from the streets of this city."[20] Samaniego further declared that he had inspected conditions in Chihuahuita that would "shame the holes of Calcutta." Calling for an investigation, he informed council members that the death rate in the area had reached an appalling level. Businessmen Félix Martínez joined the Mexican physician in protest but also blamed the Mexicans themselves. Martínez alleged that the residents of Chihuahuita would let a dead dog lie in the alleys or streets until it rotted and that they would walk around a "deposit of human filth on the sidewalk a month and never report it." Martínez concluded that authorities should force the Mexicans to obey the city's health regulations.[21]

Defensively, the mayor of El Paso stated that the city possessed the finest health department in Texas, and other council members insinuated that the Mexicans' living habits created the health hazard. One alderman observed that the council had passed an ordinance prohibiting dirt floors but that it had been unenforceable in south El Paso because Mexicans refused to report violations. He stressed that if the residents of Chihuahuita desired better sanitation they should phone in their complaints like the Americans on the northside. How the Mexicans, possessing few phones, could do this did not seem to concern the alderman. Ending its session, the council referred the entire matter to a committee for "immediate action."[22]

Although some improvements did occur in the barrios, officials took a much longer time than in American neighborhoods before they acted. Even then, the changes often proved inadequate. For example, few sidewalks were constructed in south El Paso throughout most of the period and those that existed could not be used when it rained. The streets of Chihuahuita also remained unpaved for some time. In 1895 twenty-five residents of the southside including 14 Mexicans petitioned the city council to fill up stagnant pools of water on certain streets. Two years later *El Monitor* complained about the poor condition of the streets where rubble and latrines could be found. Although none of El Paso's streets or sidewalks had been paved during the 1890s, by 1906 all had been paved north of Oregon Street in the American sections. Yet in the southside only El Paso Street had been filled by 1907. After 1910 the city finally completed the pavement of major streets and sidewalks in Chihuahuita.[23]

Because of its location by the railroad tracks the Mexican district became a dangerous area for residents, especially children and older people. In 1902 Mrs. Regina Martínez filed a $13,750 suit against the El Paso and Northeastern Railroad for injuries to her twelve-year-old son, who had been run over by the train and lost both his hands. According to Mrs. Martínez the locomotive gave no warning as it crossed near the Stanton Street intersection where it hit her son.[24] That same year a Sierra Madre car ran over and killed a fifteen-year-old Mexican boy at the Santa Fe Street crossing. Three years later the *Times* reported that a sixty-five-year-old Mexican woman had been hurt by one of the streetcars passing through Chihuahuita. The lack of playgrounds and parks for the Mexican children who played instead on streets and railroad tracks contributed to the accident rate. In 1909 while flying a kite on South Stanton Street, eleven-year-old Refugio Armenta ran into an outgoing train that instantly killed him. Neighbors stated that prior to the accident Refugio and five other Mexican companions had used the street and tracks as a playground for several weeks and had narrowly avoided accidents. While the residents of the area awaited the arrival of the police, the *Times* reporter observed:

> Meantime scenes probably as heart-rending as any that have ever been enacted drew a morbid crowd. Three or four hundred persons gathered around. When the little fellow's mother was notified she became frantic with grief. Friends took her to her home at 1220 South Stanton, while the little lad's father, shaken with sobs, knelt heart-broken, beside the crushed form of his little boy.[25]

Floods and freezing weather posed the most critical and disastrous threats for Mexicans. Not only did they have inadequate protection against these natural hazards, but they often lost what few possessions. they had as a result. This proved especially true prior to 1910, when unpaved streets turned into virtual rivers and lakes when it rained. One of the first major floods occurred in May 1891, when the north embankment of the canal that ran through Chihuahuita gave way and flooded a number of jacales. Throughout the night the residents had to transport their belongings to safer places. "On all sides could be heard the falling of houses," the *Times* reported, "intermingled with the occasional yelp of a poor canine, who in the hurry of moving had been forgotten by the owner." Some Mexicans found shelter with friends or relatives while others pitched tents on elevated ground until the flood subsided. Unfortunately, heavy July rains in 1897 led to a more severe flood than usual in Chihuahuita. Many residents lost their homes and fled to safer areas such as Stormsville. *El Monitor* pointed out that Chihuahuita had been the only place where city officials permitted poor Mexicans to build their houses, despite the fact that it was the lowest section of the city and susceptible to floods. Other floods that washed away adobe homes took place in 1903 and 1905.[26]

Although cold weather did not destroy Mexican shacks, it did bring much suffering. Those who found coal or firewood to warm themselves faced the danger of having fires burn down their jacales. In some cases lack of fuel forced Mexicans to steal coal from railroad cars stationed in Chihuahuita. Perhaps the worst devastation due to cold weather occurred in January 1906. On January 11 the police assisted 56 Mexican families with about 300 persons suffering from cold, hunger, and exhaustion. Police Captain Greet and Officers Delgado and Franco also discovered "huts and hovels where families of from three to eighteen were existing in a condition of squalor and misery indescribable."[27] To help them, the city and county began a relief program and appointed the police to go into Chihuahuita and find those in need. According to the newspaper they distributed wagons of food and provisions. "In one instance," the *Times* reported,

> a family of eighteen persons consisting of the father, mother, their nine children, grandmother and father, and five relatives, was found huddled in a "dobe" house just south of the canal in the rear of Santa Fe Street. All were seated around in the room on the dirt floor, hugging themselves up in their tattered apparal [sic] in an effort to keep from freezing to death. There was no fire in the little fireplace and in a box that served as a cupboard were a few but empty dishes.[28]

In other jacales, the police found widowed mothers with young children in total destitution. Besides snow turning dirt floors into mud puddles, most huts contained no stoves, forcing residents to cook at a fireplace. "Where the latter are missing," a reporter observed, "large tin cans serve the double purpose of heating the house and cooking." The reporter also noted that the cold weather kept the men from their work and did not allow the women to do their

washing. In two days officials, in conjunction with private charities and some businessmen, took care of more than 100 families,
which included about 500 cold and hungry persons.[29]

Living conditions in Chihuahuita further deteriorated by 1910
as larger numbers of Mexican immigrants and refugees from the
Mexican Revolution arrived. Fearing that such a concentration of
people might cause epidemics, some city officials campaigned to
"clean up" the Mexican settlements. During July of that year the
health department conducted a sanitary inspection from the old
military base at Fort Bliss in the western section of the city to
Washington Park in the east and from Second Street to the river.
The department examined 1,194 houses and found 563 to be dirty
and unsanitary. In addition, 693 had no sewers and 526 had become uninhabitable. "You can see from this report," said Dr. Anderson, the head of the department, "what a deplorable condition
exists, when almost one-half of these houses are marked uninhabitable. Taking into consideration that there are five persons to each
house and usually more, you have 2530 persons living in houses
not fit for animals." Anderson pointed out that in most cases Mexicans rented the land on which they built their homes, although
at times the landowners erected the shacks.[30]

Its report completed, the health department recommended to
the city council that it destroy many of the adobe houses. In September Dr. Anderson also informed the council that George Look, who
owned houses in Chihuahuita, had agreed to cooperate in destroying
1,500 condemned homes. When asked how long it would take to
accomplish, Look replied that it would be done as soon as tenants
could be removed, and he requested the city to use the police to
do this. A number of these residents appeared at the council meeting
and agreed to vacate their homes when told they had 30 days to do
so.[31] Where these homeless Mexicans went cannot be determined,
but they probably moved in with other families, exacerbating overcrowded conditions in south El Paso.

During the next few years the health department continued to
investigate and condemn numerous other Mexican homes in Chihuahuita. In the process it discovered that most of the land as well as
some of the jacales was owned by Americans. The department's September report in 1913, for example, disclosed unsanitary conditions

in a number of small buildings with 115 rooms on South Oregon Street and the Juárez Alley. Mexicans occupied all these residences, but ownership belonged to either the El Paso Southern Railway or T. B. Dockery. Although Mexican immigrants owned property in El Paso in the form of their jacales, it did not have much value, as city tax records reveal.[32]

Besides the destruction of the Mexican shacks, an early-day urban renewal project, by 1916 municipal officials began encouraging the construction of tenement houses. As part of the effort the city graded more of the streets on the southside and installed an improved storm and sanitary sewer system. As a result, property owners started building the tenements the city desired, which according to the *Herald* also proved to be a profitable undertaking. The newspaper related that many investors had already received handsome returns from their construction of cheap one- and two-story tenements. "There is little doubt," the *Herald* predicted, "that the old houses now being torn down will give place to tenements."[33]

While many shacks remained, contractors built several tenements in 1916 in Chihuahuita and East El Paso. These tenements were an improvement over the jacales, but they too soon became overcrowded and unsanitary owing to the Mexicans' poverty, continued immigration, and neglect by landlords. Some observers, however, subjectively blamed depressed tenement conditions throughout the Southwest on the "low-living standards" of the Mexicans. "Having few standards to begin with," Vera L. Sturges wrote in the *Survey* in 1921, "it is not surprising that the poor Mexican immigrant is content in the tenements with one toilet and one hydrant for fifteen families, four and five of these families living in one or two rooms." El Paso historian Cleofas Calleros remembered that two rooms in the early tenements could be rented for $3 per month. "And some of those are still in existence," Calleros noted in a 1972 interview, "the only improvement they have ever made is to raise the rent from $3 to $25.50 or $30.00 for two rooms." Mauricio Cordero, who arrived as a young man during the Mexican Revolution, recalls that he first lived in a tenement at the corner of Fourth and Telles in front of the Alamo School. According to Cordero, tenement residents paid $4 a month for two rooms.[34] Moreover, southside housing after 1920 failed to improve. A 1925 report by the El Paso City Plan

Commission stressed the need to proceed "with the sanitation of Chihuahuita and have a thorough cleaning up in the sections where human habitations are congested."[35] And in 1934 a city council survey of Chihuahuita pointed out that conditions had become worse. "There are 9,500 families living in the area marked 'slums,' " it stated, "in substandard housing."[36] Although many Mexicans in El Paso moved to other barrios in later years, Chihuahuita which had begun as a Mexican slum, survived as a highly congested one.[37]

Because of unsanitary conditions in the Mexican settlements a higher rate of sickness and disease existed there than anywhere else in El Paso. As early as 1883 the *Lone Star* noted that it had received warnings about the Mexican jacales as possible breeders of disease. "Whether this is true of these places or not, we are not in possession of sufficient information to say," the newspaper stated, "but they are certainly very filthy and unsightly, and might in the event of an epidemic become the harbor of disease and death." In 1892, cases of diphtheria were reported in south El Paso and health officials warned Americans to be careful in their contacts with the Mexican population. "There is no diphtheria in the city at present," one official announced, "but it has prevailed in the Mexican towns on this border for several years, and persons who take children to the circus should bear this factor in mind and keep them away from Mexican children." Cleofas Calleros remembered that around 1904, when a diphtheria epidemic hit the city, health officials deported many Mexicans across the border to Ciudad Juárez regardless of citizenship. Calleros's own brother and two sisters died in one week, "and I was the only one of the family left." The outbreak of smallpox among the immigrants had also led to a quarantine against Juárez a few years earlier that deprived many Americans of one of their border diversions. Because occasional cases of smallpox remained, E. Alexander, the United States Sanitary Inspector, had requested that Americans not attend the Sunday bullfights in the Mexican town. Those who failed to obey his request, Alexander had warned, would be held in violation of American quarantine regulations.[38]

Although El Paso claimed that its sunny and dry climate made it a perfect site for the care of tuberculosis, the disease became widespread among the Mexicans. Besides discovering that 15,000 people went hungry in El Paso, a 1909 conference of charity workers announced that large numbers of tuberculosis cases had been found in the Mexican districts. According to medical officials the problem had not existed in the city prior to large-scale Mexican immigration and they cited one case where twelve members of a Mexican family died within a year due to tuberculosis. Charity official Mrs. E. Kohlberg believed that the disease could be blamed on the city sanitation department, which swept the streets of Chihuahuita without first sprinkling them with water, "thus scattering dust in every direction and releasing million of germs." The conference further heard from Mr. F. H. McLean, the field secretary of the Russell Sage Foundation, who had arrived to investigate health conditions along the border. McLean stated that unlike other cities in the country El Paso faced a unique situation because of its location, which gave rise to a severe immigration problem. This could be seen, he reported, in the death rate from tuberculosis. In addition, McLean commented that the infant mortality rate in El Paso had increased substantially. Many Mexican babies died between the ages of four months and two years. McLean concluded that tuberculosis among Mexicans originated from their unsanitary adobe houses, which lacked fresh air and sunshine and where too many people lived in a limited amount of space. He believed, however, that the major blame for the health hazard lay with Mexican mothers, who knew nothing about sanitation. Consequently, McLean urged a campaign of education. Yet, despite efforts by city officials and private charities, *La Patria* still noted a decade later that more Mexicans died of tuberculosis in one week than from any other cause.[39]

As McLean had observed, infant mortality among Mexicans was high during the period. In May 1910 out of 36 deaths in one week, 20 involved children less than three years of age. Almost all were Mexicans. "Death seems to be a frequent and common visitor in the homes of the Mexican element," the *Times* editorialized, "but this is due, not to any neglect or oversight upon the part of the city's health department, but solely to conditions which the department is unable to control." The paper believed that this condition arose from the unsanitary nature of Chihuahuita and urged the city to do something because the health department did not have sufficient resources. Four years later, however, officials continued to report a high infant mortality rate in the barrios. Of 121 deaths during July, 52 were children under five years of age. As a result the *Times* stated that health officers were employing every means possible to protect babies during the hot summer.[40]

Typhoid fever constituted an additional hazard in Mexican neighborhoods. In 1906 W. H. Anderson, El Paso's health director, told the city council that after an investigation he had discovered evidence of typhoid fever. According to Anderson the causes for the disease lay in the unsanitary condition of certain areas. "I wish to emphasize," the health inspector stressed, "that there is not a milk dairy within the city limits that is in a sanitary condition." He had also observed unsanitary water reservoirs in addition to streets, alleys, and vacant lots filled with pools of stagnant water in the southern portion of the city. Moreover, condemned meat, fowl, and other garbage that had been deposited in the city dumping ground was being gathered by hungry people and hauled back to the city. In all, Anderson recorded 112 cases of typhoid fever in the city and called for an adequate force of sanitary inspectors.[41]

Although the city council accepted Anderson's recommendations and hired more health inspectors, ten years later with a heavier influx of Mexican immigrants and refugees El Paso again became alarmed due to typhoid fever cases in the southern neighborhoods. To contain the disease in Chihuahuita, health officers took various precautions. The *Herald* reported: "Kerosene and vinegar baths were ordered for all who had been exposed in the tenement houses and in the neighborhood, their heads were clipped and shaved, their clothing destroyed and the houses thoroughly disinfected." One year later under the continued threat of a typhoid fever epidemic, inspectors urged the city to construct public baths for the Mexicans. "Of vital importance now," stressed Dr. T. C. Galloway of the U.S. Public Health Service, "is the providing of bathing and laundry facilities for the 20,000 of El Paso's inhabitants who are without them. For the average American to live in health and decency without a chance to keep himself and his clothes clean is almost inconceivable. Yet probably 2/5 of our population live under conditions which approach this." Galloway also informed that a recent investigation indicated that in certain tenements 20 percent of the occupants were "louse infested." Because of these disclosures the city built at

least one public bath at the Beall School. According to longtime
El Paso resident José Cruz Burciaga, officials also operated public
baths close to the international bridge linking El Paso with Ciudad
Juárez. As an added precaution the school board passed a motion
that no children from across the border could attend El Paso public
schools and that city health physicians should be notified of any
such children already in attendance.[42]

Finally, influenza caused much suffering among Mexicans. In
October 1918 the worldwide "Spanish flu" epidemic hit El Paso. In
order to quarantine the sickness, city officials closed all schools,
theaters, churches, and public meeting halls. In addition the army
restricted all soldiers from the barrios as undertakers in the Mexican
district reported in one day 18 deaths from influenza. Two days
later 37 Mexicans died of the flu during a twenty-four-hour period.
On the other hand, conditions throughout the rest of the city improved rapidly and no deaths occurred. Charity workers in the southside stated that the situation there had been worse than disclosed.
For example, 22 sick people were discovered in one room. Although
the Associated Charities of the city sent some volunteers into Chihuahuita, the lack of doctors and nurses who could speak Spanish
hampered its efforts. Because of the absence of any hospital in the
vicinity, Aoy School had to be converted into a temporary one.
Nevertheless, the coroner's office indicated that many Mexicans who
died had not been treated by a physician. The epidemic ended, but
its devastation exposed the deplorable scarcity of health services for
Mexicans.[43]

While inadequate housing and epidemics reflected the Mexicans'
poverty as well as the economic exploitation directed at them,
crime in the barrios also appeared as a symptom of this relationship.
Crimes committed by Mexicans in El Paso involved people who in
many cases lacked basic necessities such as food or clothing. Moreover, it does not appear that they saw such "crime" (directed mainly
at Americans or American-owned stores) with the same disapproval
as did Americans. The most common charges brought against Mexicans were burglary, theft, and vagrancy.[44] In 1904, for example,
the *Times* reported the arrest of a Mexican woman for shoplifting
at Callisher's store. "The evil of shoplifting," the paper observed,

"is growing by leaps and bounds in El Paso." Although officials arrested shoplifters every week, similar incidents continued. Mexican women represented the majority of the violators, but the *Times* also said that "one or two Mexican men have been arrested within the past week for this offense."[45]

Crime among Mexicans conveyed a sense of frustration and despair due to unfulfilled hopes. Such feelings often led to violence as indicated by charges consisting of disturbing the peace, assault, rape, and murder. Although Americans, especially the poor, committed similar crimes, it does not seem that such acts became as widespread in the more prosperous northside neighborhoods. Paul Taylor in his 1930 report on crime among Mexicans in Chicago discovered identical conditions. Taylor noticed that disorderly conduct represented 67.3 percent of all misdemeanors.[46] Because of language and cultural differences, Mexicans had less chance to properly defend themselves when arrested. Few Mexican lawyers practiced in El Paso and the courts seldom selected Mexican jurists for service. A reporter who surveyed county jail conditions in 1900 wrote that "the Mexicans are more inclined to plead guilty and throw themselves on the mercy of the courts than the Americans. The Americans usually arrange to fight their cases."[47]

Although no organized crime operated in El Paso, except for occasional street gangs, by 1919 some residents of the Mexican settlements participated in "dope rings" in order to make more money. That year, for example, officers arrested Manuel Morales for the illegal sale of opium. According to the police, Morales owned a corral in Chihuahuita and belonged to a ring that worked both sides of the border.[48] Smuggling and selling narcotics, however, proved exceptional crimes in that most charges against Mexicans comprised lesser felonies and misdemeanors.

Unfortunately, criminal activity in the Mexican quarters led at times to violations of residents' legal rights. In September 1918, 20 patrolmen in plainclothes assisted by 18 other officers swept the city south of the downtown area in search of "gunmen" and "bootleggers." The police claimed that the raid resulted from numerous hold-ups in Chihuahuita and after the operation they reported a number of important arrests in addition to confiscating guns, knives, and liquor. Moreover, the police held the Mexicans on felony charges especially for "carrying concealed weapons." As part of their search tactics, officers stopped practically every person they saw on the streets and searched them for guns and liquor. The chief of police also announced that similar raids would continue until all undesirable characters had been locked up or driven from the city. Finally, a strict 9:00 P.M. curfew would be enforced. Although police conducted no searches in the American districts, the chief added that precautions would be applied in these neighborhoods as well.[49]

Since the majority of El Paso crimes occurred in or near the barrios, both the city and county jails contained many Mexicans who, according to one account, spent most of their time sleeping, talking, and playing cards. Jail conditions, however, do not appear to have been as pleasant as implied. Indeed, apparent negligence on the part of jail officials caused a major tragedy in March 1916. In order to clean prisoners of lice, jailors often washed them and their clothes in gasoline. Although they warned inmates not to light matches, the guards did not search them to prevent possible explosions or fires. On one occasion, a prisoner struck a match to light a cigarette, which produced an explosion of the vats filled with gasoline. The *Herald* disclosed that 25 prisoners had been fatally burned. "The smell of burning flesh," it vividly described the scene, "filled the air in the jail and made the rescue work more difficult." Those who died and the most badly burned seem to have been the men who had already been bathed in gasoline and who stood naked while guards washed their clothes. That night many Mexicans went to the police station asking for news of relatives or friends who had been inside the jail. The total number of casualties is hard to determine, but at least 16 Mexicans died out of 24 or 25 victims. Despite the disaster a grand jury investigation found no negligence on the part of the police. Furthermore, officials in their testimony suggested that although the prisoners had not been searched for matches, they had disobeyed orders and consequently the inmates could be considered responsible for the explosion. In supporting the police, Mayor Tom Lea declared that the incident had been an "unavoidable accident."[50]

The mayor's attitude exemplified the reaction of many Americans to crime among Mexicans. Some attributed it to what they called the Mexicans' inherent tendency toward violence; others more correctly saw it as the result of impoverished and unsanitary living conditions but without any relationship to racial and economic exploitation. As a result, such views failed to produce any effective solution to the problems of crime much less those of poverty. Although Paul Taylor's Chicago study was conducted in the late 1920s its conclusion appears applicable to El Paso as well. Taylor believed that similar to blacks and other immigrants, Mexicans received discriminatory treatment by police. He noted, for example, that officers displayed the same prejudice toward Mexicans that existed in the general community. "The effect of this," Taylor concluded, "is doubtless to increase arrests of Mexicans relative to arrests of native-born Americans, quite independently of criminality."[51]

In spite of the indifference of many Americans toward life in the barrios, there were some charity and reform groups, the city's "Progressives," who recognized a need to raise housing, health, and educational standards among the Mexicans. However, their programs failed to focus on the true source of the Mexican's deprivation: employers' desires for cheap labor. Instead, they stressed the improvement of the Mexican's health and his Americanization but still within a de facto segregated condition. Reformers acted, moreover, with the aim of assisting El Paso's development into a major southwestern city. Social workers, educators, journalists, and other reformers, prisoners of their own ethnocentrism and middle-class values, emphasized social changes that would make Mexicans better and more efficient workers and hence increase their contribution to the economic growth of the city.

Besides activities of the Catholic Church and some Protestant denominations, early social work in El Paso was under the direction of the Women's Charity Association organized in 1903. Composed of Americans, the association proposed to "aid and relieve destitute, sick, and friendless women and children." Among its activities, it started the El Paso Consumptive Relief Association, which in 1908 erected tenthouses in Highland Park in the northeastern section of the city to care for some tuberculosis patients from Chihuahuita. Félix Martínez and a few other Mexican businessmen supported the effort by paying the expenses of one volunteer nurse, Miss Valdez, who according to one account "did splendid work among her nationals, following up the clinic patients and educating them to live in a sanitary way."[52] The Women's Charity Association also sponsored a Save the Babies campaign during the summer of 1910 to reduce infant mortality. To accomplish this goal, it opened a baby clinic in the courthouse basement where local physicians donated their time and to which the city and county government each contributed $300 per month for milk supplies. While the association cared for the Mexicans' health needs, its director, Miss Grace Franklin, understood the benefits that would accrue to the American neighborhoods by such medical improvements in the barrios. "The same fly," she warned other Americans about typhoid germs, "may be carried by a horse to the plaza and from the plaza to your own table." Franklin emphasized that Americans should support the association as a way of improving the work performance of Mexicans: "El Paso must face her problems. She cannot shift the burden with a shrug of her shoulders. The Mexicans are here and every family in El Paso comes into close contact with them, therefore if El Paso wishes to improve her servant class she must improve the homes from which this class comes."[53]

Next to the baby clinic, Franklin requested the city to take additional steps to eradicate disease in Chihuahuita. These would include a city license and health inspection for all street food vendors and for stores in the area that sold milk. She also urged a better sewer system in south El Paso, a summer camp for Mexican children, and a baby hospital. Unable to accomplish these objectives and with little support from government or business interests, Miss Franklin resigned in disappointment in 1911. Of her departure, Mrs. Olga Kohlberg, one of the association's directors, commented: "Perhaps she was too far advanced for us and impatient of our slower minds and methods."[54]

Lack of funds as well as a need to coordinate charity work in the city and county made the association dissolve itself in 1915 and organize with other reform groups the El Paso Associated Charities. With an annual budget from city and county governments and individual contributors, the organizers aimed to take care of the "unfortunates who were unidentified religiously and who too frequently took advantage of all charities rather than doing anything to relieve their own misfortunes." The association's budget increased from $16,000 in 1915 to over $23,000 in 1918, and with a 67-member

staff operated an employment bureau, distributed tuberculosis infor-
mation in English and Spanish, and ran the Sunshine Day Nursery on
South Campbell Street in Chihuahuita, which cared for 30 to 50
Mexican children each day.[55]

Yet the activities of the Associated Charities reached only a small
percentage of the Mexican population, and some reformers headed
by the *Herald* called for a much larger program by both public and
private sources. In their opinion this had become critical by 1915
due to the significant growth in the city's Mexican population and to
increased tensions along the border as the Mexican Revolution threatened to create serious conflict in the city between Americans and
Mexicans. Although its reform campaign only partially succeeded,
the *Herald* in a series of editorials between 1915 and 1917 stressed
that it would be to the best economic interests of El Paso if
Americans established various health and educational programs for
the Mexicans. The newspaper complained, for example, that neglect
of sanitation by the Democratic Ring, in control of El Paso politics,
in the Mexican districts had hurt the city's tourist trade. The *Herald*
castigated Mayor C. E. Kelly, the head of the ring and one of El
Paso's major political figures, for his failure to institute a drainage
system in Chihuahuita, which might eliminate the threat of smallpox,
scarlet fever, and diphtheria.[56]

The health of Americans could not be divorced from the unsanitary state of Chihuahuita, the *Herald* also pointed out. It would be
for their own self-protection if they imposed sanitation reforms in
the southside. Moreover, the paper noted that high death rates among
Mexicans damaged El Paso's image as one of the healthiest areas in
the United States. It referred to the fact that the death rate in American neighborhoods was low but that disease in Chihuahuita had
raised the city's rate to 32 per 1,000 in 1914. A city like Minneapo-
lis, by contrast, had a death rate of only 11.58 per 1,000. "The
Herald will refrain from making general comparisons at this time,"
the paper editorialized. "It is enough for the present to say that
El Paso's death rate is double, or more than double, that of Minne-
apolis." The paper believed that this large number of deaths could be
lowered only if Americans recognized the Mexican settlements as part
of their responsibility. Although some citizens might denounce the
border newspaper for its unflattering revelations, the *Herald* concluded,

Americans could not avoid the serious menace of Chihuahuita and the destructive effects it had upon every family and business.[57]

In the *Herald's* opinion, educational improvements represented the most significant reforms. They would allow El Paso to make more productive and profitable use of Mexican labor. While the newspaper clearly recognized that Mexicans had become indispensable to the city's economy, it believed that industries and businesses employing them had not fully developed this valuable resource. Too many Americans, according to the *Herald*, viewed the Mexicans as inferior workers and incapable of better education or skilled labor. In addition, anti-Mexican sentiments had become more pronounced due to the irritations of the Mexican Revolution along the border and the possibility of war with Mexico. The *Herald* warned, however, that racial conflict in El Paso would be disastrous, especially for the city's economy, which depended on cheap Mexican labor and commercial ties with Mexico. "In the problem, unfortunately," it commented,

> a race question is involved. It is useless to try to deny it. The Herald has not been so blind as to fail to recognize that it does exist and has existed in recent years, to a degree that was not true in earlier days. It is a sad thing, indeed, that this spirit has been allowed to rise. It spells grave misfortune for the city, if it be not stifled and kept stifled. These people are our people, they are here to stay, their problems are our problems, and let it never be said that the English speaking people sought to raise any barrier.[58]

Mexicans, the *Herald* explained, had already proved themselves competent and intelligent. "It is a serious mistake," it pointed out, "to think that educational or improvement work of any sort or in any degree is wasted on these people. They seize eagerly upon every chance offered to them to better themselves." The *Herald* reported that one teacher who had arrived in El Paso with a prejudice against Mexicans had changed her mind and now found them to be receptive, responsive, enthusiastic, and ambitious. Yet the newspaper cautioned that as long as city leaders refused to better educate and train the Mexicans there would remain a waste of human resources. Further neglect, the *Herald* continued, could only be suicidal and it blamed Americans for the problems of Chihuahuita:

If Chihuahuita is a menace to the health and peace and welfare of the city, it is our own fault. We have only ourselves to
blame. We have set for those people the standards of the Dark
Ages and by our neglect we have compelled them to conform to
them. . . .

If Chihuahuita does not progress as we should like to have it
progress, if some of the people down there do not live as we
should like to have them live, if they fail to rise to the possibilities
of life in this splendid city, who is to blame? Can we possibly
shift the blame? Is it not all upon us? Let each El Pasoan ask
himself this question: What would become of the petted children
of the best of our homes if these children were to be condemned
to neglect and squalor and darkness of enforced ignorance to
which we El Pasoans condemn the children of Chihuahuita?[59]

As a possible solution to the underdevelopment of Mexican labor
in El Paso, the *Herald* recommended that the schools improve their
manual training programs for Mexicans and that more money be spent
in southside schools for industrial education. If El Paso could invest
$300 per English-speaking child, the newspaper observed, it could
certainly invest $50 per Spanish-speaking child. It also encouraged
the city to establish vocational schools patterned after those in
Cincinnati. The paper informed its readers that this midwestern city
had elementary industrial schools, a continuation school for appren-
tices, compulsory continuation schools, and schools for foreigners,
mental defectives, and delinquents. In addition, boys were taught how
to become machinists, printers, and carpenters, while girls learned
to be housewives, clerks, and to perform other roles commonly iden-
tified with women. The *Herald* believed that if similar facilities
could be opened in El Paso for Mexicans, their "natural manual
abilities" would be put to better use and benefit the entire economy:

The Mexicans are especially fitted to train for this class of
work. The Mexicans have much native skill as potters, metal
workers, straw weavers, leather workers, and in many other
branches of handiwork requiring practice and manual dexterity.
The supply of raw labor is unlimited; we have been very lax in
not developing it for more economic employment, and consequently for the production of greater wealth, and for the pro-

moting of human welfare through well directed and profitable industry.[60]

Furthermore, the *Herald* predicted that if El Paso augmented its vocational offerings, it would not only improve the productivity of the Mexicans (at continued cheap wages), but it would also attract Spanish-speaking students from Latin America and make El Paso an international center of industrial education.[61]

The *Herald's* views represented a slightly more advanced outlook than those of other reformers in El Paso, although the paper did not advocate racial integration in jobs, housing, and schooling. Nor did it intend to do so. Allowing for better occupational opportunities for Mexicans, the *Herald's* proposals would still maintain them in manual jobs with lower wages than American workers and in a segregated economic, political, and social condition. At the same time, improving their skills would result in greater production and profits for employers. Although the *Herald's* reform campaign put forth a middle-class, pragmatic solution to the economic and social problems arising from large-scale Mexican immigration, its consequences would still leave Mexicans in a vulnerable and exploited position. "CONTINUED NEGLECT OF OUR CHIHUAHUITA PROBLEM," the *Herald* nevertheless concluded in bold type, "IS THE MOST COSTLY AND DANGEROUS MISTAKE EL PASO IS MAKING—A GOVERNMENTAL ERROR, A SOCIAL MENACE, AND A FRIGHTFUL ECONOMIC WASTE."[62]

Yet, despite the *Herald's* efforts and although some Mexicans after 1920 managed to leave the early settlements and move into better neighborhoods, the continued reliance by El Paso and the Southwest on cheap manual labor from Mexico assured the survival of Chihuahuita and the other poverty-stricken immigrant sections of the city. Within these barrios, however, Mexicans managed not only to live and work but to maintain, develop, and accommodate their particular life-styles and culture to American society.

8

Border Politics

Living adjacent to their homeland and segregated as unskilled labor, Mexican immigrants had no political or economic interests in becoming American citizens and in participating in American politics. Still, in El Paso their large numbers influenced local politics nonetheless. Because Mexicans comprised more than half the city's population throughout the period, American politicians recognized that control of the Mexican vote ensured political dominance. As a result, a political relationship developed whereby American politicians, representing El Paso's business and professional class, supported through public jobs and patronage certain Mexican American politicos in return for their ability to organize and deliver Mexican voters. As part of this reciprocal relationship, American politicians provided a certain degree of ethnic protection for Mexicans in order to maintain their loyalty. Hence, El Paso's leaders for both political and economic reasons attempted to minimize racial friction in the city. Economically invaluable, the Mexicans also came to be regarded as a major political resource at election time.

The political importance of the Mexican population manifested itself quite early in the period after the Mexican War, especially in the valley communities southeast of El Paso. Unlike El Paso, which remained relatively small until 1880, these agricultural settlements contained a larger number of people and were more prosperous. San Elizario and Ysleta, for example, had a combined population of close to 2,400 following the American conquest. One early American resident, W. W. Mills, recalled in his autobiography that owing to the preponderance of Mexicans in both these towns, court proceedings had to be conducted in Spanish. In addition, because Mexicans constituted the majority of residents in the El Paso area and had been

155

bestowed citizenship after the Yankee conquest, American politicians courted their votes. According to Mills almost 900 Mexicans in the county voted in 1861 on the question of whether Texas would secede from the Union. Influenced by a large group of Southern Democrats, a majority of Mexicans sided with the Confederacy.[1]

Rebel rule in the El Paso area lasted only a brief period as Union soldiers from California occupied the border settlements by 1862. The departure of the Confederates also allowed the organization of the first political machine based on the Mexican vote. In his capacity as U.S. collector of customs at El Paso, Mills brought together a coalition composed of a small number of Republicans; the Mexicans led by Louis Cardis, an Italian stagecoach manager who had gained the respect and support of many Mexicans; and Father Antonio Borrajo, the Catholic priest in the valley who commanded the Mexicans' loyalty. With the Mexican vote the Mills–Cardis–Borrajo machine easily won the first postwar elections in 1866. Mexicans elected in this Republican victory included J. M. Luján, county clerk; Máximo Aranda, district clerk; and County Commissioners José María González, Julián Arias, and Gregorio N. García.[2]

Other Mexicans served in both county and municipal offices following the Civil War, although their ties with American politicians underwent various changes. In 1869 Cardis and Borrajo broke with Mills after he attempted to deprive Mexicans of their traditional salt beds 110 miles east of El Paso, which the native population tapped not only for their domestic needs but for export to Chihuahua as well. Instead, the two politicos joined with Radical Republicans and ousted Mills through the election of A. J. Fountain to the state senate. Six years later, when Fountain refused certain concessions on the salt beds to Cardis and Borrajo, the Mexicans shifted their allegiance and elected Democrats to office. Unfortunately, the transformation caused racial conflict. Although the new head of the county, District Judge Charles Howard, promised to protect the salt beds, he soon announced that the property had become his and that the Mexicans would have to pay a tax if they wished to use it. Howard's action brought on El Paso's famous Salt War in 1877, when Mexicans throughout the lower valley rose up in rebellion against Americans and killed Howard along with four other gringos. Unable to restore order, American officials had to request federal troops to enter the area and reestablish American political control.[3]

Despite the armed conflict El Paso County continued to be
dominated by machine politics. Based on their manipulation of the
lower valley Mexican vote, El Paso alderman J. P. Hague and county
clerk Manuel Flores controlled local politics following the Salt
War. Beginning in the 1882 county elections, however, an El Paso-
based reform movement of merchants and professionals sought
to replace the "jobbery and trickery" of the "ring" with what it
called "enlightenment and free thought." The "People's ticket,"
focusing its attack on Flores, resorted to racist appeals in its campaign against the county clerk. In a letter to the *Lone Star*, one
opponent called on Anglo-Saxons not to vote for a man who could
not even speak English. The *Lone Star* also accused Flores of fraudulently issuing naturalization papers to Mexican nationals so they
could vote for the Hague slate. Ironically, El Paso reformers, hoping
to divide the Mexican vote, ran Mexican candidates of their own.
"Now is the time," the *Lone Star* emphasized in its Spanish-language
column, "for all Mexicans to dissociate themselves with the dema-
gogues." Although defeated in the election, the antimachine politicians acquired revenge one year later, when they won a special
election transferring the county seat from Ysleta to El Paso, where
American businessmen and lawyers, whose numbers had increased,
could better control the area's politics.[4]

Yet the subsequent influx of Mexican immigrants into the border
town increased their significance for El Paso politics. Both Democrats and Republicans in the 1889 city election, for example, openly
purchased Mexican votes not only in El Paso but in Ciudad Juárez
as well. Besides money, the politicians offered free beer and entertainment. According to one account the festivities began on the day
before the election and continued all night. On election morning the
Mexicans discovered to their surprise that the doors of the dance hall
had been locked and that they could not leave until the polls opened
and their votes registered. At seven in the morning, therefore, the
politicians assembled the Mexicans and under guard conducted them
to the voting precincts, where they were handed a prepared ballot
and paid $3.[5] In his study of South Texas politics one scholar notes
similar tactics by politicians in that region. "In former days," he
writes, "it was not uncommon for the chief [political boss] or some
of his local henchmen literally to corral the voters several days

before the election, keeping them together by providing a barbecue for them, and voting them 'en bloc' at the proper time."[6]

Apparently possessing more money than the Democrats, the Republicans and their candidate for mayor, Adolph Krakauer, won the 1889 El Paso election. Yet officials disqualified Krakauer when they discovered that the new mayor possessed only his first citizenship papers. Given another opportunity, the Democrats elected Richard Caples mayor in a special election.[7] Caples's victory marked the beginning of an extended period of political domination of the city and county by what El Pasoans referred to as the Ring. Formed by leading merchants, bankers, lawyers, contractors, and businessmen, the Ring represented the regular or stalwart faction of the Democratic party in El Paso. It managed to succeed, however, only because it had learned from earlier experiences that since Mexicans were half or more of the population, they could not be politically ignored. Consequently, the Mexican vote constituted the base of the Ring's organization. The same class that benefited from the availability of cheap Mexican labor also gained from cheap Mexican votes. In regard to similar political organizations in the United States, one historian stresses that "had it not been for the immigrant, the city boss and his machine would not have become what they were."[8]

The Ring further recognized that the more acculturated and politicized Mexican Americans could play a key role as mediators and ward bosses in Chihuahuita and the other Mexican settlements of El Paso. Unlike the immigrants, Mexican Americans saw American politics as a way of achieving economic mobility. Although Mexican American "brokers" served under American bosses, they were not mere lackeys of the Ring. Mexican Americans organized themselves in what amounted to pressure groups within the Ring in order to extract from it not only political appointments and public employment but also ethnic protection for the Mexican population of the city and county. In addition the development of a sub-rosa machine by the Mexican Americans warned the Ring that the Mexican vote could be turned against it in favor of reform Democrats or Republicans. The *Times* reported as early as 1891 that about 75 Mexican Americans had assembled in the courthouse to discuss the organization and protection of Mexican voters. After certain speakers had addressed the group, the Mexican Americans selected Víctor Ochoa as their president, O. A. Larrazolo as vice-president, and José A. Escajeda as secretary.[9] A few weeks later the *Times* also carried a story entitled "Mexican Organizing":

> In the neighborhood of three hundred Mexican citizens assembled on Little Plaza last night, and were addressed by Victor L. Ochoa. His text was "organization for self protection." He urged the Mexican citizens of El Paso to stand shoulder to shoulder, in demands of the Mexican citizens of El Paso, as set forth in a platform promulgated at a recent meeting held in the city.[10]

These demands included that the city elect a superintendent of public works who would ensure that contractors employed only citizen and resident workers and not cheap labor from across the border in Ciudad Juárez. The second demand called for a fixed wage scale for construction workers to be set by the city and, finally, the stipulation that Mexican policemen and other Mexican municipal employees be paid the same wages as Americans doing similar work. After the rally the Mexicans attended a *baile* (dance) in Chihuahuita.[11]

Organized pressure made the Ring aware of its reliance on the Mexican vote and on the ability of the Mexican American leaders to deliver it. As a result the Ring supported Mexican American candidates, especially in county elections, and reserved certain patronage jobs for them in the sanitation and police departments. O. A. Larrazolo, who in 1918 would become governor of New Mexico as a Republican and in 1928 U.S. senator, was one Mexican American candidate whom the Ring successfully endorsed for district attorney in 1890. At a Democratic rally at the Plaza, Judge Peyton F. Edwards defended the Ring's support of Larrazolo. "They [the Republicans] bring up the cry against Larrazolo that he is a Mexican," Edwards stated. "How many of us have foreign blood in our veins. The men who first fought for Texas independence were Mexicans and they fought nobly at San Jacinto. We should feel proud to have a citizen who is Mexican by birth but American by adoption."[12]

As the organ of the Ring, the *Times* concurred with Edwards's opinion and supported the selection of Mexican American candidates such as Larrazolo. In an article entitled "The Mexican Vote," the newspaper emphasized the political importance the Ring attached to Mexicans as well as the machine's strategy to obtain their votes:

> Regularly every time a democratic ticket is nominated for county officers, there comes a cry from some source in the party against the nomination of Spanish speaking citizens on the ticket. The Mexican democratic vote in this county is fully half of the total democratic vote. Why, then, is it asking too much to place one of their men on the ticket?

> The democratic party has acted wisely in conciliating the Mexican voters and granting them all they asked on the county ticket. Where all other qualifications for office are equal the question of race should not enter. As long as the democratic party gives to its Spanish speaking members every recognition they deserve, it need not fear defeat in this county. Watch how the democratic votes will accumulate in the lower county next November.[13]

The Ring supported numerous Mexican American officeholders besides Larrazolo. The majority of them, however, served in minor county positions. Mexican Americans were elected county commissioners, justices of the peace, precinct chairmen, and local officials from San Elizario and Ysleta. For example, in 1900, voters selected B. Alderete, S. Carbajal, and Francisco González to the county commissioner's court as well as Francisco Villalobos justice of the peace in San Elizario. Moreover, the Ring appointed Carbajal, Alderete, and Esteban Serra water commissioners for Ysleta. Mexican Americans also attended Democratic county conventions as delegates and a few served on county executive committees but always in minor capacities. Mexican Americans had less representation in city politics, although they did function as ward and precinct delegates from the barrios to city Democratic conventions. Although the Ring did not hesitate to endorse Mexican Americans for certain county offices where the selection of a Mexican would be practical and beneficial, it apparently refused to nominate them for city positions for fear of offending American voters.[14]

Of the various elective offices controlled by Mexican Americans,

city clerk and district clerk became the most important. Held for
many years by José A. Escajeda and Isaac (Ike) Alderete, these positions dispensed patronage and possessed access to voter registration
procedures that the Ring used to its advantage. The political careers of both Escajeda and Alderete exemplified the political significance as well as experience of Mexican Americans in El Paso
politics. Born in San Elizario in 1866, Escajeda went to American
schools and then worked as a railroad laborer. At the age of 20 he
moved to El Paso, where he received appointments as deputy district clerk and deputy U.S. clerk. A few years later in 1892 Escajeda
obtained the support of the Ring and won election as district clerk.
Reelected for the next several terms, he met defeat in the 1898
primary. After a short business career he returned to politics in 1901,
when the Ring nominated him for city clerk. Escajeda remained in
this office until 1912, when he replaced Alderete as district clerk
and in this capacity served until 1916.[15]

Like Escajeda and other Mexican American politicos, Ike Alderete
also grew up in the older Mexican settlements of the lower valley.
His father, Benigno Alderete, had immigrated from the interior of
Mexico and had supported the Texas Revolution. After he had
settled in Ysleta, Alderete's father served as mayor as well as in other
political offices. Ike attended public school in the area and later
his parents sent him to a Jesuit college in Las Vegas, New Mexico.
Upon his graduation he returned to the border but settled in El Paso,
where he found employment with the Campbell Real Estate Company. As an agent, Alderete gained not only many business contacts
but political ties with Ring leaders.[16] Apparently more impressed
with the younger Alderete, the machine supported Ike for district
clerk in 1898 against Escajeda. "Mr. Alderete," the *Times* commented
on his candidacy, "who offers for the district clerkship is one of El
Paso's most worthy and popular young men."[17] Alderete won both
the primary and general elections and voters reelected him until
1912, when he joined with dissident Democrats in an unsuccessful
attempt to upset the Ring. Perhaps the most charismatic of Mexican
American politicians, Ike Alderete represented one of the major
factors in the Ring's ability to win heavily in the Mexican precincts.

To obtain political influence within the Ring, Mexican American

politicians like Escajeda and Alderete employed several tactics. The
principal one was organization. Mexican Americans formed political
clubs that not only applied pressure on the Democratic party but
also helped deliver the Mexican vote. The *Times* reported in 1910
that 75 members of the Club Ortiz Político Social met in a "rousing
meeting" in Chihuahuita to plan the mobilization of Mexican voters
for the Democratic candidates in the fall. Club membership had
enthusiastically increased, the newspaper noted, and promised to be
a major factor in the next county election. In addition to men,
Mexican women joined the Democratic party. Several of them began the Young Women's Democratic Club in 1912 to support the
Ring ticket in the county election. At a dance sponsored by the
mujeres and held at the Mutualista Club on the southside, the women
heard speeches from some of the Ring candidates as well as from
club officers Miss Juliet Salcido and Miss Apolonia Montañez. One
candidate told the audience that he was honored to be the first state
candidate to address a women's political club.[18] Other political
groups organized by Mexican Americans were the Mexican branch of
the Young Men's Democratic Club and the Círculo de Amigos,
composed of Mexican American city employees.

Besides jobs and occasional favors, money represented the most
effective organizing tool used by politicos. "Machine politics was
common in those days," ex-El Paso journalist Chester Chope recalls.
"It was generally conceded that buying votes was common practice."[19] Because most Mexican workers received small wages, the
offer of $1 to $3 for their vote could not be easily refused. Not
restricted to El Paso, Arizona politicians paid Mexicans as much as
$5 to vote. It is conceivable, moreover, that a tradition of political
bossism which the immigrants, like so many other newcomers to the
United States, brought from their homeland made it easier for them
to follow the directives of their new *caudillos*: the Mexican American
politicians.[20] The *Times* observed that after being paid to vote in a
1902 school election, the "peons proceeded to make a night of it.
Few arrests, however, were made by the police." Reformers denounced the practice but could not eradicate it. Opposed to vote
purchasing, the *Times* in a spurt of reformism editorialized that more
than once it had called upon responsible El Pasoans to put a stop to
it. However, the Ring's control of the political process meant that

election officials raised no obstacles to illegal voting by Mexican nationals. According to one early El Paso politician, Ring members simply provided marked official ballots to the Mexicans as they entered the polling booth.[21]

The politicos and the Ring also provided entertainment and liquor for the Mexicans on the eve of each election as well as during election day. Given their long and arduous work schedules, many Mexicans were probably enticed by the opportunity to participate in what amounted to a fiesta. Elizabeth Kelly, longtime El Pasoan, remarks that during one election around the turn of the century, Mexicans were given a keg of beer and kept in a barn until the polls opened. In addition the Ring illegally registered Mexican nationals who did not even live in the city or county but came from Ciudad Juárez to vote. In 1893 reformers requested a grand jury to investigate charges of illegal registration in the Second Ward. The *Times* commented that officials counted about 400 registered Mexicans in the Second Ward but that no one believed so many voters resided there, in which case fraud existed. Nine years later the Republicans decided not to run a full ticket against the Ring due to the corrupt practices of the Democrats. As one Republican put it, "Why . . . these men boast that they vote dead Mexicans. They assert that they have lists of every legal Mexican voter in the county and vote them whether dead or not. If the man be dead, they substitute one that is alive and use the name of the deceased at the polls."[22]

Besides having organization and money, the Ring fraudulently paid poll taxes for their Mexican supporters after the state approved a poll tax amendment in 1902. Two years later Republicans accused the Democrats of having obtained 2,000 illegal poll tax receipts and applied for an injunction to put a stop to the practice, which included paying $1 to every Mexican who held a receipt.[23] Included by Republicans as defendants in this charge were Ike Alderete and his brother Frank. According to a civil service employee, J. M. García, who secretly wrote the chairman of the Republican party in El Paso, the Republican committeeman in Ysleta, J. G. Gaal, had betrayed his party and illegally purchased poll taxes for close to 200 people—apparently Mexicans—from money that García suspected had come from Ike Alderete and the Democratic Ring. "It is a shame," stressed García, "for the Republican Organization to keep a man at

the head of the Republican party in this precinct as Mr. Gaal."[24]
A local court, however, ruled that no evidence could be found that
the Ring had acquired illegal receipts and it refused an injunction.
Consequently, the Ring continued to purchase a large number of
poll taxes, which it distributed prior to elections.[25] Similar corruption continued and twelve years later a U.S. Department of Justice
investigation reported that at least 500 poll taxes had been illegally
purchased in El Paso that year. Although no convictions resulted,
the investigation revealed that in many cases Mexicans acquired these
illegal receipts with the understanding they could also be used to
secure employment with the city or county governments.[26]

Such tactics by the Ring and their Mexican ward heelers resulted
in decisive Democratic victories at election time. The machine's
control of the Second Ward, known as the "Bloody Second" because of the many political brawls that occurred there, constituted
the most important factor in its electoral strategy. The Second Ward
not only contained the city's largest number of voters, but it consistently provided Ring candidates with substantial margins over their
opponents. In the 1893 city election W. H. Austin swept to victory
as the Ring's nominee for mayor. Austin received 1,073 total votes,
435 (or 40%) coming from the Second Ward. Three years later in
the county election won by the Ring, machine candidates also gained
large majorities in the Mexican ward. In his reelection as district
clerk, Escajeda obtained 1,901 votes, 586 (or 31%) from El Segundo
Barrio. In addition he received 224 votes from Ysleta and 153 from
San Elizario, which together were another 20 percent of Escajeda's
total vote. His success in these three Mexican areas assured the district clerk of victory.[27]

The Ring did not, however, constitute the only political vote.
Both Republicans and anti-Ring Democrats attempted to break the
machine's ascendancy in the Mexican districts. The *Times* observed
in 1892 that despite the Republicans' open antagonism toward Mexican voters, this party coveted their support. "It is well known," it
commented, "that while publically preaching through the Republican paper of the iniquity of the 'Mexican vote,' the leaders of the
party have quietly worked unceasingly to secure control of the same
vote." The Republicans had interpreted a recent incident where

a Democrat had protested the right of Mexicans to vote as proof that the Ring had turned against their Mexican followers. Consequently, the Republicans moved to take advantage of this situation and at their next convention adopted the following resolution:

> Whereas, there is in our midst as evidenced at one of the Democratic primaries in the City of El Paso, a feeling to dis-franchise on account of race our Mexican population from a part in electing delegates to their conventions, therefore be it

> Resolved, that the attention of the Mexican people is called to the Republican national platform wherein it demands that every citizen of the United States shall be allowed to cast one free and unrestricted ballot, etc.; therefore, the Republicans of El Paso County, in convention assembled, declared that this principle should extend to all primaries as well as to public elections.[28]

This opportunistic campaign by the Republicans, the *Times* argued, would fail. Evidently, the paper stated, the Republicans believed that the Mexican vote was a "brainless vote" or else they would not attempt such a "palpable fraud."[29] Lacking political power and patronage, the Republicans found it difficult to sway most Mexicans away from the Ring.

Nevertheless, on certain occasions Republicans tried very hard to outbid the machine for Mexican voters. In the 1896 city election they literally picked up Mexicans on election eve, gave them liquor and entertainment, and kept them in a cellar with beer and food until the following morning, when the Republicans marched "their" Mexicans to the polls. A *Times* reporter in interviewing an "intelligent Mexican gentleman" about the Republicans' tactics asked whether he believed they would work. No, he replied, the Republicans would not even receive half the Mexican votes since the better class of Mexicans resented their actions and refused to be treated like cattle. He went on to add that while most Mexicans would support the Democrats, the Republicans would vote the *pelados* (the uncouth Mexicans). Indeed the Republicans went down to defeat despite their strenuous efforts to capture the Second Ward, which in some contests voted almost two to one in favor of the Ring.[30]

Although unable to break the Ring's domination of the Mexican vote, the Republican party did attract some Mexican American adherents. Several attended the 1892 Republican county convention. The Ysleta contingent had five Mexican Americans out of eight delegates while Mexican Americans comprised the entire delegation from Socorro. In addition J. Silva was one of San Elizario's three delegates. Finally, a Mr. Molina served as convention interpreter. At these gatherings they at times heard speeches delivered in Spanish and intended to arouse their enthusiasm for the Republican cause. At the 1899 city convention P. A. Dwyer attacked in Spanish the Ring administration for being unfriendly to Mexicans. He also criticized the city's indifference to smallpox in Chihuahuita and received much applause from the attending Mexican Americans when he announced that he had resigned from the police force to protest its treatment of Mexicans. Besides their attendance at local meetings, the Republicans appointed Mexican Americans to various party committees, although never in major decision-making roles. Moreover, the Grand Old Party occasionally nominated Mexican Americans for lesser county offices, especially against Ring politicos such as Escajeda and Alderete, but unfortunately for the Republicans with little success.[31]

Reform Democrats, on the other hand, presented a more difficult problem for the Ring. Able to attract disgruntled Mexican American politicos, these Democrats challenged the machine in various primaries. The 1912 county primary, for example, indicated the potential strength of the anti-Ring forces. District clerk Ike Alderete broke with the machine and joined the reformers. Alderete claimed he had been forced out of the Ring because he had furnished money to an old Mexican woman who had a lawsuit against Mayor Henry Kelly over some property in Chihuahuita. "I have been with the Ring quite awhile," Ike complained, "for 20 years I have been supported by it, and the Ring threw me down." As a result, Alderete and his brother Frank helped organize an anti-Ring ticket that combined reformers with Alderete's Mexican followers. "The word has been passed down the valley," the *Times* observed, "and in the lower part of the city that Ike is out and messages are being sent to Ike to stand pat as help is on the way."[32]

Alderete's split caused the Ring particular anxiety. The *Herald*

reported that the Ring had become so concerned that it encouraged
Republicans to sponsor a ticket in the hope of taking votes away
from Alderete. This was an old political trick, commented the *Herald*,
but possibly one of desperation as the Ring stood to lose its traditional balance of power. The paper further pointed out that the
lower valley appeared to be solid for Alderete's ticket. "The Alderetes
have a number of prominent Mexicans working for them," it added,
"and they are spending money freely, it is said, in lining up the
native vote." Because of Alderete's strength among the Mexicans,
the campaign became one of the most heated in the city's history
as both sides organized their supporters. The Mexican American city
employees organization, the Círculo de Amigos, represented one
group whose endorsement the Ring and anti-Ring sides fought over.
Although the club had been reported to have first favored the district clerk, it voted to support the Ring prior to the primary in exchange for what appears to have been Kelly's and the Ring's promise
that all Mexicans hired for city jobs would have to be club members
and that the city would not discharge any Mexican without the
consent of the Círculo de Amigos. Given these assurances, the club
began to criticize Alderete. One member called Ike a "disgrace to
the Mexican race." In addition to the Círculo, the Ring also acquired
the backing of the Mexican Young Men's Democratic Club.[33]

Hurt by their inability to attract these Mexican American political organizations, Alderete and the reformers obtained help from
organized labor. At a meeting of Local 583 of the International
Brotherhood of Electrical Workers, Alderete appeared and strongly
attacked the Ring, especially Mayor Kelly. "Ike hit straight from the
shoulder," reported the *Union*, "and in his talk he intimated that he
could tell more about the Ring than it would care to have said. That
is the reason Ike said 'Old Kell' during the 15 years that he had
been running with the Ring, always compelled him to make his
speeches in Spanish. 'Kell,' he said was afraid he might say too much."[34]

Alderete further told union members that if the Ring went too
far in its charges against him, he would expose various wrong-
doings by Ring members. One machine leader, Ike told his listeners,
had already accused him of having pictures of nude women on his
office walls. "I have only the pictures of my little girl hanging on the
wall," Alderete remarked, " and some calendars from the business

houses. . . . I keep my office clean." Regardless of what the Ring said of him, he concluded, "I am a pretty good guy."[35]

The support of organized labor, however, was not enough to defeat the Ring, as it turned back the reformer's challenge. As part of their strategy, the Ring countered Alderete's candidacy by its selection of Escajeda to run against the district clerk. With the Mexican vote sufficiently divided, the Ring managed to upset Alderete by 88 votes. Nevertheless, two anti-Ring candidates won important elections: Dan Jackson for the Thirty-fourth District clerk judgeship and Tom Lea for the county chairmanship of the Democratic executive committee. Total victory had escaped reform Democrats, but as the *Union* correctly recognized it would be only a matter of time before the Ring would be ousted.[36]

Although the Ring remained in power for the next two years, anti-Ring forces organized for another confrontation. In the city primary of 1915 reformers put forth a ticket headed by Tom Lea for mayor against Kelly. No Mexican American ran with Lea, but Alderete pledged his assistance. Moreover, two of the key issues raised by Lea were the Ring's manipulation of the Mexican vote and its neglect of living conditions in Chihuahuita. The report of the special grand jury that discovered numerous poll tax frauds in El Paso greatly helped Lea in his charges of corruption against Kelly and the Ring. Besides these disclosures, the grand jury's indictment of district clerk Escajeda on a charge of lending money with which to pay poll taxes further aided the reformer's call for "More Business and Less Politics."[37] Supported by the *Herald's* proposal for reforms in Chihuahuita, Lea also emphasized the high disease rates in the Mexican neighborhoods and blamed the Ring for doing nothing to improve sanitation among the Mexicans. An ad for the Lea ticket demanded to know what steps had been taken to eliminate the existing smallpox epidemic in the city and why the incumbent administration had done nothing to improve the southside. Another anti-Ring politician also questioned the Ring's inattention to the Mexicans except at election time. "Why is it that the 'ring' is campaigning so hard below the tracks?" he inquired. "They have never done anything for these people, yet they are now asking them to give them their whole-hearted support. Why do they promise so much before election and give so little afterwards?"[38]

Forced to reply to these attacks, the Ring could produce only vague counter charges and statements of friendship for the Mexican population. Speaking before a rally of Mexican allies at Ramón Gómez Hall in south El Paso, Kelly claimed that the anti-Ring ticket had attempted two years earlier to eliminate the Mexican voters of the city. "Who went to the assistance of the Mexican citizen of El Paso then?" Kelly asked. "It was 'Henry' Kelly, and you know it." Mexican American speakers at the rally endorsed Kelly and objected to what they considered anti-Mexican sentiments by Lea and his supporters. Rafael Huerta attacked Lea for insulting and slandering the Mexican citizens of El Paso by charging that they could be bought and herded to the polls like sheep. Huerta called on Mexican Americans to show Lea that "we are real men and true Americans by voting our sentiments on election day." Escajeda then arose and defended himself against the grand jury. He claimed that the jury worked for the anti-Ring organization and that in its investigation had violated the rights and integrity of Mexicans. According to Escajeda, no honest Mexican would vote for a man like Lea, who had so grossly insulted the Mexican race.[39]

Whereas such tactics still proved to be effective for the Ring in south El Paso, they were a handicap in its relationship with American voters. Not only had the jury report damaged the Ring and given impetus to the reform movement, but a larger increase in American voters by 1915 minimized the Ring's domination of the Mexican vote, especially if it did poorly in the northern precincts. In addition, growing resentment toward Mexicans as a result of increased tensions between the United States and Mexico hurt the Ring as well. Although on election day the *Herald* noticed that Kelly's men took to the polls several hundred Mexican city employees, garbage wagon drivers, shovel men, and street cleaners, the Ring suffered its first major setback in almost 25 years of political power. According to the *Herald*, Kelly had carried only four precincts out of seventeen and these were all "below the tracks." North of the tracks the vote was overwhelmingly in favor of the Lea ticket. Kelly won the first four Mexican precincts by a vote of 1,021 to 783 for Lea but lost precincts five and six also on the southside by a combined total of 180 votes. Lea's ability to cut into the Ring's stronghold in the barrios plus his strong majorities in the other sections proved to be the undoing of the Ring in city politics. "The Ring fell apart when Papa was defeated," recalls one of Mayor Kelly's daughters. The final count revealed 4,218 votes for Lea, who carried his entire ticket, and 3,149 votes for Kelly. At the victory celebration Lea congratulated his supporters, who included Ike Alderete. Of the Mexican politico, Lea said, "I want to pay tribute for the good work Ike Alderete has done in this election. When they tried to bribe Alderete away from me several years ago, he told them he was my friend and liked me and would stay with me. He has done so. Today he went into the Mexican precincts almost alone and worked for this ticket." Alderete replied, "This is the happiest moment of my life, I said I would never stop until Henry Kelly was defeated."[40]

One year later, however, Alderete along with other leading politicos joined Kelly's attempt to reorganize the Ring for the county primaries. Why Alderete left the anti-Ring group cannot be determined, although perhaps its lack of enthusiasm for the older Mexican American politicians plus its emphasis on the American vote may have disenchanted Ike. His return to the Ring made the *Herald* comment that much of Kelly's strength would lie with the "Big Four": Alderete, Escajeda, Domingo Montoya (county constable), and Fred Delgado (deputy constable). These four expected to control the large Mexican vote on the southside. Yet the politicos no longer possessed the influence they once held and the primary was a disaster for them. Not only did anti-Ring forces win every office except three, but various Ring Mexican Americans went down in defeat. Because the Ring was strongly rejected by El Paso voters, some American members of the group began to question their traditional reliance on both the Mexican vote and the Mexican American politicos. Although Escajeda received the only patronage job left to the Ring, that of county auditor, certain reservations were expressed about his appointment. The *Herald* observed that the Ring had become ambivalent about Escajeda. Although his appointment might be an asset with Mexican voters at the next election, it might also hurt the Ring in American precincts that had voted against every Mexican candidate.[41]

The Ring never recovered from its setbacks in 1915 and 1916. Although Escajeda and the other Mexican American politicos continued to participate in both reform and "old ring" politics, their prestige and authority had diminished. How much their demise can be attributed to increased anti-Mexican sentiment in El Paso arising from such events as the American occupation of Veracruz in 1914 and Pancho Villa's raid on Columbus, New Mexico, in 1916 is hard to know, but it may have played a major role. In any event a transitional period for the politicos began with the fall of El Paso's Ring. An assessment, in retrospect, of these Mexican American politicians is difficult. Unlike the immigrants, the Mexican Americans had become sufficiently Americanized to have developed an interest in American society and to see politics as a means of economic and social mobility within the United States. Indeed, unlike other ethnic groups in the United States, it was not the Mexican immigrants but rather the Mexican Americans who experienced acculturation into American life out of their political ties with the Ring. Mexican Americans received jobs from the Ring as well as political influence in exchange for their delivery of the Mexican vote. The Ring, in turn, and the anti-Ring politicians represented employers and professionals who profited from El Paso's supply of cheap Mexican labor. Consequently, the Mexican Americans' support of the political structure reinforced the economic subordination of the Mexicans. Cheap Mexican votes sustained an economic structure dependent on cheap Mexican labor. On the other hand, Mexican American political organizations did serve as pressure groups upon American politicians and led to some political representation, patronage, and ethnic protection, especially during the tense years of the Mexican Revolution. However, these concessions benefited a minority of Mexican Americans and not the great majority of Mexican immigrants, who gained little. The continued influx of immigrants after 1920 not only expanded roles for Mexican Americans as mediators between the newcomers and local government but also reminded American politicians of the political importance of El Paso's Mexican population. Nevertheless, a pattern of political manipulation, subordination, and underrepresentation, which continues, was set in the border city and throughout much of the Southwest.[42]

9

Border Revolution

If American local politics provoked little interest among Mexican immigrants, the politics of the Mexican Revolution of 1910, by contrast, captured their attention. Because immigrants saw Mexico, not the United States, as their homeland, the civil war aroused their nationalism as well as their personal concerns for family and friends left behind. Moreover, since they saw their eventual return to Mexico as the basis of a better life, Mexicans along the border avidly followed political events in Mexico that might affect their future plans. Indeed, all of El Paso became involved in the revolution when the El Paso–Ciudad Juárez area proved to be perhaps the most strategic site for all revolutionary factions. Because of its location El Paso was a logical haven for political exiles, many of whom received support from the city's large Mexican community. By 1907 depressed economic conditions, especially in Juárez, also created fertile ground for revolutionary activity. Most important, the Pass of the North was a major supplier of armaments and munitions. Consequently, El Paso and its sister city, Ciudad Juárez, provided the stage for the acting out of varied revolutionary movements.[1]

As early as 1893 increased reports of rebellion against Porfirio Díaz's dictatorial government reached El Paso. Organized in northern Mexico and along the U.S.–Mexican border, such initial but small-scale efforts stressed Díaz's totalitarian rule and the need to implement the democratic principles of Mexico's Constitution of 1857. At first considering these actions merely an outbreak of banditry, the *Times* admitted in late 1893 that insurrection indeed existed in Mexico. "Recent disturbances," it pointed out, "in the state of Guerrero and the disorders within the state of Durango as well as the frontier troubles of Chihuahua and the threatening conditions in Coahuila . . .

all are the smoke of a revolutionary fire that has been long smoulder-
ing in the hearts of many Mexicans who believe that the Díaz government is a perpetuated tyranny daily restricting their liberty and selling
their country." Two days later the *Times* added that a Mexican rebel
by the name of Luján upon arriving in El Paso from Chihuahua had
gone to the lower valley settlement of San Elizario, where he had
taken command of 65 armed Mexicans. Luján's intentions were to
recross the border along the line of the Mexican Central and engage
Mexican federal troops. As a result of growing rebel activity, Juárez
officials announced the expected arrival of 300 federales to help
prevent a possible attack on the Mexican border town. Concurring
with the *Times* reports, although discounting a successful rebellion
against Díaz, the U.S. consul in Juárez informed the State Department of Mexican insurrectionists in western Chihuahua led by Santana
Pérez, who the consul believed had from 65 to 300 men.[2]

American authorities, concerned about violations of United
States neutrality laws and pressured by the Mexican government,
began the investigation and detention of suspected Mexican rebels
on the northern side of the frontier. In El Paso they focused on
the activities of Víctor L. Ochoa and Lauro Aguirre. First apprehended toward the end of 1893, Ochoa was accused by officers
of employing and equipping insurgents in El Paso and sending them
into Mexico to fight government forces. Ochoa's arrest, the *Times*
noted, plainly showed the American government's anxiety. However,
a few weeks later the U.S. consul in Juárez reported that Ochoa,
apparently acquitted of all charges, along with other rebels had impressed ten Mexican cowboys into their ranks 120 miles southeast
of Juárez. When rumors reached El Paso of Ochoa's return to the
border, despite some reports of his death, Mexican secret service men
swarmed around the rebel's house in Chihuahuita where his wife
still resided. "Mrs. Ochoa who is just now in the deepest grief," the
Times commented on the Mexican spies' noticeable presence, "was
not only greatly annoyed but frightened out of her wits." The
newspaper believed Ochoa to be dead but if alive did not consider
him to be foolish enough to reappear in his El Paso home.[3]

In fact quite alive, Ochoa, writing to the editor of the *Albuquerque Citizen*, announced that notwithstanding the loss of 43 of his
men in a recent battle he would continue the fight against "the usur-

pers of the right of the people. . . . I am neither dead nor wounded
and much less frightened," Ochoa defiantly stressed. "To win we
must use tricks, but I have the hope, and the day will yet come when
our cause will triumph." Ochoa's struggle ended, however, when
Texas Rangers along with federal officials captured him in Pecos
County southeast of El Paso on charges of organizing an armed force
on American territory with the intent of invading Mexico. When he
was returned to El Paso for trial, a large crowd, presumably of Mexicans, greeted the apprehended but popular revolutionary. A federal
court subsequently convicted Ochoa of violating American neutrality
laws and sentenced him to three years in prison.[4]

After Ochoa, federal investigators closely watched Lauro Aguirre.
A Chihuahua civil engineer by profession, Aguirre had actively participated in anti-Díaz protests in 1895; as a result, Mexican officials
accused Aguirre, along with Teresa Urrea, a woman believed to possess healing powers, of attempting to influence Yaqui Indians in
Sonora to rebel. Politically harassed, Aguirre crossed the border and
briefly resided in Nogales, Arizona, where he published *El Independiente*, an anti-Díaz newspaper. He arrived in El Paso shortly there-
after and carried on his work against the Díaz regime. In March 1896
the United States government without a warrant arrested Aguirre
in his Chihuahuita home along with fellow journalist Flores Chapa on
a charge by the Mexican consul that both men had plans to enter
Mexico and engage in revolution. The U.S. consul in Juárez investi-
gated the incident and informed Washington that he believed Aguirre
and Chapa innocent of the charges: "On the contrary they came to
El Paso, Texas for the purpose of gaining a livelihood by publishing
there a newspaper in the Spanish language under the name of 'El
Independiente.'" At his trial Aguirre admitted printing anti-Díaz
articles but denied any revolutionary acts. "I am publishing a paper
against Mexico," he told the court, "because I hope to remedy the
evils by pointing out what they will lead to." He further acknowledged writing that in his opinion a revolutionary process had begun
in Mexico. Yet his lawyer W. H. Burgess emphasized that such statements did not constitute evidence of overt revolutionary activity.
If the court found his client guilty, Burgess concluded, then every
American newspaper carrying news of rebellion south of the
border should also be declared guilty. The federal court agreed and
found both Aguirre and Chapa innocent.[5]

Aguirre's persistent and bold attacks on Díaz infuriated Mexican authorities, who charged the journalist along with Teresa Urrea— known to her followers as "Santa Teresa"—of fomenting revolution along the border. In 1901 the mayor of Juárez complained to the U.S. consul of "subversive" statements attributed to Aguirre in his newspaper, now called *El Progresista*. According to the Juárez official, Aguirre had misrepresented facts and had made passionate appeals against the Mexican government. One year later, informed of a Díaz plot to kidnap him, Aguirre wrote President Roosevelt asking for American protection. "I respectfully request you to issue orders to protect against [such] assaults," the Mexican editor appealed to the American head of state. "I am a political refugee and ask for the protection of the United States flag." Instructed by Washington to examine Aguirre's case, U.S. Consul Charles W. Kindrick in Juárez concluded that no kidnap scheme existed except in the newspaperman's mind.[6] Aguirre remained in El Paso, where he soon joined the most radical movement against Díaz: the revolt of Ricardo Flores Magón and the Partido Liberal Mexicano (PLM).

Flores Magón's anarchosyndicalist rebellion expressed the growing discontent among many Mexican intellectuals as well as the middle class over Díaz's refusal to broaden political decision-making in Mexico. Composed mainly of professionals and forced to leave Mexico in 1904 due to their criticisms of the government, Flores Magón and the leaders of the PLM planned revolution in San Antonio and St. Louis, where they evaded the Mexican secret service and published their newspaper *Regeneración*. Although holding to socialist and anarchist beliefs, the PLM essentially called for the establishment of bourgeois democratic principles in Mexico, which it believed could be accomplished only through armed revolution. The Magonistas hoped to stimulate a spontaneous mass uprising in Mexico by their capture of Ciudad Juárez in 1906.[7]

The PLM prepared for its attack on the key Mexican border town by organizing in El Paso a cell known as the Club Liberal. Involving Mexicans from both sides of the border, it took orders from Lauro Aguirre, who served as the organization's president, and another journalist, W. Tovar y Bueno, its vice-president. In El Paso PLM members such as Juan Sarabia and Antonio I. Villarreal also traveled into Chihuahua, where they coordinated plans with supporters and disseminated Magonista propaganda, including Aguirre's latest newspaper,

La Reforma Social.[8] Flores Magón arrived in El Paso, as prepara-
tions for the assault reached their final stages, to direct the rebellion
from the home of PLM member Modesto Díaz in Chihuahuita.
Crowded with Mexican immigrants, the rebels lived on South Oregon
and South El Paso streets and considered El Paso's Mexican district
a safe haven for their operations, besides valuing its advantageous
proximity to the international bridges and the railroad station. Expecting to recruit 200 armed men on the American side, the PLM's
objectives involved crossing into Juárez and blowing up the federal
army garrison, the police station, and the prefect's headquarters. The
Magonistas would then send a contingent by train to capture Cuidad
Chihuahua, which they believed would lead to the collapse of the
Díaz regime throughout the northern states and the beginning of its
demise in Mexico. Unfortunately, the PLM had not counted on its
plans being discovered by Díaz informers, who had successfully infil-
trated the revolutionary cells in both border towns.[9]

Before Flores Magón and his followers could complete their
strategy, El Paso police and federal officers acting in concert with the
Mexican consul raided several homes known as rebel hideouts. Most
PLM members learned of the searches just in time and escaped, including Flores Magón, who left El Paso by train for Los Angeles.
Those arrested included key Magonista lieutenants: Aguirre, Villarreal, and Rómulo Carmona. Officials also captured numerous documents linking the El Paso cell with others in Laredo, Brownsville,
Eagle Pass, Del Rio, St. Louis, and Douglas, Arizona. Such evidence,
the arresting officers believed, would be sufficient either to deport
the Mexicans or to hold them on charges of violating neutrality laws.
At the same time, Juárez police apprehended 13 known PLM members and Chihuahua authorities detained more than 100 people alleged
to be Magonista adherents. Its revolutionary plans thwarted, PLM
leaders found themselves either arrested or in hiding by the end of
1906.[10]

Undaunted, despite their constant harassment in the United
States by both American and Mexican authorities, the PLM attempted a second attack on Juárez two years later. His brother confined
in a Los Angeles jail, Enrique Flores Magón directed the plot from an
El Paso house on the corner of First and Tays near the border. Besides the raid on Juárez, the Magonistas planned assaults on several

other Mexican towns on the Texas–Mexican frontier. However, seemingly possessed of nothing but bad luck in El Paso, the PLM's strategy became known to border officials. An American barber living next door to the secret rebel headquarters reported strangers, at times armed, coming and going at all times of the night. Investigating what they believed to be a possible smuggling ring, police officers raided the house and to their surprise uncovered nine Winchester rifles, almost 1,000 rounds of ammunition, five revolvers, bombs made out of cans filled with powder and fragments of iron, and documents revealing the PLM's identity. Officials arrested eleven Mexicans suspected of being Magonistas including the four occupants of the house. After Lauro Aguirre published a special edition of *La Reforma Social*, charging the police with an illegal search, authorities also seized the editor. Aguirre, claiming to be an American citizen, denied any involvement with a revolutionary scheme. "While in my paper I have always fought the Mexican government," he insisted, "I have always fought from the front and as a citizen of the United States I am guaranteed the right under the constitution to voice my opinion and protest against wnat I consider tyranny in any part of the world."[11]

Their El Paso plans discovered, the PLM saw their additional attacks along the border likewise fail. Of the Mexicans arrested and tried, the court convicted and sentenced P. G. Silva and L. V. Treviño to two years at Fort Leavenworth for violations of the neutrality laws. The court proceedings aroused much interest among El Paso's Mexican population and many avidly attended the deliberations. Limited in followers, poorly equipped, repressed by officials, and unrealistically expecting a spontaneous mass uprising in Mexico, the PLM did not actively participate again in El Paso revolutionary politics after 1908.[12]

Where Flores Magón's movement failed, that of Francisco Madero succeeded beyond the expectations of most El Pasoans. A wealthy landowner from Coahuila in northern Mexico, Madero basically objected to Díaz's unwillingness to retire voluntarily from office and allow open elections. Don Porfirio, after suggesting that he would not stand for reelection in 1910, changed his mind and announced for still another term. In an editorial the *Times* commented

that although it had never doubted the Mexican president's desire
to remain in office, it did not agree with those who contended that
no one could ever effectively replace Díaz. The Mexican people,
according to the *Times*, had politically matured and had accepted a
peaceful transfer of power. Mexico had passed the "silly revolutionary stage," the El Paso paper asserted, and Díaz could now retire
without endangering the peace and progress of his country. The *Times*
admitted political unrest in Mexico but emphasized that foreign
investors south of the border would never allow a revolution that
would endanger their interests. Assured of Díaz's ability to maintain
the peace so essential for foreign capital, the *Times* along with many
El Pasoans, both American and Mexican, welcomed the Mexican
strongman to the border city for his celebrated visit with President
Taft on October 16, 1909. "The people of El Paso welcome you to
our midst," Mayor Joseph Sweeny proclaimed to Díaz, "greeting
not you alone, but the people of Mexico whose representative you
are, and in voicing that welcome, we but re-echo that of all our
countrymen."[13]

The *Times's* assessment of Díaz's strength proved inaccurate in
that it underestimated Mexico's economic and political crisis. After
being prevented by Díaz from effectively challenging for the presi-
dency in 1910, Madero issued from his exiled San Antonio headquarters a revolutionary call to arms: the Plan de San Luis Potosí.
Madero demanded political reforms and the revitalization of the
1857 constitution and his movement quickly gained notoriety, especially along the border. With supporters in Chihuahua and Sonora,
such as Francisco (Pancho) Villa, Abraham González, and Pascual
Orozco, the Maderistas engaged Díaz's troops in early skirmishes by
November. The Revolution of 1910, Mexico's most tragic civil war,
had commenced. In Juárez, the chief of police, fearful of an *insurrecto* attack, recruited several hundred special officers to protect the
town; in addition, Mexican customs guards patrolled the river front
to prevent any rebels from entering through El Paso. Authorities also arrested 40 Mexicans on suspicion of being revolutionaries. Not
to be left out, El Paso shared in the excitement. Thousands of Mexicans on the American side of the border flocked to the riverbank
near the smelter to better observe the expected battle, only to be
disappointed when it failed to take place.[14]

Madero arrived in El Paso a few months after his revolutionary proclamation to meet with his local junta but quickly fled when informed that U.S. authorities sought his apprehension for violation of the neutrality laws. As a result the "apostle of democracy" entered Chihuahua southeast of El Paso at Zaragoza and took formal command of his forces. However, El Paso remained a strategic location for the Maderistas, who announced early in 1911 that the Texas border city would be their central headquarters in the United States. Maintaining an office at the Planters Hotel at 110½ South Oregon and later in the Caples Building in downtown El Paso, Madero's men dispatched agents to Denver, Oakland, Kansas City, and Chicago, as well as other places, in search of recruits, arms, and financial support.[15] The *Times* accurately interpreted the establishment of the El Paso junta: "This information is taken to indicate that Madero expects to confine his operations in northern Mexico to the cities south of Juárez and to the state of Sonora, for some time to come."[16]

The Maderistas found support and sympathy from different sectors of the El Paso community including many Mexican political exiles, immigrant workers, some Mexican Americans, and various Americans who profited by selling arms and supplies to the rebel forces.[17] Among the exiles the socialist and ex-PLM member L. Gutiérrez de Lara was the most effective propagandist for the revolutionary cause. Arrested numerous times in Mexico for his opposition to Díaz, Gutiérrez de Lara had gained attention in the United States by having assisted the American journalist John Kenneth Turner in his investigative reporting, which exposed the horrid labor conditions under Díaz, especially in the rural areas.[18] By 1910 Gutiérrez de Lara traveled along the border calling for the overthrow of Díaz and gathering adherents for Madero. "Mexican Socialist to Deliver Lecture," the *Times* noted of Gutiérrez de Lara's arrival in El Paso for a series of speeches in early 1911. His first lecture delivered from the county courthouse steps attracted about 700 people, mostly Mexicans who repeatedly interrupted him with shouts of "Viva Mexico" and much applause when he referred to the revolution against Díaz. Six hundred Mexicans turned out the following day and heard Gutiérrez de Lara speak on the "Origin of Revolution in Latin America" at the corner of Overland and El Paso streets, adjacent to Chihuahuita. Possibly attracted by the festive excitement of a mass rally as well as the revolutionary polemics, an additional 2,000 Mexicans listened to the socialist at his next two streetcorner orations. "The time will come," he predicted at one gathering, "when the land will be divided among the whole people of the nation. And when this division is made they [the Mexican workers] will live the life of the millionaires of today." Gutiérrez de Lara also collected funds for Madero's field hospitals by selling political literature to his audiences.[19]

After a short excursion into Chihuahua, where he fought with the Maderistas, Gutiérrez de Lara returned to El Paso and attempted to organize a mass parade as a show of support for Madero. Unable to acquire a permit for the march when city officials, fearing a violation of neutrality statutes, refused his request, Gutiérrez de Lara nevertheless challenged the American authorities. After speaking to an evening rally attended by approximately 3,000 persons composed almost entirely of Mexicans, Gutiérrez de Lara urged the crowd to follow him through the downtown streets. Before the march could even commence, however, city police descended on the Mexicans and escorted Gutiérrez de Lara to the city jail. An angered audience pursued the police and demanded the socialist's release. Throughout the evening, a reporter observed, mounted officers had to clear the streets to prevent the Mexicans from gaining access to the police station. At one point more than 200 Mexican women approached the city jail and insisted that Gutiérrez de Lara be given his liberty. Except for some rock throwing, the *Times* noted that the irritated Mexicans remained peaceful throughout their vigil. By midnight as the streetlights went off, the Mexicans, unable to free their dynamic orator, went home. Besides Gutiérrez de Lara, El Paso police apprehended 13 of his supporters for disturbing the peace. Members of Madero's junta in the border city, apparently embarrassed by what appears to have been Gutiérrez de Lara's independent action, denounced the socialist and stressed that they had not sponsored the rally and proposed march. At a hearing attended by numerous Mexicans, the court found Gutiérrez de Lara guilty of obstructing a street and impeding traffic and fined him $25.[20]

Mexicans in El Paso assisted the revolutionary movement in other ways besides participating in pro-Madero rallies. One study of the revolution in the El Paso–Ciudad Juárez area suggests that by 1910 many unemployed Mexican immigrant workers returning to the border enlisted in Madero's army. Some with jobs and unable to leave but who sympathized with the rebels provided money. Mexican smelter workers, for example, took up a collection that they donated to the insurrectos. Still others contributed in a less orthodox fashion. "Mexican insurrecto sympathizers," the *Times* reported, "were yesterday stopped from throwing dollars and doughnuts across the river from the American side to the insurrectos camped opposite the El Paso smelting works."[21] More prominent Mexicans, including exiles and possibly Mexican Americans, helped the cause by holding fund-raisers for the rebel hospital in Chihuahuita under the direction of the American Dr. I. J. Bush. To purchase needed medical equipment for Bush, a number of young Mexican señoritas hosted a *kermes* [a Mexican fair] and dance at La Protectora lodge at the corner of Fifth and Stanton. Sponsoring lunches at a hall, older Mexican women aided the hospital as well as the Red Cross by collecting on one occasion close to $200. A Mexican women's organization, the Cinco de Febrero, chose to help relatives of dead or wounded revolutionaries by holding a bazaar at Washington Park in East El Paso, where they collected several hundred dollars. The same society held a grand ball in honor of Madero's mother and wife. "The best element of the local Mexican colony," the *Times* observed, "will turn out in force to express their sympathy for the insurrectos and to do especial honor to the mother and wife of the man who has sacrificed everything to give personal liberty to the people of Mexico." Finally, when Madero's army arrived on the outskirts of Juárez, a large crowd of El Paso Mexicans, including a Mexican band conducted by Trinidad Concha, crossed the river to welcome and serenade the Maderistas.[22]

On May 8, 1911, two weeks after their arrival on the border, the insurrectos began their attack on Juárez. Two days later, with the federales suffering heavy casualties, the strategic border town fell and a jubilant Madero proclaimed Juárez the provisional capital of Mexico. Stunned by Madero's victory, Porfirio Díaz resigned within days of the battle and abandoned Mexico for exile in Paris. In El Paso thousands of people had fought for vantage points near the border and on top of business buildings to view the fighting. "I watched the battle from the top of the then Sheldon Hotel," recalls Charles Armijo, "I took my field glasses and I watched them fight over there."

Unfortunately, stray bullets caused mishaps such as the death of José Lozano, an expressman, near the El Paso pump station. Several other Mexicans, living near the border, also suffered death or injuries because of the conflict. According to the *Times* twenty-year-old Vicente Paredes had been killed by a "wild bullet while reading a paper at his home on the corner of Santa Fe and Fifth streets." Another shot hit an eleven-year-old Mexican girl in the head, slightly injuring her. Mrs. José García, who lived two blocks north of the Santa Fe bridge, sustained a neck wound. In addition, the injured from Juárez filled the rebel hospital in El Paso.[23]

When the fighting subsided, both towns joined in celebrating Madero's great triumph. Ten thousand Mexicans, including several hundred Mexican Americans, accompanied by a brass band crossed the border one evening and paid tribute to the Maderistas. In turn many of Madero's officers shopped and dined in El Paso. "Colonel Francisco Villa made his appearance in the Sheldon Hotel lobby yesterday afternoon about 3:00 o'clock," a reporter commented, "and after walking about for several minutes entered the cafe where he ordered lunch." Yet Villa had other things on his mind than a meal. Learning that the famous Mexican revolutionary had intentions of having a shoot-out with another insurrecto personality, Italian soldier of fortune Colonel Giuseppe Garibaldi, Mayor Henry Kelly persuaded Villa to peacefully return across the river. Fascinated by the appearances of colorful figures such as Villa, Garibaldi, and Orozco, El Pasoans reserved their largest accolade for the "apostle of democracy," Madero. At a reception and banquet in Madero's honor, Kelly as well as other city dignitaries praised the man whom they expected would bring peace and prosperity to Mexico, a condition so vital for El Paso's own fortunes. "El Paso has had a warm spot in her heart for the insurrecto leader," the *Times* stressed, "and rejoices with him that newer and better things have dawned for the republic of Mexico."[24]

Despite his victory over Díaz and his election as Mexico's president, Madero faced various rebellions against his authority. In the north the most significant challenge to the new administration consisted of the Red Flaggers, the followers of ex-Maderista Pascual Orozco, who now led a conservative counterrevolution in Chihuahua. "There are more than a thousand rebels now in El Paso," the local agent of the Mexican Northwestern Railroad notified his New York employers, "most of whom would welcome an opportunity of slipping into Juárez."[25] The Red Flaggers, importing guns through El Paso with the help of a local junta, mounted a successful assault on Juárez and captured the town on February 27, 1912. However, the subsequent United States arms embargo on Mexico severely damaged Orozco's cause and the revolt failed.[26] During the struggle Orozco's opponents had often published scathing attacks on his character and had distributed them along the border. One biased flyer distributed among El Paso's Mexicans accused Orozco of being a traitor, of enjoying orgies while his men went to battle, and of hoarding thousands of dollars in El Paso banks.[27]

Although Orozco possessed a strong following in El Paso, especially among the wealthy Porfirista exiles, many local Mexicans welcomed the return of Madero's troops to the border. "The Mexican people residing in El Paso," the pro-Madero *Times* reported, "will manifest their immense satisfaction at the occupancy of Ciudad Juárez by the soldiers of the constitutional government of the southern republic by a parade of patriotic clubs, which will take place this afternoon, moving from this city over one of the international bridges to welcome and congratulate the army command." Led by Madero supporters organized in a group called the Defenders of Order, most of El Paso's Mexican clubs and societies, many of them containing Mexican American members as well as immigrants, cooperated on the parade in order to demonstrate that the border city remained a Maderista stronghold.[28]

Unfortunately for Madero, the Orozco rebellion only started a more serious counterrevolution by Porfiristas. In a little over a year after his election as president, Madero fell before the reactionary forces of General Victoriano Huerta during the "ten tragic days" of February 1913.[29] The American consul in Ciudad Juárez correctly judged that Huerta's intention was to restore the old Díaz regime although without Díaz himself. The civil war that followed between the Constitutionalists led by Carranza and Villa, on one side, and Huerta's supporters, on the other, introduced the bloodiest phase of the revolution. Seeing that both factions were using El Paso as a base of operations, American officials kept close surveillance on

possible violations of the neutrality laws. "There appears to be an
unusual number of revolutionists in El Paso at this time," one
federal agent informed the Department of Justice. Yet rebels were
not the only secret agents arriving in the border city.[30] "Conditions are just about as bad as they can be," added a railroad man.
"El Paso is simply flooded with secret service agents and representatives of the United States."[31] These investigators did not always
respect the privacy and rights of Mexican residents. For example,
in January 1914 U.S. Army troops conducted a search in the smelter
community, where they believed ammunition for the Constitutionalists had been stored. Raiding half a dozen houses and causing much
disturbance among the Mexican population, the Americans failed
to discover anything. Two days later, however, authorities captured
two Mexicans in an alley south of San Francisco Street as they attempted to transfer 12,000 rounds of 30–30 ammunition from the
warehouse of hardware dealer Krakauer, Zork & Maye to Villa's
forces in Juárez.[32]

Next to gun running, illegal enlistments in El Paso for the Mexican armies posed the most serious problem. At one point Justice
Department officers arrested the Mexican inspector of consulates,
the Mexican consul, the vice-consul, and one other official for en-
listing soldiers to Huerta's cause. According to the American investigators, the Mexican consulate in El Paso had agreed to provide
transportation to Eagle Pass for eight Mexicans on condition they
joined Huerta's army in Piedras Negras across the border. When taken
into custody, the Mexican recruits admitted that besides paying
their travel costs the consulate had coached them to say, if questioned, that they represented refugees on their way back to Mexico.
Not intimidated, Huerta agents apparently continued to recruit in
El Paso.[33]

As the Mexican civil war increased in intensity by the middle of
the decade, so too did racial tensions along the border, especially
following the Tampico Incident and the later invasion and occupation
of Veracruz by U.S. Marines in April 1914. To prevent any disturbances in the Mexican district over the international crisis or the
possibility of an attack by Villa's forces stationed in Juárez, military
patrols composed of infantry and cavalry from Fort Bliss patrolled
Chihuahuita during the week of April 21. "At the army post [Fort

Bliss] the cavalrymen were ordered to sleep with boots and saddles at their side," reported the *New York Times* correspondent in El Paso. "They can be up and away in case of an alarm in less than five minutes."[34] Mayor Kelly, although insisting that he expected no trouble, offered the army use of city facilities in case officials declared martial law. Emphasizing that the troops did not interfere with citizens, the *El Paso Times* believed that their presence was purely precautionary. In an effort to further reduce the likelihood of a retaliation on El Paso the newspaper stated in an editorial that the American action in Veracruz had not been aimed at Carranza's movement but at the Huerta government, which had insulted the U.S. flag at Tampico, and it appealed to the Constitutionalists to remember that Americans were their friends.[35]

One day after the Veracruz invasion a relieved Mayor Kelly proclaimed that no disturbance had taken place in Chihuahuita and that everything remained quiet. The resident Mexican population, the mayor disclosed, had displayed no inclination to demonstrate support for either Huerta or Carranza over the American intervention. Kelly also denied rumors that in case of a border conflict the Mexican population would be forced to cross into Juárez. "Of course nothing is more groundless, and I might say, more foolish than this," he insisted. "The American citizens of Spanish [Mexican] birth have every right here that the Americans have and we have every reason to believe they will meet the obligations resting on good citizens of supporting the government and preserving peace and quiet." The mayor added that all residents of El Paso, whether Americans or Mexicans, citizens or aliens, would be treated equally and fairly as long as they obeyed the law and did not attempt to incite disturbances. In spite of Kelly's reassurances the presence of American military forces in Chihuahuita could not help but add to American suspicions that the local Mexican population represented a possible threat to the city. A writer for *McClure's Magazine*, for example, reported rumors circulating in El Paso that Mexican domestics intended to poison their employers. The arrest of a pro-Huerta publisher in El Paso and the seizure of his press by police did not help relieve racial tensions either. According to officials, Efreno M. Franco, editor of *El Libre*, had printed an appeal to the city's Mexican population to rise up against the gringos and join Huerta in defending their homeland.[36]

Hoping to avert such an occurrence as well as to protect themselves against a growing anti-Mexican sentiment in El Paso, influential
Mexican Americans, led by the politicos, organized a mediating force
between the American establishment and the Mexican immigrants
and refugees. "I have spent the entire day," Ike Alderete told a reporter the day after the Veracruz invasion, "circulating among the
Mexican refugees in El Paso and urging them to remember that they
are in a foreign country here for protection, which they have and
are still enjoying." Alderete cautioned the Mexicans not to do or say
anything that might irritate or offend Americans. The refugees, the
Mexican American politician stated, understood the delicate situation
and as far as he knew did not intend to cause any trouble. Besides
Alderete it was reported that more than 600 other Mexican Americans led by J. A. Escajeda offered to patrol Chihuahuita as a peace
force if so needed by Mayor Kelly. The Mexican Americans pledged
their loyalty to the United States and resolved to fight on its side
in case of war with Mexico. Escajeda revealed that several months
prior to the Veracruz incident he had personally formed, trained,
and drilled a company of Mexican Americans for patrol duty in the
Mexican district or to join with American forces in the eventuality
of an attack on Mexico. "While we are called Mexicans," the district
clerk patriotically explained,

> we are not. We are Americans; born and brought up under the
> Stars and Stripes and as loyal to it as any other American. Many
> people in this city have said that we would rise up and incite
> riots in this city if President Wilson was forced to land American
> troops or bluejackets on Mexican soil, but quite on the contrary
> we are ready to shoulder a rifle and march in the ranks with the
> American soldier who is of Anglo-Saxon or Celtic origin.[37]

Although the presence of American soldiers in Chihuahuita helped
calm fears of a possible rebellion within El Paso, rumors abounded of
Villa's plans to invade the border city. As a result El Paso gun shops
faced a run on their supplies despite warnings by officials against the
illegal carrying of weapons. For their own protection many American
wives and their children left the city by train. Those unable to flee
or unwilling to abandon their homes moved farther north and east of

the areas adjacent to the border. Fearing as many as 15,000 Mexican soldiers, U.S. military authorities at Fort Bliss quickly dispatched a squadron of the Twelfth Cavalry, a battalion of the Twentieth Infantry, and a battery of the Sixth Field Artillery to El Paso. Besides guarding the reservoirs of the municipal water system, the electric light plants, and the gas works against sabotage, the troops stationed artillery where it could effectively shell Juárez and placed machine guns in positions commanding the international bridges. Expanding the American armed presence on the border, additional contingents arrived from San Antonio, San Francisco, and Columbus, New Mexico; hence, by late April El Paso hosted close to 6,500 troops under the command of General John (Black Jack) Pershing with encampments at Washington Park and on Cotton Avenue. In addition, American ranchers, sheepmen, and miners in the vicinity organized a "Rough Rider" regiment and, according to one correspondent, clamored for action in Mexico.[38] A tense and increasingly militarized city finally relaxed when Villa announced that he had no desire to invade El Paso and instead expressed friendship for the American people. "Mexico has troubles enough of her own," Villa told the American press, "and is not seeking a war with any foreign country, certainly not the United States."[39]

After Villa's anticipated attack failed to materialize, more normal conditions returned to El Paso. In the meantime the Constitutional forces deposed Huerta, but new storm clouds loomed as factionalism emerged within the victorious alliance.[40] Desiring continued peace and reflecting on the critical years of the revolution between 1910 and 1915, the *Herald* congratulated El Pasoans for maintaining order regardless of the many provocations by both the United States government and the different Mexican revolutionary juntas that had used El Paso as headquarters. "It is a record of which El Paso has a right to be proud," the *Herald* boasted. "Nothing can happen to change the temper of the El Paso people. They are not hostile toward Mexico or Mexicans, and have never been hostile." El Pasoans had respected human rights during the period, the newspaper proudly stated, and peace and order had prevailed. Astutely understanding that El Paso's dependence on Mexican commerce required tranquility and that the city's reliance on Mexican labor necessitated harmonious race relations, the *Herald* reassured Mexican immigrant workers and political refugees of the border city's hospitality as long as they refrained from political intrigue. "To El Paso's Mexicans," it concluded,

> let it be said with the convictions of sincerity and with the consciousness of power, that to them will be extended the same protection . . . that is accorded our own people always assuming, of course, that on their part they abide by the laws and do nothing calculated to create doubt, suspicion, or hostility. So long as they remain disposed, to cooperate with us to maintain order under law, and to conserve peace and safety, they will be regarded as one with us, and they need not feel the least apprehensive of any unfortunate thing happening to disturb the friendly relations always existing. They are our guests—that is enough.[41]

But peace continued to elude Mexico and the civil war between Villa and Carranza ignited a new round of racial tensions along the frontier. Recognized by the United States in the fall of 1915, Carranza's government soon reduced Villa to guerrilla tactics in Chihuahua. Isolated and short of munitions, Villa vented his frustrations against Americans. Stopping a train from Chihuahua City, Villa's men on January 10, 1916, killed 16 American employees of ASARCO in what came to be called the Santa Ysabel Massacre. News of the incident and the arrival of the bodies in El Paso caused much excitement and unrest in the city, where many of the dead Americans had been known. Literature distributed to condemn the affair read: "Remember the Alamo, Did We Watch and Wait?" Some Americans blamed the U.S. consul in Juárez, T. T. Edwards, for the killings and charged the American diplomat with not providing sufficient protection for the Americans in Chihuahua. At a local hotel three days after the tragic event a crowd of Americans surrounded Edwards and accused him of being Villa's consul. "Go back to Juárez with the Mexicans," they shouted as the consul narrowly escaped their grasp. Demanding Edwards's removal from his post, 100 El Paso citizens sent a petition to Washington. "We will either have him removed," angrily declared one man, "or will lynch him."[42]

Although Edwards and President Wilson's policy of "watchful waiting" received their share of condemnation for the Chihuahua murders, Mexicans on both sides of the border bore the brunt of American wrath over the Santa Ysabel Massacre. After soldiers had attacked two Mexicans at Broadway and San Antonio in the downtown section on the evening of January 13, fights broke out between Americans and Mexicans in a number of saloons. Following the fisticuffs, between 25 and 50 Americans attacked every Mexican they could find on the streets. They moved in the direction of Chihuahuita and called out to others to join them. "Let's get down and clean them out," the Americans yelled. "Bleeding Mexicans lined the route," a reporter on the scene observed and estimated that close to 25 Mexicans had been injured by a crowd that had rapidly expanded. "It was reported by 10 o'clock that knives frequently were used," the *New York Times* correspondent noted, "and all ambulances in El Paso were rushing through the streets, while physicians were hurried to all parts of the city." Declaring martial law, El Paso police formed a barricade along Broadway between Overland and Second streets, blockading the major Mexican barrio, and pushed the mass of Americans calculated at between 800 and 1,000 back into the central part of the city. A number of Pershing's troops along with the National Guard also arrived to reinforce local authorities. Mayor Tom Lea together with Mexican American leaders later that evening toured Chihuahuita and reported no disturbances among the Mexican residents, who had secured themselves in their homes. "We have been patient and shown a fine wisdom for the past five years through all these distressing and harrowing experiences," the mayor commented on the crisis, "and I hope we shall not lose our heads at this late hour." Faced with El Paso's most severe racial outburst, police arrested 15 Americans for disturbing the peace. Ironically, officials likewise apprehended 8 Mexicans on the same charge as well as for carrying concealed weapons although they had been the victims of the riot. Local leaders learned afterward, to their relief, that their swift control of the situation had possibly avoided a more serious conflict as Carranza's forces in Juárez upon hearing of the attack on Mexicans across the border had threatened to intervene.[43]

No more racial problems occurred, but El Paso remained nervous

for the next several days. Consul Edwards in Juárez notified the
State Department that although conditions in the Mexican border
town remained quiet they were "feverish" in El Paso, where demands for military intervention against Mexico had been made.
In letters to the newspapers El Pasoans shared some of their anxieties
and thoughts. Four Americans, including the son of one of the men
killed at Santa Ysabel, challenged their fellow citizens to live up to
their honor and manhood by revenging the dead Americans. "Can it
be that the sons of the men who have made Americans veterans of
many wars, have no true blood," they wrote. "Let us cry out until
we avenge the murdered Americans in Mexico or completely erase
all signs of the shame and outrages from the face of our beautiful flag."
Two other Americans charged Villa with barbarism and questioned
Mexico's capacity to become civilized. Expressing their displeasure at
the ease with which Mexicans could obtain jobs in El Paso, they
complained that many Americans walked around unemployed and
unable to work because of "Mexican wages." One Mexican resident empathized and wrote that most Mexicans in the city deplored
the Santa Ysabel Massacre. "We feel ashamed that such acts are
committed in our country," he noted. "It is a disgrace to humanity
that such assassins were born." Nevertheless, the Mexican believed
that although blame could be bestowed on Villa, Carranza, and other
Mexican leaders for the prevailing anarchy across the border, in his
opinion the biggest blame fell on President Wilson for pursuing an in-
terventionist policy that had intensified bad feelings between Americans and Mexicans. In contrast to most other letter writers, one
American woman called on El Pasoans to display Christian charity
toward Villa and all Mexicans as a way of perhaps ending the conflict.
"By listening to the quiet voice within," she explained, "I have
found that we can live in heaven with Mexicans, too. Villa is a divine
soul struggling upward—through darkness, through blindness, struggling upward to the light."[44]

The *Herald*, in reply, shunned the cry for revenge and expressed
a more pragmatic though no less political opinion apparently held
by most El Paso political and business leaders. Relieved that the city's
racial violence had not led to serious fatalities or injuries, the *Herald*
strongly deplored the outbreak. It pointed out that such incidents
could only further endanger American lives in Chihuahua if Villa re-

sorted to reprisals. The newspaper expressed shock that innocent Mexicans had been attacked solely because they were Mexicans. "By such acts," it exhorted El Pasoans, "we only place ourselves on the low plane of the desperate persons in Mexico who attack Americans because they are Americans, and whose morals we therefore despise and whose punishment we all justly demand." The *Herald* concluded by reminding its readers once again of the Mexican population's importance to El Paso and the need to respect their rights:

> There are tens of thousands of persons of Mexican descent in El Paso, who are our neighbors and many of whom have been our friends; they work for us and with us, they own property here, patronize the business institutions, and take part in the life of the city. The lives, acts, thoughts, and intentions of most of these people are orderly; they are citizens, or at least residents, of El Paso and entitled to the same guarantees as any other citizens or residents. They are in no sense hostile to the United States or to Americans, and they deplore the terrors and crimes of Mexicans in Mexico, as others do.[45]

Despite the *Herald's* plea for peace and harmony, two months later on March 9 Villa raided Columbus, New Mexico, just west of El Paso and precipitated Pershing's "punitive expedition" into Chihuahua. Tension gripped El Paso once again. Mario Acevedo remembers that his father warned him at the time not to leave the house because groups of Americans had begun to attack Mexicans on Santa Fe Street. One Mexican who possessed a dark complexion escaped serious injury following the Columbus incident by claiming he was a black. "I am not a Mexican," he told pursuing Americans. "I'm a nigger, I'm a nigger."[46] The *Herald*, wishing to avoid any more racial friction, urged restraint on the part of the city's population while condemning Villa's action and approving the American intervention. Americans had no quarrel with Mexico or Carranza, the newspaper stressed, but only with Villa, and it assured Mexicans on both sides of the border of Wilson's nonbelligerent policy but defended Pershing's campaign as a police action. The *Herald* explained Washington's decision by saying that there would be no interference with Mexican military or civil authorities, and no territory would be seized.

The expedition's sole objective was to capture Villa and return him to the United States.[47] General Pershing likewise issued a statement in El Paso intended to calm apprehensions, especially among the Mexican population. "It is no time to indulge in idle theories about invasion," the American commander told reporters. "I give the Mexican people too much credit for common sense to think they will not gladly accept our aid in eliminating an international outlaw."[48] Although Villa's raid and Pershing's expedition remained the principal topic of conversation and of concern for El Pasoans, no major disturbances occurred.

To ensure no repercussions and prevent a possible Villa raid on El Paso, the War Department rushed troop reinforcements to the border. "El Paso is the most important crossing along the border," the *New York Times* emphasized. "It is not only a great railroad center, but too large a place to be left without an adequate garrison."[49] In addition, police in a two-day period rounded up, apparently without warrants, more than 200 Mexicans suspected of being Villa agents or sympathizers and deported half of them to Mexico. "Heavy guards are scattered throughout the city," one report read, "especially in the Mexican quarter."[50] Those captured included four prominent Mexicans who had previously served on Villa's staff. The Texas Rangers in the area assisted local officials and apprehended two former Villa officers on charges of conspiring to commit arson, and on April 6 El Paso detectives arrested 16 Mexicans on suspicion of being ex-supporters of Villa but released them after interrogation. Besides suspected Villistas, any Mexican using language that could be interpreted by officers as inciting rebellion stood to be detained. For example, Elías Rivera, a common laborer, faced arrest on a charge of using abusive language after police alleged that in speaking to a crowd in Chihuahuita, Rivera had urged them to return to Mexico and fight against the American intervention.[51]

Local officials also stopped the presses of Mexican newspapers in El Paso that disagreed with Pershing's action in Mexico. The police explained that they had been informed that articles attacking American policies had been printed in three Mexican dailies and consequently they had been suspended. According to the *New York Times*' reporter, the editor of the confiscated *El Paso del Norte*, a pro-Villa newspaper, had called on all Mexicans to defend themselves against "the common enemy" and had predicted that all factions in Mexico would unite if the Americans crossed the border. Three additional Mexican dailies likewise had to close due to police censorship. All six resumed publication only after agreeing not to print "political news" that would "tend to excite the Mexican people." Less than a week later, however, authorities arrested editor Emilio Valenzuela and five employees of the daily *La Constitución* besides confiscating their type and printing paper for writing articles "designed to arouse anti-American feelings among the Mexicans of the city." Since copies of these newspapers could not be found, it remains impossible to prove or disprove the charges. Yet a week earlier the *New York Times* had noted that *La Constitución* had been forced to stop its presses by local police when it had compared the American military action to the 1862 French intervention in Mexico. Appearing to be overzealous, El Paso officials maintained law and order at the apparent expense of legal rights, although federal agents on the scene repeatedly informed the State Department that no cause for alarm existed.[52]

Although no significant racial violence erupted in the months following Villa's bold raid, the prolongation of Pershing's expedition kept El Paso and the entire border region in an apprehensive state. Traveling from San Antonio to El Paso, Frank B. Elser, the special correspondent of the *New York Times*, wrote:

> Everybody is talking Villa and little else. The Columbus episode has quickened the pulse of the border and worked out a paradox. It has brought a new life to the frontier by bringing back the old. Remington died too soon. He should have seen his Southwest today. Men such as he so loved to draw, spurred and booted and with a six-shooter on their hips, clumped along the station platforms or waved a hat from behind a barb-wire fence. It is men of this type who are piloting Pershing's expedition into Mexico.[53]

On the same day that anti-American riots took place in Chihuahua City in mid-June, a small-scale "riot" occurred after a baseball game between an all-Mexican team and an American one in Washington Park. After American boys, encouraged by soldiers attending the game, had pelted the Mexican players with rocks, several American men pounced on the Mexicans including the sixty-year-old father of one athlete. No serious injuries resulted, but one player suffered a face cut when hit by a bottle, and a Mexican boy at the scene had his head gashed by a flying rock. The police, claiming that only a minor scuffle had taken place, made no arrests. The incident had no overt political importance, yet the prevailing international crisis undoubtedly influenced such racial outbursts.[54]

Tensions further increased after the battle at Carrizal, Chihuahua, between Pershing's and Carranza's troops, in which a number of Americans died. Fearing a Mexican attack on El Paso, U.S. soldiers, besides patroling the downtown area, placed artillery on Golden Hill overlooking both El Paso and Juárez and once again manned machine guns at the border crossings. Juárez citizens responded to the American maneuvers by arming themselves in preparation for a rumored invasion. In addition, El Paso police and Texas Rangers closely watched the Mexican population on the American side of the Rio Grande. At a dance in Fabens, in the lower El Paso valley, Rangers arrested Maclavio Marrujo after he had yelled "Viva Mexico and death to the gringos." Another Mexican did not fare so well at the hands of the famed Texas law officers; charging him with recruiting for Villa, the Rangers shot and wounded an eighteen-year-old Mexican at Clint, also in the lower valley. In an effort to reduce the strife the *Herald* claimed that El Paso remained secure. "El Paso feels perfectly safe," the border publication emphasized, "she feels that her own people, including all those of foreign birth within her borders, are loyal to their city and friendly to each other." As a way of maintaining that security, 65,000 American troops bivouacked in El Paso by summer's end.[55]

Unable to capture Villa and faced with American involvement in the European war, Pershing abandoned Chihuahua in early 1917, thus considerably easing tensions in El Paso and throughout the border area. Whereas Villa's foray into the United States had once again raised the specter of racial conflict, El Paso's establishment had wisely recognized the damage such an outbreak would cause the border city and hence successfully deterred violence albeit with a strong military presence and the possible violation of legal rights. The *Herald* clearly explained the detrimental consequences to El Paso of racial disorders. According to the newspaper the "selfish interests" of both El Paso and Juárez required peace. Those interests for the American city involved the economic importance of the Mexican working class. The city's development as a major commercial center between the United States and Mexico also demanded peaceful conditions. "Many El Pasoans, especially those who have come here in recent years," the *Herald* informed its audience, "do not seem to realize that this city's prosperity, growth, economic power, financial and commercial prestige, and social welfare depend most largely on our retaining reasonable, just, and friendly relations with the Spanish speaking population within our own borders, and with the neighbors of the southern republic." Acknowledging the pre-American presence of Mexicans in El Paso and their cultural influence along the border, the *Herald* pointed out an obvious fact: "The Spanish speaking people are as much a permanent fixture here and hereabouts as the mountains." Perhaps the *Herald's* strongest argument for racial harmony concerned the future economic contributions of a vast local Mexican population to the growth and prosperity of El Paso. "The *Herald* firmly believes," the newspaper concluded, "that these people have, potentially, tremendous value to these communities, which has never been clearly understood, has never been developed, has never been directed or trained, has never been used, has never been acknowledged, has never been conserved. That we have not made more useful and contented and progressive citizens out of this element is chiefly our own fault, not theirs."[56]

Pershing's withdrawal ended El Paso's intense experience with revolutionary politics. Although still faced with scattered rebellion, Carranza's faction dominated the Mexican political scene and institutionalized its victory through the Constitution of 1917 with its promises of representative government, land redistribution, labor reforms, and the nationalization of the Mexican economy. For several years the scene of political intrigues, revolutionary plotting, and gun running, El Paso and its involvement with the revolution had been reduced by 1917 to efforts by political refugees to peacefully return to their homeland.[57] The revolution had affected every sector of the El Paso community, but its largest impact fell on the local Mexican population. Mexican Americans, faced with a major test of their loyalties, had been placed on the defensive and had reacted by strongly pledging their allegiance to the "Stars and Stripes." The immigrants and refugees, on the other hand, bore the brunt of the revolution's dislocating impact as well as the racial animosity generated along the border by the civil war. One historian has correctly labeled the increased anti-Mexican sentiment in the United States during this period as the Brown Scare.[58] Despite the dangers, many Mexicans not only concerned themselves with events in *la patria* but supported in their own small ways the different revolutionary juntas operating out of El Paso. The Mexican Revolution not only exposed El Paso's unavoidable ties with Mexico but had clearly revealed the nationalist consciousness of the Mexican immigrant population. To the immigrant generation of 1910 politics meant the revolution and one's country meant Mexico.

10

Border Culture

Working among themselves as manual laborers and living in segregated barrios adjacent to their homeland, Mexican immigrants in El Paso and throughout the Southwest, like other newcomers to the United States, maintained native customs that helped provide a sense of community. As one historian has correctly written of the northern movement of Mexicans: "Mexican immigration bore little resemblance to the 'uprooting' experience which Oscar Handlin depicted as characteristic of European immigration. Indeed, continuity rather than alienation, marginality and social disorganization, characterized Mexican immigration."[1] Yet, within El Paso's large Mexican population, cultural differences also existed. Mexican Americans, educated and sophisticated political refugees, and the mass of poor immigrants comprised diverse cultural enclaves although they were linked by a common language and certain Mexican traditions. Moreover, cultural continuity coexisted with some cultural change. The immigrants' adjustment to new working conditions, especially in urban areas, their relationship with more Americanized Mexican Americans, and the impact of certain gringo institutions such as the schools introduced a gradual acculturation. Cultural change among Mexican immigrants, especially children, likewise occurred because, as Ernesto Galarza indicates, working class immigration brought "no formal institutions to perpetuate its culture."[2] Cultural continuity as well as cultural change, the two in time developing a Mexican border culture, can be detected in the family, recreational activities, religion, and voluntary associations.

The family represented the most basic cultural institution transferred by Mexican immigrants and was the most resistant barrier to American assimilation. Besides young single males who entered the

197

United States seeking work, many families also arrived. The Dillingham Commission report of 1911 observed that a high percentage of
Mexican laborers in western industries had brought their wives
from Mexico. According to the commission, 81.5 percent of Mexican
railroad shop workers in the survey reported their wives in the
United States. Investigators discovered a similar condition in urban-
related work. Sixty percent of Mexicans employed as construction
workers by street railways stated they had their wives with them.[3] Although no substantial research has been done on the composition
and nature of working-class or peasant families in Mexico during the
late nineteenth and early twentieth centuries, nevertheless it appears
that the family formed a strong social and economic unit. Galarza
in his autobiography, *Barrio Boy*, recalls that his family in rural Nay-
arit included not only his mother (who had divorced his father prior
to Galarza's birth) but also his aunt, three uncles, and two cousins.
In the Galarza household the men went to labor in the fields during
the day while the women and children performed the housework
and cooking.[4]

Leaving Mexico and entering the United States, the Mexican
family, rather than weakened by the immigration process, appears
to have remained strong and retained its native character. A sample
of the 1900 manuscript census for El Paso reveals that the large
majority of Mexican immigrant households were either nuclear or
extended (see table 10.1). Out of 152 immigrant household units in
the sample, 56 percent were nuclear families living by themselves or
in an augmented relationship with nonrelated household residents,
such as boarders. In addition 13 percent were extended households
(nuclear families living with one or more relatives). Indeed, more
Mexican immigrant families lived in nuclear households than did the
non-Spanish surnamed. Perhaps reflecting more individual mobility,
a large percentage of non-Spanish surnames were recorded as single-
person households than Mexican immigrants. On the other hand,
more broken homes could be found among the Mexican immigrant
population, especially involving a mother and her children; however,
it is possible that in some cases husbands were not recorded because
they had jobs outside the city. By far most Mexican Americans
lived in nuclear households, although many apparently took in
boarders.[5] Because the 1910 and 1920 manuscript censuses are not

Table 10.1   Household Composition, El Paso, 1900 (Percentages rounded)

	M	MA	NSS
Nuclear family households			
Husband, wife, and children	38%	45%	29%
Husband, wife, no children	7	4	10
Broken families			
Husband and children	3	0	3
Wife and children	19	0	9
Single-person households	7	4	20
Extended-family households[a]	13	16	5
Augmented-family households[b]	11	30	19
Extended–augmented family households[c]	0	0	2
Total (393)	(152)	(24)	(217)

Source: Manuscript Census, 1900. See chap. 4, n. 27, for sample method.
Note: M, Mexican National; MA, Mexican American; NSS, non-Spanish surnamed.
[a]Nuclear family living with one or more relatives.
[b]Nuclear family living with nonfamily members in the same household, such as lodgers.
[c]Nuclear family living with both relatives and nonfamily members.

yet available for scholars, no comparison can be made. It is conceivable that over this 20-year period, the number of extended households among Mexican immigrants grew as more relatives arrived once a pattern of chain migration had been set, especially from the northern Mexican states. Jess López, for example, who now resides in Santa Barbara, remembers that when he left Mexico as a young boy and entered El Paso in 1910 the entire family crossed the border, including his parents, brothers and sisters, paternal grandparents, and his maternal grandmother.[6] Moreover, in another study of a Mexican immigrant community, one scholar remarks that chain migration from certain towns in Mexico reinforced not only native customs, values, and institutions but also the extended family and the traditional Mexican kinship system (*compadrazgo*).[7] It is likely that among Mexican immigrants in El Paso, and other parts of the United States, the movement from their native land to another country served to increase kinship ties as a way of finding jobs and temporary homes and of dealing with what one historian calls "critical life situations": sickness, unemployment, death, or some other form of disaster.[8]

Although some Mexican women in El Paso and throughout the

urban Southwest contributed to household incomes by taking in
wash or lodgers, no disintegration took place in the traditional
pattern of men being the chief wage earners and women doing household work (of course, certain lower-class women in Mexico were
wageworkers). The 1900 El Paso census sample shows that no
mothers and almost no daughters, most being too young, worked
outside the home in an immigrant family headed by the father
(although no data exist, some women may have worked part-time).[9]
Nevertheless, the necessity of more women having to become wageworkers over the years no doubt affected family patterns. This
appears to be true as daughters grew to working age throughout the
region. According to a Los Angeles survey taken by Paul S. Taylor
in 1928, the majority of Mexican women took jobs in industry because "of poverty, due either to the irregular work of the male
members of the family, or to the combination of large families, low
wages, high rents." However, the entrance of women into the job
market constituted, as Taylor put it, a process "contrary to their customs and traditions." Taylor believed that "such radical changes" in
the daily lives of Mexican women could not help but produce cultural changes, especially within the family. The University of California scholar observed both older as well as younger women in
industrial jobs, but he detected more profound alterations in the
habits of younger Mexicans. Not only did they adapt to the work
routine better, but what little education they secured in American
schools, especially the learning of English, made them more productive and efficient. "They look upon some sort of industrial work"
Taylor wrote, "as soon as they have completed the minimum amount
of schooling as the natural course of events." Besides acquiring some
new material and cultural tastes that they introduced into the home,
by the 1920s young Mexican working women appear to have begun
to exhibit a desire for greater independence from strict family
practices. "Her parents are apt to be ignored," Taylor stressed, "she
tends to break away from the old custom of parental authority."[10]
Whether Taylor's observations would also pertain to El Paso cannot
be determined due to a lack of similar studies in the border city. Certainly, young Mexican women who worked in the laundries and
garment factories, and possibly even as domestics, may have displayed
parallel characteristics.

The economic necessity for Mexican women to find jobs likewise appears to have challenged to a degree the traditional male-dominated Mexican family structure. Although perhaps Mexican fathers could more easily accept their daughters than their wives working outside the home, a pattern not uncommon in Mexico, still Taylor noticed that Mexican men resented women working or wanting to work. One man stated that women should not work because that was a man's duty, whereas women's consisted of keeping house. Another husband told Taylor that he could not allow his wife to work because his friends would then think he could not adequately provide for his family. Another insisted that his wife could not have a job outside the home since no women in his family had ever worked; moreover, it was neither necessary nor correct.[11] The pressure of higher living costs north of the border, however, eventually forced many Mexican women into the job market. While more research needs to be conducted into the full impact that this process had on family culture, it seems that traditional patterns slowly changed over the years. One Mexican man who had lived in the United States for over 25 years told anthropologist Manuel Gamio in the 1920s that he disliked the transformation Mexican women underwent in the Southwest. According to Carlos Ibáñez, he disliked American laws that allowed women too many rights and made them less subordinate to men. "Now the Mexican women who come here," Ibáñez emphasized, "also take advantage of the laws and want to be like the American women." Because of the change, Ibáñez concluded that if he ever married it would be in Mexico.[12] Yet accommodation in family patterns among Mexican immigrants and their children, rather than disruption, should perhaps be stressed. As Virginia Yans-McLaughlin points out in her study of Italian immigrant families in Buffalo, acculturation did not necessarily lead to a breakdown of traditional male authority in the family. Emphasizing that strong cultural traditions in addition to employment patterns sustained male authority, Yans-McLaughlin writes: "The point is that male authority did not depend entirely upon fulfillment of economic obligations; therefore, when a woman co-opted the male's economic function in whole or in part by becoming a wage-earner, she did not necessarily obtain greater bargaining power and so tip the balance of family authority in her favor."[13] What can be concluded is that the Mexican immigrant family's cultural accommodation, resulting primarily from the socializing roles of more Americanized sons and daughters, appears to have laid the foundation for a second and third generation Mexican American family structure exhibiting many of the values and characteristics common to a middle-class Anglo-Saxon family.

Outside the family it seems that the majority of Mexican immigrants did not actively participate in secondary institutions such as mutual societies, Mexican patriotic groups, or church organizations. Most Mexican immigrant workers, although they may have belonged to some of these groups and attended certain of their functions, apparently did not have the time or energy to be active members. One historian correctly observes of black working-class migrants to Cleveland in the late nineteenth century that their lives, unlike the middle and upper classes, remained simple due to a lack of options.[14] The same can be said of most Mexicans. Within the family Mexicans found their primary security for dealing with the problems of everyday life. Consequently, much Mexican popular culture in El Paso and throughout the Southwest centered on family recreational activities and existed apart from particular institutions, which tended to be under the direction of more prosperous immigrants, political refugees, and some Mexican Americans.

Within the family, Mexicans preserved many native cultural traditions that aided them in their transition to a new American setting by providing a familiar cultural environment. It is difficult to arrive at an accurate picture of family life in El Paso, but anthropologist Manuel Gamio noted certain customs being practiced in the late 1920s by Mexican immigrant families in El Paso and other southwestern locations. Gamio observed that despite the fact that Mexican immigrants accepted American material goods such as housing, clothing, domestic utensils, and machinery, they still retained earlier popular customs. These included folklore, songs and ballads, birthday celebrations, saints' days, baptisms, weddings, and funerals in the traditional style. Owing to poverty, a lack of physicians in the barrios plus traditional customs the Mexican scholar witnessed the continued use of medicinal herbs by both Mexican immigrants and Mexican Americans. "In almost all parts of America where there

are Mexicans and Mexican-Americans," he stressed, "there are
Mexican drug stores in which there is a great sale of every sort of
medicinal plant." Mexicans along the border could also find remedies
for their physical and emotional ailments by visiting Mexican healers
known as *curanderos*. "I cure by means of herbs," one *curandera* in
Tucson informed Gamio, "but I never promise to cure this one or
that one because that is something of God. . . . I have cured many
Mexicans of syphilis and tuberculosis and other diseases. I have also
helped to assist at childbirth many times, when the doctors have
let me."[15] The existence of such popular traditions illustrates what
scholars have discovered in studies of migration patterns: the persis-
tance of earlier preindustrial cultural practices within an industrializing society—or what one sociologist refers to as an "urban village."[16]

Immigrant families interviewed by Gamio further acknowledged
that for the most part they continued to cook Mexican style. "I
don't suffer in the matter of food," one woman told him in Los
Angeles, "for my mother cooks at home as if we were in Mexico.
There are some dishes which are different but we generally eat Mexican style and rice and beans are almost never lacking from our
table." According to a report by one of Gamio's associates, however,
Mexican families in certain areas purchased items such as canned
chile, canned sauces, and canned tomatoes from California. Obtaining
food processed in the United States often led to complaints about
the inadequacy and poor quality of American products in the cooking of Mexican dishes. "The food stuffs, besides costing a lot,"
another woman informed Gamio, "are no good for making good
Mexican food . . . so that it might be said that the food is half-Mexi-
can and half-American, being neither the one nor the other."[17]
Most Mexican families in El Paso avoided this dietary problem by
apparently purchasing much of their food in Juárez.

Mexican folk customs both inside and outside the family included a variety of oral traditions. Although evidence of this literature's origin is difficult to determine, some of it Mexicans created
in Texas and other southwestern states. Oral literature included
cuentos (Mexican tales), children's stories, legends, ghost and goblin
stories such as "La Llorona" (The Weeper) and "Los Duendes"
(The Goblins), and *dichos* (sayings and proverbs). Based on the
Spanish romance, perhaps the best recognized form of oral literature

has been the songs and ballads called *corridos*, which the Mexicans sang in Spanish with their families and fellow-workers. "The songs . . . are a people's heritage," Mexican American folklorist Américo Paredes stresses, "their unselfconscious record of themselves, alien for the most part to documents and books." Singing in the family involved songs sung by mothers to their children or while doing housework. Singing was part of the evening's entertainment along with prose narratives, riddles, and games. All family members participated in these performances and the singing ranged from corridos to children's songs. If a guitar was available, some songs would be accompanied by music, usually those sung by the men. Some would be preceded by a prose narrative. "The father had the role of oral historian in the family," Paredes notes, "the mother being more likely to specialize in legends and tales of the supernatural." One Mexican emphasized in the 1920s that his family always played Mexican music in the home "so that one doesn't feel the change." Besides family singing, music and songs were important at extended family gatherings, weddings, and fiestas celebrating anniversaries. Finally, men often sang at *cantinas* (bars) and usually in a much louder and boisterous fashion than done in the home.[18]

While the song form remained Mexican and in Spanish, the content increasingly centered on an immigrant experience as well as sentiments toward events in Mexico. "The 'corridos' are," Gamio wrote, "of all the songs collected, nearest to the human-interest story of the popular newspaper. Like the human-interest story, they express the interests and attitudes of the people."[19] During the Mexican Revolution hundreds of corridos appeared about the battles and heroes of the civil war. One corrido apparently written in either Juárez or El Paso commemorated Francisco Madero's victory over Díaz at Juárez. "At one time," Paredes explains, "when the events were fresh in everyone's mind, it probably was sung all up and down the Texas–Mexican borderline." Entitled "La Toma de Ciudad Juárez (The Capture of Ciudad Juárez) this corrido expresses pride in Madero's victory and in his men's courage: [translated]

Mexico is very happy, people by the thousands are giving thanks;
I will begin with Durango then Torreon and Ciudad Juárez;
where the blood of government soldiers was seen to flow.

Girls of Ciudad Juárez, you were greatly startled to find your-
selves in so many skirmishes, in so many battles,
to see the 'maderistas' setting up their machine guns.

. . .

Comet [Haley's], how true was the prophesy that you had been
announcing:
To see the 'maderistas' ruling in this land, Porfirio out of
a job and on his way to Europe.[20]

A few years later a very popular corrido dealt with the imprison-
ment of a Mexican contraband smuggler in the El Paso area. Transported out of the border city and on his way to Leavenworth, the
smuggler wonders whether he will ever see his family again. And on
the train, vowing never to smuggle again, he warns his countrymen
to avoid landing in American jails, for once in, all your friends forget
you: [translated]

Smuggling is very nice, you can make a lot of money;
but friends, do not forget what a prisoner must
    suffer.

He who will not believe it, let him try it for himself;
let them have a go at smuggling, and they'll see where
    they will end.

On the eve of St. Lawrence's day, about eleven
    in the morning,
we stepped on the threshold of the penitentiary.

Mother of mine, I leave you a sigh and an embrace;
this is the ballad of the contraband of El Paso.[21]

Many Mexican songs and corridos expressed the hardships of
life in the United States and a hope that the immigrant experience
would be short. The return to Mexico remained the goal of most
Mexicans. Based on an actual event, the corrido of "Aurelio Pompa"

relates the hanging of a Mexican in California for the murder of an American, although Pompa claimed self-defense. Twenty thousand fellow Mexicans petitioned for his pardon, but the execution took place with Pompa exclaiming: [translated]

> Farewell, my friends, farewell,
> my village;
> Dear mother, cry no more,
> Tell my race not to come here,
> For here they will suffer; there
> is no pity here.
> The jailor asked him:
> 'Were you Spanish?' and he
> answered,
> 'I am a Mexican and proud of
> being so
> Although they deny me a pardon.'
> This is the story of a compatriot
> who four years ago came there
> and through misfortune on the
> same date
> Died in a dreadful way in a
> prison.[22]

In addition to music enjoyed in the home and in cantinas, Mexicans in El Paso could take advantage of another native cultural tradition: Sunday band concerts in the plaza or park. As early as 1893 Santiago Olguín Loredo advertised in a Spanish-language newspaper that his orchestra played in an El Paso park. One year later, apparently depleted of his musicians, Olguín Loredo appealed for other musicians in order to organize a band to perform Mexican music. With the increase in Mexican immigration, larger and more sophisticated concert bands appeared. The *Herald* observed in 1916 that Rito Medina's band would present an outdoor summer concert, although no mention of the location was made, but presumably it may have taken place in the downtown plaza. The following year the most popular local band consisted of the Mexican-American Band directed by Raymundo S. González. Perhaps the most respected

Mexican musical group in El Paso during this era was Concha's Band,
led by Trinidad Concha. A former assistant director of Porfirio Díaz's
touring band, Concha arrived in El Paso around 1896 and formed
his first border city ensemble. By 1907 Concha's Band had 40 members and performed at numerous gatherings, including political
rallies of the Democratic Ring. According to the *Times*, the band
members included wageworking El Paso citizens. The highlight of
Concha's Band occurred in 1911, when they serenaded Madero,
Villa, Orozco, and the revolutionary forces camped on the Mexican
side of the Rio Grande across from the El Paso Smelter. Enter-
taining both Mexican and American audiences, bands such as Concha's played mainly European compositions that over the years had
become Mexicanized. More sophisticated in their selection of classical
tunes, which were apparently intended to appeal to Mexican as well
as American bourgeois tastes, these local bands and their music
stood in sharp contrast to the folksongs composed by Mexican
workers themselves and indicated cultural and class segmentation
within El Paso's Mexican population.[23]

Mexicans in El Paso also patronized concerts performed by
touring Mexican artists. The *Times* acknowledged the arrival in 1894
of the Mexican Female Orchestra, which had been touring the United
States. "On arriving at the smelter where jacals, burros and little
Mexicans were to be seen in abundance," the newspaper informed its
readers, "the members of the troupe were delighted and did not
hesitate to express their satisfaction at again seeing familiar scenes."
Several years later in 1916 the Mexican consul arranged for a Mexican
orquesta típica to present an outdoor concert attended by many
Mexicans from Juárez, El Paso political refugees, and Americans. Including favorite Mexican tunes, the concert proved to be a large success. "There was nothing but the most friendly feeling," the *Herald*
reporter wrote, "and the Mexican part of the audience seemed im-
mensely pleased that their native music and the musicians from their
country, were so much appreciated."[24]

Musical variety shows called *tandas de variedades* by Mexican
theaters in south El Paso proved to be popular after 1910. For 10 to
15 cents a performance Mexican workers could sit in the galleries
and be entertained by touring Mexican showpeople. "The only place
in El Paso where variety shows are performed in Spanish," boasted the

Estrella Theater.[25] Although Mexican theaters throughout the Southwest initially presented both a film and a tanda, in time, according to one critic, the moving pictures superseded both Spanish-speaking vaudeville and the legitimate theater.[26] Legitimate theater in El Paso meant that for the most part Mexican theaters appealed to the middle-class tastes of wealthier and more prominent Mexican political refugees. For example, in 1915 the El Paso Theater announced various opera performances by the touring Ricardo de la Vega Company. Included in their repertoire was "The Susana Caste" (La Casta Susana), which had been requested "by the most cultured Mexican society of El Paso." The still operating Colón Theater on South El Paso Street opened in 1919 by presenting the opera *Rigoletto*. Besides operas, these same variety houses offered touring Mexican actors such as Virginia Fabregas's troupe and the Mercedes Navarro Company, which offered plays by European playwrights.[27] "She is the first actress with reason," a Mexican drama historian wrote of Virginia Fabregas in 1932, "not of what the theater was then but of what it would be later, and consequently she is the first modern actress in Mexico."[28] In a study of an early Mexican troupe in the Southwest, one scholar emphasizes the imported as well as bourgeois character of border drama:

> The repertory contained 93 plays from foreign (i.e., non-Mexican) stages—1 by a Belgian, 2 by Germans, 3 by Italians, 7 by Frenchmen, and 80 by Spaniards. Fifty-three plays are by Mexican authors. As to the plays themselves, 84 are tragedies, dramas or melodramas and 62 are comedies, the majority are Romantic in style. Only 18 were not produced in Mexico City before the troupe brought them out: these may well have been commissioned of local authors by the managers.[29]

Although it cannot be determined if Mexican workers in large numbers attended the operas or plays, drama for them often took the form of religious plays performed during certain church celebrations such as the Feast of Our Lady of Guadalupe. "Not a single year passes," El Paso church historian Cleofas Calleros later wrote, "without a religious drama being performed and repeated two or three times."[30] Nevertheless, the existence of a Mexican "high

culture" in El Paso, as expressed through the legitimate theater and
the opera, served only to increase the social and cultural distance
between the working community and the more prominent Mexican
businessmen, professionals, and especially middle-class political
refugees.

Dancing parties in the barrio where drinking occurred were
another form of entertainment for the Mexican workers and their
families. Dance halls operated in El Paso, primarily in the red-light
district on Utah Street bordering Chihuahuita, but no evidence exists
that Mexicans attended in large numbers.[31] Instead dance parties in
their own jacales and tenements represented a less expensive diversion
and way of having a good time. Yet officials, who desired a "sober
and industrious" Mexican population, at times frowned on the
Mexicans' attempt to dance and drink. On one occasion in 1906 El
Paso police arrested two Mexican men and a Mexican woman for
disturbing the peace at a dance on Sixth Street. Evidence presented
at their trial tried to prove that much whiskey had been available
at the fiesta. Mrs. Durán, one of the defendants, acknowledged the
presence of the liquor. "Why of course everybody knows," she explained, "that one is going to drink and be jolly at a dance, drink
whiskey and wine." In an attempt to find her guilty of drunkenness,
the prosecution charged Mrs. Durán with having drunk too much at
the dance. "Yes," she replied, "but I had a right too [sic]. I was
an invited guest." The court found the Mexican woman innocent
but fined one of the men $5.[32] After 1910 the wealthier political
refugees sponsored, in contrast to the workers' dances and parties,
numerous balls in Liberty Hall, El Paso's foremost concert hall.
Social clubs organized by the refugees for such functions included
the Círculo Latino, the Centro Cultural "Porfirio Díaz," the Club
Lerdo de Tejada, and the Club Progresista.[33]

Outside the home, Mexicans patronized various other forms of
entertainment and recreation. Men visited Mexican bars, pool halls,
and gambling establishments in both El Paso and Juárez. At the
turn of the century, some Mexicans sponsored horse races in Washington Park with attendance from not only the city but the surrounding area as well. On its visits to the border the circus stood
out as a special treat for Mexican children and their parents. The
Times recorded in 1887 that many Mexicans as well as Americans

had attended John Robinson's Great Circus in back of the Santa Fe depot. Elephants, camels, and other strange beasts, a reporter observed, captured the attention of the Mexican spectators. Mexicans from the adjacent territory also came in large numbers. They camped next to the circus tents, the *Times* man wrote, and everyone spent their *dinero* freely. Mexicans along with Americans eagerly awaited the arrival of such special attractions as the Ringling Brothers' "Greatest Show on Earth" and Barnum and Bailey's circus.[34] Besides American circuses, small Mexican traveling shows with acrobats and sideshows called *carpas* visited El Paso and performed in Chihuahuita. According to one Mexican American critic, these carpas included improvised satirical skits. "The brief, topical skits of la carpa," he proposes, "with their focus on physical movement and rapid verbal gymnastics are the progenitors of today's [Chicano] 'actos.' "[35]

Mexicans also spent their limited leisure time at spectator sports that helped distract their minds from homesickness, work, and harsh living conditions. Bullfights in Juárez, for example, were a cultural link with la patria. Boxing matches on both sides of the border enticed many males. Mexican boxers such as Benny Chávez and Mexican Americans like lightweight Aurelio Herrera held special attraction for the Mexican fans. By 1900 Mexicans also began to show an interest in American baseball. In addition to its attraction as a spectator event, some Mexicans, mostly Mexican Americans, organized baseball teams of their own. The Internationals stood out as the earliest and most popular Mexican baseball team in the border city. With an all Mexican lineup and playing against Anglo-American teams, the Internationals proved to be one of the finest clubs in El Paso for several years and played games throughout the Southwest. Sportswriters considered the Mexican American players among the finest athletes. José "Curly" Villarreal, playing for a local team in 1917, was regarded as the best pitcher in the city league. One writer commented that with Curly on the pitching mound "it is a safe bet that a large number of Mexican fans will be out Sunday to see their favorite in action."[36]

The allure of American baseball for Mexicans transcended the border and began to have a cultural impact in Mexico. "Baseball is showing promise," the *Times* proudly reported in 1908, "of becoming the national game of Mexico as well as the United States." Admitting that other foreign sports such as cricket, field hockey, and polo had some following in the neighboring republic, the *Times* believed that those cultural imports could not compare with the "grand old game." The newspaper subjectively concluded that the sport physically suited the Mexicans due to their "natural quickness." Moreover, it recognized the language influence that baseball had on Mexicans with the acceptance of baseball terms such as "You're out." The *Times* further understood the political objective American baseball served in Mexico. Baseball would create a sympathetic link between Americans and Mexicans. Two men cheering for the same team, it emphasized, would find it more difficult to disagree on other matters. At the same time that the United States had become Mexico's principal trade partner and investor, the *Times* boasted that south of the border American baseball had outdistanced British, French, German, and other European sports. The border publication predicted that it would be only a matter of time before the "better classes" in Mexico would stop bullfighting and then baseball would become the national sport. "When the mob can no longer have it [bullfighting]," the *Times* stressed, "baseball will be the national game from Central America to the Great Lakes."[37]

In spite of strong Mexican cultural influences in El Paso owing to increased Mexican immigration and the city's proximity to the border, Mexicans underwent subtle cultural changes. After 1910, for example, they faced the acculturating influence of American mass culture through the silent movies. Although it does not appear that the early movie houses such as the Crawford, the Grand, the Little Wigwam, and the Bijou specifically excluded Mexicans, the attendance of Mexicans at the movies grew when several Mexican theaters opened by the period of World War I. The International Amusement Company of El Paso, owned and managed by Mexican businessmen including Mexican American politico Frank Alderete, operated seven theaters in the border city. These included the Alcázar, the Eureka, the Hidalgo, the Paris, the Iris, and Rex movie houses on South El Paso Street.[38] By 1917, these theaters showed some films produced in Mexico but for the most part Mexican audiences paid 6 or 11 cents admission, depending on where one sat, to see American movies featuring such stars as Charlie Chaplin, Mary Pickford, and

Fatty Arbuckle. "Regardless of what some may say," *La Patria*
commented in reviewing a Chaplin film at the Teatro Rex, "Carlos
Chaplin is a magnificent artist; he is not a vulgar clown, but rather
a refined and competent comic actor, whose every gesture, every grace-
ful pose, brings forth joy not only for children, but for adults."[39]

Besides exposing Mexicans to some American material and cultural values and mores, the movies also may have influenced their
ability to understand some English. Mexicans employed by the movie
houses translated English subtitles to Spanish ones, which appeared
at the bottom of the screen below the original dialogue. American
slang was no problem, remarked a *Times* reporter, for the translators
of slapstick comedies screened at Mexican theaters. Even Americans
studying Spanish took advantage of the process and visited Mexican
theaters to improve their Spanish reading ability. The reporter further noted that the technique of imposing the Spanish translation
on the films had been invented by a Mexican employee of the International Amusement Company and "is now in use wherever
American films are used for Spanish-speaking audiences."[40] Guillermo Balderas recalls that his own brother Eduardo worked as a
translator in one of the Mexican movie houses. "These were 'silent
movies,'" Balderas remembers, "that were translated into Spanish."[41]
By the 1920s American movies were an important acculturating
agent, especially on the first generation native born, on both sides
of the border. As one Mexican immigrant explained in a corrido,
Hollywood films had enticed him to leave Mexico for the "promised
land":

> I dreamed in my youth of being a movie star
> And one of these days I came to visit Hollywood.[42]

For Mexican immigrants, Catholicism provided a familiar cultural
environment as well as institutional support for their adjustment
north of the border. The Catholic Church in El Paso, under the control of Irish Americans, recognized quite early that it would have to
establish separate facilities for its Mexican members. Consequently, it
organized Mexican parishes in the barrios to serve the particular
religious and social needs of the immigrants. Unlike many national
churches in the United States, however, those in El Paso were not

staffed, for the most part, by Mexican priests, of whom there was an apparent shortage in the Southwest, but by Italian and American clergy. As a result the Church not only took into consideration Mexican cultural traditions but also became an agent of Americanization among its parishioners, especially those families, many of them political refugees, who could afford to send their children to Catholic schools. Still, the mass of Mexican immigrants retained their popular religious beliefs and practices by transferring them across the border. Regardless of economic or political backgrounds, first generation immigrants and political refugees, through their reestablishment of spiritual societies common in Mexico as well as the reenactment of native Mexican religious celebrations, successfully maintained cultural continuity and helped create a sense of community in the barrios.[43]

As an institution, the Catholic Church in El Paso pursued a bicultural approach in its treatment of Mexican immigrants. The southside parochial schools, for example, under the direction of the American Sisters of Loretto emphasized, as one part of their curriculum, the Americanization of their students and attempted to change what they considered to be the Mexicans' bad cultural habits. Sister Magdalen Dietz, who arrived as the first principal of Sacred Heart School when it opened in 1892, later wrote in her diary:

> My first experience at the Sacred Heart was with 80 over-grown Mexican boys, some of them wearing mustaches, unkempt, untidy, with shirt tails hanging out. They knew absolutely nothing of order or discipline. After a morning or two, I managed to explain to them that three signals of the bell would be given. Accordingly at the next dismissal I saw the boys leaping from every window. They were *passing out.* I had not thought to state they were to pass out *through the door.*[44]

In addition to a basic curriculum emphasizing religious and academic subjects with some industrial and domestic training, Sacred Heart School presented performances displaying both the talents of young Mexicans as well as the influences of American middle-class culture. The *Times* reported in 1895 that Sacred Heart School students would offer a musical and dramatic entertainment at the old stone church on North Oregon Street. Mainly performed in English, the school's closing exercise in 1904 took place at Myar's Opera House, where a large audience assembled. According to the *Times* critic, the entertainment not only proved to be interesting but also reflected great credit on the nuns who taught at Sacred Heart. The best acts included the singing of "The Poor Old Tramps" by a male choir and an instrumental performance by the Mandolin Club that "was rendered without a single discord, and gave promise that El Paso will have a number of skillful musicians, who, with light touch, will call forth the music that stirs men's souls." Some of the girls who presented a drama in three acts entitled "The Little Waiters" received "round upon round of applause, and demonstrated the fact that several of the young ladies had real dramatic ability." Impressed, the *Times* gave credit to the students' teachers and praised the Catholic Church for its work among the Mexican children of the city. The performance had demonstrated, the paper concluded, "that there is an efficient and practical movement on foot to educate the Catholic youths and young girls of El Paso and teach them how to become good citizens and dutiable daughters and faithful wives."[45]

Yet English and middle-class American customs at Sacred Heart shared the curriculum with Spanish and Mexican cultural traditions. Cleofas Calleros, who attended Sacred Heart during the first decade of the century, remembered that although there were only two Mexican teachers in a faculty of ten, both English and Spanish were used in instruction along with American and Mexican history. Years later, lecturing to the 1919 graduating girls of Sacred Heart, the Italian pastor of the parish encouraged them to adopt the best of other cultures but to never forget who they were: young Catholic Mexican girls, who were obliged to follow Christ and, as Mexicans, to conserve the beautiful customs and traditions of *la raza*.[46] Hence, Sacred Heart as well as the other Mexican parochial schools served a two-fold purpose. They helped transmit Mexican ethnicity and, at the same time, provided lessons in English and American culture in order to assist students to adjust and hopefully succeed in the United States.

Next to Sacred Heart, the religious and cultural activities of St. Ignatius Church at Park and Second perhaps best exemplified the Church's interest in the Mexicans' adjustment. For the spiritual needs of its members, St. Ignatius sponsored a variety of religious groups popular in Mexico. In 1905 some women formed the League of the Sacred Heart and the Congregation of the Daughters of Mary (Congregación de las Hijas de María). That same year a group of young people and children organized the Congregation of San Luis Gonzaga as a prayer union for youth. Care of the church sacristy led to the beginning of the Altar Society. Still other parishioners, expecially women, belonged to additional religious associations such as the Society of Good Death (Buena Muerte), the Society of Our Lady of Guadalupe, the Society of Divine Providence, and the Association of Christian Mothers. Besides their specific devotions, many of these organizations assisted in the more popular religious ceremonies among the Mexican working class such as the Feast of Our Lady of Guadalupe and, of course, at Christmas, when parishioners performed the Shepherds' Play (Los Pastores). The Corpus Christi procession held every June, however, was the most impressive popular religious feast day, clearly fostering a communal spirit among the entire Mexican population of El Paso. Although this event centered around Sacred Heart Church, all Mexican parishes participated. In 1919, for example, between 10,000 and 20,000 Mexicans marched in the annual procession with thousands more watching, making the *Revista Católica*, the Spanish-language Jesuit newspaper in the city, declare that the Mexican colony saw Corpus Christi as an ethnic holiday.[47]

Like other immigrant parishes in the United States, St. Ignatius, through the work of some of its members, especially women, offered a number of social services to the Mexican population. The Centro de la Unión Católica de San José provided free medical care with the aid of El Paso physicians. Started in 1903 at Sacred Heart, the organization moved in 1914 to a building at Third and Tornillo, where it assisted the members of St. Ignatius. It also began another branch at Guardian Angel School in East El Paso by 1919.[48] Besides medical attention, one of the major problems for many Mexican mothers in El Paso had been what to do with their young children while they worked. Some left them with other relatives or friends, but many mothers found it difficult to do so. As a result women from St. Ignatius, assisted by the pastor, Father R. P. C. Tranchese, organized in 1918 a day-care nursery, the Asilo Guadalupano, at 405 Park.

Under the initial direction of a board of directors composed of several Mexican women, the church transferred care of the Asilo one year later to the Sisters of the Sacred Heart of the Poor, who arrived from Puebla, Mexico. Although the Asilo listed more than 200 members in 1919, its limited facilities could care for only 36 children. In order to raise funds for a new building the nursery held *jamaicas* [carnivals] and other fund-raising events and finally in 1922 moved into larger quarters at the corner of Fifth and Virginia. As another form of assistance to the neighborhood, in 1908 some women from St. Ignatius began distributing flour to the poor. Finally, church members raised funds for the destitute by sponsoring suppers such as the first enchilada dinner ever held at St. Ignatius, which netted $60.05.[49]

St. Ignatius also provided educational services through its parochial school, which began in 1905 with two Sisters of Loretto and one lay teacher, Señora Isabel Cordona Buchanan, who taught first-year Spanish. By 1913 enrollment expanded and classes had to be held in the church building. In addition to the school, the church offered night classes one year later for adults in English, Spanish, arithmetic, chemistry, physics, and sewing. In 1917 it constructed a garage not only to repair cars but to allow instruction in auto mechanics. Moreover, when school facilities became inadequate, the church began erecting a new building in 1918 at Second and Tornillo to accommodate 600 students. According to Calleros, however, Mexican architect M. L. Cardona of El Paso, who drew up the plans for the school, encountered many difficulties in its construction including a labor strike. Nevertheless, *La Revista Católica* praised Cardona's design of the building and believed that, although few people knew of Cardona's ability, "St. Ignatius School will reveal to the present as well as future generations his intellectual and artistic qualities." Dedicated on January 26, 1919, the new school cost $30,000 gathered through fund-raising and individual contributions. It contained eleven classrooms plus an auditorium and represented one of El Paso's most modern schools. In March parishioners held a musical-literary performance to inaugurate the new 650-seat school auditorium. Besides a Mexican orchestra, Miss E. Sánchez played the opera *La Traviata* on the piano, parish members performed *Rigoletto*, the church choir under Miss Manuela Mateus sang "Caridad" by Rossini, and Rena Reyes serenaded the audience with her rendition of the American song "Smiles." Later in the year some church members staged the first drama in the auditorium: *Eliza Ronstadt* in three acts with María Mendivil as Madam Ronstadt.[50] Emphasizing a form of high culture, these church productions appear to have been quite popular among parishioners, especially the more sophisticated political refugees.

St. Ignatius supported various other cultural and recreational activities as well. Shortly after the church opened, it hired Trinidad Concha to assemble a young women's orchestra, which by 1908 appeared in public concerts. Concha further directed the church's well-known choir. In 1912 St. Ignatius obtained the benefit of another musical group when a boys' band at Sacred Heart had to leave that parish because it made too much noise and instead moved to St. Ignatius. This marked the start of the young people's band, which gained much prominence under the direction of Professor Melitón Concha. By 1918 St. Ignatius also had one of the largest Mexican athletic clubs in the city. Founded by the church to counter the success of the Mexican YMCA, the Association of Catholic Youth (Asociación Católica de Jóvenes), better known as the Club Anahuac, sponsored both athletic and cultural events. It possessed the best baseball, football, tennis, and basketball teams in south El Paso and won several city-wide contests. Moreover, its 100 members aided in the building of athletic and playground facilities for the children of the area. And, as part of its expression of loyalty to the United States during World War I, the club held picnics and athletic exhibitions to raise money for the war fund of the Knights of Columbus. "The young members of this club," it appealed to other Mexicans, "moved by a sense of duty and humanitarianism, and not being able to contribute in any other way to relieve the suffering of our own brothers, have decided to help through this exhibition. Won't you help us by attending? *Remember*: It will benefit our brothers who are fighting on the front lines."[51]

Indeed, the war gave St. Ignatius and the Catholic Church of El Paso another opportunity to stress the Americanization of the Mexicans, especially youth. After the United States declared war in 1917, the priests of St. Ignatius explained to their parishioners the alien registration provisions of the draft law and urged them to cooperate with the civil and military authorities. The church also requested Mexicans to buy Liberty Bonds (Bonas de la Libertad). Yet the parish's proudest contribution to the war came when more than 40 young Mexican men, both native born and foreign born, enlisted for military service, despite the fact that most Mexicans in the city claimed draft exemptions owing to their alien status. A few of the Mexican soldiers, moreover, served with distinction. Marcos B. Armijo, who died in battle, received the Distinguished Service Cross, while the French government honored Manuel J. Escajeda with the Croix de Guerre. Marcelino Serna, however, represented not only St. Ignatius' most distinguished soldier but one of the most decorated in El Paso and Texas. Serna received the American Distinguished Service Cross, the French Croix de Guerre and Military Medal, the Italian Cross of Merit, and the British Medal of Bravery.[52] This demonstration of American patriotism on the part of St. Ignatius' youth revealed the conviction of the Catholic Church in El Paso that, regardless of native sentiments, Mexicans for their own economic benefit should learn the language, customs, and values of the United States as quickly as possible. After the war the Church strongly supported the city's Americanization program, which included night schools for Mexican adults. In an editorial even the sometime anti-American *Revista Católica* encouraged its Mexican readers to avail themselves of this education in order to help them obtain better jobs. "The movement initiated in Washington," the Mexican Catholic paper pointed out, "to 'Americanize' all foreigners in the United States has reached El Paso, and all indicators show that it will prove more fruitful in this city than in other places. The name of this program will scare off many Mexicans and perhaps because of this fear many will not take advantage of this excellent opportunity to improve their conditions."[53]

Hence, by 1920 the Catholic Church in El Paso through its endorsement of postwar Americanization programs as well as its own efforts in the parochial schools served, along with the public schools, as a major American institution of socialization, especially for the children of Mexican immigrants. Based on a viewpoint stressing loyalty to both Church and country, which by the 1920s and 1930s increasingly meant the United States, the Catholic Church in the Southwest assisted Mexicans not only to adjust to border life but, ultimately, to believe in the American Dream. Still, the constant stream of additional immigrants into El Paso and other southwestern areas after 1920, as well as the proximity of Mexico, meant that Mexican immigrant parishes were never completely Americanized. Rather than examples of an earlier past, many of them, due to continued immigration from Mexico, remain viable though poor institutions helping to link Mexican immigrant communities in the United States with the mother country and culture.

In addition to the Catholic Church, Protestant churches in south El Paso and throughout the border helped Mexicans adjust to American society. Protestant missions, settlement houses, and schools also sought to recruit and organize Mexican converts by the social services they provided. This attempt, however, met with considerable resistance on some occasions. The *Times* noted in 1893 a disturbance over a Mexican Methodist preacher in the southside. "Last evening while a Mexican Protestant evangelist was addressing a Congregation of Mexicans in the open air not far from the Santa Fe section house in the First Ward," the newspaper informed its readers, "parties began throwing stones and clods of dirt into the crowd." The Catholic Church, itself, warned its followers to beware of the Protestants, who, according to *La Revista Católica*, posed not only a threat to the Mexicans' religion but to their culture as well. Despite the opposition, Protestant missionaries persevered in their work among the Mexican population. In their efforts they recognized the value of converting and using Mexican preachers as a way of making cultural contact with immigrants. One observer remarked in 1893 that certificates to preach among their countrymen had been granted to Eugenio Rodríguez, Epetario Madrid, and José M. Ibáñez, who were the first graduates of the Congregational training school in El Paso. The recruitment of Mexican preachers, as one Methodist official explained, would likewise be crucial for that church's efforts in Mexico. Addressing the Northwest Mexican Conference of the Southern Methodist Church meeting in El Paso in 1906, the Reverend Dr. Ward emphasized the importance of the church's work south of the border. "I know you have a difficult field of labor," he told his audience, "but am glad to know that we have men in this work in Mexico, both Americans and Mexicans, whose zest and consecration are like that of which we read in Apostolic times. We see that

Protestant countries of the world represent the highest civilization and prosperity." Dr. Ward concluded that what the church needed in Mexico was a Martin Luther "and he must be a Mexican."[54]

Because of its border location and its large Mexican population, El Paso represented a significant missionary field for Protestant denominations, which conducted missions both along the border and in Mexico. The city directory for 1898–99 listed three Protestant churches in Chihuahuita: the Young People's Society of Christian Endeavor of the Congregational Church (Mexican) with 40 members including officers I. P. Balderas, F. Ponce, A. S. Escudero, and Hilario Hernández; the Mexican Methodist Church at 519 South Stanton headed by the Reverend Thomas Howard; and the Mexican Methodist Church, South, on South Campbell Street led by the Reverend J. F. Corbin. As Mexican immigration to El Paso grew after the turn of the century, several other Protestant churches and missions sprang up in the Mexican district. They included the Mexican Baptist Church at 701 South Stanton, the Mexican Christian Church at 1100 South Stanton, the Mexican Congregational Church at 607 South Kansas, the Mexican Methodist Church (North) at 715 South Oregon, the Mexican Presbyterian Church at 619 South Florence, the Mexican Nazarene Mission at 815 South El Paso, the Salvation Army's Mexican Mission at 412 South Stanton, the Lutheran Mexican Evangelical at 1001 South Campbell, and the Mexican Temperance League at 503 South Florence. While it is difficult to know the full Protestant impact on the Mexican population, membership figures published in 1916 show that the churches had some limited success in making conversions. A total of 904 Mexicans belonged to five different Protestant sects with almost half in the Presbyterian rank. The total Mexican Protestant population included 488 women and 416 men. Although an equal number of men and women over the age of sixteen had become Protestants, a substantially higher number of Mexican females under sixteen had converted than men under that age.[55]

Perhaps the most significant contribution of Protestants to the culture of south El Paso was their educational and recreational work. Under the auspices of the Methodist Episcopal Church, Lydia Patterson Institute on South Florence Street opened its doors in 1914 with the objective of educating Mexican young men, especially political and religious refugees. Containing a gymnasium, baths, dormitories, and dining rooms, the institute sought through its courses to provide "a most excellent opportunity for the young men to receive a thorough education amid Christian surroundings and an atmosphere of the highest morality."[56] Two years later about 200 Mexican students attended the institute, which still represents one of El Paso's oldest Protestant institutions. In addition, Protestants through the local YMCA began a Mexican branch of the Y in order to assist in the Christianization and Americanization of Mexican young men. The Mexican Y, operating at first in the basement of the Lydia Patterson Institute, claimed 1,000 members when it moved into new headquarters near Chihuahuita in 1918. Working primarily among political refugees, the Mexican Y initially aided the children of wealthier exiles in El Paso. "We have in El Paso young men refugees from all parts of Mexico," J. V. Escobar, the secretary of the Mexican Y stated in an interview, "and among these are representatives of the best families of the republic. They are the hope of the Mexican people . . . because they have learned many broadening and truly democratic things in the United States that they may give to the republic."[57]

Besides providing recreation through its gymnasium facilities, the Mexican Y offered instruction in the Bible and English as well as sponsoring movies, dances, literary presentations, and counseling. Because it dealt with an immigrant population, however, the Y as well as other Protestant agencies could not divorce itself from Mexican cultural traditions. For example, the Y's most notable cultural production consisted of the lavish annual Cinco de Mayo [Fifth of May] celebration honoring the great Mexican victory over the invading French army in 1862.[58] Nevertheless, the Y aimed at eventually Americanizing Mexican youth. To this end, it expanded by 1920 its scope to include children of the Mexican working class; consequently, the Y announced that year that its functions had attracted almost 30,000 Mexican young men and boys. An additional Y branch at the El Paso Smelter claimed a total yearly attendance of more than 50,000.[59] One Mexican American official of the organization succinctly expressed the ideological and political objectives associated with such Y work among the local Mexicans. According to S. I. Esquivel, the Mexican YMCA was one of the best means for dealing with the "Mexican problem" in the United States. "Two million young men cannot reside in the midst of a foreign people," Esquivel stressed at a Y meeting, "without eventually becoming a liability, unless they are made an asset." Through its facilities, he explained, the Y could instruct the Mexicans in English and American values and customs and in so doing serve the national interest. "Work among the Mexican population of El Paso and other portions of this country will repay a thousandfold," the Mexican American officer concluded, "it will tend to avoid friction between the two republics, and will increase the loyalty of the Mexican population toward the United States."[60] Reaching a large number of Mexican young men and boys by the 1920s, the Mexican Y along with the Protestant churches in the barrios furnished additional institutional support for the acculturation of the Mexican population.

Yet, despite the cultural transitions inaugurated among the Mexicans by both Catholic and Protestant churches, the constant influx of new Mexican immigrants, many from rural areas, not only reinforced Mexican cultural traditions but, as Gamio observed in the 1920s, also aided in the survival of certain religious folk cults and superstitions.[61] One of the best examples of a folk cult in El Paso involved the appearance of a young Mexican woman called Santa Teresa. Born in the little village of Cabora in Sonora, Teresa Urrea at the age of sixteen began to attract attention by her alleged healing powers. She believed that she possessed the power to cure the poor, and villagers who claimed that Teresa had worked miracles referred to her as "Santa Teresa." However, authorities accused her of being part of a revolutionary movement against Porfirio Díaz and forced her to flee Cabora and go into exile first in Arizona in 1892 and later in El Paso in 1896. When she arrived in the border city, Santa Teresa proceeded to set up a tent in Chihuahuita where large numbers of Mexicans visited her and asked to be cured. Two years later it was reported that hundreds of Mexicans from the surrounding area were entering El Paso "in wagons and on burros" and heading to see Teresa. On one day about 3,000 persons, mostly Mexicans but including some Americans, visited the Mexican healer. After having seen the young woman, one American claimed that he could use his limp left arm once more. "But now look," he exclaimed. "I can lift it alone above my head." Tears came to his eyes as he cried out:

"Thank God, I can use it again! Santa Teresa has at least done me some good." Impressed by the attention aroused by Santa Teresa, the *Times* commented that although a large number of people scoffed at her, an even greater number were believers. Not committing itself either way, the *Times* only suggested that if the excitement over the folk healer continued, every train into El Paso would be filled with people arriving to be cured or to see a "miracle."[62]

It is not certain how long Santa Teresa resided in El Paso, but the *Times* noted in 1898 that then she lived in Clifton, Arizona. According to her friends, Teresa had left El Paso because she feared being kidnapped and returned to Mexico by Díaz's spies.[63] Although famous faith healers such as Santa Teresa were rare among Mexican immigrants, it appears that despite urbanization and secularization Mexican popular religious traditions survived along the border.

As a form of ethnic self-protection as well as an expression of ethnicity, Mexican social organizations in El Paso revealed the Mexicans' accommodation to their new American setting. Forced to organize in a new and sometimes hostile society, some of El Paso's Mexicans, especially more skilled and educated ones, formed several mutual and fraternal associations that helped provide organized leadership in the Mexican settlement. Similar societies, moreover, existed in Mexico and hence were familiar forms of association. As mediating institutions the mutual and fraternal organizations, besides aiding in the preservation and encouragement of Mexican ethnic consciousness among the immigrants, helped form a more permanent and cohesive Mexican community.

As early as 1893 the Mexican newspapaer *El Hispano-Americano* printed a notice from La Unión Occidental Mexicana (the Mexican Western Union), which was one of the first Mexican mutual aid societies in El Paso. "It is neither more nor less than what its name implies a group of persons of Mexican origin," stated organizer and political exile Víctor L. Ochoa. He went on to explain that the unión had several objectives: to aid and defend its members, to "unalterably" maintain the Spanish language, to protect the morality of its members, and to spread fraternal bonds among Mexican nationals in the United States. In addition, when a member died, his wife and children would receive $2.50 from each unión member. One year later another mutual aid society, Los Caballeros del Progreso (the Gentlemen of Progress), stressed that the poor economic conditions of Mexicans in the United States resulted from a lack of unity and that in order to alleviate this problem Los Caballeros had been organized. *El Defensor* noted that when one of the society's members who had not kept up his dues died, Los Caballeros refused to pay the funeral costs as a lesson to other negligent members.[64]

One Mexican newspaper also urged unity through organization when it observed in 1899 that despite the large numbers of Mexicans in El Paso, the city's oldest Mexican mutual benefit society (1888), the Sociedad Mutualista Mexicana "La Protectora," had only 40 members. It pointed out the validity of the motto "Unity Makes Force" and informed its readers that only through organization had the United States become a great power. "If it is true then that unity makes force," it added, "then we do not understand why Mexicans do not develop those relationships that will unite us." The Sociedad Mutualista Mexicana "La Protectora," the paper asserted, aimed to unite and protect Mexicans who lived in El Paso. Had it not been for this society, the paper believed that Mexicans in the city would have been deprived of a common meeting place where they "could exchange impressions of our beloved country." *Las Noticas* further reminded Mexicans of their obligation to one another as members of the same race "and sons of the same mother: Mexico." Among its benefits, "La Protectora" assisted members who required hospitalization and paid for funeral costs. *Las Dos Américas*, another Mexican newspaper in El Paso, expressed its gratitude in 1898 to "La Protectora's" Mexican American president, A. J. Escajeda, and its vice-president, C. Aguirre, for their consideration during the funeral of Antonio G. Gallardo, who had been killed by a Southern Pacific train at Deming, New Mexico. Although it appears that the membership of "La Protectora" remained small, it met regularly every second and fourth Monday of the month.[65] Its leadership seems to have come from Mexican Americans like Escajeda, but the entire composition of its membership cannot be determined.

As more Mexicans arrived in El Paso by the turn of the century, several other benefit and fraternal groups appeared. The *Times* announced in 1907 that seven Mexican societies of El Paso would participate in that year's 16th of September celebrations honoring

Mexican independence. These included La Benéfica patriotic society from the smelter, the Sociedad Unión Constructora, La Mutualista, Los Hijos de Hidalgo, and the Sociedad Filarmónica. "Few Americans if any," a Mexican told a *Times* reporter,

> are aware of the wonderful growth and activity to be found in the Mexican fraternal orders now existing in the Southwest.
> While the chief element of these orders is made up of the common working class, it must be remembered that there are also affiliated with these societies many Mexicans of culture —among them professional and business men. El Paso has the distinction of having the largest number of these lodges; Tucson ranking next, it being the place where two of the most important orders, the "Sociedad Zaragoza" and the "Sociedad Hispano-Americana" have their home offices.[66]

He further explained that the Hispano-American society paid $1,000 to the family of a deceased member and $200 to a member upon the death of his wife. In addition he declared that although the Sociedad Zaragoza had been operating for a shorter time than other societies, it had a larger membership with 28 branches throughout Arizona, New Mexico, and Texas. In El Paso it was represented by Lodge No. 18, founded that year with 90 members.[67]

The growing numbers of Mexican immigrants and refugees in El Paso after 1910 also influenced the expansion of these societies. "Mexicans in El Paso are interested in lodge work to an extent probably not generally known," member Pedro A. Candelaria stated in an interview in 1915. Candelaria observed that the Sociedad Mutualista Mexicana had a membership of 115 and La Constructora had 300 members. Both represented the two largest societies in the city and intended to protect the widows and orphans of deceased members. Each of these organizations assessed every member $3 whenever a death occurred and turned the amount over to the widow. Candelaria pointed out that still another lodge, La Benéfica, operated in East El Paso. These organizations had developed substantially in recent years, he concluded, owing to the arrival of Mexican refugees.[68]

The sharp rise in the Mexican population of the Southwest during the years of the Mexican Revolution encouraged consolidation among Mexican mutual aid societies and increased their emphasis on insurance practices. The best example of the change can be seen in the activities of La Sociedad Alianza Hispano-Americana. Organized in 1894 in Tucson, it grew from a small number of lodges to 88 in 1919 with more than 4,000 members from California to Texas, and with additional lodges in northern Mexico. It hoped to unite all Mexicans and Latin Americans in the United States into one "family" under the principles of "protection, morality, and education." According to the Alianza's historian, its membership consisted of both lower-middle-class and working-class people.[69] In one of the largest demonstrations of Mexican social organization in the United States, El Paso hosted a national convention of the Alianza in 1910 attended by close to 200 delegates from New Mexico, Arizona, Southern California, and Texas. At their opening session the mayors of both El Paso and Juárez welcomed the delegates and assured them they would not be molested by the police of either border town. One of the main items in the convention's agenda dealt with changes in insurance payments. Every member paid a flat rate of $1 each month for $1,000 insurance without regard to age or other conditions. However, the *Times* reported that the officers were eager to adopt a more scientific plan. The finance committee noted that the supreme lodge had $16,790 on hand of which $14,000 had been put in the reserve fund. Although the convention voted to retain a flat rate for present members, it approved a new classified assessment for future ones but kept the amount of insurance that could be secured at $500 or $1,000, with $100 and $200 funeral benefits.[70]

Nine years later *La Patria* published an advertisement for the Alianza containing both its insurance provisions and a list of its lodges in the Southwest. The notice emphasized that the Alianza had no political or religious qualifications for membership, that it treated every member equally, that each received the same benefits, and that it spent none of its members' funds for amusements. The Alianza also stressed that women could purchase a policy, "for we believe them to be as worthy and as entitled to the same right to protect their children who depend on them." Despite the fact that most of its members were "humble workers," the Alianza proudly announced that since its formation it had paid out a million and a half dollars in benefits. To share in the Alianza's protection, a

Mexican had to pay $3.50 admission fee plus $1 to $2 for a medical examination. Monthly payments would then be determined by the amount of the policy and the age of its holder. "We respectfully invite you and your family to join the 'Alianza,'" the ad told the readers of *La Patria*. In 1919 three of its lodges, apparently located in Chihuahuita, functioned in El Paso. *La Patria* observed that members of the different lodges could attend one another's meetings. In addition Jesús M. Ortiz, who had been named Alianza organizer for Texas, believed that a new chapter could be established in East El Paso since many Mexicans there had expressed an interest in the society. Besides El Paso, lodges could be found in nearby New Mexico in Silver City, Hillsboro, Santa Rita, Las Cruces, and Hurley.[71]

Like other immigrant organizations in the United States, the Mexican mutual and fraternal societies of El Paso provided social and cultural activities for their members.[72] Many of these social functions consisted of dances sponsored by different lodges. In 1911, for example, the Mexican secret societies held a grand ball at the Fraternal Brotherhood Hall. "The national colors of Mexico will be flying," the *Times* commented, "and those who cannot have one of the most enjoyable times of their life . . . will be hard to please." In 1919 the Logia Morelos held its Second Grand Ball at Liberty Hall and in 1920 the Sociedad Mutualista Zaragoza Independiente sponsored a literary and dance show to celebrate its twelfth anniversary. That same year the Alianza hosted an artistic presentation to raise funds. Moreover, the lodges sponsored the 16th of September celebrations as well as other Mexican patriotic holidays. When William Howard Taft met Porfirio Díaz in El Paso in 1909, the city's Mexican societies turned out in force to honor both leaders and the nations they represented. "As the president's carriage neared the position occupied by the Mexican societies," a reporter noticed of Taft's parade down El Paso street, "there was a tumult of applause, cheers and cries of 'Viva Taft! Viva Taft!'" After Taft had visited Díaz in Juárez, the Mexican organizations joined the parade up El Paso Street to downtown Cleveland Square. "Four different Mexican societies," the *Times* observed, "numbering about 1,000 men and all wearing natty uniforms comprised the divisions."[73]

For Mexican Americans, the social activities of the lodges became quite important because participation in Anglo-Saxon society remained limited. Although the Women's Club, the El Paso Country Club, and other American social organizations had no clear policy on the exclusion of Mexican members, businessman Félix Martínez, who belonged to the Toltec Men's Club, appears to have been one of the few persons of Mexican descent throughout the period who claimed membership in an American social group. Social intercourse between Mexicans and Americans on an organized level seems to have occurred only during special political or patriotic events or the arrival of major Mexican dignitaries such as Díaz. Because of this de facto social separation as well as their own cultural affinity, Mexican Americans either formed their own clubs or joined immigrant organizations. In 1907 the Logia Fraternal No. 30, composed exclusively of Mexican Americans, held a banquet in honor of Mexican Independence Day at the Sheldon Hotel attended by 132 persons including 35 prominent American politicians. The walls of the big dining room had been decorated with a number of Mexican and American flags, "while at the south end of the hall facing the toastmaster was an immense Mexican and a huge American flag leaning so close together that their folds embraced each other." After some of the American guests spoke, lodge officer Agapito Martínez emphasized that it gave him great pride to say that every member of the lodge held American citizenship and yet could also be proud of Mexico's achievements. "Freedom," said editor Lauro Aguirre, "started the fire at Philadelphia, at Paris and in Mexico." Z. M. Oriza ended the speeches by a toast to the menu motto "After All, What is Better than Friendship."[74]

The annual 16th of September celebration proved to be not only the most important Mexican cultural event in El Paso, and throughout the Southwest, but also an indication of the level of social organization and cooperation that could occur among the different Mexican societies. The 1897 ceremonies, for example, stood out as one of the most successful holidays in El Paso and revealed the various cultural activities that often took place during this community fiesta. As early as July, the Mexican newspaper *El Monitor* announced a meeting of La Junta Patriótica Mexicana (the Mexican Patriotic Council) to select a board of directors and decide on the best format for the 16th of September celebration. One month later the paper criticized some Mexican Americans who did not believe that the

16th of September had any meaning for them and refused to support the festivities: "To these 'Agringados' (Americanized Mexicans) who negate that they are Mexicans because they were born in the United States, we ask: what blood runs through their veins? Do they think they are members of the Anglo-Saxon race who only happen to have dark skins because they were born on the border! What nonsense! (Qué barbaridad!)."[75] *El Monitor* went on to add that this did not mean that Mexican Americans should not be good citizens of the United States and even fight for "Tío Samuel" if it went to war against a European or an Asiatic nation. However, in the event of conflict between the United States and Mexico or a Latin American nation, *El Monitor* believed that every Mexican living north of the border should go to the defense of their "blood brothers" and the country of their parents' birth. The paper concluded by asking: "Why should there be any reason now for us to feel ashamed of being a Mexican?"[76]

Led by the Junta Patriótica, the Mexicans of El Paso prepared to celebrate the independence of Mexico. In its September 12th edition, *El Monitor* dedicated its coverage to the Mexican workers of the city, "to whom we wish all kinds of happiness during these glorious days." It also reminded its readers of the events to be held on both the fifteenth and the sixteenth, and commented that the prepared program left nothing to be desired, thanks to the work of the Junta. Similar festivities would occur in other areas of Texas, as well as in New Mexico, Arizona, and California, but the paper predicted that one of the best 16th of Septembers would be held in El Paso. To stimulate patriotic sentiments, *El Monitor* retold the story of the fathers of Mexican independence, Hidalgo and Morelos, and of the independence struggle against the "tyranny of Spain." "Long live the illustrious Liberator," the article eulogized Hidalgo, "and 'Viva Mexico!' "[77]

Organized in honor of the Mexican colony, especially the Junta Patriótica and the Mexican consul Francisco Mallén, only rain spotted an otherwise flawless event. The celebration began on the morning of the fifteenth, when Consul Mallén dedicated the observance to Don Porfirio Díaz. That evening the Junta, the Mexican mutual benefit society "La Protectora," and the Mexican students of Sacred Heart School marched from Fifth Street, bordering the downtown area, to Sacred Heart Church in Chihuahuita preceded by a Mexican band. Throughout the route the homes and businesses of both Mexicans and Americans had been decorated with the Mexican tricolors. At 8:00 P.M. Consul Mallén and the president of the Junta, Dr. Rechy, accompanied by their wives arrived at the platform in front of the church and the program commenced by the playing of the Mexican national anthem. The more than 3,000 people who attended also heard recitations by several young people as well as songs and piano recitals. A speech in English by lawyer T. J. Beall that praised Mexican independence and Hidalgo received much applause. After several songs Don Esteban Gómez del Campo delivered the main speech touching on various Mexican historical themes. The band then played both the Mexican and American anthems followed by two tunes originally composed by Trinidad Concha entitled "On the Shores of the Rio Grande" and "Through El Paso." At last the secretary of the Junta read Hidalgo's act of independence ("El grito de Dolores") and Consul Mallén said a few words. The program concluded with the Mexican national anthem sung by a chorus of young Mexican women. The following morning of the sixteenth, a parade through downtown El Paso containing both Mexican and American units ended the independence day celebrations.[78]

As the 16th of September festivities partly indicated, different cultural influences touched the Mexican population of El Paso. Given diverse cultural levels within the Mexican settlement, these influences also had varied effects and responses. More acculturated than the immigrants, the minority of Mexican Americans felt the pull of both cultures much more strongly. "This civilization is American nominally," Gamio observed of Mexican Americans in the 1920s, "and exhibits the principal material aspects of modern American civilization, but intellectually and emotionally it lives in local Mexican traditions."[79] On the other hand, the recently arrived immigrants retained to a considerable degree their native traditions in the form of language, folklore, superstitions, songs, and religious holidays, which expressed their national origins. However, the impact of American industrialization and urbanization forced the immigrants to adjust to changed conditions. In the process many of El Paso's Mexicans formed relationships with one another through family, recreational, mutual aid, fraternal, and patriotic organizations that, on the one hand, provided a cultural security and continuity and, on the other, revealed new American conditions and influences. Moreover, the schools, both public and parochial, American material goods, and, to a degree, churches represented institutions and attractions within the barrios that affected the subtle and gradual Americanization of the Mexicans.

Although their culture underwent some transformation as they adjusted to immigrant life, Mexicans, as Gamio further recognized, "never became integrally assimilated to American civilization." He believed that the problem retarding the complete Americanization of the Mexicans lay in the large gulf between what he called "purely American culture" and "purely Mexican culture."[80] The economic discrimination and segregation aimed at Mexicans in El Paso also made it difficult to assimilate them as well as Mexican Americans because employers desired to keep them as a source of cheap labor. Furthermore, unlike European immigration, which slowed to a trickle in the 1920s, Mexican immigration persisted and reinforced a distinct Mexican presence in El Paso. Too, most Mexicans believed they would soon return to their homeland and therefore felt no strong motivation to discard their cultural traditions. Mexico, of course, was right next door. Consequently, a dialectical relationship existed between the immigrant's native culture and the attempt by American institutions and reformers to restructure earlier habits and instill a new urban-industrial discipline among the Mexicans. The eventual result: a Mexican border culture, neither completely Mexican nor American, but one revealing contrasting attractions and pressures between both cultures. Yet Mexican border culture was and is by no means monolithic because different experiences are represented. Recent arrivals display what Galarza calls "the most authentic transplant of Mexican working-class culture,"[81] whereas middle-class newcomers, such as many of the political refugees during the Revolutionary period, bring with them a more sophisticated bourgeois one of both Mexican and European origins. Finally, Mexican Americans, especially the children and grandchildren of immigrants, have faced an erosion of their Mexican culture as American institutions, including an acculturated family environment, bring them into the fold of American mass culture. Cultural attrition, according to Galarza, must be seen as a result of the destruction of Mexican institutions, including the loss of land through the migration process both into and within the United States and through the elimination of such earlier Mexican cultural units in the Southwest as villages, mining towns, presidios [military outposts], haciendas, and the missions. "For that is what happens," Galarza concludes,

> when two social groups [American and Mexican] palpably unequal in technology or some other vital factor intersect each other. Those who are overcome, if they are not annihilated, are left with the residues of culture, those resources and institutions which are least useful or threatening to the winner— indeed, which might even be amusing to him. Thus cultural pluralism can conceal paraplegic subcultures that were not born that way. Mexican Southwestern culture has been crippled; that is the essence of its history.[82]

11

Conclusion

The Mexicans' economic, political, and cultural experiences in El Paso and throughout the Southwest during the late nineteenth and early twentieth centuries were inextricably linked with the economic boom of the region. Indeed material growth continued until 1929 and as a result more than half a million Mexicans emigrated to the United States during the Roaring Twenties. Those who arrived in El Paso, however, no longer entered an "instant city" but a more established American border metropolis. In a short period of time this once remote area of the United States had undergone profound development, primarily as a supplier of raw materials, and quickly became integrated into an expanded American industrial economy. As part of the process Mexican immigrant labor played a significant role. The railroads, mines, smelters, farms, and a variety of other industries and businesses found Mexicans not only to be a source of reliable and manageable workers but also an extremely cheap one. Moreover, lax immigration restrictions and a special exemption from the 1917 Immigration Law allowed employers to obtain a surplus of Mexican laborers. Consequently, Mexicans formed the labor base for the Southwest's prosperity.

Mexican immigrants, of course, shared a common tie with the larger wave of Eastern and Southern European immigrants as well as with black workers who migrated from the rural South to the urban North. Despite racial and cultural differences these mass movements of diverse people resulted from economic dislocation in their homelands and the availability of employment in the United States. Mexican immigrants, like black migrants to the North, may have experienced less economic and social advances owing to persistent racial and cultural discrimination, yet they were significant additions to an expanded multiracial American working class by World War I.[1]

European immigrants, Mexicans, and blacks represented a major factor in industrial stability and prosperity.[2] Although heavily concentrated in one particular region of the United States, the Mexican immigrant worker proved to be part of a wider historical process.

As an important center of southwestern development El Paso grew to be the largest city in West Texas, New Mexico, Arizona, and northern Mexico. In addition, owing to its location on the border and its railroad network, El Paso served as the major labor market for the area. Besides supplying Mexican workers to industries throughout the Southwest, El Paso profitably used its own vast pool of Mexican labor. Employers in the city hired Mexicans in numerous unskilled, semiskilled, and even some skilled occupations in almost every significant business in the city. Notwithstanding a popular view of El Paso as a "cowboy town" on the border, the city became one of the most prominent railroad, mining, commercial, and ranching locations in the Southwest and West.[3] In this expansion the labor of Mexicans, both men and women, became indispensable.

While economic development and cheap labor constitute one basic theme of the Mexican saga in El Paso, the exploitable condition of the Mexican immigrant forms another. Like other immigrants to the United States at the time, the Mexicans believed they would reside only temporarily in the United States.[4] Indeed, because of the proximity of Mexico to the Southwest, this belief was a practical possibility for Mexicans. As a result they possessed only a limited interest in American society: to acquire a job and enough money to return to Mexico and perhaps purchase some land. Because employment could be secured in the United States, the Mexicans also experienced economic advancement not possible in Mexico. However, such improved conditions involved much labor exploitation and discrimination. Mexicans acquired jobs, mostly unskilled, but did not have the same opportunities to move into better paying skilled and managerial ones monopolized by Americans. Mexicans received lower wages than American workers, sometimes even for similar work, and because of economic discrimination as well as racial and cultural prejudice, they lived in the most depressed and unsanitary sections of the city. Not only did employers reap the benefits of cheap Mexican labor, but the political bosses of the city with the assistance of Mexican American politicos exploited the Mexicans in order to remain in power. In return the Mexicans received few economic or political benefits. Representing perhaps the most essential factor in the growth of El Paso, the majority remained economically under-developed, politically manipulated, and socially segregated.

El Paso's Mexicans tolerated these conditions because they be-lieved they would remain in the United States for only a brief period and because they feared reprisals if they objected to their harsh surroundings. Some Mexicans did resort to strikes as an expression of discontent, but most Mexicans shied away from such activity and saw no reason for these "radical" manifestations. Accommoda-tion rather than resistance characterized the Mexican immigrant experience. Moreover, they adjusted their cultural habits to better serve themselves in a more modernized and urban society. Although they retained many Mexican cultural traditions, they also under-went a degree of Americanization due to the influences of the schools, the churches, and their new material and recreational interests. The retention of familiar life-styles plus the acceptance of new in-fluences helped Mexicans adjust to what they hoped would be a short stay. Accommodation made conditions more tolerable for the Mexicans to live and work in the United States but unfortunately made them vulnerable to exploitation as well.

By 1920 the Mexicans of El Paso had grown to more than half the city's total population of almost 80,000 and probably closer to 100,000. Ten years later both Los Angeles and San Antonio would contain more Mexicans than El Paso, yet this border city represented not only one of the first major urban concentrations of Mexican immigrants in the United States, but more significantly the only metropolitan area in the Southwest with a Mexican majority. According to the 1930 census, the total Mexican population of El Paso stood at 58,291, or 56.9 percent of the entire community, and this did not include Mexicans of American citizenship.[5] While most studies of Mexicans in the United States have tended to concentrate on the Mexican's rural migratory life during the early part of the twentieth century, the urban dimension as reflected by the Mexicans of El Paso provides a fuller understanding of the part Mexicans played in the economic development of the Southwest and of the United States. Some historians of the Southwest and West have emphasized that these regions developed as urban societies, and the history of El Paso reveals that the Mexicans had performed an early and important role in the process. Clearly, "desert immigrants" from Mexico have been, and continue to be, despite recent concerns over "illegal aliens," a productive force in American life. If, at the same time, they and their descendants have not been completely integrated into the mainstream of American society, the history of the early immigrants in places like El Paso provides us with clues as to the origin and nature of this dilemma.

Notes

CHAPTER 2

1. Samuel P. Hays, *The Response to Industrialism, 1885–1914*, pp. 4–5, 15–17. Also see Robert H. Wiebe, *The Search for Order, 1877–1920*; Tomas C. Cochran and William Miller, *The Age of Enterprise*; and Gerald D. Nash, *The American West in the Twentieth Century: A Short History of an Urban Oasis*, pp. 34–38.
2. Perhaps using an inappropriate term, Gerald D. Nash refers to the Southwest as a "colonial economy" dominated by eastern interests. Using a similar colonial analogy, D. W. Meinig in his interpretative essay on Texas emphasizes that "by 1900, the economy of Texas, in terms of the state's leading components had become integrated thoroughly with that of the rest of the United States on the colonial basis of supplying raw materials to the industrialized sectors and importing manufactured products." See Nash, *American West*, p. 18, and D. W. Meinig, *Imperial Texas: An Interpretive Essay in Cultural Geography*, p. 77.
3. Gunther Barth, *Instant Cities: Urbanization and the Rise of San Francisco and Denver*, p. xiii.
4. See Nancy Lee Hammons, "A History of El Paso County, Texas to 1900," p. 9; Ruth Harris, *Geography of El Paso County*; Russel A. White, "El Paso del Norte: the Geography of a Pass and Border Area Through 1906"; and C. L. Sonnichsen, *Pass of the North: Four Centuries on the Rio Grande*, pp. 1–99. For a brief overview of El Paso's history, see W. H. Timmons, "Continental Crossroads: El Paso in History," pp. 7–10.
5. Owen White, *Out of the Desert: The Historical Romance of El Paso*, pp. 20–21; J. Lawrence McConville, "A History of Population in the El Paso–Juárez Area," pp. 53–54. For a history of the Chihuahua Trail see Max L. Moorhead, *New Mexico's Royal Road: Trade and Travel on the Chihuahua Trail*.
6. Sonnichsen, *Pass*, pp. 100–23; White, *Desert*, pp. 31, 37–50.
7. White, *Desert*, pp. 31, 37–50; Oscar J. Martínez, *Border Boom Town: Ciudad Juárez since 1848*, p. 10.
8. W. W. Mills, *Forty Years at El Paso 1858–1898*, pp. 24–25. For a short account of early American inhabitants in El Paso see Rex W. Strickland, "Six Who Came to El Paso: Pioneers of the 1840's."

9. White, *Desert*, pp. 57–60; Mills, *Forty Years*, p. 13; Strickland, "Six Who Came," p. 5; Rhoda Milnarich, "A Study of the El Paso County Census of 1860"; U.S. Department of Interior, *Manuscript Census, 1880*, El Paso (microfilm), roll no. 1301, pp. 2–20.

10. White, *Desert*, pp. 49–73. A proclamation issued on July 24, 1888, by the state government of Chihuahua changed the name of Paso del Norte to Ciudad Juárez: "That in consideration of the progress made by the town of Paso del Norte and the glorious incidents of which the said town was the scene during the French intervention the town of Paso del Norte be elevated to the rank of city under the title of City of Juárez." See Beckford Mackey, U.S. Consul at Paso del Norte, to George L. Rines, Assistant Secretary of State, Paso del Norte, August 30, 1888, in General Records of the Department of State, Washington, D.C., Record Group 59, Microfilm roll 3. Hereinafter cited as RG 59, M—.

11. White, *Desert*, pp. 74, 177–178. As early as the 1850s American companies, such as the Sonora Exploring and Mining Company, operated mines in Arizona. See Joseph F. Park, "The History of Mexican Labor in Arizona during the Territorial Period," pp. 50–51.

12. Ira G. Clark, *Then Came the Railroads: The Century from Steam to Diesel in the Southwest*, p. 197. Other Texas towns that prospered due to the entrance of the railroads included San Antonio, Dallas, Houston, and Galveston.

13. White, *Desert*, p. 124.

14. As quoted in C. L. Sonnichsen and M. G. McKinney, *The State National Since 1881: The Pioneer Bank of El Paso*, p. 6.

15. See El Paso Division Southern Pacific Papers, ACC 610, University of Texas, El Paso Archives (hereinafter cited as UTEP Archives); *El Paso City Directory*, 1885, pp. 5–6; *Lone Star*, Nov. 5, 1881, p. 2; Nov. 31, 1881, p. 2; Mar. 8, 1899, p. 2; and John H. McNeely, "The Railways of Mexico: A Study in Nationalization." The Mexican Central was chartered under the laws of Massachusetts and backed by the same investors who promoted the Santa Fe Railroad.

16. Clark, *Railroads*, p. 195; also see Robert L. Martin, *The City Moves West: Economic and Industrial Growth in Central West Texas*, p. 20.

17. Floyd S. Fierman, *Some Early Jewish Settlers in the Southwestern Frontier*, p. 6.

18. White, *Desert*, p. 124.

19. *El Paso Daily Times*, Oct. 31, 1901, p. 4; hereinafter cited as *Times*. For a history of the *Times*, see John Middagh, *Frontier Newspaper: The El Paso Times*. Also see El Paso Bureau of Information, "The City and County of El Paso, Texas Containing Useful and Reliable Information Concerning the Future Great Metropolis of the Southwest Its Resources and Advantage for the Agriculturist, Artisan and Capitalist" (El Paso, 1886). Copies of this report can be found in the Bancroft Library at Berkeley and in the Southwestern Collection, El Paso Public Library.

20. Although I do not equate southwestern underdevelopment with that of Latin America, some developmental models used for Latin America can be useful in explaining the Southwest's, and especially El Paso's, relationship to the industrial sections of the United States. See André Gunder Frank, *Latin America: Underdevelopment or Revolution*, pp. 3–17, and Cyril Edward Black, "Change as a Condition of Modern Life."

21. Barth, *Instant Cities*, p. xxiii.

22. See D. W. Meinig, *Southwest: Three Peoples in Geographical Change, 1600–1970*, chap. 5, and *Times*, Jan. 14, 1902, p. 21. In 1901 the El Paso city council adopted a chamber of commerce resolution that assured the city's railroads "of our profound friendship and recognition of the investments of each to the welfare and prosperity of our city, and we are mindful that our interests are identical" (see El Paso City Council, *Minutes*, Jan. 10, 1901). Also see *El Paso City Directory*, 1920, pp. 214–15.

23. Meinig, *Southwest*, p. 45.

24. As quoted in James L. Marshall, *Santa Fe: The Railroad that Built an Empire*, p. 160. In 1882 on a trip to Paso del Norte the American writer Helen Hunt Jackson predicted the modernizing impact the railroads would have on Mexico: "But it does not need statistics of today to give the imagination foundations for picturing the future of Mexico, once her vast empire is threaded by railways, her revolutionary blood kept quiet by that eminent conciliator and enforcer of peace, the steam engine, and her lazy millions inoculated with the inevitable contagion of new industries and gains" (Helen Hunt Jackson, "By Horse-Cars Into Mexico," p. 362.

25. *Times*, Feb. 21, 1900, p. 2. For a study of American railroad promotion in Mexico, see David M. Pletcher, *Rails, Mines, and Progress: Seven American Promoters in Mexico, 1867–1911*, and V. S. Mason to Grant B. Schley, Esq., The Development Company of America, New York, Oct. 11, 1904, in Chihuahua and Pacific Railroad Correspondence, box 8, John H. McNeely Collection, ACC 795, UTEP Archives.

26. As quoted in *Times*, May 4, 1900, p. 3.

27. Ibid., Jan 14, 1902, p. 10; *El Paso Herald*, Dec. 4, 1915, hereinafter cited as *Herald*. Clark emphasizes that railroads also influenced the social growth of the Southwest. "They were the one contact with the outside world," Clark writes, "which tended to break down extreme provincialism before the coming of motion pictures, automobiles, and radios" (*Railroads*, p. 316).

28. *Times* (internat. ed.), Mar. 1903, sec. 4, p. 1: *Herald*, June 22–23, 1918, p. 8; Robert Glass Cleland, *A History of Phelps Dodge, 1834–1950*, p. 161; *Times*, Aug. 24, 1913, sec. 17, p. 7; El Paso Chamber of Commerce, *El Paso, the Story of a City*.

29. *Mexican Mining Journal* 5 (Dec. 1907): 10. American investors cornered much of Mexico's mineral production. United States investments in Mexican industrial metals rose from $18 million in 1897 to $162 million in 1914. See Marvin D. Bernstein, *The Mexican Mining Industry 1890–1950*, p. 7; also see *Times*, Mar. 4, 1902, p. 1, and *Washington Star*, July 5, 1914, p. 4,

contained in Mexico Northwestern Railway Company Correspondence, box 13, Miscellaneous, McNeely Collection, UTEP Archives.

30. *Times*, Feb. 7, 1892, p. 2; Jan. 4, 1900, p. 4.
31. Ibid., Jan. 5, 1900, p. 7; Dec. 10, 1908; Feb. 18, 1900, p. 3; and *International Industrial Record* 3 (July 20, 1901): 1.
32. *Lone Star*, Nov. 10, 1883, p. 1; *Times*, Sept. 12, 1886, p. 2, and Feb. 28, 1900, p. 3.
33. Mary Antoine Lee, "A Historical Survey of the American Smelting and Refining Company in El Paso, 1887–1950," pp. 3–18. Eastern capitalists invested in two other El Paso smelters, which operated for only a brief period (see City Council, *Minutes*, Mar. 17, 1887; *Times*, Mar. 18, 1887, p. 4; Mar. 27, 1887, pp. 2, 4; Mar. 21, 1888, p. 5; and Bernstein, *Mexican Mining*, p. 22).
34. Lee, "American Smelting," pp. 43–46. For ASARCO activities in Chihuahua, see Chihuahua and Pacific Railroad Correspondence, box 8, 1906 letters, McNeely Collection, UTEP Archives.
35. *International Industrial Record* 3 (July 20, 1901): 1; see Lee, "American Smelting," p. 80, and John Sneed, ed., *El Paso—The Queen City of the Southwest*, pp. 8–9.
36. Lee, "American Smelting," pp. 84–87; *Times*, Aug. 24, 1913, sec. D, p. 3; El Paso Chamber of Commerce, *What to See in El Paso, Texas*, p. 69; *El Paso City Directory*, 1917. By the 1920s ASARCO converted the El Paso Smelter to a copper operation to treat Guggenheim ore from Arizona (Bernstein, *Mexican Mining*, p. 54).
37. *Lone Star*, Nov. 12, 1881, p. 2; *Times*, Sept. 30, 1903, p. 5; Feb. 1, 1903, p. 4; U.S. Department of State, *Commercial Relations of the United States with Foreign Countries, 1910* (1913), p. 42; *Times*, Sept. 27, 1890, p. 4; *Herald*, May 8, 1916, p. 6; *Times*, Dec. 29, 1906, p. 3.
38. After the United States, Great Britain (29.1% of total) and France (26.7%) constituted the largest investors in Mexico by 1911. See Roger D. Hanson, *Mexican Economic Development: The Roots of Rapid Growth*, pp. 15–16; also see *Times* (internat. ed.), Mar. 1903, pp. 2, 5.
39. *Times*, Jan. 17, 1902, p. 4; J. Harvey Brigham to James D. Porter, Assistant Secretary of State, Paso del Norte, Jan. 19, 1886, RG 59, M-3. Besides commerce with the United States that passed through Juárez, this Mexican border town also experienced some growth in agriculture, retail trade, and local industries; however, the termination of the town's duty-free zone in 1905 shifted Juárez's economy to a dependency on American tourism. For the economic history of Ciudad Juárez, see Martínez, *Boom Town*. Also see Armando B. Chávez, *Historia de Ciudad Juárez*.
40. *Times*, Dec. 31, 1893, p. 7; Jan. 17, 1902, p. 4; Nov. 18, 1903, p. 5; Oct. 16, 1909, sec. 3, p. 7; *Herald*, Jan. 26–27, 1918, p. 10.
41. U.S. Department of State, *Commercial Relations of the United States*, vol. 1 (1901). Also see U.S. Consul Buckford Mackey to Assistant Secretary of State, Paso del Norte, Mar. 22, 1889, RG 59, M-4, and A. J. Sampson

to William Wharton, Paso del Norte, Mar. 22, 1890, RG 59, M-4.

42. Pletcher, *Rails, Mines, and Progress*, p. 3.

43. *Mexican Mining Journal* 9 (July 1911): 5. U.S. Consul Edwards in 1905 listed 67 American citizens or corporations within the Cuidad Juárez consular district with the majority engaged in mining or ranching (see Thomas D. Edwards to Robert Bacon, Assistant Secretary of State, Ciudad Juárez, Nov. 16, 1905, RG 59, M-6).

44. *Lone Star*, Nov. 28, 1885, p. 4; Charles W. Kindrick to W. R. Day, Assistant Secretary of State, Ciudad Juárez, Jan. 12, 1898, RG 59, M-6; *Times*, Apr. 27, 1902, p. 11; U.S. Department of State, *Reports From the Consuls of the United States, 1895*, p. 488.

45. U.S. Department of State, *Commercial Relations* (1909), pp. 525–26; Chamber of Commerce, *El Paso, the Story of a City*, no p. nos.; El Paso Chamber of Commerce, *Prosperity and Opportunities in El Paso and El Paso's Territory for the Investor–Manufacturer–Jobber–Miner–Farmer–Home Seeker*, p. 19; *Herald*, Jan. 6, 1920, p. 2; *El Paso City Directory*, 1918, p. 76. For the cattle industry in West Texas, see Martin, *City Moves West*, pp. 3–15.

46. El Paso Chamber of Commerce, *Somewhat About El Paso, Texas—Its Resources, Advantages, Attractions 1903 and 1904*, p. 25; *Times*, Oct. 11, 1910, p. 4; Mar. 19, 1902, p. 7.

47. *El Paso City Directory*, 1920, p. 196.

48. *Lone Star*, Nov. 31, 1881, p. 2; *Official Proceedings of the Twelfth National Irrigation Congress, El Paso, Nov. 15–18, 1904*, p. 16; Chamber of Commerce, *El Paso, the Story of a City*; idem, *Prosperity and Opportunities*, p. 19; *El Paso City Directory*, 1917, p. 72; idem, *What to See*, p. 9.

49. *El Paso City Directory*, 1918, p. 76; ibid., 1920, p. 195.

50. For a detailed description of the free zone, see Martínez, *Boom Town*, pp. 19–37. According to Martínez, merchants in Ciudad Juárez who took advantage of the "zona libre" included many Americans and Europeans. Department stores in Juárez during this period sold imported American, European, and Asian goods such as carpets, silks, linens, laces, and jewelry.

51. *Times*, May 1, 1900, p. 8.

52. Ibid., Nov. 26, 1901, p. 4; Aug. 20, 1910, p. 1. During the Mexican Revolution, El Paso retail merchants benefited from sales to both Mexican and U.S. troops stationed along the border (Martínez, *Boom Town*, p. 46).

53. *Lone Star*, Oct. 29, 1881, p. 2; *Times*, Jan. 6, 1893, p. 4; Feb. 7, 1900, p. 3.

54. *Times*, May 30, 1900, p. 3; Nov. 30, 1902, p. 4; Sept. 28, 1909, p. 4; Chamber of Commerce, *El Paso, the Story of a City*.

55. Chamber of Commerce, *El Paso, the Story of a City*; Sneed, ed., *Queen City*, p. 15; *Times*, Sept. 28, 1887, p. 1; Oct. 6, 1911, p. 3; June 9, 1901, p. 1. The Pearson Box Factory was part of the holdings of Dr. Frederick Stork Pearson and his Canadian firm, Madera Company, Ltd. The Madera Company held more than 1 million hectares of Chihuahua land, the third largest holding in that state; material for the box factory came from

Pearson's mills at Madera, Chihuahua. See McNeely, "Railways of Mexico," p. 21.

56. *El Paso City Directory*, 1920, p. 196; also see U.S. Department of Commerce, *Fifteenth Census of the United States, 1930, Manufactures*, 3 (1933), pp. 1470–79.

57. *Lone Star*, Dec. 17, 1881, p. 2; Chamber of Commerce, *El Paso, the Story of a City*; Billy M. Jones, *Health-Seekers in the Southwest, 1817–1900*, pp. vii–viii; *Times*, Sept. 17, 1891, p. 4; May 1, 1900, p. 8. El Paso physician J. T. Harrington wrote the city council in 1890 that "the reputation of your city as a Sanatorium is now firmly established, and no work upon the Health resorts of the United States is all complete without a full mention of El Paso" (see City Council, *Minutes*, Feb. 21, 1890).

58. Jones, *Health-Seekers*, pp. 169–70; *Times*, Dec. 1, 1900, p. 1; *El Paso City Directory*, 1889, p. 155; ibid., 1920, pp. 592–93. For the early development of tourism in the West, see Earl Pomeroy, *In Search of the Golden West: The Tourist in Western America*.

59. *Historical and Descriptive Review of El Paso*, p. 46.

60. Chamber of Commerce, *Somewhat About El Paso*, p. 32. In 1887 the El Paso City Council wired President Grover Cleveland that on his scheduled Pacific trip he should stop in El Paso and rest. A visit to the border city, the council informed Cleveland, would not only allow him to inspect the city's progress but also give him an opportunity to compare "the American and Mexican civilizations as they contrast themselves in this the largest American and Mexican city situated on the border of the two republics" (see City Council, *Minutes*, Sept. 2, 1887).

61. See Oscar J. Martínez, "Border Boom Town: Ciudad Juárez Since 1880," pp. 57–59, 100–04.

62. *City Directory*, 1889, pp. 149–50; ibid., 1920, pp. 931–32; *Times* (internat. ed.), Mar. 1903, sec. 5, p. 7. The *Lone Star* noted in 1885 that "the building boom in El Paso is a big thing for everybody. It is giving employment to a large number of skilled and unskilled laborers, and puts money in the pockets of merchants and boarding house keepers, and directly or indirectly benefits every man, woman, and child in the city" (*Lone Star*, May 9, 1885, p. 3).

63. *Times*, Jan. 2, 1903, p. 3; Nov. 24, 1901, p. 4. A Mexican newspaper in El Paso also applauded the city's construction. *El Defensor* in 1894 stated: "Four days ago work began on a building to go up at the corner of Texas and Stanton. El Paso is progressing" (*El Defensor*, Sept. 24, 1894, p. 2); also see *Times*, Jan. 11, 1913, p. 6, and *Herald*, Dec. 30, 1915, p. 7.

64. *City Directory*, 1920, p. 196; C. G. Benfield to P. C. Thede, c/o H. C. Ferris, General Manager, Mexico Northwestern Railway Co., New York, n.d., in Dav Book, Madera Co., Nov. 13, 1911–Apr. 11, 1912, box 12, Railroads-Mexico Northwestern Railway Co. Correspondence, McNeely Collection, UTEP Archives; Treasurer, Mexico Northwestern Railway Co., New York, Apr. 6, 1911, in Letter Book, Mexico Northwestern Railway Co., box 9,

McNeely Collection; *Herald*, Jan. 22–23, 1916, p. 8, and Jan. 1, 1920, p. 2; Sonnichsen and McKinney, *The State National*, p. 74; *Times*, Oct. 11, 1901, p. 1.

65. Chamber of Commerce, *El Paso, the Story of a City*, no p. nos.; U.S. Department of Commerce, *Fourteenth Census of the United States, 1920, Agriculture*, 6 (1922), pp. 670, 722; *Thirteenth Census of the United States, 1910, Agriculture*, 7 (1913), pp. 808–09.

66. Chester Chope Transcript, ACC 29, Institute of Oral History, University of Texas at El Paso, July 27, 1968, p. 8. Institute of Oral History hereinafter will be cited as IOH.

67. U.S. Department of Commerce, *Fourteenth Census, Agriculture*, 1920, vol. 6, pp. 670–740. For a view of West Texas agriculture, which also remained limited during this period, see Martin, *City Moves West*, pp. 35–49, 50–72. The principal crops in West Texas during this period were cotton, corn, oats, Kaffir corn, and milo maize.

68. U.S. Department of the Interior, *Eleventh Census of the United States, 1890, Population* 1 (1895), pp. 332, 382, *Fourteenth Census, 1920: Abstract*, p. 57. El Paso ranked twelfth in growth in the United States in 1910 and was one of 22 cities that doubled their population between 1900 and 1910 (see Martínez, *Boom Town*, p. 32, and *Times*, Aug. 28, 1891, p. 4).

69. Ray C. West, Jr., "El Paso: Big Mountain Town," p. 91.

CHAPTER 3

1. For a breakdown of various ethnic groups employed by western and southwestern industries, see U.S., Congress, Senate, Dillingham Commission, *Immigrants in Industries*, pt. 25: *Japanese and Other Immigrant Races in the Pacific Coast and Rocky Mountain States*, vol. III, pts. I–IV, VI, hereinafter cited as Dillingham Commission.

2. *Times*, Jan. 23, 1909, p. 2; Lesley Byrd Simpson, *Many Mexicos*, p. 260.

3. *Times*, June 5, 1900, p. 1.

4. Friedrich Katz, "Labor Conditions on Haciendas in Porfirian Mexico: Some Trends and Tendencies," and Lawrence Anthony Cardoso, "Mexican Emigration to the United States, 1900 to 1930: An Analysis of Socio-Economic Factors," pp. 14–23. For the Porfirian period see Daniel Cosío Villegas, ed., *Historia Moderna de México*. Also see Roger D. Hanson, *The Politics of Mexican Development*, pp. 23–29.

5. Katz, "Labor Conditions," pp. 33–46; also see Marvin D. Bernstein, *The Mexican Mining Industry 1890–1950*, p. 86. Workers on Chihuahua haciendas received from 35 centavos (17.5 U.S. cents) to 1 peso and 50 centavos (75 U.S. cents) a day (Robert Lynn Sandels, "Silvestre Terrazas, the Press, and the Origins of the Mexican Revolution in Chihuahua," pp. 159–60). The Mexican peso was valued at 2 to the dollar.

6. Oscar J. Martínez, "Border Boom Town: Ciudad Juárez Since 1880," p. 41, and Victor S. Clark, "Mexican Labor in the United States," p. 480.

7. World War I Draft Registration Cards, El Paso City Boards 1 and 2, Federal Records Center, East Point, Georgia. There are eleven boxes for both draft boards with approximately 19,660 names. In order to get a representative sample of at least 385 every thirty-fourth name was counted starting with the fifth card. The total number of names in the sample amounted to 578. Of the total, 274 were detected as Mexicans, both citizens and aliens. Of these, 113 listed only Mexico as their place of birth; in addition, 17 had no birthplaces listed. It is my belief that a good number of them were born in the northern states, given the breakdown of those who listed their place of birth. Of the 144 who gave their birthplace, 103 were born in the northern states: 68 in Chihuahua, 16 in Zacatecas, 11 in Durango, 4 in Coahuila, and 4 in Aguascalientes. This represented 71.76 % of the Mexicans who recorded a birthplace. For sample methodology see Peter R. Knights, *The Plain People of Boston, 1830-1860: A Study in City Growth*, pp. 3-10. I wish to thank Dr. Carl V. Harris of the Department of History, University of California, Santa Barbara, for his assistance in utilizing the sample methodology.
8. Park, "Mexican Labor in Arizona," pp. 228-29; also see Glenn E. Hoover, "Our Mexican Immigrants," p. 100. See also Max Sylvius Handman, "Economic Reasons for the Coming of the Mexican Immigrant," and Arthur F. Corwin, "Causes of Mexican Migration to the United States: A Summary View," pp. 557-67.
9. Samuel Bryan, "Mexican Immigration in the United States," p. 726; Ricardo Romo, "Mexican Workers in the City: Los Angeles, 1915-1930," pp. 1, 50, 65; U.S. Department of Commerce, *Fifteenth Census, Population*, vol. 2, p. 27.
10. Clark, "Mexican Labor," pp. 473-74; Charles Armijo Transcript, ACC 117, IOH, Jan. 30, 1973, p. 3; Romo, "Mexican Workers," p. 53; *Fifteenth Census, Population*, vol. 2, p. 27. For a comparative view of Mexicans in El Paso, San Antonio, and Los Angeles, see Romo, "The Urbanization of Southwestern Chicanos in the Early Twentieth Century."
11. *Times*, Oct. 2, 1907, p. 3; Armijo Transcript, IOH, p. 3; Cleofas Calleros Transcript, IOH, Sept. 14, 1972, p. 7.
12. *El Defensor*, Sept. 24, 1894, p. 3; Oct. 15, 1894, p. 2; Park, "Mexican Labor in Arizona," p. 212.
13. Calleros Transcript, IOH, p. 3; Dillingham Commission, pt. 25, vol. III, pt. I, pp. 11-12; Judith Fincher Laird, "Argentine, Kansas: the Evolution of a Mexican-American Community: 1905-1940," p. 121. Romo estimates that during the 1920s, 69% of Mexican immigrants represented males, compared to 56% for other immigrants. Moreover, most Mexican immigrants were quite young; the medium age in 1930 for Mexicans in the United States being 20 years against the medium age of 26 for U.S. citizens (Romo, "Mexican Workers," pp. 9, 11).
14. *Times*, May 17, 1902, p. 2.
15. Ibid., Jan. 27, 1903, p. 1.
16. Ibid., July 4, 1906, p. 3; July 16, 1906, p. 4; Sept. 1, 1907, p. 2; *El Clarín*

del Norte, Feb. 9, 1907, p. 1; Clark, "Mexican Labor," p. 467. Clark observed that in both Ciudad Juárez and El Paso used clothing stores thrived. *El Correo de Chihuahua* reported in 1907 that 22,000 men had entered the United States the previous year through El Paso; this number equaled approximately half Chihuahua's entire agricultural work force (Sandels, "Silvestre Terrazas," p. 162).

17. Dillingham Commission, pt. 25, vol. III, pt. I, pp. 7–8; Laird, "Argentine, Kansas," p. 131.

18. Dillingham Commission, pt. 25, vol. III, pt. I, pp. 7, 13–14, 19, 23.

19. *Times,* Feb. 2, 1911, p. 1; Feb. 4, 1911, pp. 1, 10; Mar. 28, 1911, p. 10; Aug. 22, 1911, p. 10; Feb. 2, 1912, p. 1; May 3, 1912, p. 1; May 3, 1912, p. 2; Dec. 21, 1913, p. 10.

20. Interviewed by Ricardo Romo in Los Angeles, Nov. 1972 (see Romo, "Mexican Workers," pp. 32–33). El Pasoan Mario Acevedo, who arrived in 1916, remembers that every hour of the day and night, large numbers of Mexican political refugees could be seen on the streets of south El Paso (Mario Acevedo Transcript, IOH, May 1, 1975, p. 10). Also see T. T. Edwards, U.S. Consul, to Secretary of State, Ciudad Juárez, Apr. 13, 1911, in U.S. Department of State, Records of the Department of State Relating to Internal Affairs of Mexico, 1910–1929, microcopy no. 274, 812.00/1309, hereinafter cited as Internal Affairs.

21. *Times,* Jan. 13, 1914, p. 1; Apr. 7, 1914, p. 9; Mar. 21, 1914, p. 4; Jan. 14, 1914, p. 1; Jan. 16, 1914, p. 1.

22. Ibid., Jan. 17, 1914, p. 6; Feb. 7, 1914, p. 6; Feb. 8, 1914, p. 6; Feb. 14, 1914, p. 4; Feb. 15, 1914, p. 6. Also see Edwards to Secretary of State, Ciudad Juárez, Feb. 21, 1914, Internal Affairs, 812.00/11006.

23. *Times,* Jan. 23, 1914, p. 3; Apr. 30, 1914, p. 7; May 6, 1914, p. 7; Sept. 22, 1914, p. 1; Sept. 20, 1914, p. 1; Sept. 23, 1914, p. 1; Jan. 27, 1914, p. 3. Officers of the Huerta army were also later released and allowed the choice of remaining in the United States or returning to Mexico.

24. Ibid., Mar. 29, 1911, p. 8; June 14, 1911, p. 10.

25. Ibid., Oct. 4, 1914, p. 15; interview conducted by Paul S. Taylor with Mr. Myers, Watkins Labor Agency, St. Louis, Missouri, Manuscript 102-273, Paul S. Taylor Papers, Bancroft Library, University of California, Berkeley. Taylor's interviews were conducted between 1927 and 1930. By the 1920s, sociologist Emory L. Bogardus also observed that "American motion pictures in Mexico act as incentives of Mexican immigration to the United States" (Bogardus, "The Mexican Immigrant," p. 476). A Mexico City newspaper, *La Convención,* reported in 1915 that much mail was being received in Mexico from the United States, apparently due to increased immigration (Jan. 16, 1915, p. 7, in Mexican Newspaper Collection, ACC 829, box 2, UTEP Archives).

26. *Herald,* June 16, 1916, p. 4; June 21, 1916, p. 5; Aug. 22, 1916, p. 2; Félix López Urdiales Transcript, IOH, Jan. 4, 1974, p. 4. Also see Edwards to Secretary of State, El Paso, Sept. 24, 1916, Internal Affairs, 812.00/19282.

27. "The Mexican 'Invaders' of El Paso," *Survey* 36 (July 8, 1916): 380. The *Survey* reporter informed his readers that in 1915 more than 4,000 Mexicans had been refused entry at El Paso out of 65,248 immigrants. "None have ever looked so hungry and forsaken," he wrote, "as those who have come over the last few months. They seem to be getting worse all the time."
28. *Herald*, Feb. 29, 1916, p. 3.
29. Ibid., Mar. 3, 1910, p. 11; June 15, 1916, p. 5; June 16, 1916, p. 5.
30. Ibid., June 19, 1916, p. 4.
31. U.S. Department of Commerce, *Special Census of the Population of El Paso, Texas* (Jan. 15, 1916), pp. 3, 4. Concern about the "invasion" of Mexican immigrants arose again during the 1920s. Former Congressman James L. Slayden wrote in 1921 that hundreds of "ragged, filthy paupers" had entered the United States from Mexico (see James L. Slayden, "Some Observations on Mexican Immigration," p. 123).
32. John Martínez, *Mexican Emigration to the U.S. 1910–30*, p. 17; Martínez, "Border Boom Town," p. 86. According to Oscar Martínez, the Mexicans' fears were not unfounded, for some political refugees actually were drafted.
33. *Herald*, May 11, 1917, p. 8; Romo, "Mexican Workers," p. 57; *Herald*, May 11, 1917, p. 8.
34. *Herald*, May 14, 1917, p. 6; Romo, "Mexican Workers," p. 57. The demand for increased immigration characterized a basic position taken by employers in other developing economies. In writing of Argentine and Chilean economic interests who supported liberal immigration policies between 1890 and 1914, Solberg notes that "these groups were convinced that prosperity and growth required a steady flow of cheap labor" (Carl Solberg, *Immigration and Nationalism: Argentina and Chile, 1890–1914*, pp. 17–21).
35. Martínez, *Mexican Emigration*, p. 18; *Herald*, May 24, 1917, p. 6.
36. *Herald*, Aug. 25, 1917, p. 6.
37. Ibid., Mar. 7, 1918, p. 3; Urdiales Transcript, IOH, p. 8. The baths, according to Urdiales, were located underneath the bridge. Such health facilities, however, left much to be desired. Vera Sturges, writing for the *Survey*, noted a few years later that "when five or six hundred steaming people, men, women, and children, are crowded into the room at one time, sanitation becomes a farce" (Vera L. Sturges, "The Mexican Immigrant," p. 470).
38. *Herald*, June 17, 1918, p. 12; June 28, 1918, p. 9; *Times*, June 20, 1918, p. 3.
39. *Times*, July 6, 1918, p. 3.
40. Ibid., July 18, p. 3; *Herald*, July 19, 1918, p. 6.
41. Ibid., July 26, 1918, p. 4; July 27–28, 1918, p. 6. Cleofas Calleros remembered that these "houses" consisted of boxcars. According to him, communities such as Vado and Rincon, New Mexico, began as clusters of boxcars with Mexican families (Calleros Transcript, IOH, p. 3). In Argentine, Kansas, Mexican workers for the Santa Fe lived in converted boxes on the side tracks near the roundhouse (Laird, "Argentine, Kansas," p. 62).
42. *Times*, Dec. 31, 1918, p. 3; Jan. 3, 1919, p. 6; *Herald*, Oct. 22, 1919, p. 3.

For Mexican immigration in the 1920s see Romo, "Mexican Workers," pp.
61–72; Enrique Santibañez, *Ensayo Acerca de la Inmigración Mexicana en
los Estados Unidos*; Cardoso, "Mexican Emigration," pp. 93–130; and Mark
Reisler, *By the Sweat of their Brow: Mexican Immigrant Labor in the United
States*, pp. 49–76, 127–226.

43. *Times*, May 29, 1912, p. 6; Clark, "Mexican Labor," p. 475.

44. *El Latino-Americano*, Feb. 28, 1891, p. 4; *Times*, Mar. 25, 1888, p. 5; Apr.
19, 1888, p. 8; Apr. 11, 1888, p. 5. Notwithstanding violations of the contract labor law it appears that the large majority of Mexican immigrants
arrived in El Paso without contracts, as did other immigrants to the United
States at the time. For a comparative view, see Charlotte Erickson, *American Industry and the European Immigrant, 1860–85.*

45. *Times*, Jan. 24, 1900, p. 7; Jan. 25, 1900, p. 5; June 2, 1903, p. 5; T. T.
Edwards, U.S. Consul at Ciudad Juárez, to Robert Bacon, Assistant Secretary of State, Ciudad Juárez, Nov. 25, 1905, RG, M-6. Victor Clark believed
that unlike seaports, where the contract labor law could better be enforced,
the U.S.-Mexican border represented an unenforceable area ("Mexican
Labor," p. 471).

46. *El Paso City Directory*, 1910, p. 506; *Times*, Nov. 28, 1905, p. 3; Oct. 7,
1908, p. 3; Feb. 6, 1907, p. 5. González was also listed in the city directory
of 1905 as a city policeman. In the early 1920s the González Labor Agency
still supplied thousands of Mexican workers. In 1923, for example, it
transported 5,000 Mexicans to the Santa Fe Railroad and to various agricultural interests. (See interview conducted by Taylor with J. R. Silva,
employment agent for Mexican agricultural laborers, El Paso, Manuscript
103–107a, Taylor Papers.)

47. *El Clarín del Norte*, Nov. 24, 1906, p. 7; José Cruz Burciaga Transcript,
ACC 154, IOH, Feb. 16, 1974, p. 33; Manuel Gamio, *The Life Story of the
Mexican Immigrant*, p. 16. Gamio conducted a series of interviews with
Mexican immigrants in the United States during 1926 and 1927.

48. Bryan, "Mexican Immigration," pp. 727–28; *Times*, Oct. 27, 1906, p. 7;
Apr. 1, 1910, p. 8; Calleros Transcript, IOH, p. 2. The Dillingham Commission estimated that supply deductions averaged about one-third of Mexican
railroad workers' earnings (Dillingham Commission, pt. 25, vol. III, pt. I,
p. 27).

49. Dillingham Commission, pt. 25, vol. III, pt. I, p. 26; *Times*, July 27, 1910,
p. 8; May 21, 1911, p. 4.

50. *Times*, Dec. 24, 1909, p. 2.

51. Mauricio Cordero Transcript, IOH, Feb. 15, 1974, p. 27.

52. *Times*, Oct. 2, 1907, p. 3; Apr. 1, 1910, p. 8. According to one labor contractor, Mexicans in 1903 were shipped out of El Paso in "coaches in the
back of freight trains," which took 8 to 10 days to get to Los Angeles,
among other locations (see interview conducted by Taylor with Mr. Clark,
El Paso, Manuscript 98–103, Taylor Papers).

53. *Times*, Sept. 14, 1907, p. 8.

54. Ibid.; interview conducted by Taylor with Mr. Kennedy, S. W. & A. Labor Agency, San Antonio, Manuscript 26–31, Taylor Papers. Sociologist Helen W. Walker observed in 1928 that "it was not uncommon for the 'enganchadores' and employment bureaus to use 'unscrupulous methods' to recruit Mexican laborers, since their object [was] to get as many as possible" (as quoted in Romo, "Mexican Workers," p. 52).

55. See Taylor interviews with R. P. Zárate, El Paso, Manuscript 110–114; with personnel at Zárate-Avina Labor Agency, El Paso, Manuscript 17–189; with W. H. Talbot, Los Angeles, Manuscript 56–61; with Mr. Johnson, El Paso, Manuscript 102–107; with B. J. Kerley, El Paso, Manuscript 18–190; with C. R. Howard, El Paso, Manuscript 27–199; and with Mr. Marril, Los Angeles, Manuscript 1–173. For Taylor's studies, see Taylor, *Mexican Labor in the United States*, vols. 1–3, and *An American-Mexican Frontier, Nueces County, Texas*.

56. *Times*, Oct. 28, 1894, p. 6; Nov. 22, 1901, p. 7; Sept. 18, 1902, p. 3; Oct. 8, 1908, p. 2. Some of the railroad labor agents were Mexicans or of Latin backgrounds.

57. Ibid., Apr. 23, 1911, p. 1; Apr. 25, 1911, p. 1.

58. *Herald*, June 19, 1916, p. 4; Nov. 23, 1917, p. 6; *Times*, Sept. 6, 1918, p. 4; *Labor Advocate*, Aug. 2, 1911, p. 1. The *Advocate* was the official newspaper of the Central Labor Union, AFL, in El Paso; hereinafter cited as *Advocate*. According to Laird, the Santa Fe line established its own labor agency by 1917 due to increased complaints by Mexicans concerning bad treatment at the hands of independent labor agents ("Argentine, Kansas," pp. 131–32).

59. June 23–24, 1917, p. 4; *Herald*, Mar. 1, 1918, p. 2; Mar. 13, 1918, p. 4; *Times*, May 21, 1919, p. 4. The American Beet Sugar Company contracted Mexican workers in El Paso as early as 1905 (Taylor interview with Silva, Manuscript 103–107a, Taylor Papers).

60. *Herald*, June 5, 1918, p. 3; June 6, 1918, p. 3; *Advocate*, June 14, 1918, p. 8; *Times*, June 30, 1918, p. 20; *Advocate*, May 31, 1918, p. 1; Nov. 28, 1919, pp. 1, 8.

61. *Times*, Sept. 17, 1918, p. 3.

62. Various Mexicans to A. V. Lomelí, Mexican Consul at El Paso, El Paso, Mar. 12, 1910, Topográfica 18–25–64; Eduardo Soriano Bravo, Mexican Consul at El Paso, Gobierno Constitucionalista, to Al. C. General Candido Aguilar, Secretaría de Relaciones Exteriores, El Paso, Jan. 6, 1917, Topográfica 17–17–12, Asuntos Secretaría de Relaciones Exteriores, Mexico City; hereinafter, cited as ASRE. A Mexico City newspaper later complained in 1921 of the often drunken condition of U.S. immigration officials (Sturges, "Mexican Immigrant," p. 470).

63. Soriano Bravo to Aguilar, El Paso, Feb. 19, 1917, Topográfica 28–9–46, ASRE. For additional information on abuses by immigration officers and labor contractors, see Helen W. Walker, "Mexican Immigrants as Laborers." In the 1920s complaints included not only *enganchadores* but *coyotes—*

the individuals who illegally transferred Mexicans across the border due to the imposition of the head tax and visa fee; a Mexican newspaper in El Paso, *El Sol*, referred to the *coyotes* as "Traficantes de Carne Humana" (Transporters of Human Meat), June 11, 1924, pp. 1–4, in Mexican Newspaper Collection, ACC 829, box 6, UTEP Archives. For additional information on the attempt by Mexican consulates in the United States to protect Mexican immigrants, see Cardoso, "Mexican Emigration," pp. 130–61.

64. Dillingham Commission, pt. 25, vol. III, pt. III, pp. 146, 206; Park, "Mexican Labor in Arizona," p. 266. The employment of Mexican miners in Arizona had a long history; as early as 1878, almost 200 Mexican miners worked at the Clifton mines.

65. *El Paso del Norte*, May 14, 1904, p. 3; *Times*, Oct. 15, 1911, p. 7.

66. *Times*, July 25, 1919, p. 1; Oct. 21, 1912, p. 3; Taylor interview with Mr. Lindsay, U.S. Immigration Service, Houston, Manuscript 116–287, Taylor Papers; and for an early account of Mexican immigration patterns, see Manuel Gamio, *Mexican Immigration to the United States*. Gamio compiled his data between 1926 and 1927.

67. Gamio, *Mexican Immigration*, pp. 84–86. This particular song was composed in Chicago.

CHAPTER 4

1. For a comparison with black workers in Chicago see Allan H. Spears, *Black Chicago: The Making of a Negro Ghetto, 1890–1920*, esp. chap. 8, "The Struggle for Homes and Jobs," pp. 147–66. Glenn E. Hoover in a 1929 article in *Foreign Affairs* incorrectly observed that "it is almost impossible for a newly arrived [Mexican] immigrant, ignorant of our language, to work in a factory or shop or on a small farm" ("Our Mexican Immigrants," p. 101).

2. *Times*, June 2, 1914, p. 6. Humbert Nelli in his study of Chicago's Italian immigrants discovered that they also performed a variety of work activities besides common labor. For a comparison with Mexican immigrants see chap. 3, "Economic Activity: The Padrone Era and After," in Nelli, *The Italians in Chicago, 1880–1930*, pp. 55–87.

3. See *El Paso City Directories*, 1900, 1910, 1920; see World War I Draft Registration Cards, El Paso City Boards 1 and 2; *Times*, Nov. 28, 1902, p. 3; Feb. 26, 1914, p. 3. Victor S. Clark observed in 1908 that Mexican smelter workers in El Paso received from $1.10 to $1.25 a day. In Arizona smelters, according to Clark, wages for Mexican common labor averaged about $2 a day for 8 hours of work, for "though the Mexicans can stand hot work, they cannot work long hours in the very hot surroundings of a desert smelter." See Clark, "Mexican Labor," p. 493; also, Chamber of Commerce, *Prosperity and Opportunities*, p. 19; *Times*, Nov. 26, 1904, p. 5.

4. See *City Directories*, 1900, 1910, 1920.

5. Charles Armijo Transcript, IOH, p. 4; Calleros Transcript, IOH, pp. 4–5. Calleros also recalled that during his tenure as an assistant cashier in the

Santa Fe offices he encountered hostility from the Masons and the Ku Klux Klan. According to Calleros, both groups opposed white-collar jobs for Mexicans and unsuccessfully attempted to have him fired. R. B. Gutiérrez worked as a Spanish–English telegraph operator for the Mexico Northwestern Railway in El Paso until the railroad dismissed him in 1912 after the Mexican consul in El Paso accused Gutiérrez of being a "rebel." See A. L. L. to Mr. Crocket, El Paso, Oct. 14, 1912, box 13, Folder–Mexico Northwestern Railway, Miscellaneous, 1912, 1913, 1914, in the McNeely Collection, ACC 795, UTEP Archives.

6. As quoted in the *Times*, Dec. 17, 1908, p. 8. In his statements about Mexican labor, Clark only repeated earlier rationalizations for the exploitation of cheap Maxican labor. Capitalist Sylvester Mowry in his 1864 history of Arizona and Sonora wrote: "The question of labor is one which commends itself to the attraction of the capitalists; cheap, and, under proper management, efficient and permanent. My own experience has taught me that the lower class of Mexicans . . . are docile, faithful, good servants, capable of strong attachment when fairly and kindly treated. They have been 'peons' (servants) for generations. They will always remain so, as it is their natural condition" (Park, "Mexican Labor in Arizona," p. 61).

7. *Times*, Feb. 3, 1908, p. 6.

8. *Herald*, Dec. 17, 1917, p. 5; May 19–20, 1917, p. 7; June 2–3, 1917, p. 17; Cordero Transcript, IOH, p. 2. The Southwestern Line in 1917 listed 58 employees in its shops, 46 having Spanish surnames, and half the workers in both the machine shop (51 of 102) and the roundhouse (19 of 38) of the G.H. & S.A. possessed Spanish surnames.

9. *Lone Star*, May 9, 1885, p. 3. Clark observed in 1908 that in other southwestern cities where Mexican settlements could be found, construction firms also utilized Mexican unskilled labor. "In Los Angeles," Clark wrote, "Mexicans of California descent and immigrants are employed as builders' helpers and in minor occupations connected with construction." Clark further noted that in cities such as Tucson and Laredo, Mexicans dominated the less skilled building trades and had formed unions separate from Anglo-Americans. See Clark, "Mexican Labor," pp. 494–85. For a study of Mexican occupations in Los Angeles during the 1920s, see Robin F. Scott, "The Mexican–American in the Los Angeles Area, 1920–1950: From Acquiescence to Activity," pp. 20–24.

10. Clark, "Mexican Labor," p. 495; *Times*, Aug. 20, 1912, p. 8; *El Paso del Norte*, Mar. 12, 1904, p. 2. For earlier reports of construction accidents involving Mexicans, see *Lone Star*, Dec. 3, 1881, p. 3, and Nov. 17, 1883, p. 3. A later study, which analyzed Mexican immigration workers in both rural and urban occupations during the 1920s, is Gamio, *Mexican Immigrants*, "The Mexican Immigrant Wage-Earner," esp. pp. 30–50.

11. *Herald*, May 5–6, 1917, p. 15; May 12–13, 1917, p. 7; June 16–17, 1917, p. 7. Paul S. Taylor in his 1928 study of Chicago noted the growth of Mexi-

can industrial workers since World War I in steel and meat packing (see *Mexican Labor in the United States: Chicago and the Calumet Region*, pp. 27–48, 68–70). Also see Mark Reisler, "The Mexican Immigrant in the Chicago Area during the 1920s," pp. 147–49.

12. *Times*, Oct. 14, 1905, p. 8; Feb. 22, 1904, p. 1; Nov. 19, 1908, p. 6; Jan. 5, 1910, p. 6; Martínez, "Border Boom Town," p. 96. Clark also observed that in Los Angeles and other southwestern cities a minority of immigrant Mexicans worked in semiskilled or skilled positions ("Mexican Labor," p. 495).

13. Leonard A. Goodman III, "The First Cigar Factory in El Paso"; *Times*, Oct. 10, 1911, p. 5; *Herald*, Dec. 21, 1915, p. 6; Chamber of Commerce, *Prosperity and Opportunities*, p. 75; *Advocate*, Oct. 16, 1909, p. 5. Also see *Herald*, June 9–10, 1917, p. 15, and Mario Acevedo Transcript, IOH, pp. 3–4.

14. *Times*, Jan. 4, 1914, p. 6; Urdiales Transcript, IOH, p. 11; *Herald*, Dec. 4, 1915, p. 21. Mauricio Cordero, who worked after 1910 in several downtown stores operated by Jewish merchants, remembered that in some establishments all the clientele were Mexicans. According to Cordero, the busiest day was Saturday, when the stores remained open until midnight to service Mexican laborers who had been paid that day. Some of the most sought after merchandise were workers' overalls. See Cordero Transcript, IOH, pp. 1, 20. Félix Urdiales recalled that on Saturdays, most Mexicans, even those who lived in Ciudad Juárez, shopped in El Paso, where they could receive credit (Urdiales Transcript, pp. 10–11).

15. *Herald*, July 19, 1916, p. 10; Robert Gustave King, "The Popular Dry Goods Company," pp. 9, 25; *La Patria*, Sept. 16, 1920, p. 33; Cordero Transcript, IOH, pp. 3, 5. Although it appears to be a unique case, Cordero also recalled that when he was in charge of men's clothing at the Bazar Store between World War I and 1923, he sold so much merchandise that he averaged $600 a month on a commission of 1% (Cordero Transcript, p. 29).

16. Cleofas Calleros, *El Paso . . . Then and Now*, p. 183.

17. Martínez, "Border Boom Town," p. 96; also Alma María García, "The Occupational Distribution of El Paso Ethnicity, 1900–1940," p. 10; *Advocate*, Feb. 4, 1913, p. 1. Taylor observed in his Chicago study that no more than 200 Mexican clerks could be found in the city. Although employed by a variety of American stores, they exclusively served a Mexican clientele (Taylor, *Chicago and the Calumet Region*, p. 166).

18. See Pay Roll of Mills Building, June 5, 1915, in H. Stevens Collection, ACC 761, UTEP Archives; El Paso School Board, *Minutes*, Mar. 3, 1902; Sept. 17, 1918 (hereinafter cited as *School Minutes*); *Times*, Sept. 7, 1905, p. 3; Chris P. Fox Transcript, IOH, July 25, 1972, p. 14; *Times*, May 21, 1913, p. 12. In a 1968 interview Mrs. Hugh White commented that one reason few blacks could be found in El Paso in the early part of the century was that "there [were] too many Mexicans to do the jobs" (Mrs. Hugh White Transcript, ACC 52, IOH, June 3, 1968, p. 22).

19. *Advocate*, July 16, 1915, p. 5; *Herald*, Aug. 22, 1917, p. 6; *Advocate*, Oct. 18, 1918, p. 4; Nov. 29, 1918, p. 8. Chester Chope, who arrived in El Paso in 1917, remembered that the jitneys were Fords that operated from the the north side of San Jacinto Plaza in the downtown section. According to Chope, the standard fare was 5 cents, or a jitney as a nickel was called, hence the popular name for the early taxicabs. See Chope Transcript, IOH, p. 29.

20. See the Judge Joseph Sweeney Collection (2 boxes), UTEP Archives; *Times*, Apr. 29, 1894, p. 7; Nov. 19, 1908, p. 1; El Paso City Council, *Minutes*, Aug. 27, 1886; Oct. 18, 1889; June 24, 1897; Feb. 2, 1899; Apr. 11, 1901; Sept. 2, 1889; Nov. 17, 1898; Apr. 13, 1899; Nov. 17, 1898; Dec. 8, 1898; Jan. 3, 1901.

21. Sweeney to El Paso City Council, El Paso, June 18, 1908, in Sweeney Collection, letterbook, box 2.

22. *Texas Union* (El Paso), Mar. 1, 1912, p. 4. Public jobs as a form of patronage were not unique to Mexican immigrants; for a comparison with Italians, see Nelli, *Italians*, pp. 75–76.

23. *Times*, Mar. 20, 1896, p. 20. Employers and their supporters throughout the Southwest often rationalized their exploitation of cheap Mexican labor by suggesting that Mexicans were unreliable, lazy, and sought any excuse not to work. Helen W. Walker in a 1928 article quoted Eva Frank of the *Nation*, who had written that Mexicans cared little for making money and that "until the Mexican-Indian wants money to buy things that money can buy more than he wants mastery over time, he will not labor consistently like the American, except by force" ("Mexican Immigrants as Laborers," p. 60).

24. City Council, *Minutes*, Sept. 8, 1890; May 16, 1890; Aug. 31, 1894; Feb. 28, 1896; June 3, 1897; *Herald*, Jan. 26–27, 1918, p. 6; *Times*, Apr. 22, 1905, p. 3; *Times*, Aug. 6, 1950, in the El Paso Police Department Newspaper Files, El Paso Public Library.

25. See *El Paso Herald-Post*, Mar. 20, 1930, in the politics file of the El Paso Vertical Files, El Paso Public Library; see the city directories for lists of El Paso public officials, 1890–1920.

26. Calleros, *El Paso*, p. 177; *Herald-Post*, July 12, 1935, p. 9, in Vertical Files—Pioneer M, El Paso Public Library; *Times*, Dec. 25, 1901, p. 1; June 4, 1902, p. 8; June 14, 1904, p. 5. Federal officials also hired Mexican common laborers at nearby Fort Bliss. Félix Urdiales recalled working at the Fort Bliss stables during World War I and being paid $2.40 a day. If Urdiales's memory is correct, this wage was much higher than the standard rate of $1 a day for Mexican common labor in El Paso. See Urdiales Transcript, IOH, p. 6.

27. U.S. Department of the Interior, *Manuscript Census, 1900*, El Paso County, vols. 35, 36. There are 3,123 total family units included in the 1900 census for El Paso city. To acquire a representative sample of as close to 385 units as possible, every eighth unit was counted commencing with the second listing of the First Ward (the census encompassed El Paso's four wards). The total number of units in the sample amounted to 393. For sample method-

ology see Peter R. Knights, *The Plain People of Boston, 1830–1860: A Study in City Growth*, pp. 3–10. I wish to thank Dr. Carl V. Harris of the Department of History, University of California, Santa Barbara, for his assistance in utilizing the sample methodology.

28. Ibid. Of married Mexican immigrant women 41.08% were between 15 and 30 years of age; 38.44% were between 30 and 40 years of age.

29. For attitudes of Mexican men toward wage-working women see Paul S. Taylor, "Mexican Labor in Los Angeles Industry," unpublished manuscript, pt. 2, Taylor Papers, and Gamio, *Life Story*, p. 46.

30. As quoted in Margaret Towner, "Monopoly Capitalism and Women's Work during the Porfiriato," p. 93. Like Mexican men, most males in the United States did not look with favor on women, especially married ones with children, working outside the home (see Valerie Kincade Oppenheimer, *The Female Labor Force in the United States*, pp. 40–42).

31. *Fourteenth Census, Population*, vol. 4, p. 263. Spears in his study of black Chicago recorded a similar occupational trend among black women (*Black Chicago*, p. 151).

32. The 1900 census sample of 393 households reveals significant differences between occupations of Mexican female heads of household and those of American female heads. Of 33 households with Mexican female heads, the distribution consisted of 19 with no occupation listed; 6 washing women; 3 servants; and 1 each of the rest—laundress, dressmaker, seamstress, ironer and washer, and grocer. By contrast, American heads of households had these occupations: 11 with no occupations listed; 6 who operated boarding-houses; 3 nurses; and 1 each of the rest—housekeeper, laundress, operator of a bakery; chambermaid; typist, dairy woman; schoolteacher; hotel keeper; dressmaker; and, finally, 1 nun and 1 prostitute (whose occupation the census taker listed as "lewd").

33. Clark, "Mexican Labor," p. 496. Almost 20 years after Clark's report, Emory S. Bogardus observed that in Los Angeles, unlike El Paso, American women as a rule did not hire Mexican domestics because they lacked "knowledge and training." Moreover, Mexican women who labored as domestics were "handicapped because of this lack of knowledge of American household methods." See Bogardus, "The Mexican Immigrant." In Chicago during the 1920s Taylor reported that few Mexican women served as domestics due to the scarcity of Mexican females. Those who did received about $7 or $8 a week plus room and board; Taylor also recorded that in some Mexican boardinghouses, Mexican domestics doubled as prostitutes. See Taylor, *Chicago and the Calumet Region*, p. 79.

34. Mary Wilson Barton, "Methodism at Work Among the Spanish-Speaking People of El Paso, Texas," p. 15. Some Mexican women, such as Bertha Luján, who was employed by the Mills Building for $5.75 a week, also worked as maids in office buildings (see Pay Roll, Mills Building, Sept. 1, 1911, H. Stevens Collection).

35. Mrs. Jane Perrenot Transcript, ACC 62, IOH, Feb. 14, 1973, pp. 12–15;

Times, Nov. 17, 1919, p. 5; July 16, 1907, p. 4. The only minor source of competition that Mexican domestics encountered came from the Chinese, who entered El Paso from Mexico. Those who remained worked as cooks. For a survey of the Chinese in El Paso, see Nancy Farrar, "The Chinese in El Paso." Also see U.S. Department of the Interior, *Manuscript Census, 1900.* From the sample of 393 household units, 23 reported live-in domestics; of these 19 represented American middle-class families with a head of household classified as a professional, such as a physician or lawyer. Of these 23, only 1 Mexican had a live-in domestic: Jacobo Blanco, the Mexican consul in El Paso.

36. *Advocate*, Oct. 31, 1919, p. 4; *Herald*, June 23–24, 1917, p. 7; July 28–29, 1917, p.16; May 26–27, 1917, p. 15; Dec. 15–16, 1917, p. 4; telephone interview with Mrs. Frank Fletcher, Jr., El Paso, Aug. 15, 1975.

37. *Times*, Sept. 26, 1902, p. 8; *La Patria*, Oct. 30, 1919, p. 4; *Herald*, June 9–11, 1917, p. 15; *Times*, Dec. 19, 1905, p. 7; *El Día*, Feb. 18, 1919, p. 3; *La Patria*, Oct. 30, 1919, p. 4; *Times*, Dec. 8, 1903, p. 7; *Herald*, Aug. 1, 1916, p. 14. In 1908 Clark noted that in the United States Mexican women as well as children did not usually work in factories. Although this condition changed after 1910 because of the availability of cheap Mexican female workers, Clark had concluded that the omission of Mexican women from factories was due "partly because husbands and fathers oppose it, having a peasant prejudice to their women leaving home, and it is partly because these women lack the foundations of industrial training." See Clark, "Mexican Labor," p. 495. Governor C. C. Young's 1930 report in California pointed out that many Los Angeles Mexican women worked in the canning industry (Scott, "Mexican-American in Los Angeles," p. 20). Taylor observed in 1928 that a considerable proportion of Chicago's Mexican clerks were young women, especially in those 10-cent stores that had a Mexican clientele (see Taylor, *Chicago and the Calumet Region*, p. 166).

38. *Lone Star*, Aug. 22, 1885, p. 3; *Times*, Feb. 4, 1903, p. 2; Feb. 3, 1905, p. 3. For a study of El Paso's red-light district see "Sin City," in Sonnichsen, *Pass*, pp. 277–309.

39. Guillermo Balderas Transcript, IOH, Apr. 18, 1974, p. 5; Enrique L. Acevedo Transcript, IOH, ACC 141, May 17, 1974, p. 13; *Times*, Feb. 19, 1908, p. 3; Aug. 6, 1895, p. 7; Sept. 2, 1902, p. 8; Aug. 11, 1919, p. 12; Feb. 7, 1914, p. 6; Feb. 14, 1912, p. 2.

40. See the *Times* and *Herald* for this period and El Paso Chamber of Commerce, *Minutes* (1899–1908); *Times*, Apr. 16, 1910, p. 5; Apr. 22, 1910, p. 8. Chris P. Fox remembered that some Mexican stores could be found in East El Paso with names such as El Porvenir, El Buen Tomo, and El Ultimo Balazo (Fox Transcript, IOH, p. 15). Nelli noted in his study of Chicago's Italian immigrants that a variety of businesses could be found in the Italian settlement such as grocers, butchers, shoemakers, blacksmiths, tailors, and so on (*Italians*, pp. 73–74). Taylor observed that in Chicago by 1928, with the increase in the city's Mexican population, the number of Mexican businesses

also grew. Most of the businesses remained small and catered to an exclusive Mexican clientele. Taylor found that the majority of Mexican businesses were pool halls, restaurants, or barbershops. See Taylor, *Chicago and the Calumet Region*, pp. 167–71.

41. *El Defensor*, Sept. 24, 1894, p. 1; also see the rest of the 1894 issues. Since it appears no Spansih-language newspapers operated in El Paso during the 1880s, it is difficult to know the extent of Mexican businesses in that decade. The *Lone Star* carried an ad in 1884 for Romero and Maxwell, owners of the El Paso Planning Mill on San Antonio Street, which sold lumber and other wood products (*Lone Star*, June 28, 1884, p. 3). See *El Paso del Norte* from Mar. 12, 1904 to May 12, 1904. For Calderón Brothers correspondence, see A. Calderón to Silvestre Terrazas, El Paso, May 20, 1916, Calderón Hermanos, Sucs., Inc., El Paso, 10 letters, 1903–23, boxes 85–91 (1919–25), M-B, 18, pt. 1, Silvestre Terrazas Collection, MSS, Bancroft Library, University of California, Berkeley. For examples of Mexican stores that advertised in the Spanish-language press, see the following: *Las Dos Américas*, Mar. 7, 1898, p. 3; Apr. 18, 1898, pp. 2, 4; July 11, 1898, p. 2; *El Monitor*, Oct. 10, 1897, p. 3; *El Progresista*, June 17, 1901, p. 2; *El Día*, Feb. 18, 1919, p. 4; *El Correo del Bravo*, Mar. 13, 1913, p. 4.

42. See *La Patria* from June 18, 1919 to Dec. 31, 1919; *Times*, Aug. 17, 1919, p. 70. The appearance of Mexican silent movie houses in El Paso also created a new occupation. Guillermo Balderas recalled that his brother, Eduardo, translated English-language subtitles into Spanish (Balderas Transcript, IOH, p. 14).

43. See the various El Paso Spanish-language newspapers during this period.

44. *La Patria*, Sept. 16, 1920, p. 50.

45. *El Hispano-Americano*, Aug. 7, 1893, p. 4; *El Correo del Bravo*, May 1, 1913, p. 4.

46. Terrazas to U.S. Secretary of State, El Paso, May 27, 1920, in C. B. Hudspeth Collection, ACC 738, box 3, folder 78, UTEP Archives. A list of El Paso's Spanish-language newspapers can be found in the Chicano Studies Library, University of California, Berkeley. The price of a Mexican newspaper in El Paso ranged from $2.75 per year's subscription to *La Democracía* in 1906 to $5 per year for *La Patria* in 1919. For Silvestre Terrazas's business as well as political activities in Chihuahua and El Paso see Sandels, "Silvestre Terrazas." Also see an interview with his daughter in Margarita Terrazas Transcript, IOH, ACC 17, Oct. 24, 1964.

47. See *City Directory*, 1900, p. 321; 1920, pp. 918–19; ibid., 1900, p. 322; 1920, pp. 921–22; ibid., 1900, pp. 328–29; 1920, pp. 934–50; *Times*, Jan. 9, 1919, p. 3; see the city directories for home and business addresses. Still alive in 1973 at the age of 102, when he was named El Paso's "Oldest Father," Francisco Noriega recalled that he became a barber when he moved to El Paso in 1901 from Jalisco, Mexico. He established his barbershop at 304 South El Paso Street and when he finally retired in 1955 he owned six barbershops in south El Paso. See *Times*, June 17, 1973, p. 8-A. Guillermo

Balderas also remembered that about 1917 his father operated a barbershop in East El Paso; as a youngster, Balderas worked as a shoeshine boy in his father's shop (Balderas Transcript, IOH, pp. 1, 10). The Spanish Speaking Retail Grocers' Association was affiliated but separate from the American-dominated El Paso County Retail Grocers Association. Mexican grocers who had to be licensed by the city attempted to prevent unlicensed Mexican fruit-vendors from selling on the streets and sidewalks (see City Council, *Minutes*, Aug. 2, 1889).

48. See the *City Directory*, 1920.
49. White, *Out of the Desert*, p. 365; *El Monitor*, Dec. 16, 1897, p. 3; *Times*, Apr. 20, 1905, p. 5; Jan. 18, 1905, p. 4; Anson Mills Collection, UTEP Archives; *Times*, Jan. 13, 1963, in Félix Martínez Vertical File, Pioneers M, Southwestern Collection.
50. *Times*, Jan. 28, 1904, p. 5; Apr. 11, 1907, p. 3; Jan. 29, 1908, p. 5; Martínez Vertical File; White, *Out of the Desert*, p. 365; *Times*, Jan. 13, 1963 in Martínez Vertical File. Miss Elizabeth Kelly, a longtime El Paso librarian, remembered that "Don Félix" also served on the first El Paso Public Library Board of Directors (Elizabeth and Ann Kelly and Mary Quinn Transcript, IOH, Mar. 1973, p. 6).
51. See *City Directory*, 1900, pp. 326, 335; ibid., 1920, pp. 934, 975–76; Acevedo Transcript, p. 42; *Times*, Feb. 14, 1895, p. 6; *El Progresista*, June 17, 1901, p. 2; *El Monitor*, Nov. 28, 1897, p. 1; Dec. 30, 1897, p. 3; June 26, 1897, p. 4; *El Clarín del Norte*, Feb. 9, 1907, p. 5; *Herald*, May 5, 1917, p. 2.
52. See *City Directory*, 1900, pp. 320–21; ibid., 1920, pp. 911–12; *El Monitor*, Aug. 29, 1897, p. 4; *La Patria*, June 18, 1919, p. 4; *El Hispano-Americano*, Aug. 7, 1893, p. 3; *El Correo del Bravo*, Mar. 13, 1913, p. 2.

CHAPTER 5

1. For an earlier version of this chapter see my article "Racial Dualism in the El Paso Labor Market, 1880–1920."
2. *City Directories*, 1900, 1920, 1940. Taken from unpublished paper by Alma María García, "The Occupational Distribution of El Paso by Ethnicity, 1900–1940," p. 10.
3. Ibid.
4. *Herald*, May 26, 1917, p. 6.
5. Dillingham Commission, pt. 25, vol. III, pt. I, p. 44.
6. García, "Occupational Distribution," p. 10.
7. Calleros Transcript, IOH, p. 9.
8. Stephen Thernstrom, *The Other Bostonians: Poverty and Progress in the American Metropolis, 1880–1970*, p. 218. See "Blacks and Whites," esp. pp. 176–219.
9. Martínez, *Boom Town*. For additional studies that stress occupational segmentation influenced by race between Mexicans and Americans, see Romo, "Mexican Workers," pp. 132–68; Albert M. Camarillo, "The Making of a

Chicano Community: A History of the Chicanos in Santa Barbara, California, 1850-1930"; idem, *Chicanos in a Changing Society: From Mexican Pueblos to American Barrios in Santa Barbara and Southern California, 1848-1930*; and Mario Barrera, *Race and Class in the Southwest*.

10. See the *Advocate* during this period; U.S. Department of the Interior, *Manuscript Census, 1900*; World War I Draft Registration Cards; and interview conducted by Taylor with Juan Machuca, immigrant inspector, along the Rio Grande, Manuscript 100-105, Taylor Papers.

11. Dillingham Commission, pt. 25, vol. III, pt. I, p. 19; pt. III, pp. 192-93.

12. Park, "Mexican Labor in Arizona," p. 261.

13. *Times*, Nov. 20, 1919, p. 5.

14. Ibid.

15. Ibid.

16. *Herald*, Nov. 20, 1919, p. 10.

17. Ibid. Fletcher's indictment of Mexican inefficiency contrasted with the El Paso public school's opinion that Mexican children excelled at manual work.

18. *Herald*, Nov. 21, 1919, p. 11.

19. Ibid.

20. *Times*, Nov. 20, 1919, p. 5.

21. *Herald*, Nov. 20, 1919, p. 10.

22. Ibid.

23. Ibid., Nov. 21, 1919, p. 11.

24. *Advocate*, June 26, 1909, p. 1; Sept. 2, 1910, p. 1. Prior to the AFL's appearance in El Paso, Knights of Labor locals operated in the border city, but no evidence exists of Mexican members or of attempts to organize Mexican workers.

25. See ibid., Feb. 20, 1909, p. 2; Mar. 6, 1909, p. 4; Mar. 13, 1909, p. 2; Mar. 20, 1909, p. 4; Mar. 12, 1920, p. 2.

26. American Federation of Labor, *Proceedings of the Twenty-Second Annual Convention*, 1902, p. 152; *Proceedings of the Thirtieth Annual Convention*, 1910, p. 212; *Advocate*, Jan. 21, 1910, p. 3.

27. *Advocate*, Feb. 14, 1913, p. 8; Apr. 8, 1913, p. 3; Oct. 31, 1913, p. 1; June 12, 1914, p. 6; June 19, 1914, p. 1; June 26, 1914, p. 1.

28. Ibid., Feb. 13, 1909, p. 2; Jan. 14, 1910, p. 3; July 22, 1910, p. 6.

29. Ibid., Oct. 24, 1919, p. 1; Oct. 31, 1919, p. 1.

30. Ibid., Oct. 31, 1919, p. 4.

31. Ibid., Nov. 7, 1919, p. 1; *La Patria*, Nov. 1, 1919, p. 1; *Advocate*, Nov. 7, 1919, p. 1; Nov. 14, 1919, p. 1. The term *Raza* was used by Mexicans in El Paso during the period.

32. *Advocate*, Dec. 19, 1919, p. 1. In a 1923 railroad shop strike in Argentine, Kansas, the Santa Fe railroad rather than recruiting strikebreakers simply promoted some of its unskilled Mexican workers to more skilled positions as replacements for American workers (Laird, "Argentine, Kansas," p. 139).

33. *Advocate*, July 31, 1909, p. 1; Aug. 1, 1919, p. 1; *Texas Union*, Jan. 31, 1913, p. 1; Sept. 26, 1913, p. 5; Jan. 9, 1914, p. 1; *Advocate*, Apr. 21, 1916,

p. 1. The *Advocate's* name was changed to the *Texas Union* on Sept. 8, 1911, because the editor believed the word *Labor* might be objectionable to business; it was later changed back to the *Advocate* in 1915.

34. *Advocate*, Sept. 2, 1910, p. 1; Samuel Gompers, "United States–Mexico–Labor–Their Relations," p. 633.

35. American Federation of Labor, *Proceedings of the Thirty-Sixth Annual Convention*, 1916, p. 63; *Proceedings of the Thirty-Seventh Annual Convention*, 1917, p. 264; also see *Pan-American Labor Press*, Dec. 4, 1918, p. 8, in Pan-American Federation of Labor, 1st Congress, *Proceedings and Conference*, Laredo, Texas, in the AFL-CIO Library, AFL-CIO headquarters, Washington, D.C. One successful effort with Mexican workers occurred in the Clifton–Morenci–Metcalf mining districts in Arizona, where after strikes in 1915 and 1917 the Western Federation of Miners and its successor, the International Union of Mine, Mill and Smelter Workers, organized the Mexican workers into three locals (see C. A. Vargas, "A Short History of the Organized Labor Movement in the Clifton–Morenci–Metcalf District in Arizona," pp. 1, 3). Also see James R. Kluger, *The Clifton–Morenci Strike: Labor Difficulty in Arizona, 1915–1916*. For a history of relations between organized labor in the United States and Mexico, see Harvey Levenstein, *Labor Organizations in the United States and Mexico: A History of Their Relations*. With increased Mexican immigration by the 1920s the national policy of the AFL turned toward restricting Mexican immigration by placing it on a quota system. Although no quota was established, the onset of the 1929 depression sharply curtailed Mexican immigration until World War II.

36. Park, "Mexican Labor in Arizona," p. 244.

37. *Advocate*, Jan. 7, 1910, p. 1; *Texas Union*, Mar. 13, 1914, p. 1; *Advocate*, Nov. 17, 1916, p. 4; Jan. 9, 1920, p. 4. The AFL failed to recognize that in certain southwestern locations employers advanced the wages of skilled American workers as an effective way of preventing unionization (see Park, "Mexican Labor in Arizona," p. 263).

38. *Advocate*, Apr. 22, 1910, p. 1; July 21, 1911, p. 4.

39. Ibid., Apr. 7, 1911, p. 4; May 6, 1910, p. 1.

40. Ibid., Sept. 10, 1915, p. 4. According to Park, the Western Federation of Miners also attempted to organize American workers in Arizona around a strong anti-Mexican policy. However, Park believes "this course merely increased the dilemma of unionism in Arizona, since it played directly into the hands of the employers by further perpetuating the existence of two competing classes of workmen." See Park, "Mexican Labor in Arizona," pp. 253–54.

41. *Advocate*, May 6, 1910, p. 1.

42. *Texas Union*, Jan. 16, 1914, p. 1.

43. *Advocate*, June 24, 1910, p. 4.

44. American Federation of Labor, *Proceedings of the Thirty-Ninth Annual Convention*, 1919, pp. 384–85.

45. See the *Advocate* and *Texas Union* between 1909 and 1920. In Arizona,

union organizers introduced anti-alien measures at the 1910 State Constitutional Convention at Phoenix. Key propositions included the prohibition of contract labor, the exclusion of aliens from public works jobs, the prohibition of non-English speaking persons in hazardous work, and the limitation of alien labor to no more than 20% of an employers' work force; of these, only the public works measure was adopted (Park, "Mexican Labor in Arizona," pp. 269–78).

46. *Pan-American Labor Press,* Sept. 18, 1918, p. 4.
47. U.S. Department of Commerce, *Fourteenth Census, Abstract,* pp. 57, 117.
48. Gamio, *Life Story of the Mexican Immigrant,* p. 182.
49. Armijo Transcript, IOH, p. 13.
50. Gerald Rosenblum, *Immigrant Workers: Their Impact on American Labor Radicalism.*
51. *Times,* Nov. 27, 1901, p. 1; Nov. 29, 1901, p. 2; Apr. 18, 1905, p. 3; June 6, 1917, p. 5; June 7, 1907, p. 3; June 8, 1907, p. 8; June 9, 1907, p. 7; June 10, 1907, p. 8.
52. Ibid., Apr. 9, 1913, p. 12; Apr. 10, 1913, p. 2; Apr. 12, 1913, p. 2; Apr. 24, 1913, p. 1.
53. Ibid., Apr. 23, 1913, p. 12; May 13, 1913, p. 2; Apr. 29, 1913, p. 5.
54. Ibid., Mar. 30, 1911, p. 2; June 21, 1914, p. 1; Oct. 30, 1919, p. 10; Aug. 3, 1919, p. 4.
55. Rosenblum, *Immigrant Workers,* p. 36. Greene in his study of Slav coal miners in Pennsylvania noted that their support for unionization and strikes stemmed from either economic factors or ethnic solidarity (Victor R. Greene, *The Slavic Community on Strike: Immigrant Labor in Pennsylvania Anthracite,* p. 211).
56. Greene, *Slavic Community,* p. 31. Juan Gómez-Quiñones, on the other hand, inaccurately suggests that the prevailing characteristic of Mexican labor in the United States between 1900 and 1920 was militancy as expressed in strike actions (see Gómez-Quiñones, "The First Steps: Chicano Labor Conflict and Organizing, 1900 to 1920").

CHAPTER 6

1. *Lone Star,* Jan. 16, 1883, p. 3; Aug. 18, 1883, p. 3.
2. *Times,* Nov. 3, 1887, p. 8; Jan. 5, 1888, p. 5.
3. Ibid., Sept. 2, 1890, p. 7; *School Minutes,* Nov. 5, 1894; *El Defensor,* Jan. 13, 1895, p. 3; Bertha Archer Schaer, *Historical Sketch of Aoy School,* p. 7.
4. *School Minutes,* June 1, 1895; June 7, 1897; June 16, 1899; Sept. 5, 1900; *Times,* Dec. 3, 1901, p. 3. Principal López resigned as principal in 1902 to take a position as an interpreter for the American government in the Philippines.
5. *Times,* Sept. 8, 1908, p. 8.
6. Ibid., Oct. 16, 1909, sec. 3, p. 3; Letitia S. Fitzpatrick, ed., *El Paso,* pp. 76–77. Taylor in an interview with the principal of the Beall School in El Paso

in the late 1920s found a continuation of similar views about the Mexican children's limited potentials (interview conducted by Taylor with Mr. Clark, principal of Beall School, El Paso, Manuscript 116–120, Taylor Papers).

7. Paul W. Horn, "Survey of the City Schools of El Paso, Texas," pp. 33–34.
8. *School Minutes,* Auditors' Monthly Report of Expenditures, Sept. 1910; Sept. 9, 1912; Schaer, *Aoy,* pp. 14–15.
9. J. C. Ross, "Industrial Education for the Spanish-Speaking People," *New Mexico Journal of Education* 7 (Feb. 1911): 19–21, as quoted in Gilbert G. González, "The System of Public Education and its Function within the Chicano Communities, 1920–1930," pp. 115–16; Romo, "Mexican Workers," p. 196; González, "Public Education," pp. 89–90.
10. González, "Public Education," pp. 76, 72, 81–82, 107, 78.
11. Ibid., pp. 119, 174–75.
12. Ibid., p. 174.
13. Ibid., p. 178.
14. González, "Crisis of Urbanization: Racism, Education, and the Mexican Community in Los Angeles, 1920–1930." Also see González, "The Relationship between Progressive Educational Theory and Practice and Monopoly Capital." For a similar analysis of American educational developments, see Samuel Bowles and Herbert Gintes, *Schooling in Capitalist America.*
15. *Times,* Sept. 2, 1913, p. 12. On Americanization and the Mexican immigrant, see Mario T. García, "Americanization and the Mexican Immigrant, 1880–1930."
16. As quoted in Schaer, *Aoy,* p. 17. For an analysis of "time" in pre-industrial culture, see E. P. Thompson, "Time, Work-Discipline, and Industrial Capitalism."
17. *Herald,* Feb. 22, 1916, p. 4. The *Lone Star* in 1883 also accused Mexican students of another vice: smoking (Jan. 16, 1883, p. 3).
18. González, "Public Education," pp. 135–36.
19. See *Reports of the Public Schools,* El Paso, 1903–04, p. 26, Southwestern Collection.
20. *Times,* Sept. 8, 1903, p. 3; *School Minutes,* "Report from External Committee," Jan. 6, 1899, and noted in minutes of Jan. 16, 1899; see the list of teachers published each year by the *Times.* During the 1920s a small number of Spanish-surnamed teachers were hired (see *School Minutes,* "List of Teachers and Salaries, 1922–23"; "Comparison of Teachers' Salaries, Size of Classes, Cost of Instruction, 1927–28 and 1928–29").
21. *Times,* Nov. 21, 1906, p. 3.
22. Horn, "Survey," p. 33.
23. González, "Public Education," pp. 99, 102–04.
24. *Lone Star,* Feb. 1, 1882, p. 3; *Times,* Feb. 18, 1899, p. 3; *School Minutes,* Aug. 12, 1912; Apr. 28, 1913.
25. See *Reports of Public Schools,* 1903–04, p. 27.
26. Horn, "Survey," p. 64.
27. Schaer, *Aoy,* p. 23.

28. *School Minutes*, Sept. 9, 1912.
29. Horn, "Survey," pp. 19–22; *Times*, July 6, 1908, p. 8; see *Report of the Public Schools*, El Paso, 1914–16, p. 5; U.S. Department of Commerce, Bureau of the Census, *Special Census*, 1916, p. 5; *Herald*, Sept. 4, 1916, p. 12; *School Minutes*, Nov. 17, 1913; also see *Herald*, Feb. 18, 1915, p. 5. According to the enrollment figures in 1928, out of a total school population of 17,485, students of Mexican nationality constituted 10,229; however, it is conceivable that many Mexican Americans were counted as simply Americans (*School Minutes*, Feb. 19, 1929).
30. *School Minutes*, Sept. 19, 1918; Oct. 21, 1919; June 17, 1919; *La Patria*, Aug. 30, 1919; *Herald*, June 2, 1917, p. 6. By 1917 night schools had been established by both public and charitable organizations for Mexican adults in order to teach them more practical skills, hygiene, and American principles. Mexican community leaders in El Paso supported such vocational and civic training (see J. A. Escajeda et al., to President and Members of "Sociedad Mexicana Protectora de Instrucción Publica," El Paso, June 7, 1919, in Pedro E. Portillo, El Paso, 109 letters and one folder of statements, 1914–24, boxes 85–91 [1919–25], Terrazas Collection, MSS).
31. Schaer, *Aoy*, pp. 3–11; *Times*, Sept. 17, 1919, p. 5; *School Minutes*, Sept. 12, 17, 1910.
32. Horn, "Survey," p. 8.
33. *Times*, Sept. 17, 1919, p. 5. Also see Edna Snowden Foley, "A History of Beall School, El Paso, Texas"; Ruth Cummings, "History of Alamo School"; and Elma Galentine Ramírez, "A Brief History of Franklin School." One of Franklin's most distinguished Mexican alumni was Mexican American actor Gilbert Roland, who attended in 1916.
34. Balderas Transcript, IOH, p. 3.
35. *Times*, Sept. 17, 1919, p. 5.
36. *Herald*, Jan. 26, 1915, p. 2; Horn, "Survey," p. 41. See the list of graduates of El Paso High School to be found in the principal's office, El Paso High School. During the 1920s the number of Mexicans at the high school increased, although the figures remained low compared to American students; in May of 1930, 19 Spanish-surnamed students graduated from a class of 195 (*School Minutes*, "List of High School Grads," May 1930).
37. Calleros Transcript, IOH, p. 9; Balderas Transcript, IOH, p. 4.
38. See *Times*, Feb. 15, 1907, p. 5; School Records—Sacred Heart School, 1909–45, one box (this source can be found at the Sacred Heart Church Rectory on South Oregon Street); Calleros Transcript, IOH, p. 10. Also see City of El Paso, Department of Planning, *A Short History of South El Paso*, p. 9, and Cleofas Calleros, *Historia de la Parroquia de San Ignacio de Loyola*, El Paso, Texas.

CHAPTER 7

1. Although there is little supporting evidence, longtime El Paso resident,

Enrique L. Acevedo, suggested in a 1974 interview that the term *Chicano* derived from Chihuahuita (Enrique L. Acevedo Transcript, IOH, p. 4).

2. Chihuahuita received its name from the large number of Mexican immigrants from the northern Mexican state of Chihuahua. The concentrations of Mexicans where jobs could be found on the edge of the central business district represented a characteristic of other immigrant groups in the United States. See David Ward, "The Making of Immigrant Ghettos, 1840–1920," in Alexander Callow, Jr., ed., *American Urban History*, pp. 296–307, and Louise Año Nuevo de Kerr, "Chicano Settlements in Chicago: A Brief History." Año Nuevo de Kerr points out that by 1920 Mexican settlements in Chicago were determined by their proximity to the railroad yards, steel mills, and packing houses that had recruited Mexican labor. Also see Taylor, *Chicago and the Calumet Region*, pp. 56–61.

3. Similar to a pattern observed by Nelli in his study of Italian immigrants in Chicago, Mexicans in El Paso also formed communities away from the central city colony at an early date (see Nelli, *Italians*, pp. 22-54). According to Spears, enclaves of blacks likewise existed in other sections of Chicago around the turn of the century in addition to the dominant black southside (see Spears, *Black Chicago*, pp. 11–27).

4. See the preface in City of El Paso, Department of Planning, *A Short History of South El Paso*; *Times*, Jan. 17, 1899, p. 3; and Gladys Gregory, "El Chamizal: A Boundary Problem Between the United States and Mexico." In 1911 an international arbitration commission composed of the United States, Mexico, and Canada voted to award most of the Chamizal back to Mexico; however, the United States refused to accept the decision. The 1963 treaty returned some of the disputed area to Mexico in exchange for some Mexican land east of the Chamizal. For correspondence concerning aspects of the Chamizal problem see the Richard Burgess Papers in the Southwest Collection Archives, boxes 293 and 294, El Paso Public Library. Burgess was an El Paso lawyer in the 1920s. Also see Gladys Gregory, "The Chamizal Settlement; A View from El Paso"; Sheldon B. Liss, *A Century of Disagreement: The Chamizal Conflict, 1854-1964*; Kenneth Duane Yielding, "The Chamizal Dispute: An Exercise in Arbitration"; and Salvador Mendoza, *El Mito y la Mística de El Chamizal*.

5. *Manuscript Census, 1900*.

6. *City Directory*, 1902, p. 1; Robert Neal Blake, "A History of the Catholic Church in El Paso," pp. 52-70.

7. *Times*, June 5, 1906, p. 3; Feb. 4, 1908, p. 3; Sept. 13, 1910, p. 5. Unlike the racial violence directed toward blacks in various northern cities as they expanded into white neighborhoods, no evidence exists of similar racial disturbances in El Paso. It seems that few Anglos in El Paso lived in the southeastern areas, which became predominantly Mexican settlements (see *Manuscript Census, 1900*).

8. Blake, "Catholic Church," pp. 113-14; *El Monitor*, Sept. 12, 1897, p. 4; *Times*, July 26, 1902, p. 8.

9. City of El Paso, *South El Paso*, p. 2; according to long-term El Paso resident Chris P. Fox, "Those Mexican families got tired of being flooded out each year, so they packed up their goods, wares, and merchandise, and went up to the Mesa" (Fox Transcript, IOH, p. 13).

10. Armijo Transcript, IOH, p. 12. Armijo also believed that the Mexicans of Stormsville acquired water in barrels from the downtown area.

11. See Cleofas Calleros, *El Paso . . . Then and Now*, p. 81. In a 1968 interview, Mrs. Hugh White commented that she did not remember hearing of any trouble with the Mexicans in Stormsville, but she "wouldn't be surprised if they didn't come down into town and do some stealing" (White Transcript, IOH, p. 15).

12. Eugene O. Porter, "The Great Flood of 1897." According to Chester Chope, who arrived in El Paso in 1917 and worked as a reporter for the *Times*, politician J. Porter Bender, who also lived in Stormsville, voted the Mexicans "as a block" (see Chope Transcript, IOH, p. 7).

13. Enrique L. Acevedo Transcript, IOH, pp. 16–17; Mario Acevedo Transcript, IOH, p. 11; Blake, "Catholic Church," p. 76. Mauricio Cordero, who arrived in El Paso in 1907, recalled that some of the wealthy Mexican refugees in Sunset Heights collected money among themselves to construct Holy Family (see Cordero Transcript, IOH, p. 37). Also see Mardee de Wetter, "Revolutionary El Paso, 1910–1917," p. 159.

14. World War I Draft Registration Cards, El Paso City Boards 1 and 2. See chap. 3, n. 7, for sample method. Also see *Herald*, Jan. 20, 1916, p. 10. According to Chester Chope, houses in Anglo neighborhoods after World War I sold for about $6,000. This factor alone would have excluded most Mexican residents. See Chope Transcript, IOH, p. 8. Guillermo Balderas remembered that as late as 1937, a landlord of an apartment on Myrtle Avenue in the predominantly American Cotton Addition refused to rent him a room. "We don't rent to Mexicans," Balderas recalled the landlord's words. See Balderas Transcript, IOH, pp. 15–16.

15. Thirty-four years later journalist Ray C. West, Jr. could still detect a physical and social separation between Mexicans and Americans in El Paso. "An intangible but rarely escapable line divides the 'Mexican' from the so-called 'American' element. It is not, except now and then, a line setting peoples apart in bitter race prejudice and hatreds. It is more, on both sides, a matter of greater or less racial 'indrawing' of one element from its opposite number." See West, Jr., "El Paso: Big Mountain Town," p. 84.

16. *Times*, Jan. 9, 1900, p. 6.

17. Ibid., June 16, 1892, p. 7; July 21, 1903, p. 3; July 26, 1905, p. 2; July 29, 1905, p. 3.

18. Ibid., Aug. 11, 1905, p. 3. Three years earlier, on behalf of other Mexicans in Chihuahuita, Francisco Martínez unsuccessfully petitioned the city council to extend sewer lines through the alleys between Stanton and Oregon streets and to the city limits (see City Council, *Minutes*, Dec. 4, 1902).

19. *Times*, Aug. 11, 1905, p. 3. According to a petition from Guillermo Mena

on behalf of other Mexican residents of the southern wards, the city already charged them too much for the few sanitary facilities that existed. Mena called for a reduction to at least 50 cents per month for the cleaning of "water closets." See City Council, *Minutes*, Sept. 25, 1902. One year later Alderman James W. Magoffin called the city council's attention to the construction of some adobe houses in the lower part of the city that used "open water closets" (ibid, Aug. 20, 1903).

20. *Times*, June 17, 1910, p. 8.
21. Ibid.
22. Ibid.
23. City Council, *Minutes*, July 26, 1895; *El Monitor*, Oct. 31, 1897, p. 3; City of El Paso, *South El Paso*, p. 21. Enrique L. Acevedo recalled that in 1910 most of the paved streets in El Paso could be found in the center of the city, and streets such as Montana, Magoffin, Rio Grande, Mesa, and San Antonio in the American neighborhoods (Acevedo Transcript, IOH, p. 16).
24. *Times*, Aug. 15, 1902, p. 21. Although not as many accidents occurred in the American sections of the city, the police committee of the city council recommended in 1889 that strict measures be used to halt the high rate of speed of railroads on the northern tracks because it posed "a menace to the safety of our citizens" (City Council, *Minutes*, July 19, 1889).
25. *Times*, Oct. 10, 1902, p. 2; Feb. 23, 1905, p. 3; Jan. 21, 1909, pp. 1, 6.
26. Ibid., May 7, 1891, p. 7; *El Monitor*, July 3, 1897, p. 1; *Times*, June 6, 1903, p. 3; May 26, 1905, p. 1. Enrique L. Acevedo recalled the frequent floodings that according to him often inundated Chihuahuita as far north as Sixth Street and sometimes beyond. Most of the floods occurred, so Acevedo remembered, during the rainy months of May, June, and July. See Acevedo Transcript, IOH, pp. 15–16.
27. *Times*, Jan. 18, 1906, p. 5; Jan. 11, 1906, p. 2. As early as 1881 the County Commission's court received a petition from James Marr about the depressed conditions of certain Mexican women in south El Paso (see City Council, *Minutes*, Sept. 24, 1881).
28. *Times*, Jan. 11, 1906, p. 2.
29. Ibid., Jan. 12, 1906, p. 5.
30. Ibid., July 29, 1910, p. 5. As early as 1893 Alderman Magoffin as well as the chief of police had warned of the dilapidated condition of some of the Mexican jacales (City Council, *Minutes*, May 5, 1893).
31. *Times*, Sept. 16, 1910, p. 8.
32. Ibid., Sept. 19, 1913, p. 12; El Paso City Tax Rolls in the County Tax Office, El Paso City–County Building.
33. *Herald*, May 29, 1916, p. 14.
34. Ibid., Jan. 22, 1916, p. 2; Vera L. Sturges, "The Mexican Immigrant," p. 470; Calleros also recalled that most of the tenements had been built by Armenians, Jews, and Syrians; Cordero further remembered that in the 1930s Mexican families literally fought for occupancy in the tenements even though they remained overcrowded and with only one toilet for each two-story build-

ing (see Calleros Transcript, IOH, p. 8, and Cordero Transcript, pp. 3, 8, 17).

35. City of El Paso, *South El Paso*, p. 23. As early as 1907 Victor S. Clark commented on the Mexican tenements in Los Angeles, where rooms rented for $3 a month ("Mexican Labor," pp. 507–08). In his 1927 examination of Mexican immigrants in the United States, anthropologist Manuel Gamio observed that many Mexicans in San Antonio likewise lived in one- or two-room tenements (*Mexican Immigration*, p. 146).

36. Ibid., pp. 26–27. Substandard housing also affected other Mexican urban settlements in the United States. In his 1932 study of Chicago Paul S. Taylor observed, "In general, the Mexicans live in poor quarters. They [Mexicans and Negroes] are the latest heirs to the city's worst housing." See Taylor, *Chicago and the Calumet Region*, p. 184.

37. See Duane W. Thomforde, "Political Socialization in South El Paso."

38. *Lone Star*, Oct. 21, 1882, p. 2; *Times*, Oct. 7, 1892, p. 7; Calleros Transcript, IOH, p. 12; *Times*, Mar. 19, 1899, p. 1. In 1901, when health officers discovered diphtheria among children of the city, the Board of Health requested examinations of all school children until the disease abated; the Board also asked the city newspapers not to report the outbreak of diphtheria (see *School Minutes*, Dec. 2, 1901). For city health ordinances on contagious and infectious diseases, see City Council, *Minutes*, Apr. 13, 1882, and Nov. 21, 1901. In a 1973 interview, longtime resident Mrs. Jane Perrenot recalled that "as a child . . . it was unusual to see a Mexican who was not pock marked" due to small pox (Perrenot Transcript, IOH, p. 6).

39. *Times*, Nov. 24, 1909, pp. 1, 2; *La Patria*, Sept. 5, 1919, p. 3. Tuberculosis also proved to be a major health hazard in other Mexican urban settlements in the Southwest. Of 461 cases of tuberculosis reported in Los Angeles County in 1929, 98, or 21.2%, involved Mexicans, who represented only 10% of the total population. See Scott, "Mexican-American in Los Angeles," p. 82.

40. *Times*, May 13, 1910, p. 4; Aug. 19, 1914, p. 12.

41. City Council, *Minutes*, Dec. 20, 1906. Two years later the city council approved a recommendation by Anderson and the city sanitary commission that tighter regulations on contagious diseases be instituted including compulsory fumigation (May 8, 1908).

42. *Herald*, Feb. 29, 1916, p. 5; May 3, 1917, p. 8; Burciaga Transcript, IOH, pp. 23–24; *School Minutes*, Jan. 16, Aug. 27, 1917. In 1916 the principal of Beall had requested the school board to provide an extra teacher to bathe the Mexican children; although the board did not approve the request, it did instruct teachers to inspect children daily and return those home who were not "apparently clean" (ibid., Mar. 9, 1916).

43. *Times*, Oct. 13, 1918, p. 22; Oct. 15, 1918, p. 7; Oct. 17, 1918, p. 3. Also see White Transcript, IOH. The Red Cross operated Aoy as a hospital during the flu epidemic (*School Minutes*, Oct. 16, 1918). The effect of slum conditions on the health of other ghetto populations during the period can be seen in Gilbert Osofsky, *Harlem: The Making of a Ghetto*. "Whatever

the causes of Harlem's health problem . . .," Osofsky noted, "a good deal can be laid at the door of slum environment," as quoted in Osofsky, "Harlem Tragedy: An Emerging Slum," in Callow, *Urban History,* p. 391.

44. See the *Times* and *Herald* for this period; El Paso County Court, Docket Records, 1899–1902, Archives, Southwest Collection, El Paso Public Library; El Paso City, *Civil Docket Precinct No. 1* (1915) and *Criminal Docket Precinct No. 1* (1916–17) in the University of Texas, El Paso, Archives (ACC 755). Mexican residents of Chihuahuita themselves at times petitioned the city council for increased police protection (see City Council, *Minutes,* Apr. 23, 1908). According to Governor C. C. Young's report on Mexicans in California in 1930, most Mexicans in that state were arrested for burglary. While burglary was also the most common arrest for the general population, Mexicans exhibited a higher percentage than their percentage of the total population (see Paul S. Taylor, "Crime and the Foreign Born," pp. 201–204; also see Scott, "Mexican-American in Los Angeles," pp. 82–86).

45. *Times,* Feb. 2, 1904, p. 5.

46. See various editions of the *Times* and *Herald* for this period; Taylor, "Crime and the Foreign Born," pp. 224, 225; and Taylor, *Chicago and the Calumet Region,* pp. 145–55.

47. *Times,* Jan. 2, 1900, p. 8. Governor Young's 1930 report in California noted a similar condition among the Mexicans in that state. "Police officials," the report commented, "generally state a greater tendency among arrested Mexicans to plead guilty to charges and the common financial inability extended to defense and appeal cases, both of which causes undoubtedly increase the apparent crime among the Mexicans." Taylor also believed that a higher percentage of burglary, theft, disorderly conduct, and assault charges among the Mexicans in Chicago was in part due to their higher percentage of young men than the general population (see Taylor, "Crime and the Foreign Born," pp. 204, 225).

48. *Herald,* Oct. 15, 1919, p. 16.

49. *Times,* Sept. 18, 1918, p. 19. Ten years later Taylor recorded a tendency by Chicago police to stereotype the Mexicans as knife-users ("Crime and the Foreign Born," p. 235). One officer told Taylor that policemen in Chicago had been instructed not to take any chances with Mexicans; according to Chicago officers, Mexicans were "quick on the knife and are hot tempered, and do the damage before you know it."

50. *Times,* Jan. 2, 1900, p. 8; *Herald,* Mar. 7, 1916, pp. 1, 3; Mar. 6, 1916, p. 1; Mar. 6–14, 1916; Mar. 8, 1916, p. 5; Mar. 24, 1916, p. 13.

51. Taylor, "Crime and the Foreign Born," p. 238.

52. Helen Rainey, "A History of Organized Welfare in El Paso, 1892–1948," pp. 12, 20–22. Roy Lubove in his study of Progressive housing reformers refers to similar settlement and charity workers as employers of the "retail" method of reform: face-to-face relations with the poor (see Lubove, *The Progressives and the Slums,* p. 185).

53. Eddie Lou Miller, "The History of Private Welfare Agencies in El Paso, 1886–1930," pp. 72–73.

54. Ibid. The association also operated a kindergarten at Aoy School, which had to be closed in 1914 due to apparent lack of funds (*School Minutes,* Jan. 20, 1914).

55. Rainey, "Organized Welfare," pp. 40, 46–49. Ten years later a member of the Los Angeles Chamber of Commerce praised El Paso for what he believed to be its adequate handling of Mexican charity cases despite the border city's small expenditure of only 6% of its budget on Mexicans, who comprised 58% of El Paso's total population. By contrast the writer deplored the fact that in Los Angeles 68% of the charitable budget went to Mexicans, who represented only 5% of the total population (see Scott, "Mexican American in Los Angeles," pp. 74–75). To care for the needs of Mexican refugees, prominent American and Mexican residents of El Paso, including Mrs. Albert Madero, the aunt of Francisco Madero, and General John J. Pershing, organized in 1915 the Mexican Relief Association (*Herald,* Jan. 30–31, 1915, p. 3–B).

56. *Herald,* Feb. 9, 1915, p. 4. According to Lubove, reformers who called for sweeping legislative and environmental changes for the poor during the Progressive Era utilized the "wholesale" method of reform (*Progressives,* p. 185).

57. *Herald,* Feb. 13, 1915, p. 4–A.

58. Ibid.

59. Ibid., May 26, 1917, p. 6; May 1, 1915, Educational Section, p. 1; Feb. 4, 1915, p. 4.

60. Ibid., Feb. 11, 1915, p. 4; Feb. 25, 1915, p. 4; May 3, 1916, p. 6.

61. Ibid., May 26, 1917, p. 6.

62. Ibid., Feb. 4, 1915, p. 4. For a view of social reformers and their attitudes toward other immigrants as well as blacks during the Progressive Period, see Allen F. Davis., *Spearheads for Reform: The Social Settlements and the Progressive Movement, 1890–1914.* According to Davis, the settlement approach to the problem of the immigrant concerned first understanding the peculiar customs of each group and then finding as much opportunity for them as possible. "This was the settlement workers ideal," Davis wrote, "but not all were able to avoid the extremes of bigotry and hatred on the one hand, and sentimentality and condescension on the other" (p. 85).

CHAPTER 8

1. W. W. Mills, *Forty Years at El Paso 1858–1898,* p. 16; Jack C. Vowell, Jr., "Politics at El Paso: 1850–1920," p. 43. For a comparative view of the early political role of Mexicans in San Antonio see Edwin Larry Dickens, "The Political Role of Mexican-Americans in San Antonio, Texas," pp. 13–51.

2. Vowell, "Politics," p. 52; also see Sonnichsen, *Pass,* pp. 154–67.

3. Salomon Schutz, U.S. Consul at Paso del Norte, to Second Assistant Secre-

tary of State, Paso del Norte, Oct. 21, 1877, RG 59, M–2. According to Consul Schutz the salt beds belonged to the state of Texas, which donated them to the Texas and Pacific Railroad, whose agent was Howard; also see Vowell, "Politics," pp. 55–71; Sonnichsen, *Pass,* pp. 173–210; and Sonnichsen, *The El Paso Salt War.* The conflict was likewise the result of Howard's murder of Cardis in an El Paso store in 1877 (see White, *Desert,* pp. 101–02). For a biased view of the Salt War see Walter Prescott Webb, *The Texas Rangers: A Century of Frontier Defense,* pp. 345–67; also see Charles Francis Ward, "The Salt War of San Elizario (1887)."

4. *Lone Star,* Oct. 7, 1882, p. 2; Sept. 13, 1882, p. 3; Oct. 7, 1882, p. 2; Oct. 21, 1882, p. 4; White, *Desert,* pp. 101–02.

5. Vowell, "Politics," p. 198.

6. O. Douglas Weeks, "The Texas-Mexican and the Politics of South Texas," p. 625. In general where Mexicans remained numerically large such as in El Paso, San Antonio, South Texas, Northern New Mexico, and Arizona, they exercised a greater political influence; on the other hand, in places such as California, where by the turn of the century the Mexican percentage of the population had significantly declined, the Mexicans' political role likewise decreased. See Leonard Pitt, *The Decline of the Californios;* Mario T. García, "The Californios of San Diego and the Politics of Accommodation, 1846–1860"; Robert W. Larson, *New Mexico's Quest for Statehood, 1846–1912;* and Miguel Antonio Otero, *My Nine Years as Governor of the Territory of New Mexico, 1897–1906.*

7. Vowell, "Politics," pp. 101–02. For additional information on the 1889 election see City Council, *Minutes,* June 14, 1889.

8. Alexander B. Callow, Jr., ed., *The City Boss in America,* p. 91. Also see Elmer E. Cornwall, Jr., "Bosses, Machines, and Ethnic Groups."

9. *Times,* Mar. 20, 1891, p. 2. Prominent as a political foe of Porfirio Díaz and the Mexican government, Ochoa apparently was a Mexican citizen.

10. Ibid., Apr. 5, 1891, p. 7.

11. Ibid.

12. Ibid., Oct. 28, 1890, p. 7. A former principal of the public school in San Elizario in El Paso County, Larrazolo was a naturalized American who had been appointed in 1885 as the chief deputy in the district court and in the El Paso county clerk's office. One year later he was elected clerk of the Thirty-fourth Judicial District of Texas, a position to which he was reelected in 1888 as a Democrat. For a brief and critical view of Larrazolo's political career in New Mexico see Paul A. F. Walter, "Octaviano Ambrosio Larrazolo."

13. *Times,* Oct. 16, 1890, p. 4.

14. Ibid., Jan. 9, 1900, p. 5.

15. Ibid., Jan. 14, 1902, p. 30.

16. Ibid; also see *Herald,* May 31, 1916, p. 9.

17. *Times,* July 10, 1898, p. 3.

18. Ibid., Apr. 22, 1910, p. 2; Apr. 8, 1912, p. 10.

19. Chope Transcript, IOH, p. 7.
20. Park, "Mexican Labor," pp. 241–42. "It is not through the generalized appeal to large public concerns that the machine operates," sociologist Robert K. Merton correctly emphasizes about American machine politics, "but through the direct, quasifeudal relationships between local representatives of the machine and voters in their neighborhood" (Merton, *Social Theory and Social Structure* [New York: Free Press, 1957], reprinted in Callow, *City Boss*, p. 25).
21. *Times*, May 4, 1902, p. 3; Sept. 11, 1902, p. 4; Clarence Harper Transcript, ACC 41, IOH, July 17, 1968, p. 8. For vote buying in South Texas see William E. Leonard, "Where Both Bullets and Ballots are Dangerous."
22. Kelly Interview, Aug. 17, 1975; *Times*, Apr. 4, 1893, p. 4; Oct. 8, 1902, p. 2.
23. Charles B. Stevens, Republican County Chairman, to M. M. Rogers, El Paso, Nov. 21, 1904, no. 686, Mills Building Collection, Southwestern Collection.
24. J. M. García to C. B. Stevens, Ysleta, Oct. 27, 1904, no. 707, Mills Building Collection.
25. *Times*, Nov. 5, 1904, p. 4; Nov. 6, 1904, p. 1. According to Dickens, American political bosses in San Antonio likewise fraudulently purchased poll taxes for Mexicans ("Mexican-Americans in San Antonio," p. 36).
26. *Herald*, Feb. 3, 1916, p. 1. A few years later Paul S. Taylor discovered similar political corruption in San Antonio and South Texas. According to one immigration official the possession of a poll tax receipt plus residency constituted enough evidence of citizenship to satisfy election clerks (interview conducted by Taylor with District Director William A. Whalen, U.S. Immigration Service, San Antonio, Manuscript 155–155, Taylor Papers).
27. *Times*, Apr. 12, 1893, p. 7; Nov. 11, 1896, p. 2.
28. Ibid., Sept. 4, 1892, p. 4.
29. Ibid.
30. Ibid., Apr. 15, 1896, p. 3; Apr. 14, 1896, p. 3.
31. Ibid., Mar. 23, 1899, p. 8. See the Proceedings of the Republican Party, El Paso, July 10, 1904, no. 684, Mills Building Collection.
32. *Union*, July 12, 1912, p. 1; *Times*, Dec. 19, 1911, p. 12.
33. *Herald*, Jan. 8, 1912, p. 1; *Union*, Mar. 1, 1912, p. 1; *Times*, July 25, 1912, p. 1. For some correspondence on the Círculo de Amigos, see Círculo de Amigos, 10 letters, 1919–22, boxes 85–91, Terrazas Collection MSS.
34. *Union*, July 12, 1912, p. 1.
35. Ibid.
36. *Times*, July 30, 1912, pp. 1–2; *Union*, Aug. 2, 1912, p. 1.
37. *Times*, Jan. 3, 1915, pp. 1–2; *Herald*, Jan. 5, 1915, p. 2; Feb. 6, 1915. p. 1; Feb. 1, 1915, p. 1; Feb. 15, 1915, p. 2.
38. *Times*, Jan. 29, 1915, p. 12; *Herald*, Jan. 30–31, 1915, p. 4–A.
39. Ibid., Feb. 9, 1915, p. 3.
40. Ibid., Feb. 16, 1915, p. 1; Feb. 17, 1915, pp. 1, 4; Kelly Interview.
41. Ibid., Feb. 17, 1915, p. 4; Aug. 1, 1916, p. 14.

42. Despite their role as political mediators, Mexican Americans have still found it difficult to assimilate into El Paso's political structure. The city, for example, has had only two Mexican American mayors since 1873, and between 1881 and 1951 Mexican Americans had absolutely no representation on the city council (Oscar J. Martínez, "The Chicanos of El Paso: An Assessment of Progress," p. 12). Also see Melvin P. Strauss, "The Mexican-American in El Paso Politics," and Rudolph O. de la Garza, "Voting Patterns in 'Bicultural' El Paso—A Contextual Analysis of Chicano Voting Behavior."

CHAPTER 9

1. Richard Medina Estrada, "Border Revolution: The Mexican Revolution in the Ciudad Juárez–El Paso Area, 1906–1915," pp. i, ii.
2. *Times*, Nov. 16, 1893, p. 4; Dec. 3, 1893, p. 1; Feb. 11, 1892, p. 4; May 15, 1892, p. 7; Nov. 18, 1893, p. 1; Theodore Huston to Department of State, Paso del Norte, Nov. 30, 1893, RG 59, M–5; also see *Times*, Dec. 3, 1893, p. 6; Dec. 5, 1893, p. 6; and Feb. 25, 1894, p. 7.
3. *Times*, Dec. 2, 1893, p. 4; Dec. 7, 1893, p. 7; Huston to Edwin F. Uhl, Assistant Secretary of State, Paso del Norte, Jan. 10, 1894, RG 59, M–5; *Times*, Feb. 1, 1894, p. 7.
4. Ibid., Mar. 6, 1894, p. 7; Oct. 14, 1894, p. 6; Oct. 24, 1894, p. 7; Oct. 25, 1894, p. 7; Oct. 26, 1894, p. 7; Oct. 16, 1894, p. 7; Apr. 12, 1895, p. 7.
5. Ibid., Mar. 27, 1895, p. 3; U.S. Consul Charles W. Kindrick to David J. Hill, Ciudad Juárez, Nov. 3, 1902, RG 59, M–6; Louis M. Bufford to William W. Rockhill, Assistant Secretary of State, Paso del Norte, Mar. 13, 1896, RG 59, M–5; *Times*, Mar. 27, 1896, p. 3; Mar. 13, 1893, p. 3; Mar. 25, 1896, p. 3; Mar. 26, 1896, p. 3.
6. Bufford to Rockhill, Paso del Norte, Sept. 9, 1896, RG 59, M–5; Kindrick to Hill, Juárez, Aug. 7, 1906, RG 59, M–6; *Times*, Oct. 29, 1902, p. 3; Kindrick to Hill, Juárez, Nov. 3, 1902, RG 59, M–6.
7. Estrada, "Border Revolution," pp. 32–33.
8. Ibid., pp. 34–36. For correspondence by Chihuahua officials on their concern about PLM operations in El Paso see Enrique Creel to A. Calderon Urrutia, Chihuahua, Oct. 6, 1906; S. Montemayor to Mexican consul in El Paso, Juárez, Oct. 20, 1906; and Montemayor to Creel, Juárez, Oct. 23, 1906, in Flores Magón Correspondence, file 12A in Terrazas Collection, Pt. I, MSS. Two other Liberal newspapers in El Paso were *La Democracia* and *La Bandera Roja;* see Francisco Mallén, Mexican consul in El Paso, to Enrique Creel, El Paso, Nov. 20, 1906, Flores Magón Correspondence, file 9A in Terrazas Collection, MSS, and Juan Gómez-Quiñones, *Sembradores: Ricardo Flores Magón y el Partido Liberal Mexicano: A Eulogy and Critique*, p. 29.
9. See "Acuerdos de la Junta Revolucionaria Establecida en El Paso Texas, Bajo La Presidencia de Ricardo Flores Magón," in Ricardo Flores Magón

Correspondence, file 13A, box 1, Terrazas Collection, Pt. I, MSS. The Díaz government enlisted the services not only of the U.S. Post Office and Justice Department to investigate violations of neutrality laws but also of private American detectives (see William Dirk Raat, "The Diplomacy of Suppression: 'Los Revoltosos,' Mexico, and the United States, 1906–1911," pp. 529–50, and William H. Beezley, *Insurgent Governor: Abraham González and the Mexican Revolution in Chihuahua,* pp. 10–11).

10. *Times,* Oct. 20, 1906, p. 3; Estrada, "Border Revolution," pp. 42–43; Robert Lynn Sandels, "Silvestre Terrazas, The Press, and the Origins of the Mexican Revolution in Chihuahua," pp. 177–83; for copies of captured documents including list of members of PLM in the United States and Mexico see Francisco Mallén to Enrique Creel, El Paso, Oct. 21, 1906, in Flores Magón Correspondence, files 9B and 13A in Terrazas Collection, Pt. I, MSS. Villarreal escaped from El Paso officers only to be rearrested and subsequently serve time in a Yuma, Arizona, jail for violation of neutrality laws. After serving four days in the county jail Aguirre was released due to lack of evidence (*Times,* Nov. 20, 1906, p. 5; Feb. 20, 1907, p. 3; Dec. 23, 1906, p. 2; Oct. 29, 1909, p. 2). Wanted for possible violations of neutrality laws, Flores Magón was arrested within a year in Los Angeles, where he remained until 1910 (Charles C. Cumberland, "Mexican Revolutionary Movements from Texas, 1906–1912," pp. 303–04).

11. Estrada, "Border Revolution," pp. 45–47; *Times,* June 26, 1908, p. 3; Sandels, "Silvestre Terrazas," p. 189. It is not clear that Aguirre was in fact an American citizen at the time of his arrest; the *Times* reported in December of the same year that Aguirre had become a naturalized citizen (Dec. 8, 1908, p. 3).

12. *Times,* June 28, 1908, p. 1; July 16, 1908, p. 5; July 17, 1908, p. 8; July 18, 1908, p. 8; Oct. 25, 1908, p. 2. In a later extradition case involving an anti-Díaz journalist, Enrique C. Villaseñor, more than 200 Mexicans packed the federal courtroom for four days in support of Villaseñor, whose case was dismissed (*Times,* Aug. 26, 1909, p. 2; Sept. 24, 1909, pp. 1, 2). For other PLM attacks on the Texas–Mexican border see Cumberland, "Mexican Revolutionary Movements," pp. 304–05. For an account of the Magonista movement see James D. Cockcroft, *Intellectual Precursors of the Mexican Revolution, 1910–1913;* also Gómez-Quiñones, *Sembradores,* and Lowell L. Blaisdell, *The Desert Revolution: Baja California 1911.*

13. *Times,* Apr. 12, 1909, p. 4; June 29, 1909, p. 4; Oct. 16, 1909, p. 2. Prominent Mexican Americans in El Paso such as Félix Martínez and J. A. Escajeda served on the arrangements and welcome committees for the Taft-Díaz visit. The actual meeting of the two chief executives occurred on Santa Fe Street at Seventh while hundreds of Mexicans from Chihuahuita looked on. See *Times,* Aug. 2, 1909, p. 1; Aug. 22, 1909, p. 2; Sept. 2, 1909, p. 8; and Oct. 17, 1909, p. 1. For an account of the Taft-Díaz meeting see Armando B. Chávez, *Historia de Ciudad Juárez,* pp. 343–59.

14. Estrada, "Border Revolution," pp. 57–59; *Times,* Nov. 22, 1910, p. 2; Dec. 27, 1910, p. 1.
15. Estrada, "Border Revolution," pp. 66–67, 76–77; *Times,* Apr. 20, 1911, p. 1; Michael C. Meyer, *Mexican Rebel: Pascual Orozco and the Mexican Revolution 1910-1915,* p. 27. In El Paso the junta also recruited foreigners wishing to participate in the revolution such as the Italian Giuseppe Garibaldi (see Beezley, *Insurgent Governor,* p. 46).
16. *Times,* Mar. 8, 1911, p. 1.
17. Estrada, "Border Revolution," p. 65. The best account of El Paso arms sales to the varied revolutionary factions is in Estrada, "Border Revolution."
18. Turner's accounts, first published in the *American Magazine,* were subsequently reprinted in 1911 as a book entitled *Barbarous Mexico.* Gutiérrez de Lara, who had also been arrested at Cananea during the famous copper strike in 1906, had testified along with Turner before a U.S. Congressional Committee on the illegal activities of Mexican secret service agents in the United States (see *Times,* Oct. 22, 1909, p. 5; Jan. 8, 1911, p. 8; June 11, 1910, p. 2; and June 12, 1910, p. 1).
19. *Times,* Jan. 8, 1911, p. 8; Jan. 10, 1911, p. 5; Jan. 13, 1911, p. 1; Jan. 16, 1911, p. 3.
20. Ibid., Apr. 9, 1911, p. 5; Apr. 10, 1911, p. 8; Apr. 11, 1911, pp. 1 and 5; Apr. 12, 1911, p. 10; May 7, 1911, p. 4.
21. Estrada, "Border Revolution," pp. 67–69, 73–74; *Times,* Feb. 9, 1910, p. 1.
22. First operating in Mexico as a Red Cross volunteer, Bush later accepted the position of chief surgeon of Madero's army with the rank of colonel (see Beezley, *Insurgent Governor,* pp. 51–52; also Bush's own account, *Gringo Doctor*). Besides the work of Dr. Bush, the American Red Cross proved to be active along the border (see "The Red Cross on the Mexican Border," and J. B. Gwin, "Making Friends of Invaders: Mexican Refugees in Advance of the Returning Troops"). Also see *Times,* Feb. 2, 1911, p. 1; Feb. 5, 1911, p. 5; Mar. 26, 1911, p. 2; May 1, 1911, p. 3; May 6, 1911, p. 10; Apr. 26, 1911, p. 10; Apr. 27, 1911, p. 1; and de Wetter, "Revolutionary El Paso," pp. 43–46.
23. For an account of the Battle of Juárez see Chávez, *Historia de Ciudad Juárez,* pp. 360–406. Also see T. T. Edwards to Secretary of State, Ciudad Juárez, May 10, 1911, Internal Affairs, 812.00/1701; Armijo Transcript, IOH, p. 4; and *Times,* May 9, 1911, p. 1, and May 10, 1911, p. 1. In total Mexican bullets killed 5 El Pasoans and wounded 14.
24. Ibid., May 12, 1911, p. 1; May 15, 1911, p. 8; May 18, 1911, p. 11; May 29, 1911, p. 4; May 31, 1911, p. 2. Mayor Kelly's daughter, Elizabeth, remembers that her father escorted Villa to the Kelly drugstore adjacent to the Sheldon Hotel, where he offered the colonel a drink; according to Miss Kelly, the mayor then gave Villa a police escort to the border to make sure he returned to Juárez and to avoid his being killed in El Paso (Kelly Interview).
25. H. C. Ferris to H. I. Miller, El Paso, Oct. 25, 1912; also see similar corre-

spondence dated Oct. 6, 1912, Oct. 20, 1912, and Oct. 22, 1912, in Mexico Northwestern Railroad Correspondence, box 13, McNeely Collection, UTEP Archives.

26. Estrada, "Border Revolution," pp. 98–100. Madero apparently did not contest the Orozco move on Juárez for fear of U.S. intervention if a battle should affect El Paso or American citizens (see Cumberland, "Mexican Revolutionary Movements," p. 321). For activities of federal agents in El Paso see Assistant Attorney General to Secretary of State, Washington, D.C., Nov. 27, 1912, Internal Affairs, 812.00/5608. See also same to same, Feb. 18, 1913, 812.00/6260; Feb. 28, 1913, 812.00/6528; Nov. 21, 1912, 812.00/5562; Nov. 27, 1912, 812.00/5608; and Sept. 23, 1913, 812.00/8972.

27. Meyer, *Orozco*, p. 86. According to Meyer the causes of Orozquismo were multiple and varied; although Orozco may have sincerely believed that Madero had failed to implement his promised reforms and hence rebelled, at the same time much of his financial support came from the Porfiristas of Chihuahua.

28. *Times*, Aug. 21, 1912, p. 1; Meyer, *Orozco*, p. 87. Besides those already in El Paso, prominent Porfiristas arrived in El Paso after 1912. The most noted exile was Governor Luis Terrazas, who resided for a time in El Paso, both at the Hotel Paso del Norte and at the home of Senator Albert Fall of New Mexico on Arizona Avenue. One of the wealthiest landowners in Chihuahua, "Don Luis" symbolized the old Porfirian ruling class. See Estrada, "Border Revolution," p. 115, and de Wetter, "Revolutionary El Paso," pp. 105–06, 110.

29. On Madero, see Stanley R. Ross, *Francisco I. Madero: Apostle of Democracy*, and Charles C. Cumberland, *Mexican Revolution: Genesis Under Madero*. Among the exiles in El Paso following Madero's downfall was Pancho Villa, who maintained residence at the Hotel La Roma in Chihuahuita (see Edgcumb Pinchon, *Viva Villa!* pp. 218–20).

30. T. T. Edwards to Secretary of State, Ciudad Juárez, Feb. 7, 1913, Internal Affairs, 812.00/6613; see report of special agent in J. C. Adkins, Assistant Attorney General, to Secretary of State, Washington, D.C., Feb. 18, 1913, Internal Affairs, 812,00/6260.

31. J. O. C. to H. I. Miller, El Paso, Mar. 16, 1914, Mexico Northwestern Railroad Correspondence, box 13, McNeely Collection.

32. *Times*, Jan. 15, 1914, p. 4; Jan. 16, 1914, p. 1. Besides Krakauer, Zork & Maye, another prominent El Paso supplier of Villa was Hayman Krupp and Company (see Martín Luis Guzmán, *Memoirs of Pancho Villa*, p. 181; also see Silvestre Terrazas to Krakauer, Zork & Maye, Chihuahua, Jan. 14, 1915, in Letters from Terrazas, box 84, 1914–18, Terrazas Collection, Pt. I, MSS). Also see reports of special agents in Assistant Attorney General to Secretary of State, Washington, D.C., Jan. 30, 1914, Internal Affairs, 812.00/10751.

33. *Times*, Mar. 10, 1914, p. 1; Mar. 15, 1914, p. 2; Mar. 20, 1914, p. 1.

34. *New York Times*, Apr. 21, 1914, p. 2. Consul Edwards in Juárez warned the State Department prior to the Veracruz invasion that no anti-American feelings had surfaced in his station but that he feared this would change if Americans occupied Mexican terrory (see Edwards to Secretary of State, Ciudad Juárez, Apr. 21, 1914, Internal Affairs, 812.00/11583, and same to same, Apr. 21, 1914, 812.00/11600).

35. *El Paso Times*, Apr. 21, 1914, pp. 1, 6.

36. Ibid., Apr. 22, 1914, p. 11; Apr. 23, 1914, p. 2; Clarence Clendenen, *The United States and Pancho Villa: A Study in Unconventional Diplomacy*, p. 83.

37. *Times*, Apr. 23, 1914, pp. 6, 9. Mexican Americans in Phoenix organized a similar regiment and in San Antonio 50 Mexican Americans dispatched a telegram to President Wilson endorsing his Veracruz action and offering their services in case of war with Mexico (*New York Times*, Apr. 22, 1914, p. 4; Apr. 28, 1914, p. 4).

38. *El Paso Times*, Apr. 24, 1914, pp. 1, 2; Apr. 25, 1914, p. 1; Apr. 26, 1914, p. 1; May 14, 1914, p. 10; *New York Times*, Apr. 24, 1914, p. 6; Apr. 27, 1914, p. 2.

39. *New York Times*, Apr. 24, 1914, p. 1. Villa three days earlier had also issued orders that any Mexican attempting to start an anti-American demonstration was to be shot; the *New York Times* believed that Villa saw the U.S. invasion of Veracruz as a pro-Constitutionalist move on Wilson's part (*New York Times*, Apr. 21, 1914, p. 1). Also see Edwards to Secretary of State, Ciudad Juárez, Apr. 24, 1914, Internal Affairs, 812.00/11685.

40. Not seriously affecting El Paso, increased border conflict developed in 1915 in the South Texas region. In one instance American officials discovered a Mexican plan, called the Plan de San Diego, which called for the reconquest of the Mexican Cession lost in the Mexican War. See William M. Hager, "The Plan of San Diego: Unrest on the Texas Border in 1915"; Allen Gerlach, "Conditions Along the Border–1915: The Plan de San Diego"; Charles C. Cumberland, "Border Raids in the Lower Rio Grande Valley–1915"; Juan Gómez-Quiñones, "Plan of San Diego Reviewed"; and James A. Sandos, "The Plan of San Diego: War & Diplomacy on the Texas Border, 1915–1916."

41. *Herald*, June 1, 1915, p. 12.

42. Estrada, "Border Revolution," p. 136; *New York Times*, Jan. 14, 1916, pp. 1–2; *Herald*, Jan. 13, 1916, pp. 1–3. Until the Wilson administration imposed an arms embargo on Mexico in 1915, Villa had been able to import large amounts of arms and munitions; during a two-week period in April 1915, for example, U.S. Customs at El Paso recorded more than 1 million bullets destined for Villa (Estrada, "Border Revolution," pp. 126–28).

43. *Herald*, Jan. 14, 1916, pp. 1–2; Jan. 17, 1916, p. 6; *New York Times*, Jan. 14, 1916, pp. 1–2. Hoping to avoid further trouble, officials arrested several Villa representatives in the city and ordered them to leave. In a 1945 interview Mayor Lea stated that if the mob had not been controlled they

would have "massacred" the Mexicans living in Chihuahuita (de Wetter, "Revolutionary El Paso," pp. 142–43).

44. Edwards to Secretary of State, El Paso, Jan. 14, 1916, Internal Affairs, 812.00/17095; *Herald*, Jan. 14, 1916, p. 7; Jan. 19, 1916, p. 9.

45. Ibid., Jan. 14, 1916, p. 6.

46. Acevedo Transcript, IOH, p. 25; Cordero Transcript, IOH, p. 41. On the Columbus raid, see Friedrich Katz, "Pancho Villa and the Attack on Columbus, New Mexico."

47. *Herald*, Mar. 9, 1916, p. 1; Mar. 11, 1916, p. 6; Mar. 24, 1916, p. 6; Mar. 18, 1916, p. 1.

48. *New York Times*, Mar. 12, 1916, p. 1. Pershing had 10,000 troops in Chihuahua; on the Pershing expedition, see Haldren Braddy, *Pershing's Mission in Mexico*, and Colonel Frank Tompkins, *Chasing Villa.*

49. *New York Times*, Mar. 13, 1916, p. 1. Besides the military reinforcements, El Pasoans organized a "home defense league" composed of 400 men (*New York Times*, Mar. 16, 1916, p. 2).

50. Ibid., Mar. 10, 1916, p. 2. Federal troops also guarded the smelter, the cement plant, and the electric light and gas plants to prevent any attempts to dynamite them.

51. *Herald*, Mar. 13, 1916, p. 3; Mar. 25, 1916, p. 2; Apr. 6, 1916, p. 4; June 5, 1916, p. 2. Mauricio Cordero remembers that immediately after the Columbus raid officials prohibited American soldiers from entering Chihuahuita for fear of violence (Cordero Transcript, IOH, p. 41). Mass arrests of Mexicans accused of being Villa spies were also made in Columbus (*New York Times*, Mar. 12, 1916, p. 2).

52. *Herald*, Mar. 13, 1916, p. 6; Mar. 18–19, 1916, p. 4; Mar. 24, 1916, p. 7; *New York Times*, Mar. 15, 1916, p. 2; Mar. 12, 1916, p. 3. According to the *New York Times*, *La Constitución* was a Porfirista newspaper. Also see Edwards to Secretary of State, El Paso, Mar. 14, 1916, Internal Affairs, 812.00/17469; same to same, Mar. 14, 1916, 812.00/117490; and Mar. 24, 1916, 812.00/17620; and Collector of Customs to Secretary of State, El Paso, Mar. 16, 1916, 812.00/17493, and same to same, Mar. 27, 1916, 812.00/17640.

53. *New York Times*, Mar. 18, 1916, p. 1.

54. *Herald*, June 12, 1916, p. 10.

55. Ibid., June 22, 1916, pp. 1–2; June 23, 1916, p. 1; June 24–25, 1916, p. 3; June 26, 1916, p. 5; July 8, 1916, p. 2; June 27, 1916, p. 6; Aug. 26–27, 1916, sec. 4, p. 9. On the Carrizal Incident, see Braddy, *Pershing's Mission*, p. 56. When Dr. David Starr Jordan of Stanford University and a member of the recently established Inter-American Committee (a private peace organization) arrived in El Paso in July to obtain information on border conditions, numbers of Americans expressed their exasperation over recent events (see Paul U. Kellogg, "A New Era of Friendship for North America").

56. *Herald*, June 17, 1916, p. 6.

57. For correspondence on the activities of Mexican political exiles in El Paso

see Alianza Liberal Mexicana, El Paso, 20 letters, 1919-23, box 86, and
Manuel Ayala Correspondence, 1906-40, box 85, Terrazas Collection, MSS.
58. See "The 'Brown Scare' in Los Angeles," in Romo, "Mexican Workers,"
pp. 104-31.

CHAPTER 10

1. Laird, "Argentine, Kansas," p. 159. Also see Herbert G. Gutman, *Work Culture, and Society in Industrializing America,* pp. 3-78.
2. Ernesto Galarza, "Mexicans in the Southwest: A Culture in Process,"
p. 269.
3. Dillingham Commission, pt. 25, vol. III, pts. I, II, pp. 39, 86.
4. Ernesto Galarza, *Barrio Boy,* pp. 3-71.
5. *Manuscript Census, 1900.* See chap. 4, n. 27, for sample method.
6. Interview with Jess López conducted by Gregory S. Fisher, Feb. 15, 1977,
Center for Chicano Studies, University of California, Santa Barbara, pp. 1-2.
7. Laird, "Argentine, Kansas," pp. 164-86. Of chain migration to Argentine,
Laird writes: "Within the city, migration streams separated into specific
sub-groups with locality bases. In particular, immigrants from one Mexican
town, Tangancícuaro, Michoacán, settled almost exclusively in Argentine,
and worked, almost without exception, as shop laborers" (p. 80). Also see
Eugene Litwack, "Geographic Mobility and Extended Family Cohesion";
Harvey M. Chaldin, "Kinship Networks in the Migration Process"; and Ted
J. Jitadi, "Migration and Kinship Contacts."
8. Michael Anderson, *Family Structure in Nineteenth Century Lancashire,*
pp. 1, 101, 134, 136.
9. *Manuscript Census, 1900.* In the sample of 152 immigrant households, of
those with a working father, not one unit contained a mother working outside the home and only 7 units had working daughters (see chap. 4, n. 27,
for sample method).
10. Taylor, "Mexican Labor in Los Angeles Industry," pt. 2, p. 1; pt. 3, pp. 1-
11, in Taylor Papers.
11. Ibid., pt. 3, p. 12.
12. Gamio, *Life Story,* p. 46.
13. Virginia Yans-McLaughlin, "Patterns of Work and Family Organization:
Buffalo's Italians," p. 140.
14. Kenneth L. Kusmer, *A Ghetto Takes Shape: Black Cleveland, 1870-1930,*
p. 109.
15. Gamio, *Mexican Immigration,* pp. 76-83; idem, *Life Story,* pp. 82-83.
16. Emilio Willems, "Peasantry and City: Cultural Persistence and Change in
Historical Perspective, a European Case"; and Herbert J. Gans, *The Urban
Villagers.*
17. Gamio, *Life Story,* pp. 161, 166.
18. Américo Paredes, *A Texas-Mexican Cancionero: Folksongs of the Lower
Border,* pp. xvii, xix, xx, xxi, xxii; Gamio, *Life Story,* p. 218.

19. Gamio, *Life Story*, p. 96.
20. Paredes, *Cancionero*, p. 36, pp. 82–83.
21. Ibid., pp. 104–05.
22. Gamio, *Mexican Immigration*, pp. 104–07.
23. *La Justicia*, Sept. 5, 1893, p. 3; *El Defensor*, Dec. 3, 1894, p. 4; *Herald*, June 5, 1916, p. 2; June 2–3, 1917, p. 13; *El Monitor*, July 3, 1897, p. 4; *City Directory*, 1907, p. 29; *Times*, Jan. 12, 1908, p. 3; Oct. 4, 1903, p. 7; Apr. 27, 1911, p. 1; *Herald*, May 11, 1917, p. 2.
24. *Times*, Feb. 15, 1894, p. 2; *Herald*, Aug. 15, 1916, p. 16.
25. *Times*, Jan. 24, 1915, Spanish Section, p. 1; *La Patria*, Sept. 15, 1919, p. 4; June 5, 1920, p. 4.
26. Tomás Ybarra-Frausto, "El Teatro Chicano and Its Traditions." I wish to thank Professor Ybarra-Frausto for permission to use his study.
27. *Times*, Jan. 24, 1915, Spanish Section, p. 1; *La Patria*, Nov. 11, 1919, p. 1; Oct. 11, 1919, pp. 1, 2; Jan. 31, 1920, p. 6; Nov. 4, 1920, p. 4; *El Día*, Feb. 18, 1919, p. 1.
28. Rodolfo Usigli, *Mexico in the Theater*, p. 116.
29. John W. Brokaw, "The Repertory of a Mexican-American Theatrical Troupe: 1849–1924," p. 26.
30. Cleofas Calleros, *Historia de la Parroquia de San Ignacio de Loyola*, p. 147. Other religious dramas popular among the Mexican population in the Southwest included New Testament subjects such as "Los Pastores" (The Shepherd's Play) and "La Pasión" (The Passion Play). Such dramas originated during the Spanish colonial period and in New Mexico have been performed for centuries. See C. B. Morten, "The Survivals of Medieval Religious Drama in New Mexico," and Arthur Campa, "Religious Spanish Folkdrama in New Mexico." For a sample text of "Los Pastores" see Carmelo Tranchese and Carmela Montalvo, eds., *Los Pastores*.
31. *Times*, Feb. 22, 1904, p. 1; Enrique L. Acevedo Transcript, IOH, p. 20.
32. *Times*, Mar. 1, 1906, p. 3.
33. *El Día*, Feb. 23, 1919, p. 2; *La Patria*, Jan. 3, 1920, pp. 1, 4; Jan. 20, 1920, pp. 1, 6; June 14, 1920, p. 1; Nov. 14, 1920, p. 4; Nov. 15, 1920, p. 1.
34. *Times*, Aug. 10, 1886, p. 4; Nov. 11, 1904, p. 1; Mar. 19, 1910, p. 8; Jan. 18, 1913, p. 10; *Las Noticias*, Nov. 18, 1899, p. 2; Oct. 14, 1899, p. 2; *Times*, Oct. 25, 1887, p. 5; Oct. 9, 1903, p. 3; Oct. 8, 1905, p. 2.
35. The carpas received their name after the canvas tents in which they were housed (Paredes, *Cancionero*, p. 134). Also see, *Times*, Oct. 18, 1906, p. 3; *Las Dos Américas*, July 25, 1898, p. 2; *La Justicia*, Oct. 12, 1893, p. 3; *La Patria*, Sept. 6, 1919, p. 4; and Ybarra-Frausto, "Teatro Chicano," p. 10.
36. *Times*, Sept. 24, 1893, p. 7; Aug. 14, 1903, p. 5; Sept. 20, 1907, p. 2; May 30, 1908, p. 2; June 18, 1908, p. 2; Sept. 14, 1908, p. 2; Apr. 9, 1911, p. 4; Nov. 12, 1914, p. 4; Apr. 3, 1916, p. 10; *Herald*, May 20–21, 1916, p. 17; June 2–3, 1917, p. 16; June 24, 1918, p. 9; Nov. 10, 1919, p. 14.
37. *Times*, May 3, 1908, pt. II, p. 6.
38. Ibid., Apr. 11, 1907, p. 2; *Herald*, Aug. 3, 1917, p. 9; Aug. 13, 1917, p. 5;

Juan de la C. Alarcón to Silvestre Terrazas, El Paso, July 5, 1920, in Juan de la C. Alarcón Correspondence, 6 letters, 1918-32, Terrazas Collection MSS; *La Patria,* Aug. 29, 1919, p. 4. The International Amusement Company, also called the International Picture Company with other offices in New York and Mexico City, was capitalized at $60,000 and distributed movies in Mexico and Central America (de la C. Alarcón to Terrazas, El Paso, Oct. 1, 1919, Alarcón Correspondence, Terrazas Collection, MSS).

39. *Times,* Aug. 2, 1914, p. 5; Jan. 20, 1915, p. 2; *Herald,* Aug. 13, 1917, pp. 5, 9; *La Patria,* Aug. 29, 1919, p. 4; Oct. 4, 1919, p. 8; June 5, 1920, p. 2.

40. *Times,* Mar. 18, 1919, p. 8.

41. Balderas Transcript, IOH, p. 14.

42. See transcript of "El Lavaplatos" (The Dishwasher) in Philip Sonnichsen's album *Texas-Mexican Border Music,* p. 9.

43. For popular religion among other immigrants as well as the role of the Catholic Church, see Jay P. Dolan, *The Immigrant Church: New York's Irish and German Catholics, 1815-1865,* and Randall M. Miller and Thomas D. Marzik, eds., *Immigrants and Religion in Urban America.*

44. M. Lilliana Owens, *Loretto in El Paso,* p. 24; also see Cleofas Calleros, "En el Aureo de la Venida de la Companía de Jesús, 1881-1931."

45. Owens, *Loretto,* p. 31; also see "Parroquia Del Sagrado Corazón" (May 10, 1931) bulletin in Sacred Heart Church Records, and *Times,* Jan. 30, 1895, p. 7.

46. Calleros Transcript, IOH, p. 10; *La Revisita Católica,* June 15, 1919, no p.

47. Calleros, *San Ignacio,* pp. 7-39, 83-87; *La Revista Católica,* July 13, 1919, p. 562.

48. *La Revista Católica,* Mar. 31, 1918, p. iii; May 4, 1919, p. vii; Feb. 2, 1919, p. 7; Calleros, *San Ignacio,* pp. 43, 46.

49. Calleros, *San Ignacio,* pp. 19-22, 77; *La Revisita Católica,* Jan. 19, 1919, p. 7; Feb. 16, 1919, p. 7; also see Calleros, "Historia del Asilo de San José de El Paso, Tex.," p. 2. A similar Asilo was established by Guardian Angel School in 1926 (Calleros, "Asilo," pp. 2-3).

50. Calleros, *San Ignacio,* pp. 13, 49, 66, 79, 81-82; *La Revista Católica,* Feb. 2, 1919, p. 5.

51. Calleros, *San Ignacio,* pp. 17, 39, 69. By 1918 a similar youth club called the Asociación Católica de Jóvenes "El Azteca" was organized at Guardian Angel School (*La Revista Católica,* Jan. 6, 1918, p. iii). In the early 1920s St. Ignatius also sponsored a boy scout troop (Calleros, *San Ignacio,* p. 147). At Holy Family Church on 701 West Main in the Sunset Heights district, the church sponsored classes in Spanish grammar, literature, philosophy, and Mexican history for the youth of the predominantly political refugee population (*La Revista Católica,* Jan. 20, 1918, p. vi; Feb. 3, 1918, p. v; Mar. 3, 1918, p. vi).

52. Calleros, *San Ignacio,* pp. 49-68.

53. *La Revista Católica,* Jan. 19, 1919, p. vi. One such night school emphasizing citizenship classes was sponsored by St. Ignatius. Other organizations

that the Catholic Church in El Paso supported in the 1920s included a branch of the National Catholic Welfare Conference that aided Mexican immigrants and a de facto segregated branch of the Knights of Columbus, El Concilio Del Norte, No. 2592 (Calleros, *San Ignacio*, pp. 101, 121, 131). For Americanization programs by the Catholic Church in the Mexican settlement in Los Angeles see Romo, "Mexican Workers," p. 190; also see José Roberto Juárez, "La Iglesia Católica y el Chicano en Sud Texas 1836–1911."

54. May Wilson Barton, "Methodism at Work Among the Spanish-Speaking People of El Paso, Texas"; *Times*, Aug. 24, 1893, p. 7; *La Revista Católica*, Feb. 2, 1919, p. iv; *Times*, May 31, 1893, p. 7; Feb. 24, 1906, p. 3.

55. *City Directory*, 1898–99, p. 59; 1905, pp. 24–25; 1909, p. 27; 1913, p. 55; 1914, p. 62; 1916, p. 79; 1916, p. 83; *Herald*, Mar. 18–19, 1916, p. 22.

56. *Times*, Aug. 23, 1914, p. 20.

57. *Herald*, May 25, 1916, p. 9; Mar. 30–31, 1918, p. 3; Apr. 13, 1916, p. 12.

58. Ibid. May 6–7, 1916, p. 11; May 3, 1917, p. 2; Apr. 27–28, 1918, p. 11; May 4–5, 1918, p. 10; May 7, 1918, p. 5. Also see N. B. Stump, Branch Secretary, "Associación Cristiana de Jóvenes, Rama Mexicana," report of July 1919, in Pedro E. Portillo Correspondence, 109 letters, 1914–24, in Terrazas Collection, MSS.

59. P. E. Portillo to Silvestre Terrazas, El Paso, Mar. 3, 1919, Portillo Correspondence, Terrazas Collection MSS; "Four Beehives of Activity and Service," YMCA pamphlet, Portillo Correspondence, Terrazas Collection MSS; N. B. Stump to Board of Management of the San Antonio Street Branch of the YMCA, El Paso, July 2, 1919, Portillo Correspondence, Terrazas Collection MSS; "Ins and Outs of a Great Community Service," pamphlet, Portillo Correspondence, Terrazas Collection, MSS.

60. *Herald*, July 13–14, 1918, p. 15.

61. Gamio, *Mexican Immigration*, p. 122.

62. *Times*, June 18, 1896, p. 3. In August 1896, Santa Teresa also engaged in a debate with a representative of *La Revista Católica* over the woman's healing powers (*El Independiente*, Aug. 7, 1896, p. 1).

63. *Times*, Jan. 8, 1898, p. 2. For more on Teresa Urrea see Frank Bishop Putnam, "Teresa Urrea, 'The Saint of Cabora'"; Mario Gill, "Teresa Urrea, La Santa de Cabora"; and Richard Rodríguez and Gloria L. Rodríguez, "Teresa Urrea: Her Life As It Affected the Mexican–U.S. Frontier." Another noted Mexican folk healer along the border at the turn of the century was Don Pedrito Jaramillo (see Elena Gonzales, "The Role of Chicano Folk Beliefs and Practices in Mental Health," pp. 268–69).

64. *El Hispano-Americano*, Aug. 7, 1893, p. 3; *El Defensor*, Oct. 16, 1894, p. 1; Jan. 13, 1895, p. 1.

65. *Las Noticias*, Nov. 11, 1899, p. 1; *Las Dos Américas*, Mar. 7, 1898, p. 3; *El Monitor*, Jan. 30, 1897, p. 2.

66. *Times*, Sept. 15, 1907, p. 3.

67. Ibid.

68. *Herald,* Jan. 22, 1915, p. 4. In his study of Santa Barbara Camarillo observes that in some cases Mexican mutual societies restricted membership to Mexican nationals as a way of minimizing acculturating influences by Mexican Americans (Camarillo, "The Making of a Chicano Community," p. 208).

69. *La Patria,* Sept. 5, 1919, p. 6. Charter organizers of the Alianza consisted primarily of Mexican American businessmen who desired to use the organization as a means of preserving their political influence in Tucson (see Kaye Lynn Briegel, "Alianza Hispano-Americana, 1894-1965: A Mexican American Fraternal Insurance Society," pp. 40-42, 77).

70. *Times,* Jan. 5, 1910, p. 2; Jan. 18, 1910, p. 2; Jan. 19, 1910, p. 2; Jan. 20, 1910, p. 2; Jan. 23, 1910, p. 1.

71. *La Patria,* Sept. 5, 1919, p. 6; Sept. 6, 1919, p. 3. By 1920 Mexicans in the Southwest also began to join American insurance societies such as the Woodman of the World (see Woodman of the World, El Paso, 7 letters, 1920, in the Terrazas Collection, MSS). The Alianza itself continued to grow and reached its apex in 1939, when total membership reached 17,366; in 1942, moreover, it had 373 lodges in the United States. By 1961, however, it had for all practical purposes dissolved due to decreased financial support (Briegel, "Alianza," pp. 214-15, 128-34).

72. See, e.g., Josef J. Barton, *Peasants and Strangers: Italians, Rumanians, and Slovaks in an American City, 1890-1950,* pp. 64-90.

73. *Times,* Feb. 20, 1911, p. 4; *La Patria,* Aug. 29, 1919, p. 3; Nov. 4, 1920, pp. 2, 4; *Times,* Oct. 17, 1909, p. 1.

74. Ibid. Feb. 4, 1903, p. 2; Sept. 17, 1907, p. 5.

75. *El Monitor,* July 21, 1897, p. 1; Aug. 15, 1897, p. 1. Spanish-language newspapers in El Paso such as *El Monitor* were characterized by their strong Mexican nationalism. What little remains of the press, which from 1890 to 1920 involved between 20 and 30 publications, reveals that the press must be considered an institution that helped preserve and maintain a Mexican national consciousness along the border. Besides its main concern with views from Mexico, the Spanish-language press published essays, poems, and even in the case of *El Paso del Norte* serialized Mariano Azuela's famous novel of the Mexican Revolution, *The Underdogs* (Los de Abajo) in 1915.

76. Ibid.

77. Ibid., Sept. 12, 1897, p. 4.

78. Ibid., Sept. 19, 1897, pp. 1, 2.

79. Gamio, *Mexican Immigration,* p. 65.

80. Ibid., pp. 65, 73.

81. Galarza, "Mexicans in the Southwest," p. 279.

82. Ibid., p. 294.

CHAPTER 11

1. See Thernstrom, *The Other Bostonians,* pp. 176-219.

2. See David Brody, *Steelworkers in America: The Nonunion Era.*
3. See Sonnichsen, *Pass.*
4. See Rosenblum, *Immigrant Workers.*
5. U.S. Department of Commerce, *Fourteenth Census, Abstract,* p. 57; *Fifteenth Census, Population,* 2, pp. 67–73.

Bibliography

PRIMARY SOURCES

Newspapers   *English Language*
Lone Star   1880-90
El Paso Daily Times   1890-1920
Labor Advocate   1909-20
El Paso Herald   1910-20
New York Times   1914-16
Pan-American Labor Press   1918
Texas Union   1911-15

Newspapers   *Spanish Language*
El Latino-Americano   Jan. 14-Mar. 28, 1891
Sancho Panza   Nov. 8-28, 1891
El Hispano-Americano   Aug. 7, 1893
La Justicia   Sept. 5-Nov. 4, 1893
El Defensor   Sept. 24, 1894-Mar. 3, 1895
La Opinión Pública   May 11, 1895
El Eco Fronterizo   Oct. 3, 1896
El Independiente   May 6-Aug. 7, 1896
El Monitor   Jan. 30-Dec. 30, 1897; June 30, 1899-Jan. 26, 1900
Las Dos Américas   Mar. 7-June 25, 1898
Las Noticias   Oct. 14, 1899-Jan. 20, 1900
El Progresista   June 17, 1901
El Paso del Norte   Mar. 12-Sept. 18, 1904; Nov. 18, 1915
El Clarín del Norte   Oct. 8, 1905-Oct. 27, 1906; Nov. 10, 1906-Feb. 9,
     1907
La Democracia   Jan. 14, 1906
El Correo del Bravo   Mar. 13-May 1, 1913
La Convención   Jan. 16, 1915

La Revista Católica Jan. 1918–Jan. 1920
El Día Feb. 18–Feb. 23, 1919
El Sol June 11, 1924
La Patria June 18, 1919–Aug. 12, 1924

Government Documents*

Clark, Victor S. "Mexican Labor in the United States," Department of Commerce and Labor, *Bureau of Labor Bulletin* (no. 78, 1908), reprinted in Carlos E. Cortes, Rodolfo Acuña, Juan Gomez-Quiñones, and George Fred Rivera, eds., *Mexican Labor in the United States.* New York: Arno Press, 1974.

El Paso City. *Civil Docket Precinct No. 1* (1915; Nov. 8, 1916–May 19, 1917).

El Paso City Council. *Minutes* 1880–1908, 32 vols.

El Paso County. *Marriage License Records.* Books 3, 5, 10, 20, 21 (1890, 1900, 1910, 1920).

El Paso County. *El Paso City Tax Rolls* (1901, 1919).

El Paso Police Department Newspaper Files. El Paso Public Library.

El Paso School Board. *Minutes.* Vols. 1–19, 1891–1930.

Secretaría de Relaciones Exteriores. Mexico. Asuntos Secretaría de Relaciones Exteriores (consular documents, 1877–1920).

U.S. Congress. Senate. Dillingham Commission. *Immigrants in Industries.* 61st Cong., 2d sess., 1911, Doc. no. 633.

U.S. Department of the Interior. Census Office. *Manuscript Census, 1860,* El Paso County.

———. ———. *Manuscript Census, 1880,* El Paso County.

———. ———. *Eleventh Census of the United States, 1890: Population,* vol. 1.

———. ———. *Eleventh Census of the United States, 1890: Agriculture by Irrigation,* vol. 5.

———. ———. *Eleventh Census of the United States, 1890: Manufacturing Industries,* vol. 6.

———. ———. *Manuscript Census, 1900.* El Paso County.

———. ———. *Twelfth Census of the United States, 1900: Population,* vols. 1, 2.

———. ———. *Twelfth Census of the United States, 1900: Agriculture,* vols. 5, 6.

———. ———. *Twelfth Census of the United States, 1900: Manufactures,* vols. 7, 8.

*The Government Printing Office, Washington, D.C., is the publisher of all United States federal publications cited in the bibliography.

U.S. Department of Commerce. Bureau of the Census. *Thirteenth Census of the United States, 1910: Population*, vols. 1, 3, 4.
——. ——. *Thirteenth Census of the United States, 1910: Agriculture*, vol. 7.
——. ——. *Thirteenth Census of the United States, 1910: Manufactures*, vol. 9.
——. ——. *Thirteenth Census of the United States, 1910: Mines and Quarries*, vol. 11.
——. ——. *Special Census of the Population of El Paso, Texas, Jan. 15, 1916.*
——. ——. *Fourteenth Census Abstract, 1920: Abstract.*
——. ——. *Fourteenth Census of the United States, 1920: Population*, vols. 2-4.
——. ——. *Fourteenth Census of the United States, 1920: Agriculture*, vol. 6.
——. ——. *Fourteenth Census of the United States, 1920: Manufactures*, vol. 9.
——. ——. *Fourteenth Census of the United States, 1920: Mines and Quarries*, vol. 11.
——. ——. *Fifteenth Census of the United States, 1930: Abstract.*
——. ——. *Fifteenth Census of the United States, 1930: Population*, vols. 1-5.
——. ——. *Fifteenth Census of the United States, 1930: Manufactures*, vols. 1, 3.
——. ——. *Fifteenth Census of the United States, 1930: Distribution*, vol. 1.
——. ——. *Fifteenth Census of the United States, 1930: Metropolitan Districts.*
U.S. Department of State. *Commercial Relations of the United States with Foreign Countries*, 1890–91; 1900; 1909; 1910.
——. *Reports from the Consuls of the United States, 1890 and 1895*, vols. 32 and 47.
——. General Records of the Department of State, Record Group 59.
——. Records of the Department of State Relating to Internal Affairs of Mexico, 1910–29. Microcopy No. 274.
World War I Draft Registration Cards. El Paso City, Boards 1 and 2.

Miscellaneous Documents

American Federation of Labor. *Proceedings of the Twenty-Second Annual Convention, New Orleans, 1902.*
——. *Proceedings of the Thirtieth Annual Convention, St. Louis, 1910.*

——. *Proceedings of the Thirty-Sixth Annual Convention, Baltimore, 1916.*
——. *Proceedings of the Thirty-Seventh Annual Convention, Buffalo, 1917.*
——. *Proceedings of the Thirty-Ninth Annual Convention, Atlantic City, 1919.*
El Paso Chamber of Commerce. *Minutes.* 2 vols., 1899–1908 (typewritten).
El Paso City Directories, 1885–1920.
El Paso High School. List of Graduates, 1898–1920.
Official Proceedings of the Twelfth National Irrigation Congress, El Paso, Nov. 15–18, 1904. Galveston, 1905.
Pan-American Federation of Labor. 1st Congress, *Proceedings and Conference.* Laredo, 1918.
——. 2d Congress, *Proceedings and Conference.* New York City, 1919.
Reports of the Public Schools of El Paso, 1897–98; 1903–04; 1905–06; 1914–15; 1915–16.
Sacred Heart Church. Register of Baptismarum. 2 vols., 1885–92; 1892–95.
Sacred Heart School. School Records. 1909–45 (typewritten).

Manuscript Collection

Berkeley. Bancroft Library. Silvestre Terrazas Collection, MSS.
——. ——. Paul S. Taylor Papers.
El Paso. Southwest Collection, El Paso Public Library. Richard Burgess Papers.
——. University of Texas at El Paso Archives. Chihuahua and Pacific Railroad Correspondence.
——. ——. William Flournoy Collection.
——. ——. Josephine Clardy Fox Collection.
——. ——. C. B. Hudspeth Collection.
——. ——. John H. McNeely Collection.
——. ——. Mexico Northwestern Railway Company Correspondence.
——. ——. Anson Mills Collection.
——. ——. C. L. Sonnichsen Collection.
——. ——. El Paso Division, Southern Pacific Collection.
——. ——. H. Stevens Collection.
——. ——. Laurence Stevens Collection.
——. ——. Judge Joseph Sweeney Collection.
——. ——. Owen P. White Collection

Miscellaneous Published Sources

Calleros, Cleofas. "En el Aureo de la Venida de la Companía de Jesús, 1881–
1931. Pamphlet. El Paso: no publisher given, 1931.

El Paso Bureau of Information. "The City and County of El Paso, Texas Containing Useful and Reliable Information Concerning the Future Great
Metropolis of the Southwest Its Resources and Advantages for the Agriculturist, Artisan and Capitalist." El Paso, 1886.

El Paso Chamber of Commerce. *El Paso, the Story of a City.* El Paso: Chamber
of Commerce, 1910.

———. *El Paso, What It Is and Why.* El Paso: Chamber of Commerce, no date
but appears to have been published about 1910.

———. *Prosperity and Opportunities in El Paso and El Paso's Territory for the
Investor–Manufacturer–Jobber–Miner–Farmer–Home Seeker.* El Paso:
Chamber of Commerce, 1911.

———. *Somewhat About El Paso, Texas–Its Resources, Advantages, Attractions
1903 and 1904.* El Paso: Chamber of Commerce, 1904.

———. *What to See in El Paso, Texas.* El Paso: Chamber of Commerce, 1917.

El Paso Gateway Club. *El Paso and the New Southwest.* El Paso: Gateway Club,
1924.

Fitzpatrick, Letitia, S. *El Paso:* no publisher listed, apparently published between 1910 and 1917.

Historical and Descriptive Review of El Paso. El Paso: Trade and Commerce
Publishing Company, 1890.

Horn, Paul W. "Survey of the City Schools of El Paso, Texas." Publications of
El Paso Public Schools no. 1 (Nov. 1, 1922).

Sneed, John, ed. *El Paso–The Queen City of the Southwest.* El Paso: 1904.

Sonnichsen, Philip. *Texas–Mexican Border Music.* Vols. 2 and 3, Corridos, pts.
1 and 2. Berkeley: Arhoolie Productions, 1975.

Southwestern Opportunities. El Paso: Opportunities Publishing Company,
1908.

Books

Bush, I. J. *Gringo Doctor.* Caldwell, Idaho: Caxton Printers, 1939.

Calleros, Cleofas. *El Paso . . . Then and Now.* El Paso: American Printing Co.,
1954.

———. *Historia de la Parroquia de San Ignacio de Loyola.* El Paso: American
Printing Co., 1935.

Galarza, Ernesto. *Barrio Boy.* Notre Dame: Notre Dame University Press, 1971.

Gamio, Manuel. *Mexican Immigration to the United States.* Chicago: University of Chicago Press, 1930. Reprint. New York: Dover Publications, 1971.

——. *The Life Story of the Mexican Immigrant.* Chicago: University of Chicago Press, 1931. Reprint. New York: Dover Publications, 1971.

Guzmán, Martín Luis. *Memoirs of Pancho Villa.* Austin: University of Texas Press, 1965.

Mills, W. W. *Forty Years at El Paso 1858-1898.* El Paso: W. W. Mills, 1901.

Otero, Miguel Antonio. *My Nine Years as Governor of the Territory of New Mexico, 1897-1906.* Albuquerque: University of New Mexico Press, 1940.

Santibáñez, Enrique. *Ensayo Acerca de la Inmigración Mexicana en los Estados Unidos.* San Antonio: Clegg Co., 1930.

Taylor, Paul S. *An American-Mexican Frontier, Nueces County Texas.* Chapel Hill: University of North Carolina Press, 1934.

——. *Mexican Labor in the United States.* Vols. 1-3. Berkeley: University of California Press, 1928-34.

——. *Mexican Labor in the United States: Chicago and the Calumet Region. University of California Publications in Economics,* vol. 7 (1932).

Tompkins, Colonel Frank. *Chasing Villa.* Harrisburg, Penn.: Military Service Publishing Co., 1934.

Turner, John Kenneth. *Barbarous Mexico.* Chicago: C. H. Kerr & Co., 1910.

White, Owen. *Out of the Desert: The Historical Romance of El Paso.* (El Paso: McMath Co., 1923).

Articles

Bogardus, Emory L. "The Mexican Immigrant." *Sociology and Social Research* 2 (1926-27): 470-88.

Bryan, Samuel. "Mexican Immigrants in the United States." *Survey* 28 (Apr.-Sept. 1912): 726-30.

Calleros, Cleofas. "Historia del Asilo de San José de El Paso, Tex." *Estudios Preliminarios de la Sociedad Histórica Católica del Estado de Texas* 1 (Dec. 1931): 1-11.

Gompers, Samuel. "United States-Mexico-Labor—Their Relations." *American Federationist* 23 (Aug. 1916): 633-52.

Gwin, J. B. "Making Friends of Invaders: Mexican Refugees in Advance of the Returning Troops." *Survey* 37 (Mar. 3, 1917): 621-23.

Handman, Max Sylvius. "Economic Reasons for the Coming of the Mexican Immigrant." *American Journal of Sociology* 35 (July-May 1929-30): 601-11.

Hoover, Glenn E. "Our Mexican Immigrants." *Foreign Affairs* 8 (Oct. 1929): 99–107.

International Industrial Record 3 (July 1901): 1.

Jackson, Helen Hunt. "By Horse-Cars into Mexico." *Atlantic Monthly* 51 (Mar. 1883): 350–62.

Kellogg, Paul U. "A New Era of Friendship for North America." *Survey* 36 (July 15, 1916): 415–16.

Leonard, William E. "Where Both Bullets and Ballots are Dangerous." *Survey* 37 (Oct. 28, 1916): 86–87.

Mexican Mining Journal 5 (Oct. 1904)–19 (June 1915).

Slaydon, James L. "Some Observations on Mexican Immigration." *Annals of the American Academy of Political and Social Sciences* 93 (Jan. 1921): 121–26.

Sturges, Vera L. "The Mexican Immigrant." *Survey* 46 (Apr.–Sept. 1921): 470–71.

Taylor, Paul S. "Crime and the Foreign Born." In National Commission on Law Observance and Enforcement. *The Mexican Immigrant and the Problem of Crime and Criminal Justice.* Pt. III. Washington, D.C.: Government Printing Office, 1931.

"The Mexican 'Invaders' of El Paso." *Survey* 36 (July 8, 1916): 380–82.

"The Red Cross on the Mexican Border." *Survey* 32 (July 25, 1914): 429–30.

Vargas, C. A. "A Short History of the Organized Labor Movement in the Clifton-Morenci-Metcalf District." *Pan-American Labor Press* Oct. 16, 1918.

Walker, Helen W. "Mexican Immigrants as Laborers." *Sociology and Social Research* 13 (Sept. 1928): 55–62.

Oral History

Enrique L. Acevedo, May 17, 1974. Interviewed by Robert H. Novak. Institute of Oral History, University of Texas at El Paso.

Mario Acevedo, May 1, 1975. Interviewed by Oscar J. Martínez. IOH, UTEP.

Charles Armijo, Jan. 30, 1973. Interviewed by Leon Metz, David Salazar, and Cristina García. IOH, UTEP.

Guillermo Balderas, Apr. 18, 1974. Interviewed by José H. Maese. IOH, UTEP.

José Cruz Burciaga, Feb. 16, 1974. Interviewed by Oscar J. Martínez. IOH, UTEP.

Cleofas Calleros, Sept. 14, 1972. Interviewed by Oscar J. Martínez. IOH, UTEP.

Chester Chope, July 27, 1968. Interviewed by Wilma Cleveland. IOH, UTEP.

Mauricio Cordero, Feb. 15, 1974. Interviewed by Oscar J. Martínez. IOH, UTEP.

Frank Fletcher, July 1968. Interviewed by Wilma Cleveland. IOH, UTEP.

Mrs. Frank Fletcher, Jr., Aug. 15, 1975. Interviewed by Mario T. García.

Chris P. Fox, July 25, 1972. Interviewed by Leon Metz. IOH, UTEP.

Modesto Gómez, July 26, 1968. Interviewed by Wilma Cleveland. IOH, UTEP.

Eleanor Greet, July 26, 1968. Interviewed by Wilma Cleveland. IOH, UTEP.

Clarence Harper, July 17, 1968. Interviewed by Wilma Cleveland. IOH, UTEP.

Aileen Hague Hill, Apr. 10, 1973. Interviewed by Jo Ann Hovious. IOH, UTEP.

Elizabeth Kelly, May 18, 1973. Interviewed by David Salazar. IOH, UTEP.

Elizabeth Kelly, Aug. 17, 1975. Interviewed by Mario T. García.

Elizabeth Kelly, Ann Kelly, and Mary Quinn, Mar. 1973. Interviewed by Mildred Torok and David Salazar. IOH, UTEP.

Jess López, Feb. 15, 1977. Interviewed by Gregory S. Fisher.

Francisco Noriega, Oct. 29, 1973. Interviewed by Robert H. Novak. IOH, UTEP.

Mrs. Leigh White Osborn, Apr. 3 and 10, 1973. Interviewed by Jo Ann Hovious. IOH, UTEP.

Mrs. Jane Perenot, Feb. 14, 1973. Interviewed by Jo Ann Hovious. IOH, UTEP.

Margarita Terrazas, Oct. 24, 1964. Interviewed by Leon Metz. IOH, UTEP.

Félix López Urdiales, Jan. 4, 1974. Interviewed by Oscar J. Martínez. IOH, UTEP.

Mrs. Hugh White, June 3, 1968. Interviewed by Robin Fuller and Leon Metz. IOH, UTEP.

SECONDARY SOURCES

Books

Aikman, Duncan, ed. *Rocky Mountain Cities.* New York: Norton, 1949.

Anderson, Michael. *Family Structure in Nineteenth Century Lancashire.* London: University Press, 1971.

Apter, David E. *The Politics of Modernization.* Chicago: University of Chicago Press, 1965.

Barrera, Mario. *Race and Class in the Southwest.* Notre Dame: Notre Dame University Press, 1979.

Barth, Gunther. *Instant Cities: Urbanization and the Rise of San Francisco and Denver.* New York: Oxford University Press, 1975.

Barton, Joseph J. *Peasants and Strangers: Italians, Rumanians, and Slovaks in an American City, 1890–1950.* Cambridge: Harvard University Press, 1975.

Beezley, William H. *Insurgent Governor: Abraham González and the Mexican Revolution in Chihuahua.* Lincoln: University of Nebraska Press, 1973.

Bernstein, Marvin D. *The Mexican Mining Industry 1890–1950.* Albany: State University of New York, 1965.

Blaisdell, Lowell L. *The Desert Revolution: Baja California 1911.* Madison: University of Wisconsin Press, 1962.

Bowles, Samuel, and Gintes, Herbert. *Schooling in Capitalist America.* New York: Basic Books, 1976.

Braddy, Haldren. *Pershing's Mission in Mexico.* El Paso: Texas Western Press, 1966.

Brody, David. *Steelworkers in America: The Nonunion Era.* Cambridge: Harvard University Press, 1960.

Callow, Jr., Alexander B., ed. *American Urban History.* New York: Oxford University Press, 1973.

———. *The City Boss in America.* New York: Oxford University Press, 1976.

Camarillo, Albert. *Chicanos in a Changing Society: From Mexican Pueblos to American Barrios in Santa Barbara and Southern California, 1848–1930.* Cambridge: Harvard University Press, 1979.

Chávez, Armando B. *Historia de Ciudad Juárez.* Ciudad Juárez: 1970.

City of El Paso, Department of Planning. *A Short History of South El Paso.* El Paso: City of El Paso, 1967.

Clark, Ira G. *Then Came the Railroads: The Century from Steam to Diesel in the Southwest.* Norman: University of Oklahoma Press, 1958.

Cleland, Robert Glass. *A History of Phelps Dodge, 1834–1950.* New York: Knopf, 1952.

Clendenen, Clarence. *The United States and Pancho Villa: A Study in Unconventional Diplomacy.* Ithaca: Cornell University Press, 1961.

Cochran, Thomas C., and Miller, William. Rev. ed. *The Age of Enterprise.* New York: Harper & Row, 1961.

Cockroft, James D. *Intellectual Precursors of the Mexican Revolution, 1910–1913.* Austin: University of Texas Press, 1968.

Cumberland, Charles C. *Mexican Revolution: Genesis Under Madero.* Austin: University of Texas, 1952.

Davis, Allen F. *Spearheads for Reform: The Social Settlements and the Progressive Movement, 1890–1914.* New York: Oxford University Press, 1967.

Dolan, Jay P. *The Immigrant Church: New York's Irish and German Catholics, 1815–1865.* Baltimore: Johns Hopkins University Press, 1975.

Eisenstadt, Shmuel Noah. *Modernization: Protest and Change.* Englewood, N.J.: Prentice-Hall, 1969.

Erickson, Charlotte. *American Industry and the European Immigrant, 1860–85.* Cambridge: Harvard University Press, 1957.

Fierman, Floyd S. *Some Early Jewish Settlers in the Southwest Frontier.* El Paso: Texas Western Press, 1960.

Frank, Andre Gunder. *Latin America: Underdevelopment or Revolution.* New York: Monthly Review Press, 1969.

Fuchs, Lawrence H., ed. *American Ethnic Politics.* New York: Harper & Row, 1968.

Gans, Herbert J. *The Urban Villagers.* New York: Free Press of Glencoe, 1962.

Gómez-Quiñones, Juan. *Sembradores: Ricardo Flores Magón y El Partido Liberal Mexicano: A Eulogy and Critique.* Los Angeles: Aztlán Publications, 1973.

Gordon, Michael, ed. *The American Family in Social-Historical Perspective.* New York: St. Martin's Press, 1973.

Greene, Victor R. *The Slavic Community on Strike: Immigrant Labor in Pennsylvania Anthracite.* Notre Dame: University of Notre Dame Press, 1968.

Gutman, Herbert G. *Work, Culture, and Society in Industrializing America.* New York: Knopf, 1976.

Hanson, Roger D. *Mexican Economic Development: The Roots of Rapid Growth.* Washington, D.C.: National Planning Associates, 1971.

———. *The Politics of Mexican Development.* Baltimore: Johns Hopkins Press, 1971.

Harris, Ruth. *Geography of El Paso County.* El Paso: El Paso Vocational School, 1931.

Hays, Samuel P. *The Response to Industrialism, 1885–1914.* Chicago: University of Chicago Press, 1957.

Hernández, Carol A.; Haug, Marsha J.; and Wagner, Nathaniel N., eds. *Chicanos: Social and Psychological Perspectives.* St. Louis: C. V. Mosby, 1976.

Hufford, Charles H. *The Social and Economic Effects of the Mexican Migration into Texas.* San Francisco: R & E Research Associates, 1971.

Jones, Billy M. *Health-Seekers in the Southwest, 1817–1900.* Norman: University of Oklahoma Press, 1967.

Kluger, James R. *The Clifton–Morenci Strike: Labor Difficulty in Arizona, 1915–1916.* Tucson: University of Arizona Press, 1970.

Knights, Peter R. *The Plain People of Boston, 1830–1860: A Study in City Growth.* New York: Oxford University Press, 1971.

Kusmer, Kenneth L. *A Ghetto Takes Shape: Black Cleveland, 1870–1930.* Urbana: University of Illinois Press, 1976.

Larson, Robert W. *New Mexico's Quest for Statehood, 1846–1912.* Albuquerque: University of New Mexico Press, 1968.

Levenstein, Harvey A. *Labor Organizations in the United States and Mexico: A History of Their Relations.* Westport, Ct.: Greenwood Press, 1971.

Liss, Sheldon B. *A Century of Disagreement: The Chamizal Conflict, 1854–1964.* Washington, D.C.: University Press, 1965.

Lubove, Roy. *The Progressives and the Slums.* Pittsburgh: University of Pittsburgh Press, 1962.

Marshall, James L. *Santa Fe: The Railroad that Built an Empire.* New York: Random House, 1945.

Martin, Robert L. *The City Moves West: Economic and Industrial Growth in Central West Texas.* Austin: University of Texas Press, 1969.

Martínez, John. *Mexican Emigration to the U.S., 1910–30.* San Francisco: R & E Research Associates, 1972.

Martínez, Oscar J. *Border Boom Town: Ciudad Juárez since 1848.* Austin: University of Texas Press, 1978.

Meinig, D. W. *Imperial Texas: An Interpretive Essay in Cultural Geography.* Austin: University of Texas Press, 1969.

———. *Southwest: Three Peoples in Geographical Change, 1600–1970.* New York: Oxford University Press, 1971.

Mendoza, Salvador. *El Mito y la Mística de El Chamizal.* Mexico City: Editorial Periodística e Impresora de México, 1963.

Meyer, Michael C. *Mexican Rebel: Pascual Orozco and the Mexican Revolution 1910–1915.* Lincoln: University of Nebraska Press, 1967.

Middagh, John. *Frontier Newspaper: The El Paso Times.* El Paso: Texas Western Press, 1958.

Miller, Randall M., and Marzik, Thomas D., eds. *Immigrants and Religion in Urban America.* Philadelphia: Temple University Press, 1977.

Moorhead, Max L. *New Mexico's Royal Road: Trade and Travel on the Chihuahua Trail.* Norman: University of Oklahoma Press, 1958.

Nash, Gerald D. *The American West in the Twentieth Century: A Short History of an Urban Oasis.* Englewood Cliffs, N.J.: Prentice-Hall, 1973.

Nelli, Humbert. *The Italians in Chicago, 1880–1930.* New York: Oxford University Press, 1970.

Oppenheimer, Valerie Kincade. *The Female Labor Force in the United States.* Berkeley: Institute of International Studies, 1970.

Osofsky, Gilbert. *Harlem: The Making of a Ghetto*. New York: Harper & Row, 1963.

Owens, M. Lilliana. *Loretto in El Paso*. St. Louis: McMullen, 1964.

Paredes, Américo. *A Texas–Mexican Cancionero: Folksongs of the Lower Border*. Urbana: University of Illinois Press, 1976.

Pinchon, Edgcumb. *Viva Villa!* New York: Arno Press, 1970; 1st ed., 1933.

Pitt, Leonard. *The Decline of the Californios*. Berkeley: University of California Press, 1966.

Pletcher, David M. *Rails, Mines, and Progress: Seven American Promoters in Mexico, 1867–1911*. Ithaca: Cornell University Press, 1958.

Pomeroy, Earl. *In Search of the Golden West: The Tourist in Western America*. New York: Knopf, 1957.

Reisler, Mark. *By the Sweat of Their Brow: Mexican Immigrant Labor in the United States*. Westport, Ct.: Greenwood Press, 1976.

Rosenblum, Gerald. *Immigrant Workers: Their Impact on American Labor Radicalism*. New York: Basic Books, 1973.

Ross, Stanley R. *Francisco I. Madero: Apostle of Democracy*. New York: Columbia University Press, 1955.

Schaer, Bertha Archer. *Historical Sketch of Aoy School*. El Paso: El Paso Public Schools, 1951.

Simpson, Lesley Byrd. *Many Mexicos*. Berkeley: University of California Press, 1959.

Solberg, Carl. *Immigration and Nationalism: Argentina and Chile, 1890–1914*. Austin: University of Texas Press, 1970.

Sonnichsen, C. L. *Pass of the North: Four Centuries on the Rio Grande*. El Paso: Texas Western Press, 1968.

———. *The El Paso Salt War*. El Paso: Texas Western Press, 1961.

———, and McKinney, M. G. *The State National Since 1881: The Pioneer Bank of El Paso*. El Paso. Texas Western Press, 1971.

Spears, Allan H. *Black Chicago: The Making of a Negro Ghetto, 1890–1920*. Chicago: University of Chicago Press, 1967.

Spicer, Edward H., and Thompson, Raymond H., eds. *Plural Society in the Southwest*. New York: Interbank Inc., 1972.

Thernstrom, Stephen. *The Other Bostonians: Poverty and Progress in the American Metropolis, 1880–1970*. Cambridge: Harvard University Press, 1973.

Tranchese, Carmelo, and Montalvo, Carmela, eds. *Los Pastores*. San Antonio: Trevino Printing & Lithograph, 1976.

Usigli, Rodolfo. *Mexico in the Theater.* University, Miss.: Romance Mono-
graphs, 1976.
Villegas, Daniel Cosío, ed. *Historia Moderna de México.* Vols. 1-7. Mexico City:
Editorial Hermes, 1955-72.
Webb, Walter Prescott. *The Texas Rangers: A Century of Frontier Defense.* Aus-
tin: University of Texas Press, 1935.
Weiner, Myron, ed. *Modernization: The Dynamics of Growth.* New York: Basic
Books, 1966.
Wiebe, Robert H. *The Search For Order, 1877-1920.* New York: Hill & Wang,
1967.
Wingfield, Clyde J., ed. *Urbanization in the Southwest.* El Paso: Texas Western
Press, 1968.

Articles
Año Nuevo de Kerr, Louise. "Chicano Settlements in Chicago: A Brief History."
Journal of Ethnic Studies 2 (Winter 1975): 22-32.
Black, Cyril Edward. "Change as a Condition of Modern Life." In Myron
Weiner, ed., *Modernization: The Dynamics of Growth,* pp. 17-27.
Brokaw, John W. "The Repertory of a Mexican-American Theatrical Troupe:
1849-1924." *Latin American Theatre Review* 8 (Fall 1974): 25-36.
Campa, Arthur. "Religious Spanish Folkdrama in New Mexico." *New Mexico
Quarterly* 2 (1932): 3-13.
Chaldin, Harvey M. "Kinship Networks in the Migration Process." *International
Migration Review* 7 (Summer 1973): 163-75.
Cornwall, Elmer E., Jr. "Bosses, Machines, and Ethnic Groups." In Lawrence
H. Fuchs, ed., *American Ethnic Politics,* pp. 194-216.
Corwin, Arthur F. "Causes of Mexican Migration to the United States: A
Summary View." *Perspectives in American History* 7 (1973): 557-635.
Cumberland, Charles C. "Border Raids in the Lower Rio Grande Valley—1915."
Southwestern Historical Quarterly 57 (Jan. 1954): 285-311.
———. "Mexican Revolutionary Movements from Texas, 1906-1912." *South-
western Historical Quarterly* 52 (Jan. 1949): 301-24.
Farrar, Nancy. "The Chinese in El Paso." *Southwestern Studies* 33 (1972): 3-44.
Galarza, Ernesto. "Mexicans in the Southwest: A Culture in Process." In Edward
H. Spicer and Raymond H. Thompson, eds., *Plural Society in the Southwest,*
pp. 261-97.

García, Mario T. "Americanization and the Mexican Immigrant, 1880-1930." *Journal of Ethnic Studies* 6 (Summer 1978): 19-34.

——. "Racial Dualism in the El Paso Labor Market, 1880-1920." *Aztlán* (Special Issue on Chicano Labor History) 6 (Summer 1975): 197-217.

——. "The Californios of San Diego and the Politics of Accommodation, 1846-1860." *Aztlán* 6 (Spring 1975): 69-85.

de la Garza, Rudolph O. "Voting Patterns in 'Bi-Cultural' El Paso—A Contextual Analysis of Chicano Voting Behavior." *Aztlán* 5 (Spring and Fall 1974): 235-60.

Gerlach, Allen. "Conditions Along the Border—1915: The Plan de San Diego." *New Mexico Historical Review* 42 (July 1968): 195-212.

Gill, Mario. "Teresa Urrea, La Santa de Cabora." *Historia Mexicana* 6 (Apr.-June 1957): 626-44.

Gómez-Quiñones, Juan. "Plan of San Diego Reviewed." *Aztlán* 1 (Spring 1970): 124-32.

——. "The First Steps: Chicano Labor Conflict and Organizing, 1900 to 1920." *Aztlán* 3 (1973): 13-45.

Gonzalez, Elena. "The Role of Chicano Folk Beliefs and Practice in Mental Health." In Carol A. Hernandez, Marsha J. Haug, and Nathaniel N. Wagner, eds., *Chicanos: Social and Psychological Perspectives,* pp. 263-81.

Goodman, III, Leonard A. "The First Cigar Factory in El Paso." *Password* 10 (Fall 1965): III.

Gregory, Gladys. "The Chamizal Settlement: A View from El Paso." *Southwestern Studies* 1 (Summer 1963): 3-52.

Hager, William M. "The Plan of San Diego: Unrest on the Texas Border in 1915." *Arizona and the West* 5 (Winter 1963): 327-36.

Jitadi, Ted J. "Migration and Kinship Contacts." *Pacific Sociological Review* 6 (Fall 1963): 49-55.

Juárez, José Roberto. "La Iglesia Católica y el Chicano en Sud Texas 1836-1911." *Aztlán* 4 (Fall 1973): 217-70.

Katz, Friedrich. "Labor Conditions on Haciendas in Porfirian Mexico: Some Trends and Tendencies." *Hispanic American Historical Review* 54 (Feb. 1974): 1-47.

——. "Pancho Villa and the Attack on Columbus, New Mexico." *American Historical Review* 83 (Feb. 1978): 101-30.

Litwack, Eugene. "Geographic Mobility and Extended Family Cohesion." *American Sociological Review* 25 (June 1960): 385-95.

McNeely, John H. "The Railways of Mexico." *Southwestern Studies* 2 (Spring 1964): 1–56.

Porter, Eugene O. "The Great Flood of 1897." *Password* 18 (Fall 1973): 99.

Putnam, Frank Bishop. "Teresa Urrea, 'The Saint of Cabora.'" *Southern California Quarterly* 45 (Sept. 1963): 245–64.

Raat, William Dirk. "The Diplomacy of Suppression: 'Los Revoltosos,' Mexico, and the United States, 1906–1911." *Hispanic American Historical Review* 56 (Nov. 1976): 529–50.

Reisler, Mark. "The Mexican Immigrant in the Chicago Area during the 1920s." *Journal of the Illinois State Historical Society* 66 (Summer 1973): 144–58.

Rodríguez, Richard, and Rodríguez, Gloria L. "Teresa Urrea: Her Life As It Affected the Mexican–U.S. Frontier." *El Grito* 5 (Summer 1972): 48–68.

Romo, Ricardo. "The Urbanization of Southwestern Chicanos in the Early Twentieth Century." *New Scholar* 6 (Fall 1977): 183–207.

Sandos, James A. "The Plan of San Diego: War and Diplomacy on the Texas Border, 1915–1916." *Arizona and the West* 14 (1972): 5–24.

Strauss, Melvin P. "The Mexican-American in El Paso Politics." In Clyde J. Wingfield, ed., *Urbanization in the Southwest*, pp. 56–74.

Strickland, Rex W. "Six Who Came to El Paso: Pioneers of the 1840s." *Southwestern Studies* 1 (Fall 1963): 3–48.

Thompson, E. P. "Time, Work-Discipline, and Industrial Capitalism." *Past and Present* 38 (1967): 56–97.

Timmons, W. H. "Continental Crossroads: El Paso in History." *Nova* 9 (June 1974): 7–10.

Towner, Margaret. "Monopoly Capitalism and Women's Work during the Porfiriato." *Latin American Perspectives* 9 (Winter and Spring 1977): 90–105.

Walter, Paul A. "Octaviano Ambrosio Larrazolo." *New Mexico Historical Review* 7 (Apr. 1932): 97–104.

Ward, David. "The Making of Immigrant Ghettos, 1840–1920." In Alexander Callow, Jr., ed., *American Urban History*, pp. 296–307.

Weeks, O. Douglas. "The Texas-Mexican and the Politics of South Texas." *American Political Science Review* 24 (Aug. 1930): 606–27.

Willems, Emilio. "Peasantry and City: Cultural Persistence and Change in Historical Perspective, a European Case." *American Anthropologist* 72 (1970): 528–43.

Yans-McLaughlin, Virginia. "Patterns of Work and Family Organization: Buffalo's

Italians." In Michael Gordon, ed., *The American Family in Social-Historical Perspective,* pp. 136-51.

Theses and Other Papers

Barton, May Wilson. "Methodism at Work among the Spanish-Speaking People of El Paso, Texas." M.A. thesis, University of Texas, El Paso, 1950.

Blake, Robert Neal. "A History of the Catholic Church in El Paso." M.A. thesis, University of Texas, El Paso, 1948.

Briegel, Kaye Lynn. "Alianza Hispano-Americana, 1894-1965: A Mexican American Fraternal Insurance Society." Ph.D. diss., University of Southern California, 1974.

Camarillo, Albert M. "The Making of a Chicano Community: A History of the Chicanos in Santa Barbara, California, 1850-1930." Ph.D. diss., University of California, Los Angeles, 1975.

Cardoso, Lawrence Anthony. "Mexican Emigration to the United States, 1900 to 1930: An Analysis of Socio-Economic Factors." Ph.D. diss., University of Connecticut, 1974.

Cummings, Ruth. "History of Alamo School." History Seminar Paper no. 10, University of Texas, El Paso, Jan. 1951. UTEP Archives.

Dickens, Edwin Larry. "The Political Role of Mexican-Americans in San Antonio, Texas." Ph.D. diss., Texas Tech University, 1969.

Estrada, Richard Medina. "Border Revolution: The Mexican Revolution in the Ciudad Juárez-El Paso Area, 1906-1915." M.A. thesis, University of Texas, El Paso, 1975.

Foley, Edna Snowden. "A History of Beall School, El Paso, Texas." History Seminar Paper no. 12, University of Texas, El Paso, July 6, 1950. UTEP Archives.

García, Alma María. "The Occupational Distribution of El Paso by Ethnicity, 1900-1940." Seminar Paper, Dept. of Sociology, University of Texas, El Paso, 1974.

González, Gilbert G. "Crisis of Urbanization: Racism, Education, and the Mexican Community in Los Angeles, 1920-1930." Paper presented at the American Historical Association, San Francisco, Dec. 1973.

———. "The Relationship between Progressive Educational Theory and Practice and Monopoly Capital." Occasional Papers no. 1, Program in Comparative Cultures, University of California, Irvine, 1976.

———. "The System of Public Education and its Function within the Chicano

Communities, 1920-1930." Ph.D. diss., University of California, Los Angeles, 1974.

Gregory, Gladys. "El Chamizal: A Boundary Problem between the United States and Mexico." Ph.D. diss., University of Texas, Austin, 1937.

Hammons, Nancy Lee. "A History of El Paso County, Texas to 1900." M.A. thesis, Texas College of Mines and Metallurgy, 1942.

King, Robert Gustave. "The Popular Dry Goods Company," History Seminar Paper no. 58, University of Texas, El Paso, 1953. UTEP Archives.

Laird, Judith Fincher. "Argentine, Kansas: The Evolution of a Mexican–American Community: 1905-1940." Ph.D. diss., University of Kansas, 1975.

Lee, Mary Antoine. "A Historical Survey of the American Smelting and Refining Company in El Paso, 1887-1950." M.A. thesis, University of Texas, El Paso, 1950.

McConville, J. Lawrence. "A History of Population in the El Paso-Ciudad Juárez Area." M.A. thesis, University of New Mexico, 1966.

Martínez, Oscar J. "Border Boom Town: Ciudad Juárez Since 1880." Ph.D. diss., University of California, Los Angeles, 1975.

———. "The Chicanos of El Paso: An Assessment of Progress." Unpublished paper.

Miller, Eddie Lou. "The History of Private Welfare Agencies in El Paso, 1886-1930." M.A. thesis, University of Texas, El Paso, 1969.

Milnarich, Rhoda. "A Study of the El Paso County Census of 1860." History Term Paper, University of Texas, El Paso, n.d. UTEP Archives.

Morten, Charles B. "The Survivals of Medieval Religious Drama in New Mexico." Ph.D. diss., University of Missouri, 1959.

Park, Joseph F. "The History of Mexican Labor in Arizona during the Territorial Period." M.A. thesis, University of Arizona, 1961.

Rainey, Helen. "A History of Organized Welfare in El Paso, 1892-1948." M.A. thesis, University of Texas, El Paso, 1949.

Ramírez, Elma Galentine. "A Brief History of Franklin School." History Seminar Paper no. 40, University of Texas, El Paso, 1950. UTEP Archives.

Romo, Ricardo. "Mexican Workers in the City: Los Angeles, 1915-1930." Ph.D. diss., University of California, Los Angeles, 1975.

Sandels, Robert Lynn. "Silvestre Terrazas, the Press, and the Origins of the Mexican Revolution in Chihuahua." Ph.D. diss., University of Oregon, 1967.

Scott, Robin F. "The Mexican-American in the Los Angeles Area, 1920-1950: From Acquiescence to Activity." Ph.D. diss., University of Southern California, 1971.

Thomforde, Duane W. "Political Socialization in South El Paso." M.A. thesis, University of Texas, El Paso, 1969.

Vowell, Jr., Jack C. "Politics at El Paso: 1850–1920." M.A. thesis, University of Texas, El Paso, 1952.

Ward, Charles Francis. "The Salt War of San Elizario (1887)." M.A. thesis, University of Texas, Austin, 1932.

de Wetter, Mardee. "Revolutionary El Paso, 1910–1917." M.A. thesis, University of Texas, El Paso, 1946.

White, Russel A. "El Paso del Norte: the Geography of a Pass and Border Area Through 1906." Ph.D. diss., Columbia University, 1968.

Ybarra-Frausto, Tómas. "El Teatro Chicano and its Traditions." Unpublished paper.

Yielding, Kenneth Duane. "The Chamizal Dispute: An Exercise in Arbitration." Ph.D. thesis, Texas Tech University, 1973.

Index